Metropolis:

values in conflict

Metropolis:

values in conflict

C. E. Elias, Jr.
REAL ESTATE RESEARCH PROGRAM
UNIVERSITY OF CALIFORNIA, LOS ANGELES

James Gillies
PROFESSOR OF URBAN LAND ECONOMICS
UNIVERSITY OF CALIFORNIA, LOS ANGELES

Svend Riemer
PROFESSOR OF SOCIOLOGY
UNIVERSITY OF CALIFORNIA, LOS ANGELES

Wadsworth Publishing Co., Inc.
Belmont, California

L. C. Cat. Card No.: 64–13106

Printed in the United States of America

preface

One of the fundamental processes of social change today is the increasing tendency of men to conduct their affairs in a congested urban environment. This book is about the problems and value conflicts which this increasing urbanization produces.

The conflicts are clearly established early in the book. After an introductory chapter on the historical perspective, the two chapters of Part One set forth the basic value questions that recur throughout the book. Chapter 2 is concerned particularly with two issues. First, there is the feeling of many Americans (including intellectuals, as the Whites make clear) that something is wrong, destructive, unnatural about the city, and that the life of virtue is to be found only in the rural area and the small town. Second, there is the view of those who believe in the city, but are enraged by the forms taken by most contemporary cities; Lewis Mumford is the representative prophet here, and his anger at today's metropolis is basically an attack on the direction of Western civilization itself.

Chapter 3 makes it clear that the major value conflicts of urban life today are no longer limited to "the city." This is a book about the entire metropolis; and it is suburban life that contains perhaps the most characteristic issues of our time. David Riesman and Gibson Winter, in particular, discuss those aspects of the suburbs which are not conducive to a vigorous and variegated culture.

Neither of these chapters, however, is designed to evoke an inevitably hostile response to metropolitan life. Not everyone thinks that the city is a destroyer of sound values. Robert Moses has no use for Mumford's thunderings. John Burchard suggests that small populations cannot produce great cultural centers. Paul Ylvisaker believes that the urban spread is irreversible and has many positive features. And other voices in these two chapters are raised in support of the view that the metropolis, for all of its defects, can be a creator of new and worthwhile values.

Thus Part One establishes a dialogue, and raises issues which can be debated.

Part One sets the pattern for the remainder of the book. Inherent in each of the problems of urban renewal and design and land use, of transportation, housing, race, crime, finances, and politics is the basic question of what view of life we want to embody in our cities and our suburbs. And on this question the value choices are presented in the contrasting views of Jane Jacobs and Lewis Mumford, of John Dyckman and Henry Churchill, of Robert Heilbroner and Gilbert Burck, of C. Wright Mills and Scott Greer. Not every problem, of course, can be viewed on a simple pro and con basis, and many of the pieces are simply expository and analytical rather than didactic. Just the same, in the metropolis the great issues of our day are to be found in their most immediate and inescapable form; and the excitement in these issues can be revealed only by a confrontation of ideas such as is to be found in this anthology.

The organization of the material makes the book suitable, we believe, for two kinds of users. First, it suits the requirements of a variety of college and university courses dealing with urban problems. Second, it provides a sound and lively basis for adult classes and groups organized through university extension divisions, other adult education agencies, and the many organizations interested in urban problems.

The need for a book of readings on urbanism for study and discussion purposes, both in conjunction with a television series, and as a self-contained program for discussion groups, led to the creation of the present book. Early in 1962 a group of university extension deans and directors began meeting as a program committee under the auspices of the University Council on Education for Public Responsibility.* This group had agreed to work together each year in an attempt to focus public attention on a major area of public policy. For 1964 the public-policy area selected was that of urbanism. National Educational Television (N.E.T.) was approached; and it agreed, out of its own resources, to produce a television series on urbanism by March 1964.†

The final plan of this book and the decision on the selections to be used are, of course, the responsibility of the three editors alone. The editors are happy to acknowledge, however, the major help rendered to them by members of the University Council program committee, particularly Leonard Freedman, Eugene Johnson, Granville Davis, Carl Tjerandsen, A. A. Liveright, Martin Chamberlain and Cyril Hager, together with Henry Alter of N.E.T. and Kenneth Haygood of C.S.L.E.A. We wish also to express our gratitude to James Bell and Marilyn Affleck, who provided invaluable research assistance, and to Diana Collister and Linda Dalton for undertaking the crucial secretarial services involved.

* The Council consists of the presidents of universities that were recipients of grants from the Fund for Adult Education. The Center for the Study of Liberal Education for Adults (C.S.L.E.A.) functioned as a secretariat for the planning group while this book was being developed.
† Information on this series can be obtained from The Director of Program Utilization, N.E.T., 10 Columbus Circle, N.Y. 19.

contents

x   Contents

1
Perspectives

In our time increasing numbers of people are becoming city dwellers or suburbanites—so that urbanism is becoming the dominant pattern of life. Within this urban framework—that is, within our own specific, immediate environment—this book of readings focuses on some of the most compelling issues of our time. Although most of us probably feel more comfortable talking about issues in abstractions or in distant contexts, these readings force us to talk about our own neighborhoods. And it is there, localized and particularized, that we have to confront the issues —and perhaps do something about them.

On the other hand, since we cannot understand local situations unless we can make comparisons that give perspective, throughout this book there are comparisons between cities in America, between those here and abroad, and between modern cities and cities of the past.

The city as such goes far back into history. So, at the outset, we must ask whether in fact the urban problems examined here are merely variations on familiar themes or whether, in their present form, they constitute essentially new phenomena. Much will depend, obviously, on the perspective from which the question is asked. Consider, for instance, the transportation problem. Accident victims, whether produced by a Roman chariot or an automobile, have existed as long as there have been cities. But only since the advent of the automobile has a means of transportation caused air pollution.

Again, change has always been associated with urbanization. But has the increased pace of change introduced a new dimension? Certainly, in no previous period has urban growth proceeded at anything like its present rate. To point out that as many people will be added to cities in the next 35 years in the United States as were added from the colonial beginnings to 1960 is to do more than illustrate the fact of population growth. It is to indicate a fundamental shift in the manner in which people live.

The selections in this introductory chapter provide some essential insights into the character of this urban development from the earliest origins of the city.

Jean Gottmann, utilizing the perspectives of history, points out that the current wave of urbanization is beginning to make demands on mankind that have never been made before: "Mankind is reshaping its habitat. The much maligned trend towards urbanization has become so rapid and massive as to overshadow many other modern problems." Urbanization, Gottmann comments, is a worldwide force: "most countries today want more industries, more and better cities, fewer people on their farms." The cities that have developed in response to this desire are different from those of the past; we now have "urban districts of great variety and of such size as to become sections within the national state." In essence, according to Gottmann's analysis, modern urbanization represents a break with the past and hence requires new solutions. The old approaches will not do.

Kingsley Davis, in his contribution, explores the origin and growth of urbanization. He is unequivocal in his attitude toward modern cities; like Gottmann he regards them as something fundamentally different from cities of the past. "Such cities are creatures of the twentieth century. Their sheer quantitative difference means a qualitative change as well."

Hathaway, in the final selection in this introductory chapter, considers the three great migrations that have coincided with the rise of metropolitan areas—the migration from the south to the north, from the east to the west, and from the farm to the city. In Hathaway's opinion, the migration from farm to city has been the most persistent and has produced the most significant changes in the national culture.

Mankind Is Reshaping Its Habitat*

Jean Gottmann

. . . For many thousands of years the majority of mankind lived in the rural countryside and worked at making the soil yield the raw materials necessary to feed and occupy everybody. Only a minority inhabited cities—densely built-up small areas, set aside from the "open country" as separate entities, endowed with a set of laws and regulations peculiarly their own. Walls, ramparts, or at least legal lines enclosed them. In some cases city people may have engaged in farming outside the walls; they may have drawn most of their income from agricultural revenues. But the city was more typically specialized in trade, manufacture, administration, and in large gatherings for religious, political, recreational, or commercial purposes. These specially *urban* functions carried power, and with power, prestige. For whether it was a temple, a market, a tribunal, or a king's residence that originally determined the city's growth on a given site, a city was always a seat of some kind of power. A scholarly international meeting recently held in Chicago to examine the origins of the urban process in ancient times published its proceedings under the title: *The City Invincible*. Indeed, the city was a place from which the open country was dominated, where wealth was gathered, the locus of authority and responsibility. It claimed a long, lasting future of dominance.

Many cities were defeated, and even destroyed. Some rose again and again, to be vanquished and deserted in the end. The plains and valleys of the Middle East, where highly civilized peoples early started building cities, are now dotted with *tells*, hills shaped like truncated pyramids, erected by stratas of cities built each on top of the preceding one's ruins, upon a site which had thus become "naturally" dominant and fortified. But whatever the fate of individual cities, the urban way of life, urban occupations, and the prestige of the city have constantly attracted larger crowds of people all over the earth. Recently the urban population of our globe has become a majority of mankind. In the more advanced, better developed countries city dwellers form an overwhelming majority. Farming still occupies only a small and shrinking portion of the labor

* Jean Gottmann, *Economics, Esthetics, and Ethics in Modern Urbanization* (New York, The Twentieth Century Fund, 1962), pp. 2–10. Copyright © 1962 by The Twentieth Century Fund, Inc. Reprinted by permission.
  Jean Gottmann is with The Twentieth Century Fund. One of the world's outstanding geographers, he is the author of *Megalopolis*.

force, less than ten per cent even in a country with as plethoric an agricultural production as the United States. As a way of life, as an economic system the city has certainly won out through history and appears invincible today.

This special role of dominance, of authority and responsibility within the society it administers becomes diluted, however, as the urban population comes to coincide with the vast majority of the nation. What prestige is left to a condition which almost everybody shares? There is nothing "special" any more about residence in a city. This change affects much more than the attitude of the rural population towards the modern urban centers. It modifies the very structure of the city, the means and the aims of those who plan, build, and govern cities. Architects and urbanists used to be concerned mainly with beauty and prestige: their job was to build churches and castles, fortresses and ramparts. Because all these buildings housed prestigious and respected functions and people, they had to be spectacular, to impress the outsider, the people passing by. A certain kind of beauty, of esthetics was indeed one of the buildings' functions. It may have been functional to decorate and overstress the esthetic features. This past of architecture and urbanism has brought us an extraordinary artistic heritage, in fact most of the world's marvels. A great art thus evolved, going through many styles, schools, and stages.

The people of our century are more intent than ever on preserving the monuments of the past, on treasuring and admiring the art and techniques of architectural and urbanistic beauty. Every city retains, for the various aspects of community life, an urgent need of spectacular buildings, the materials, design, and appearance of which give expression to the beauty, dignity, and authority of the functions performed within and to the virtues of the owner, whether private or public, individual or corporate. But this is no longer the main market for the talents of the architect, urbanist, and builder. Those talents and endeavors are also and increasingly to be exercised for a completely different market of mass consumption, mass transportation, mass production, for the daily use of the rank and file as much as and perhaps more than for the use of those who hold power and prestige. And still we all want the city to be beautiful, as well as comfortable and accessible to all. The urbanization of the world carries with it social progress: a more urbane way of life for the vast majority of the people, more comfort, better education, more leisure, and better taste. Two centuries ago people craved more happiness for all; now we talk of the opportunity for excellence. Our social and political ethics require the greatest possible equality in distribution of benefits. Are such requirements consistent with esthetic demands inherited from a very different past, and with the economic mechanisms of the time?

These are not purely academic questions. The solutions provided are molding the environment of our generation and the next. Their discussion has already aroused strong feelings; for the appearance and structure of cities reach much deeper than just matters of habit, comfort, and landscape. As a seat of prestige and power in the midst of the open country, the city was a symbol of high moral values. Here religion was administered, government managed, trade transacted, all functions requiring that moral principles be elaborated and upheld there—for how could society survive and progress be made without such guarantees? But it was also well known that as loci of power and wealth the cities offered to the less virtuous the broad opportunity and frequent temptation of lax moral conduct in business or in private life. Many an angry voice cried out against the city's vices, condemning it to an apocalyptic downfall. Such castigations and prophecies are repeatedly found in the Bible, directed at Nineveh and Babylon, Jerusalem and Rome. Long would be the list of famous outbursts against one city or another in more recent times. Still, every voice so raised to condemn a city or a group of cities would also announce some new, clean, shining, saintly city to come, which would replace the corruption of the day. The behavior of the cityfolks and the morality of the city fathers are potent factors in the general esthetic feeling about the city. Operations of urban renewal that beautify a city miss their aim in terms of power and prestige if they pay little attention to the deep moral and ethical instincts easily aroused in the urban population.

Our very concept of the city has been exploded by the massive expansion of modern urbanization. A city which, with its suburbs, gathered a million people or more in a densely built-up area was an infrequent occurrence as recently as half a century ago. In the United States only three cities measured up to this standard in 1910; by 1960 five cities counted over a million inhabitants and 24 "standard metropolitan statistical areas" were in that category. In the same fifty years the number of urban places in the United States having a population between 250,000 and a million rose from 16 to 46 and the number inhabited by 50,000 to 250,000 people rose from 90 to 282. Although no other country could boast as many large cities, several smaller nations were even more urbanized: Great Britain, the Netherlands, Belgium, possibly Switzerland. The world outside the United States counted at least 72 cities of more than a million population by 1960; and if the concept of metropolitan area (or of the British conurbation) were adopted more generally, that figure would be above one hundred.

For, breaking out of the old bounds, walls, boulevards, or administrative limits, which set it apart, the city has massively invaded the "open country," though parts of the countryside may have kept their rural appearance. The growth in size of population has also meant a spectacular growth in area for the modern metropolis. Some metropolises, the expansion of which has been recent, sudden, and yet rather limited (such as the case with Madrid, for instance), still show a sharp demarcation between city-and-suburbs densely built up with multistoried structures and the surrounding areas where buildings are few and scattered. But such urban growths today bear witness to a rather underdeveloped kind of economy. The modern metropolis of a rapidly expanding economy floods the land around it, irregularly but over a wide radius.

The distinction between city growth and metropolitan growth refers to two stages in the process of urbanization: until recently the city grew in more or less orderly fashion, adding to the built-up area of yesterday new developments which could some day, when convenient, be included by consolidation in the city's administrative limits. Nowadays urbanization is so massive that entire administrative divisions, previously considered of a rank above the municipal one, are suburbanized, and occasionally the metropolitan area thus formed may claim more than one central city. A polynuclear structure often makes the pattern of relations between the component parts of the metropolitan region quite complex.

Modern urbanization increases city volume, or size, in several dimensions: to the expansion in area and in population is usually added an expansion in the variety of economic activities performed. This last results both from the mass of the urban or metropolitan system itself and from the ever deepening and developing division of labor, the intricacies of which are bound to multiply as the size of the market increases. Fifty years ago most small and medium-size cities in industrialized countries were "specialized": each lived from one special product or service supplied to the outside. There were mill towns, developed around one plant: a textile or steel mill, for instance. There were company towns built and controlled by a corporation to house a plant or two and the workers. There were university towns; cities that were political capitals, or fishing ports, or market towns, or military strongholds. It is becoming increasingly difficult in the better developed countries to find cities of some size which have remained so specialized. One can occasionally see a factory standing almost alone near a small village and draining its labor force from a radius of a dozen or more miles, but a community the size of a city will usually combine several functions, a whole collection of interrelated economic activities.

At the same time a new classification has been evolving, applying mainly in larger metropolitan areas: central city, satellite city, dormitory town, manufacturing city; and we believe that a category of "brains towns" is forming out of university towns to which further activities of an intellectual kind—research, mass media, and so on—are attracted. The enormous scale of modern urbanization multiplies the metropolitan centers around which entire constellations of towns are developing. For increases in population, area, and diversity proceed together, one pulling the other, and the whole process shapes urban districts of great variety and of such size as to become sections within the national state.

The rhythm of urbanization and industrialization has been accelerated since World War II. To a large extent this was the result of increased mechanization and automation in agriculture and in the simpler stages of industry. Smaller numbers of people can now produce more and more of a widening variety of goods. The technological revolution that made this mechanization and automation possible was accelerated by the great wars. Its application to a rapidly broadening area which is close to encompassing our entire planet was precipitated and helped by the new eminence taken by the United States in international relations and in the world economy. Many countries in various parts of the world began, sometimes almost unconsciously, to imitate the American way of life, at least in its external, more material aspects. Rapid urbanization has been one of the major characteristics of this way of life in our time.

Whether or not they wanted to organize their ways of living and working along American-inspired patterns, most countries today want more industries, more and better cities, fewer people on their farms. This state of mind, added to the normal play of economic forces chasing most of the available manpower from the primary towards the secondary and even the tertiary stages of economic activity, speeds up the pace of urbanization. The coming of age of the generations born since 1940 (much more numerous in most lands than the preceding generations had been) presents an abundance of new needs to be taken care of, and they can be taken care of only in the urban way: through employment and residence of an urban kind.

Mankind is reshaping its habitat. The much maligned trend towards urbanization has become so rapid and massive as to overshadow many other modern problems. The critics of modern urbanization are many. Much of what they say is right; but the parallels they draw with past cases hardly apply. The modern city takes on a volume that calls for new concepts as well as new methods. The change in scale produces a change in the nature of the city's problems and in the nature of the planning necessary to provide for the urban people's needs. . . .

Origin and Growth of Urbanization*

Kingsley Davis

. . . The first cities, doubtless small and hard to distinguish from towns, seem to have appeared in the most favorable places sometime between 6000 and 5000 B.C. From that time on, it can be assumed that some of the inventions which made larger settlements possible were due to towns and cities themselves—viz., writing and accountancy, bronze, the beginnings of science, a solar calendar, bureaucracy. By 3000 B.C., when these innovations were all exercising an influence in Egypt, Mesopotamia, and India, there were in existence what may be called "true" cities. After that there appears to have been, for some 2,000 years, a lull during which the most important innovations, toward the end of the period, were alphabetic writing and the smelting of iron. Curiously, the cities in the regions where city life had originated eventually went into eclipse, and it was not until Greco-Roman times that new principles made possible, in new regions, a marked gain in city existence. The fact that the greatest subsequent cultural developments did not occur primarily in the regions where the first cities arose suggests that cities are not always and everywhere a stimulant of economic and social advance. . . . If anything, the first cities had a stultifying effect on cultural progress, due perhaps to the unproductive insulation and excessive power of the urban elite. There is no doubt that the religio-magical traditionalism of the early cities was profound.

Why was there so little urbanization in ancient times, and why did it proceed so slowly from that point? The sites of the earliest "cities" themselves show that they were small affairs. The walls of ancient Babylon, for example, embraced an area of very roughly 3.2 square miles, and "Ur, with its canals, harbors, and temples, occupied some 220 acres; the walls of Erech encompass an area of just on two square miles." This suggests that the famous Ur could hardly have boasted more than 5,000 inhabitants and Erech hardly more than 25,000. The mounds of Mohenjo-daro in Sind cover a square mile, and Harappa in the Punjab had a walled area visible in 1853 with a perimeter of 2½ miles. These were evidently "cities" of 5,000–15,000 inhabitants, yet they were the chief centers for the entire Indus region, an area nearly two-thirds the size of Texas. Less is

* Kingsley Davis, "The Origin and Growth of Urbanization in the World," *The American Journal of Sociology*, 61 (March 1955), 430–437. Reprinted by permission of the University of Chicago Press. Copyright 1955 by the University of Chicago. Kingsley Davis is Professor of Sociology at the University of California, Berkeley.

known about the earliest Egyptian cities, for they were built with mud bricks and have long since disappeared beneath the alluvial soil. Tell el 'Amarna, the temporary capital built much later, about 1400 B.C., perhaps held something like 40,000 people. The wall of Hotep-Sanusert, an earlier capital built about 1900 B.C. on the Fayum, measured 350 by 400 meters and inclosed an area of approximately one-twentieth of a square mile. Thebes, at the height of its splendor as the capital of Egypt about 1600, was described by Greek writers as having a circumference of 14 miles. By a liberal estimate it may have contained 225,000 inhabitants.

To the questions why even the largest cities prior to 1000 B.C. were small by modern standards, why even the small ones were relatively few, and why the degree of urbanization even in the most advanced regions was very slight, the answer seems as follows: Agriculture was so cumbersome, static, and labor-intensive that it took many cultivators to support one man in the city. The ox-drawn plow, the wooden plowshare, inundation irrigation, stone hoes, sickles, and axes were instruments of production, to be sure, but clumsy ones. Not until iron came into use in Asia Minor about 1300 B.C. could general improvement in agriculture be achieved. The static character of agriculture and of the economy generally was fostered perhaps by the insulation of the religio-political officials from the practical arts and the reduction of the peasant to virtually the status of a beast of burden. The technology of transport was as labor-intensive as that of agriculture. The only means of conveying bulky goods for mass consumption was by boat, and, though sails had been invented, the sailboat was so inefficient that rowing was still necessary. The oxcart, with its solid wheels and rigidly attached axle, the pack animal, and the human burden-bearer were all short-distance means of transport, the only exception being the camel caravan. Long-distance transport was reserved largely for goods which had high value and small bulk—i.e., goods for the elite—which could not maintain a large urban population. The size of the early cities was therefore limited by the amount of food, fibers, and other bulky materials that could be obtained from the immediate hinterland by labor-intensive methods, a severe limitation which the Greek cities of a later period, small as they remained, nevertheless had to escape before they could attain their full size.

There were political limitations as well. The difficulty of communication and transport and the existence of multifarious local tribal cultures made the formation of large national units virtually impossible. The first urban-centered units were city-states, and when so-called "empires" were formed, as in Egypt, in the Sumerian region, and later in Assyria, much local autonomy was left to the subordinated areas, and the constant danger of revolt prevented the extension of the hinterlands of the cities very far or very effectively. It is symptomatic of the weakness of the early cities that they were constantly threatened and frequently conquered not only by neighboring towns but also by nonurban barbarians. Each wave of barbarians tended to rebuild the urban centers and to become agricultural and sedentary, only to be eventually overwhelmed in turn by new invaders. Other limiting factors were the lack of scientific medicine (which made urban living deadly), the fixity of the peasant on the land (which minimized rural-urban migration), the absence of large-scale manufacturing (which would have derived more advantage from urban concentration than did handicraft), the bureaucratic control of the peasantry (which stifled free trade in the hinterland), and the traditionalism and religiosity of all classes (which hampered technological and economic advance).

The limitations explain why we find, when the sites furnish adequate evidence, that the earliest cities were small affairs, usually no more than towns. Whether in the new or in the old world, even the biggest places could scarcely have exceeded 200,000 inhabitants, and the proportion of the total population living in them must have been not more than 1 or 2 per cent. From 50 to 90 farmers must have been required to support one man in a city.

If urbanization was to escape its early limitations, it had to do so in a new region, a region more open to innovation and new conceptions. As it turned out, the region that saw a later and greater urban development was farther north, the Greco-Roman world of Europe, flourishing approximately during the period from 600 B.C. to 400 A.D. Iron tools and weapons, alphabetic writing, improved sailboats, cheap coinage, more democratic institutions, systematic colonization—all tended to increase production, stimulate trade, and expand the effective political unit. Towns and cities became more numerous, the degree of urbanization greater. A few cities reached a substantial size. Athens, at its peak in the fifth century B.C., achieved a population of between 120,000 and 180,000. Syracuse and Carthage were perhaps larger.

The full potentialities of the ancient world to support a large city were realized only with the Romans. Through their ability to conquer, organize, and govern an empire, to put the immediate Italian hinterland to fruitful cultivation, to use both force and trade to bring slaves, goods, food, and culture to the imperial capital, they were able to create in Rome (with the possible exception of Constantinople some centuries later) the largest city that was to be known in the world until the rise of London in the nineteenth century. Yet, despite the fact that Rome and Constantinople came to hold populations of several hundred thousand, they were not able to resist conquest by far less urbanized outsiders. The eclipse of cities in Europe was striking. Commerce declined to the barest minimum; each locale became isolated and virtually self-sufficient; the social system congealed into a hereditary system. When finally towns and cities began to revive, they were small, as the following estimates suggest: Florence (1338), 90,000; Venice (1422), 190,000; Antwerp (sixteenth century), 200,000; London (1377), 30,000; Nuremberg (1450), 20,165; Frankfort (1440), 8,719.

Yet it was precisely in western Europe, where cities and urbanization had reached a nadir during the Dark Ages, that the limitations that had characterized the ancient world were finally to be overcome. The cities of Mesopotamia, India, and Egypt, of Persia, Greece, and Rome, had all been tied to an economy that was primarily agricultural, where handicraft played at best a secondary role and where the city was still attempting to supplement its economic weakness with military strength, to command its sustenance rather than to buy it honestly. In western Europe, starting at the zero point, the development of cities not only reached the stage that the ancient world had achieved but kept going after that. It kept going on the basis of improvements in agriculture and transport, the opening of new lands and new trade routes, and, above all, the rise in productive activity, first in highly organized handicraft and eventually in a revolutionary new form of production—the factory run by machinery and fossil fuel. The transformation thus achieved in the nineteenth century was the true urban revolution, for it meant not only the rise of a few scattered towns and cities but the appearance of genuine urbanization, in the sense that a substantial portion of the population lived in towns and cities.

Urbanization has, in fact, gone ahead much faster and reached proportions far greater during the last century and a half than at any previous time in world history. The tremendous growth in world trade during this period has enabled the urban population to draw its sustenance from an ever wider area. Indeed, it can truly be said that the hinterland of today's cities is the entire world. Contemporary Britain, Holland, and Japan, for example, could not maintain their urban population solely from their own territory. The number of rural inhabitants required to maintain one urban inhabitant is still great—greater than one would imagine from the rural-urban ratio *within* each of the highly urbanized countries. The reason is that much of agriculture around the world is still technologically and economically backward. Yet there can be no doubt that, whether for particular countries or for the entire globe, the ratio of urban dwellers to those who grow their food has risen remarkably. This is shown by the fact that the proportion of people living in cities in 1950 is higher than that found in any particular country prior to modern times and many times higher than that formerly characterizing the earth as a whole.

The rapidity of urbanization in recent times can be seen by looking at the most urbanized country, England. In 1801, although London had already reached nearly the million mark (865,000), England and Wales had less than 10 per cent of their population in cities of 100,000 or more. By 1901 no less than 35 per cent of the population of England and Wales was living in cities of 100,000 or more, and 58 per cent was living in cities of 20,000 or more. By 1951 these two proportions had risen to 38.4 and 69.3 per cent, respectively.

Britain was in the van of urban development. A degree of urbanization equal to that she had attained in 1801 was not achieved by

TABLE 1. PERCENTAGE OF WORLD'S POPULATION
LIVING IN CITIES

	Cities of 20,000 or More	Cities of 100,000 or More
1800	2.4	1.7
1850	4.3	2.3
1900	9.2	5.5
1950	20.9	13.1

any other country until after 1850. Thereafter the British rate of urbanization began slowly to decline, whereas that of most other countries continued at a high level. By assembling available data and preparing estimates where data were lacking, we have arrived at figures on urbanization in the world as a whole, beginning with 1800, the earliest date for which anything like a reasonable estimate can be obtained. The percentage of the world's population found living in cities is as shown in Table 1. It can be seen that the proportion has tended to do a bit better than double itself each half-century and that by 1950 the world as a whole was considerably more urbanized than Britain was in 1800. As everyone knows, the earth's total population has grown at an extremely rapid rate since 1800, reaching 2.4 billion by 1950. But the urban population has grown much faster. In 1800 there were about 15.6 million people living in cities of 100,000 or more. By 1950 it was 313.7 million, more than twenty times the earlier figure. Much of this increase has obviously come from rural-urban migration, clearly the most massive migration in modern times.

In 1800 there were apparently less than 50 cities with 100,-000 or more inhabitants. This was less than the number in the million class today and less than the number of 100,000-plus cities currently found in many single countries. By 1950 there were close to 900 cities of 100,000 or more people, which is more than the number of towns and cities of 5,000 or more in 1800.

TABLE 2. PERCENTAGE OF WORLD'S POPULATION
LIVING IN CITIES, BY REGIONS

	In Cities of 20,000 Plus	In Cities of 100,000 Plus
World	21	13
Oceania	47	41
North America (Canada and U.S.A.)	42	29
Europe (except U.S.S.R.)	35	21
U.S.S.R.	31	18
South America	26	18
Middle America and Caribbean	21	12
Asia (except U.S.S.R.)	13	8
Africa	9	5

As yet there is no indication of a slackening of the rate of urbanization in the world as a whole. If the present rate should continue, more than a fourth of the earth's people will be living in cities of 100,000 or more in the year 2000, and more than half in the year 2050. For places of 20,000 or more, the proportions at the two dates would be something like 45 per cent and 90 per cent. Whether such figures prove too low or too high, they nevertheless suggest that the human species is moving rapidly in the direction of an almost exclusively urban existence. We have used the proportion of the population in cities of 20,000 and 100,000 or more as a convenient index of differences and changes in degree of urbanization. Places of less than 20,000 also fit a demographic definition of "urban." When, therefore, more than a third of the population of a country lives in cities of the 100,000 class (38.4 per cent in England and Wales in 1951), the country can be described as almost completely urbanized (81 per cent being designated as "urban" in the English case in 1951). We thus have today what can be called "urbanized societies," nations in which the great majority of inhabitants live in cities. The prospect is that, as time goes on, a greater and greater proportion of humanity will be members of such societies.

The question may be raised as to how such an extreme degree of world urbanization will prove possible. Who will grow the food and fibers necessary for the enormous urban population? The answer is that agriculture may prove to be an archaic mode of production. Already, one of the great factors giving rise to urbanization is the rather late and as yet very incomplete industrialization of agriculture. As farming becomes increasingly mechanized and rationalized, fewer people are needed on the land. On the average, the more urbanized a country, the lower is its rural density. If, in addition to industrialized agriculture, food and fiber come to be increasingly produced by manufacturing processes using materials that utilize the sun's energy more efficiently than plants do, there is no technological reason why nearly all of mankind could not live in conurbations of large size.

The highest levels of urbanization are found today in northwestern Europe and in those new regions where northwest Europeans have settled and extended their industrial civilization. The figures are as shown in Table 2. Oceania is the most urbanized of the world's major regions, because Australia and New Zealand are its principal components. North America is next, if it is defined as including only Canada and the United States. The regions least urbanized are those least affected by northwest European culture, namely, Asia and Africa.

The figures for world regions are less valuable for purposes of analysis than are those for individual countries. The latter show clearly that urbanization has tended to reach its highest point wherever economic productivity has been greatest—that is, where the economy is industrialized and rationalized. This explains why urbanization is so closely associated with northwest Europeans and their culture, since they were mainly responsible for the industrial revolution. Of the fifteen most urbanized countries in the world, all but one, Japan, are European in culture, and all but four derive that culture from the northwest or central part of Europe.

The rate of urbanization in the older, industrial countries, however, is slowing down. During the twenty years from 1870 to 1890 Germany's proportion in large cities more than doubled; it nearly doubled again from 1890 to 1910; but from 1910 to 1940 the increase was only 36 per cent. In Sweden the gain slowed down noticeably after 1920. In England and Wales the most rapid urbanization occurred between 1811 and 1851. Contrary to popular belief, the fastest rate in the United States occurred between 1861 and 1891. Since, as we noted earlier, there has been no slowing-down of urbanization in the world as a whole, it must be that, as the more established industrial countries have slackened, the less-developed countries have exhibited a faster rate. In fact, such historical evidence as we have for underdeveloped areas seems to show that their rates of urbanization have been rising in recent decades. This has been the case in Egypt, where the rate is higher after 1920 than before; in India, where the fastest urbanization has occurred since 1941; in Mexico, where the speed-up began in 1921; and in Greece, where the fastest period ran from 1900 to 1930. Asia, for example, had only 22 per cent of the world's city population in 1900 but 34 per cent of it in 1950, and Africa had 1.5 per cent in 1900 but 3.2 per cent at the later date.

With respect to urbanization, then, the gap between the industrial and the preindustrial nations is beginning to diminish. The less-developed parts of the world will eventually, it seems, begin in their turn to move gradually toward a saturation point. As the degree of urbanization rises, it of course becomes impossible for the rate of gain to continue. The growth in the urban proportion is made possible by the movement of people from rural areas to the cities. As the rural population becomes a progressively smaller percentage of the total, the cities no longer can draw on a noncity population of any size. Yet in no country can it be said that the process of urbanization is yet finished. Although there have been short periods in recent times in England, the United States, and Japan when the city population increased at a slightly slower rate than the rural, these were mere interludes in the ongoing but ever slower progress of urban concentration.

The continuance of urbanization in the world does not mean the persistence of something that remains the same in detail. A city of a million inhabitants today is not the sort of place that a city of the same number was in 1900 or in 1850. Moreover, with the emergence of giant cities of five to fifteen million, something new has been added. Such cities are creatures of the twentieth century. Their sheer quantitative difference means a qualitative change as well.

One of the most noticeable developments is the ever stronger tendency of cities to expand outward—a development already observed in the nineteenth century. Since 1861, the first date when the comparison can be made, the Outer Ring of Greater London has been growing more rapidly than London itself. French writers prior to 1900 pointed out the dispersive tendency, as did Adna Weber in 1899. There is no doubt, however, that the process of metropolitan dispersion has increased with time. This fact is shown for the United States by comparing the percentage gains in population made by the central cities with those made by their satellite areas in forty-four metropolitan districts for which Thompson could get comparable data going back to 1900. The gains are as shown in

TABLE 3. PERCENTAGE INCREASE IN POPULATION IN 44 METROPOLITAN DISTRICTS IN THE UNITED STATES, 1900–1940

	Central Cities	Rest of Districts
1900–1910	33.6	38.2
1910–20	23.4	31.3
1920–30	20.5	48.7
1930–40	4.2	13.0

Table 3. The difference increases, until in 1930–40 the population outside the central city is growing more than three times as fast as that inside the central city. Furthermore, Thompson has shown that *within the metropolitan area outside the central cities* it was the "rural" parts which gained

faster than the urban parts, as the percentage increases per decade shown in Table 4 indicate. Clearly, the metropolitan districts were increasingly dependent on the areas outside the central cities, and especially upon the sparsely settled parts at the periphery of these areas, for their continued growth. Thompson showed that, the greater the distance from the center of the city, the faster the rate of growth.

The same forces which have made extreme urbanization possible have also made metropolitan dispersion possible, and the dispersion itself has contributed to further urbanization by making large conurbations more efficient and more endurable. The outward movement of urban residences, of urban services and commercial establishments, and of light industry—all facilitated by improvements in motor transport and communications—has made it possible for huge agglomerations to keep on growing without the inconveniences of proportionate increases in density. In many ways the metropolis of three million today is an easier place to live and work in than the city of five hundred thousand yesterday. Granted that the economic advantages of urban concentration still

TABLE 4. PERCENTAGE POPULATION INCREASE
OUTSIDE CENTRAL CITIES IN 44
METROPOLITAN DISTRICTS

	Urban Parts	Rural Parts
1900–1910	35.9	43.2
1910–20	30.2	34.5
1920–30	40.6	68.1
1930–40	7.3	28.1

continue and still push populations in the direction of urbanization, the effect of metropolitan dispersion is thus to minimize the disadvantages of this continued urban growth.

The new type of metropolitan expansion occurring in the highly industrial countries is not without its repercussions in less-developed lands as well. Most of the rapid urbanization now occurring in Africa and Asia, for example, is affected by direct contact with industrial nations and by a concomitant rise in consumption standards. Although private automobiles may not be available to the urban masses, bicycles and busses generally are. Hence Brazzaville and Abidjan, Takoradi and Nairobi, Jamshedpur and New Delhi, Ankara and Colombo, are not evolving in the same manner as did the cities of the eighteenth and nineteenth centuries. Their ecological pattern, their technological base, their economic activity, all reflect the twentieth century, no matter how primitive or backward their hinterlands may be. Thus the fact that their main growth is occurring in the present century is not without significance for the kind of cities they are turning out to be.

Speculation concerning the future of urbanization is as hazardous as that concerning any other aspect of human society. Following the direction of modern trends, however, one may conclude that, with the industrial revolution, for the first time in history urbanization began to reach a stage from which there was no return. The cities of antiquity were vulnerable, and the degree of urbanization reached was so thin in many societies as to be transitory. Today virtually every part of the world is more urbanized than any region was in antiquity. Urbanization is so widespread, so much a part of industrial civilization, and gaining so rapidly, that any return to rurality, even with major catastrophes, appears unlikely. On the contrary, since every city is obsolescent to some degree —more obsolescent the older it is—the massive destruction of many would probably add eventually to the impetus of urban growth.

The fact that the rate of world urbanization has shown no slackening since 1800 suggests that we are far from the end of this process, perhaps not yet at the peak. Although the industrial countries have shown a decline in their rates, these countries, because they embrace only about a fourth of the world's population, have not dampened the world trend. The three-fourths of humanity who live in underdeveloped countries are still in the early stages of an urbanization that promises to be more rapid than that which occurred earlier in the areas of northwest European culture.

How urbanized the world will eventually become is an unanswerable question. As stated earlier, there is no apparent reason why it should not become as urbanized as the most urban countries today—with perhaps 85–90 per cent of the population living in cities and towns of 5,000 or more and practicing urban occupations. Our present degree of urbanization in advanced countries is still so new that we have no clear idea of how such complete world urbanization would affect human society; but the chances are that the effects would be profound.

In visualizing the nature and effects of complete urbanization in the future, however, one must guard against assuming that cities will retain their present form. The tendency to form huge metropolitan aggregates which are increasingly decentralized will undoubtedly continue but probably will not go so far as to eliminate the central business district altogether, though it may greatly weaken it. At the periphery, it may well be that the metropolis and the countryside, as the one expands and the other shrinks, will merge together, until the boundaries of one sprawling conurbation will touch those of another, with no intervening pure countryside at all. The world's population doubles itself twice in a century, becoming at the same time highly urbanized, and as new sources of energy are tapped, the possibility of centrifugal metropolitan growth is enormously enhanced. If commuting to work could be done with the speed of sound and cheaply, one would not mind living two hundred miles from work. Almost any technological advance from now on is likely to contribute more to the centrifugal than to the centripetal tendency. It may turn out that urbanization in the sense of emptying the countryside and concentrating huge numbers in little space will reverse itself—not, however, in the direction of returning people to the farm but rather in that of spreading them more evenly over the land for purposes of residence and industrial work. "Rurality" would have disappeared, leaving only a new kind of urban existence.

Migration from Agriculture*

Dale E. Hathaway

. . . For the last four decades there has been a large out-migration from agriculture to the nonfarm economy. . . .

Because it has become so commonplace in our society we sometimes fail to grasp the magnitude of the migration from agriculture. Yet, for a nation lacking a positive policy to induce migration and which has fortunately largely avoided widespread natural or man-made disaster, the record is truly amazing. Since 1920 more than 25 million people have migrated from farms to urban areas and nonfarm occupations. Migration from farms has persisted through depressions and wars. Although the farm population in 1950 was only about two-thirds that of 1920, the absolute number of migrants during the past decade has been above earlier periods.

However, economic conditions have had a strong influence on the rate of out-migration from agriculture. In the 1920–30 decade more than 6 million people left agriculture—a rate of 19 per cent of the beginning population. During the thirties only slightly over 3.5 million

* Dale E. Hathaway, "Migration from Agriculture: The Historical Record and Its Meaning," *American Economic Review*, 50 (May 1960), 379–391. Reprinted by permission.

Dale E. Hathaway is Professor of Agricultural Economics at Michigan State University.

migrated, a rate of about 13 per cent. In the ten years from 1940 to 1950 the net migration exceeded 9 million persons, giving a rate of 31 per cent. It appears that the number of out-migrants during the 1950–60 decade has been about the same as in the forties, so that the rate probably has exceeded one-third.

All regions of the country have experienced an out-migration from agriculture. However, the rates have varied between regions in different ways at different times (Table 1). The variation between regions in rate of out-migration was relatively low during the twenties. During the thirties, however, there was a wide variation between regions, with

TABLE 1. NET CHANGE IN RURAL-FARM POPULATION BY MIGRATION, UNITED STATES AND REGIONS, 1920–30, 1930–40, 1940–50

Area	Rate of Change in Farm Population due to Migration		
	1920–30	1930–40	1940–50
United States	−19.3	−12.7	−30.9
New England	−13.0	+ 2.6	−21.8
Middle Atlantic	−18.7	− 1.3	−20.7
East North Central	−19.7	− 5.3	−22.6
West North Central	−17.5	−17.7	−29.2
South Atlantic	−25.0	−13.8	−31.9
East South Central	−19.8	−13.2	−33.4
West South Central	−17.3	−19.9	−44.0
Mountain	−19.4	−16.3	−32.6
Pacific	− .3	+ 4.9	−15.1

Source: *Net Migration from the Rural Farm Population, 1940–50*, Statistical Bulletin No. 176, June 1956, Table 1, p. 16.

the west North Central and west South Central having the highest rates. During the 1940–50 period the relative variation between geographical regions was again reduced, although the entire south and the west North Central regions experienced rates of out-migration above those for other regions.

One should not conclude immediately that this has been entirely a movement of people from what we generally classify as "the low-income areas" in agriculture (Table 2). For the decade 1940–50 the net migration from serious low-income farming areas was only one-third above that of the higher income areas. Among the generalized low-income farming areas classified by the Department of Agriculture there were many geographical regions from which the rate of out-migration was below that from medium- and high-income areas. Thus the rate of out-migration from a specific area depends upon a complex of socio-economic factors of which relative income level is but one.

A majority of the migrants from agriculture have gone to the large urban metropolitan areas of the North and West. The popular concept of large-scale movements from the South to Detroit and Chicago

TABLE 2. NET MIGRATION RATES FROM DIFFERENT FARMING AREAS CLASSIFIED BY INCOME LEVELS, UNITED STATES

Area	Rate of Net Migration*	
	1930–40	1940–50
Rural-farm	−12.7	−30.9
Medium and high-income farming areas	−13.2	−28.0
Low-income farming areas	−12.5	−33.8
Moderate low-income farming areas	− 8.3	−27.8
Substantial low-income farming areas	−13.9	−34.9
Serious low-income farming areas	−14.2	−36.9
Generalized low-income farming areas		
Appalachian Mountains and border areas		−27.8
Southern Piedmont and Coastal Plains		−34.8
Southeastern Hilly		−34.5
Mississippi Delta		−39.9
Sandy Coastal Plains of Arkansas, Louisiana, and Texas		−49.1
Ozark-Ouachita Mountains and Border		−33.4
Northern Lake States		−29.2
Northwestern New Mexico		−39.6
Cascade and Rocky Mountain areas		−16.0

* Change due to migration expressed as a percentage of farm population alive at both beginning and end of decade.

SOURCE: *Net Migration from the Rural Farm Population, 1940–50*, Statistical Bulletin No. 176, June 1956, Table A, p. 13.

are based on fact. The 1950–57 net migration to Michigan is estimated at about 520,000 persons. The high concentration of the in-migrants is illustrated by the estimate that two-thirds of the in-migrants went to the three counties including and adjacent to Detroit. Other northern and western metropolitan areas have had approximately similar experiences.

What has been true generally for migration from agriculture has been particularly true of nonwhites. They have concentrated very heavily in large urban areas. Thus the migration from farm areas has contributed very significantly to the growth of the labor force of the large urban areas. Some of the impacts of these movements upon the receiving areas will be discussed in a subsequent section.

Much economic theory has as an underlying assumption that units of resources are homogeneous and that, therefore, resource transfers

part one

Underlying Value Conflicts

As was pointed out in the Preface, these readings revolve around some of the fundamental value conflicts of our age. However, certain underlying issues will come up over and over again; the purpose of this section is to set forth these issues explicitly, so that the arena for discussion in the remainder of the book is clearly defined at the outset.

The two chapters in this section emphasize two primary sources of the controversy that surrounds urban life: (1) the rural and small-town hostility to the metropolis as a source of corruption of traditional values; and (2) criticism by those who believe in the city as the maker of civilization, but who see contemporary urban and suburban life as alien to civilized values.

2
Metropolis: Destroyer or Creator?

The city has elicited a generally unfavorable response from the American intellectual, and Morton and Lucia White document this fact carefully. They also point out the significant, and negative, influence this view of the city has had on the American planner, who feels that ". . . he has no mythology or mystique on which he can rest or depend." Moreover, this tradition of bias against the city has shaped the contemporary notions of the city's form and function—*vide* Frank Lloyd Wright.

But, says the sociologist Georg Simmel, intellectuality and the metropolitan way of life go hand in hand. In arriving at this conclusion, Simmel goes directly to a consideration of the impact on the individual of the monetary basis of the modern city. Now, intellectualism and money do not at first glance seem to be compatible; and certainly if intellectualism is to be viewed primarily as an attribute of writers and philosophers, as the Whites tended to view it, the attempt to connect it with money seems illogical. But there is much to be drawn from Simmel's careful and unemotional observations about the loss of life's richness and color in the metropolis; about the attempts by the individual to preserve his discrete qualities in the face of the leveling impact of money; and about the paradoxically high regard that city dwellers have for the most violent critics of city life.

26

The next two selections represent the confrontation of two absolutely opposite views of the modern city. Lewis Mumford recognizes that the city, in the course of history, has developed into a goods-producing mechanism; but he argues that the future requires another kind of shift in city function: ". . . significant improvements will come only through applying art and thought to the city's central human concerns, with a fresh dedication to the cosmic and ecological processes that enfold all being. We must restore to the city the maternal, life-nurturing functions, the autonomous activities, the symbiotic associations that have long been neglected or suppressed." Mumford's view is met head on by Robert Moses, New York's city planner extraordinary. What are these symbiotic associations and how may they be revived, asks Moses. After posing a series of practical questions to the critics of the modern city, Moses concludes: "Pending answers to these questions, those of us who have work to do and obstacles to overcome, who cannot hide in ivory towers writing encyclopedic theses, whose usefulness is measured by results, must carry on." It is the classic confrontation of the idealist and the practical man.

In Moses's view, those responsible for planning and administering the city are exhibiting competence in their jobs. But behind this argument lies a fundamental belief in the city. For exactly the opposite reason that Thoreau, for example, was anti-city, Moses is pro-city—that is, because he believes that the city enables man to live a richer, fuller life. However, Moses does not spell out the details of that better life. It remains for John Burchard to furnish us with some of the advantages of the metropolis over the village and the small town. Burchard's comment on the relationship between city size and its potential for enrichment is prompted by the often-voiced criticism of Lewis Mumford (who lives in the village of Amenia, New York) that cities have grown beyond the "human scale." According to Burchard, the real failure of the large city is not in its size but in its frequent failure to realize this potential for enrichment. "Our big cities are gradually declining to the dead level of the 50,000 town without shedding any of their metropolitan disadvantages. We are not going to have the little places that Wordsworth mourned the passing of a few hundred years ago; Amenia would not be much except for Manhattan; and our problem is not that of arresting the metropolis but of making it justify itself." Thus, at least one intellectual no longer regards the city as inherently a baneful influence and an unmitigated evil.

There remains the long-lived conflict between the rural and urban areas of America. As the Whites have pointed out, the strongest push in favor of the rural ways of life came from Jefferson; and the defenders of the city have had difficulty in shaking off the weight of authority he represents. It is to the rural-urban conflict that the National Resources Committee addresses itself in a short selection. The Committee concludes that rural problems are much the same as urban problems. If this is true, then the intellectuals and other critics of the city have no place to hide.

American Intellectual versus American City*

Morton and Lucia White

Although the city has become one of the most absorbing and most intensively studied social problems in America today, and although it is now fashionable for intellectuals to express an almost tender concern for its future, to hope that its decay can be arrested, and to offer plans for its revitalization, this has not always been the attitude of our greatest American thinkers. For a variety of reasons they have expressed different degrees of hostility toward urban life in America, hostility which may be partly responsible for a feeling on the part of today's city planner and urban reformer that he has no mythology or mystique on which he can rest or depend. We have no tradition of romantic attachment to the city in our highbrow literature, nothing that remotely resembles the Greek philosopher's attachment to the *polis* or the French writer's affection for Paris. And this fits very well with the frequently defended thesis that the American writer has been more than usually alienated from the society in which he lives, that he is typically in revolt against it. Throughout the nineteenth century our society was becoming more and more urbanized, but the literary tendency to denigrate the American city hardly declined in proportion. If anything, it increased in intensity.

Faced with this fact about the history of American thought, the contemporary student of the city can take one of two opposing attitudes. He, at his peril, can turn his back on the tradition of Jefferson, Emerson, Thoreau, Hawthorne, Melville, Poe, Henry Adams, Henry

* Morton and Lucia White, "The American Intellectual versus the American City," *Daedalus, Proceedings of the American Academy of Arts and Sciences*, 90, No. 1 (Winter 1961), 166–176. Copyright 1961 by Morton and Lucia White. Reprinted by permission.
Morton White is Professor of Philosophy at Harvard University.

James, Louis Sullivan, Frank Lloyd Wright, and John Dewey. In this case he will treat some of the American city's profoundest critics as irresponsible literary men or as idle metaphysicians who fled the city rather than face its problems. Or he can regard this critical tradition as a repository of deep, though troubling, wisdom, one which raises basic questions for any urban reformer, and some of whose premonitions and fears have been more than justified by the passage of time. There is no doubt that the second is the wiser course. He who would improve the American city can only profit by an awareness of what some of our greatest minds have said, felt, and thought about one of the most conspicuous and most troubling features of our national life.

One cannot deny, of course, that there were pro-urban literary voices like Whitman's, or that there were urban sociologists like Robert Park who tried to speak up for the city. But they are voices in "the city wilderness," never comparing in volume with the anti-urban roar in the national literary pantheon. The urbanist must face the fact that the anti-urbanist does not live only in the Kentucky hills, in the Rockies, in the Ozarks, in the Cracker country, or the bayous. He lives in the mind and heart of America as conceived by the intellectual historian. The intellect, whose home is the city, according to some sociologists, has been the American city's sharpest critic. Everyone knows that Jefferson once hoped to discourage the development of the city in America, but he was only the first of a long and varied list of critics of the city.

Jefferson despised the manners and principles of the urban "mob" as he knew it in Europe and he hoped to keep it from crossing the Atlantic intact. He certainly did not think of the city as "The Hope of Democracy," as some Progressive theorists did at the turn of the twentieth century. He adopted a conciliatory tone about the city in his old age when he said in 1816 that we could not possibly depend on England for manufactures, as he had originally thought, and therefore we *needed* cities. But this does not show any *love* for the city. The country and its yeomen Jefferson loved all his life; in his old age he grudgingly accepted the manufacturing city as a necessity.

The same War of 1812 which led Jefferson to reassess his views was followed by a great expansion of the American city. It inaugurated a major phase of urban civilization between the Revolution and the Civil War. By 1860 the urban population was eleven times what it had been in 1820. The early decades of the nineteenth century saw the decline of Jefferson's empiricism among American intellectuals, and the emergence of philosophical transcendentalism, but a distaste for the city persisted among American writers.

The growth of the city in the North produced an even sharper reaction in Ralph Waldo Emerson than the European city had produced in Jefferson. Emerson's first philosophical work, *Nature*, appeared in 1836, in the middle of that interval which witnessed an eleven-fold increase in our urban population. Its very title was a protest against what he thought was happening. Partly under the influence of English romanticism, Emerson and some of his friends took to deprecating manufacture, art, and civilization, and so it was not long before they took to criticizing the city, the greatest of artifacts. The distaste for the city as an artificial creation was associated in Emerson's mind, as it was in the case of many romantic thinkers, with doubts about the value of science as an avenue to truth. And yet Emerson agreed with the scientifically minded Jefferson about the nasty manners and principles of the city. Whereas Jefferson was given to arguing the defects of the city in common-sense political terms, Emerson sought to buttress his feelings by a metaphysical theory. Hence we may label his period as the metaphysical period of anti-urbanism. To be is to be natural for Emerson. In the wilderness he said he found "something more dear and connate than in streets or villages." The life of the city was "artificial and curtailed"; it destroyed solitude, poetry, and philosophy.

One will find passages in which Emerson extolled the application of science and the virtues of civilization, the need for sociability to educate a man's sympathies, and the advantages of specialization that allow each man to develop his own talents. This suggests a more friendly view of the industrial urban society which was emerging in his own lifetime. But he always harped on the human failings of State Street and commercialism. At times Emerson could celebrate the artifice of pure technology, but he persistently attacked the debasement of moral standards by those who pursued nothing but wealth in the cities as he knew them. One is reminded of Thorstein Veblen's praise of urban industry even as he attacked its financial captains, for it was Veblen who saw the modern industrial city as the *locus classicus* of conspicuous waste.

Thoreau went even farther than Emerson in his distaste for civilization and the city, for Thoreau also attacked the village and the farm. *Walden* is a bible of anti-urbanism, in which Thoreau celebrates the life of the isolated individual, living in Nature and free of *all* social attachments. No wonder that Thoreau refused to visit the Saturday Club, which provided one of the few values of Boston in Emerson's eyes: intellectual conversation. And when Thoreau refused, Perry Miller reminds us, he put his refusal in no uncertain terms: "The only room in Boston which I visit with alacrity is the Gentlemen's Room at the Fitchburg Depot, where I wait for cars, sometimes for two hours, in order to get out of town." No wonder Henry James said that Thoreau "was essentially a sylvan personage."

If Jefferson attacked the city on political grounds, and if Emerson and Thoreau may be represented as criticizing it from the point of view of transcendental metaphysics, what shall we say of Poe, Hawthorne and Melville, all of whom may be added to our list of pre-Civil War critics of the city? They were far from political theorists or meta-physicians but all of them saw the city as the scene of sin and crime. Speaking of them, Harry Levin says: "For our dreamers, America was a garden, an agrarian Eden, which was losing its innocence by becoming citified. Melville had located his City of Woe in London or Liverpool; Poe had tracked down imaginary crimes in the streets of an imagined Paris; and Hawthorne had exposed sins most luridly among the ruins of Rome." As in Jefferson's case, the urban models of extreme crime and sin-fulness were not located in the United States by most of our pre-Civil War anti-urbanists, but they saw dark omens in the streets of American cities which made them fear that they might become like Paris, London, Liverpool or Rome. . . .

Among the most influential and most fastidious observers . . . were Henry Adams and the younger Henry James. Both were men of literary genius, both were members of cultivated families with wealth in their backgrounds, and for both of them the American city provided a profound spiritual problem. Because Henry Adams and Henry James lived in the age of the city's supremacy, they did not speak of it, as Jeffer-son had, as a remote future phenomenon or as something existing in Europe alone. And, unlike Thoreau, they did not feel as though they had only the American city and the American wilderness to choose between. Adams and James were both refined, civilized, indeed urban men whose animadversions on the American city are made more significant precisely because they were not opposed to cities in principle. They demonstrate what a hard time the American city had at the hands of nineteenth-century intellectuals. For here at last were two *city* types who also found the American city sadly wanting. Their reaction to the American city is more esthetic, more literary, more psychological than that of their pred-ecessors Jefferson and Emerson. . . .

Although we are primarily concerned with recording the theme of *anti*-urbanism in American writing and thinking, it would be absurd to argue that *every* great writer or thinker in the American pan-theon was hostile to urban life. The fact is that at the end of the nine-teenth century there emerged a tendency to view the American city in a more friendly manner. By contrast to his brother Henry, William James had very little desire to escape from the American city into the past. His philosophy was one of hope, of optimism, of possibility—indeed, a little bit too much so—and it was this that allowed him to view the urbaniza-tion of America in a way that might encourage Americans to do some-thing about urban problems. Unlike Henry, he did not adore the great cities of Western Europe. For ten days after his arrival in Florence in 1875 he "was so disgusted with the swarming and reeking blackness of the streets and the age of everything, that enjoyment took place under protest." As for London, during his visit of 1889 he wrote his sister that he was "thoroughly sated" with it, and "never cared to see its yellow-brownness and stale spaciousness again."

William James loved the country but his love of nature was tempered by a fondness for sociability, and therefore he was unable to subscribe either to Thoreau's primitivism or to the ultracivilized sentiments of his brother. With Emerson he looked to the future, but unlike Emerson he did not think that the future excluded the possibility of a decent life in the cities of America. Many of William James's reactions to the buzzing confusion of New York of 1880 and 1900 had been unfavorable because of "the clangor, disorder and permanent earthquake conditions" which he experienced on his customary daylong visits. But in 1907 he spent a longer time there and, as he says, "caught the pulse of the machine, took up the rhythm, and vibrated *mit*, and found it simply magnificent." He spoke of it as an "*entirely* new New York, in soul as well as in body, from the old one, which looks like a village in retrospect. The courage, the heaven-scaling audacity of it all, and the *lightness* withal, as if there were nothing that was not easy, and the great pulses and bounds of progress, so many in directions all simultaneous that the coordination is indefinitely future, give a drumming background of life that I have never felt before. I'm sure that once *in* that movement, and at home, all other places would seem insipid." This was written to his brother, of all people, after the appearance of the latter's *The American Scene*, but William had evidently read the manuscript, for he says: "I observe that your book—'The American Scene,'—dear H., is just out. I must get it and devour again the chapters relative to New York." William would not have liked them upon rereading them, and one can imagine how Henry must have winced when William exclaimed, "I'm surprised at you, Henry, not having been more enthusiastic, but perhaps the superbly powerful subway was not opened when you were there!"

William James, like Walt Whitman, saw virtue and promise in the American city. Both William James and Whitman not only accept the city as an inescapable part of America, but they *enjoy* it, as Jefferson most certainly did not. The year of William James's discovery of what he called "the new New York" was 1907, when he delivered his most famous set of lectures, entitled *Pragmatism*, at Columbia. James thought his philosophy would mediate between the views of those whom he called "tenderfoot Bostonians" and those he labeled "Rocky Mountain toughs" in philosophy. It is not too fanciful to suppose that James identified the great future city, along with his pragmatic philosophy, as a blend of, a compromise between, the insipidity of Boston and the craggy brutality of the Rockies. A livable city on earth, one is tempted to say, is the social counterpart of James's pragmatism, and therefore he is one of the first great American writers to associate himself with the effort to accept what is good and to root out what is bad in the American city. He does not escape to the country with Emerson and Thoreau, or to the past with his brother and Henry Adams. He revives the wisdom of the older Jefferson after a century of transcendentalism, Brook-farming and expatriation, and adds to it a love of the city. In doing so he becomes the herald of a pragmatic phase in urban thinking.

But this pragmatic phase, in which the city was joyfully described by Frederic C. Howe in 1905 as "The Hope of Democracy," did not last very long. Indeed, Howe's book contained within itself the classical argument for the central city's impending destruction. "The open fields about the city are inviting occupancy," Howe said, "and there the homes of the future will surely be. The city proper will not remain the permanent home of the people. Population must be dispersed. The great cities of Australia are spread out into the suburbs in a splendid way. For miles about are broad roads, with small houses, gardens, and an opportunity for touch with the freer, sweeter life which the country offers." Howe calls the city the hope of democracy, but he is, it would appear, a suburban booster rather than a city-lover. He shares the basic inability of greater American intellectuals to go all out in their admiration for the modern American city.

A more striking illustration of the same thing may be found in the writings of John Dewey, the disciple of William James, who sympathized with so much of James's interest in the American city. In his earlier writing Dewey expressed a typically progressive interest in the city. This was part of the political liberalism of the period, with its interest in urban planning, social work, socialism, the single tax, and muckraking. The city was not regarded as a perfect form of life, but it was seen as having promise. And, to the extent to which it showed promise, it became the concern of all sorts of people who could criticize it in a constructive spirit quite different from that which dominated the work of militant anti-urbanists from Jefferson to Henry James. For a variety of reasons Chicago became the most conspicuous locale of this new way of looking at the city. It was the home of a great university, which had opened its doors in the 'nineties and which became a center of urban sociology and, it might be said, of urban philosophy. One can understand, therefore, why William James looked to Dewey and other Chicago intellectuals as his friends, and why they regarded him as their spiritual leader. For Chicago at the turn of the century was the home of James's pupil, Robert Park, his worshipper, Jane Addams, and his disciple, John Dewey.

As early as 1899 Dewey was urging that the congregation of men into cities was one of the most conspicuous features of the modern world and that no theory of education could possibly disregard the fact of urbanization. Indeed, *the* problem of education, as Dewey saw it in his *School and Society*, was how to adjust the child to life in the city. The earlier kind of rural environment, in which he had been raised as a boy in Vermont, had its virtues, he admitted. It encouraged habits of personal orderliness, industry, and responsibility; it led to a firsthand acquaintance with nature. But, Dewey said in 1899, "it was useless to bemoan the departure of the good old days . . . if we expect merely by bemoaning and by exhortation to bring them back." The problem, as Dewey saw it, was that of retaining some advantages of the older mode of life while training the child to cope with the new urban world. The school, therefore, was to be a miniature urban community, a microcosmic duplication of macrocosmic Chicago, much as Hull House was in Jane Addams' eyes. The essence of society, said Dewey—and in this he was joined by Robert Park and other sociologists—was communication—and therefore the school was to encourage and develop this peculiarly social phenomenon, this salient feature of the urban age. Dewey's progressivism in educational theory was defined by his broad conception of communication, his idea that it takes place while children are building blocks, dancing, and cooking, as well as on the more formal level of asserting propositions.

Soon, however, a new and more critical attitude toward the city began to enter Dewey's writing. In *The Public and Its Problems* (1927) he concluded that steam and electricity, the very forces that had created modern society, that had provided it with the means of transportation and communication that made urban concentration possible, were creating a situation in which communication at its most human level was being destroyed. The very forces which brought Bangkok and Chicago closer to each other and which brought people from isolated farms to urban centers had diminished the possibility of "face-to-face" relationships. The primary group, in the phrase of the sociologist, Charles Horton Cooley, was disappearing rapidly. And while Dewey did not use our current jargon, he said, in effect, that modern society was becoming a lonely crowd of organization men.

Dewey warned: "Unless local communal life can be restored, the public cannot adequately resolve its most urgent problem: to find and identify itself." But the local communal unit of which Dewey spoke now was not the enormous city as it was coming to be known in the twentieth century. It was more like the University Elementary School at the University of Chicago, or Hull House. "Democracy must begin at home," Dewey said, "and its home is the neighborly community." As a result, a curious reversal takes place in Dewey's thinking. Instead of taking the city as the model *for* the progressive school, he almost speaks as though the urban community should be modeled *on* the progressive school. Jefferson wrote at the end of his life: "As Cato concluded every speech with the words, 'Carthago delenda est,' so do I every opinion with the injunction, 'Divide the counties into wards.'" At the end of his life Dewey seemed to conclude every speech with the words, "Divide the cities into settlement houses." . . .

The moral message of the intellectual critic of the city today is not fundamentally different from what it was in the age of Jefferson, Emerson, and Dewey. For today's serious thinker must also build upon a respect for the fundamental values of education, individuality, and easy communication among men. But, unlike his predecessors, he cannot deceive himself about the *place* in which those values must be realized today. The wilderness, the isolated farm, the plantation, the self-contained New England town, the detached neighborhood are things of the past. All the world's a city now and there is no escaping urbanization, not even in outer space.

The Metropolis and Mental Life*

Georg Simmel

The deepest problems of modern life derive from the claim of the individual to preserve the autonomy and individuality of his existence in the face of overwhelming social forces, of historical heritage, of external culture, and of the technique of life. The fight with nature which primitive man has to wage for his *bodily* existence attains in this modern form its latest transformation. The eighteenth century called upon man to free himself of all the historical bonds in the state and in religion, in morals and in economics. Man's nature, originally good and common to all, should develop unhampered. In addition to more liberty, the nineteenth century demanded the functional specialization of man and his work; this specialization makes one individual incomparable to another, and each of them indispensable to the highest possible extent. However, this specialization makes each man the more directly dependent upon the

* Reprinted with permission of the publisher from *The Sociology of Georg Simmel*, by Georg Simmel, translated by Kurt H. Wolff (New York: The Free Press, 1950), pp. 409–422. Copyright 1950 by The Free Press.

Georg Simmel, although known in America as a sociologist, was Professor of Philosophy at the universities of Berlin and Strasbourg. He died in 1918.

supplementary activities of all others. Nietzsche sees the full development of the individual conditioned by the most ruthless struggle of individuals; socialism believes in the suppression of all competition for the same reason. Be that as it may, in all these positions the same basic motive is at work: the person resists to being leveled down and worn out by a social-techno-logical mechanism. An inquiry into the inner meaning of specifically modern life and its products, into the soul of the cultural body, so to speak, must seek to solve the equation which structures like the metropolis set up between the individual and the super-individual contents of life. Such an inquiry must answer the question of how the personality accommodates itself in the adjustments to external forces. This will be my task today.

The psychological basis of the metropolitan type of individuality consists in the *intensification of nervous stimulation* which results from the swift and uninterrupted change of outer and inner stimuli. Man is a differentiating creature. His mind is stimulated by the difference between a momentary impression and the one which preceded it. Lasting impressions, impressions which differ only slightly from one another, impressions which take a regular and habitual course and show regular and habitual contrasts—all these use up, so to speak, less consciousness than does the rapid crowding of changing images, the sharp discontinuity in the grasp of a single glance, and the unexpectedness of onrushing impressions. These are the psychological conditions which the metropolis creates. With each crossing of the street, with the tempo and multiplicity of economic, occupational and social life, the city sets up a deep contrast with small town and rural life with reference to the sensory foundations of psychic life. The metropolis exacts from man as a discriminating creature a different amount of consciousness than does rural life. Here the rhythm of life and sensory mental imagery flows more slowly, more habitually, and more evenly. Precisely in this connection the sophisticated character of metropolitan psychic life becomes understandable—as over against small town life which rests more upon deeply felt and emotional relationships. These latter are rooted in the more unconscious layers of the psyche and grow most readily in the steady rhythm of uninterrupted habituations. The intellect, however, has its locus in the transparent, conscious, higher layers of the psyche; it is the most adaptable of our inner forces. In order to accommodate to change and to the contrast of phenomena, the intellect does not require any shocks and inner upheavals; it is only through such upheavals that the more conservative mind could accommodate to the metropolitan rhythm of events. Thus the metropolitan type of man—which, of course, exists in a thousand individual variants—develops an organ protecting him against the threatening currents and discrepancies of his external environment which would uproot him. He reacts with his head instead of his heart. In this an increased awareness assumes the psychic prerogative. Metropolitan life, thus, underlies a heightened awareness and a predominance of intelligence in metropolitan man. The reaction to metropolitan phenomena is shifted to that organ which is least sensitive and quite remote from the depth of the personality. Intellectuality is thus seen to preserve subjective life against the overwhelming power of metropolitan life, and intellectuality branches out in many directions and is integrated with numerous discrete phenomena.

The metropolis has always been the seat of the money economy. Here the multiplicity and concentration of economic exchange gives an importance to the means of exchange which the scantiness of rural commerce would not have allowed. Money economy and the dominance of the intellect are intrinsically connected. They share a matter-of-fact attitude in dealing with men and with things; and, in this attitude, a formal justice is often coupled with an inconsiderate hardness. The intellectually sophisticated person is indifferent to all genuine individuality, because relationships and reactions result from it which cannot be exhausted with logical operations. In the same manner, the individuality of phenomena is not commensurate with the pecuniary principle. Money is concerned only with what is common to all: it asks for the exchange value, it reduces all quality and individuality to the question: How much? All intimate emotional relations between persons are founded in their individuality, whereas in rational relations man is reckoned with like a number, like an element which is in itself indifferent. Only the objective measurable achievement is of interest. Thus metropolitan man reckons with his merchants and customers, his domestic servants and often even with persons with whom he is obliged to have social intercourse. These features of intellectuality contrast with the nature of the small circle in which the inevitable knowledge of individuality as inevitably produces a warmer tone of behavior, a behavior which is beyond a mere objective balancing of service and return. In the sphere of the economic psychology of the small group it is of importance that under primitive conditions production serves the customer who orders the good, so that the producer and the consumer are acquainted. The modern metropolis, however, is supplied almost entirely by production for the market, that is, for entirely unknown purchasers who never personally enter the producer's actual field of vision. Through this anonymity the interests of each party acquire an unmerciful matter-of-factness; and the intellectually calculating economic egoisms of both parties need not fear any deflection because of the imponderables of personal relationships. The money economy dominates the metropolis; it has displaced the last survivals of domestic production and the direct barter of goods; it minimizes, from day to day, the amount of work ordered by customers. The matter-of-fact attitude is obviously so intimately interrelated with the money economy, which is dominant in the metropolis, that nobody can say whether the intellectualistic mentality first promoted the money economy or whether the latter determined the former. The metropolitan way of life is certainly the most fertile soil for this reciprocity, a point which I shall document merely by citing the dictum of the most eminent English constitutional historian: throughout the whole course of English history, London has never acted as England's heart but often as England's intellect and always as her moneybag!

In certain seemingly insignificant traits, which lie upon the surface of life, the same psychic currents characteristically unite. Modern mind has become more and more calculating. The calculative exactness of practical life which the money economy has brought about corresponds to the ideal of natural science: to transform the world into an arithmetic problem, to fix every part of the world by mathematical formulas. Only money economy has filled the days of so many people with weighing, calculating, with numerical determinations, with a reduction of qualitative values to quantitative ones. Through the calculative nature of money a new precision, a certainty in the definition of identities and differences, an unambiguousness in agreements and arrangements has been brought about in the relations of life-elements—just as externally this precision has been effected by the universal diffusion of pocket watches. However, the conditions of metropolitan life are at once cause and effect of this trait. The relationships and affairs of the typical metropolitan usually are so varied and complex that without the strictest punctuality in promises and services the whole structure would break down into an inextricable chaos. Above all, this necessity is brought about by the aggregation of so many people with such differentiated interests, who must integrate their relations and activities into a highly complex organism. If all clocks and watches in Berlin would suddenly go wrong in different ways, even if only by one hour, all economic life and communication of the city would be disrupted for a long time. In addition an apparently mere external factor: long distances, would make all waiting and broken appointments result in an ill-afforded waste of time. Thus, the technique of metropolitan life is unimaginable without the most punctual integration of all activities and mutual relations into a stable and impersonal time schedule. Here again the general conclusions of this entire task of reflection become obvious, namely, that from each point on the surface of existence—however closely attached to the surface alone—one may drop a sounding into the depth of the psyche so that all the most banal externalities of life finally are connected with the ultimate decisions concerning the meaning and style of life. Punctuality, calculability, exactness are forced upon life by the complexity and extension of metropolitan existence and are not only most intimately connected with its money economy and intellectualistic character. These traits must also color the contents of life and favor the exclusion of those irrational, instinctive, sovereign traits and impulses which aim at determining the mode of life from within, instead of receiving the general and precisely schematized form of life from without. Even though sovereign types of personality, characterized by irrational impulses, are by no means impossible in the city, they are, nevertheless, opposed to typical city life. The passionate hatred of men like Ruskin and Nietzsche for the metropolis is understandable in these terms. Their natures discovered the value of life alone in the unschematized existence which cannot be defined with precision for all alike. From the same source of this hatred of the metropolis surged their hatred of money economy and of the intellectualism of modern existence. . . .

Whereas the subject of this form of existence has to come to terms with it entirely for himself, his self-preservation in the face of the large city demands from him a no less negative behavior of a social nature. This mental attitude of metropolitans toward one another we may designate, from a formal point of view, as reserve. If so many inner reactions were responses to the continuous external contacts with innumerable people as are those in the small town, where one knows almost everybody one meets and where one has a positive relation to almost everyone, one would be completely atomized internally and come to an unimaginable psychic state. Partly this psychological fact, partly the right to distrust which men have in the face of the touch-and-go elements of metropolitan life, necessitates our reserve. As a result of this reserve we frequently do not even know by sight those who have been our neighbors for years. And it is this reserve which in the eyes of the small-town people makes us appear to be cold and heartless. Indeed, if I do not deceive myself, the inner aspect of this outer reserve is not only indifference but, more often than we are aware, it is a slight aversion, a mutual strangeness and repulsion, which will break into hatred and fight at the moment of a closer contact, however caused. The whole inner organization of such an extensive communicative life rests upon an extremely varied hierarchy of sympathies, indifferences, and aversions of the briefest as well as of the most permanent nature. The sphere of indifference in this hierarchy is not as large as might appear on the surface. Our psychic activity still responds to almost every impression of somebody else with a somewhat distinct feeling. The unconscious, fluid and changing character of this impression seems to result in a state of indifference. Actually this indifference would be just as unnatural as the diffusion of indiscriminate mutual suggestion would be unbearable. From both these typical dangers of the metropolis, indifference and indiscriminate suggestibility, antipathy protects us. A latent antipathy and the preparatory stage of practical antagonism effect the distances and aversions without which this mode of life could not at all be led. The extent and the mixture of this style of life, the rhythm of its emergence and disappearance, the forms in which it is satisfied—all these, with the unifying motives in the narrower sense, form the inseparable whole of the metropolitan style of life. What appears in the metropolitan style of life directly as dissociation is in reality only one of its elemental forms of socialization.

This reserve with its overtone of hidden aversion appears in turn as the form or the cloak of a more general mental phenomenon of the metropolis: it grants to the individual a kind and an amount of personal freedom which has no analogy whatsoever under other conditions. The metropolis goes back to one of the large developmental tendencies of social life as such, to one of the few tendencies for which an approximately universal formula can be discovered. The earliest phase of social formations found in historical as well as in contemporary social structures is this: a relatively small circle firmly closed against neighboring, strange, or in some way antagonistic circles. However, this circle is closely coherent and allows its individual members only a narrow field for the development of unique qualities and free, self-responsible movements. Political and kinship groups, parties and religious associations begin in this way. The self-preservation of very young associations requires the establishment of strict boundaries and a centripetal unity. Therefore they cannot allow the individual freedom and unique inner and outer development. From this stage social development proceeds at once in two different, yet corresponding, directions. To the extent to which the group grows—numerically, spatially, in significance and in content of life—to the same degree the group's direct, inner unity loosens, and the rigidity of the original demarcation against others is softened through mutual relations and connections. At the same time, the individual gains freedom of movement, far beyond the first jealous delimitation. The individual also gains a specific individuality to which the division of labor in the enlarged group gives both occasion and necessity. The state and Christianity, guilds and political parties, and innumerable other groups have developed according to this formula, however much, of course, the special conditions and forces of the respective groups have modified the general scheme. This scheme seems to me distinctly recognizable also in the evolution of individuality within urban life. The small-town life in Antiquity and in the Middle Ages set barriers against movement and relations of the individual toward the outside, and it set up barriers against individual independence and differentiation within the individual self. These barriers were such that under them modern man could not have breathed. Even today a metropolitan man who is placed in a small town feels a restriction similar, at least, in kind. The smaller the circle which forms our milieu is, and the more restricted those relations to others are which dissolve the boundaries of the individual, the more anxiously the circle guards the achievements, the conduct of life, and the outlook of the individual, and the more readily a quantitative and qualitative specialization would break up the framework of the whole little circle.

The ancient *polis* in this respect seems to have had the very character of a small town. The constant threat to its existence at the hands of enemies from near and afar effected strict coherence in political and military respects, a supervision of the citizen by the citizen, a jealousy of the whole against the individual whose particular life was suppressed to such a degree that he could compensate only by acting as a despot in his own household. The tremendous agitation and excitement, the unique colorfulness of Athenian life, can perhaps be understood in terms of the fact that a people of incomparably individualized personalities struggled against the constant inner and outer pressure of a de-individualizing small town. This produced a tense atmosphere in which the weaker individuals were suppressed and those of stronger natures were incited to prove themselves in the most passionate manner. This is precisely why it was that there blossomed in Athens what must be called, without defining it exactly, "the general human character" in the intellectual development of our species. For we maintain factual as well as historical validity for the following connection: the most extensive and the most general contents and forms of life are most intimately connected with the most individual ones. They have a preparatory stage in common, that is, they find their enemy in narrow formations and groupings the maintenance of which places both of them into a state of defense against expanse and generality lying without and the freely moving individuality within. Just as in the feudal age, the "free" man was the one who stood under the law of the land, that is, under the law of the largest social orbit, and the unfree man was the one who derived his right merely from the narrow circle of a feudal association and was excluded from the larger social orbit—so today metropolitan man is "free" in a spiritualized and refined sense, in contrast to the pettiness and prejudices which hem in the small-town man. For the reciprocal reserve and indifference and the intellectual life conditions of large circles are never felt more strongly by the individual in their impact upon his independence than in the thickest crowd of the big city. This is because the bodily proximity and narrowness of space makes the mental distance only the more visible. It is obviously only the obverse of this freedom if, under certain circumstances, one nowhere feels as lonely and lost as in the metropolitan crowd. For here as elsewhere it is by no means necessary that the freedom of man be reflected in his emotional life as comfort. . . .

Cities are, first of all, seats of the highest economic division of labor. They produce thereby such extreme phenomena as in Paris the remunerative occupation of the *quatorzième*. They are persons who identify themselves by signs on their residences and who are ready at the dinner hour in correct attire, so that they can be quickly called upon if a dinner party should consist of thirteen persons. In the measure of its expansion, the city offers more and more the decisive conditions of the division of labor. It offers a circle which through its size can absorb a highly diverse variety of services. At the same time, the concentration of individuals and their struggle for customers compel the individual to specialize in a function from which he cannot be readily displaced by another. It is decisive that city life has transformed the struggle with nature for livelihood into an inter-human struggle for gain, which here is not granted by nature but by other men. For specialization does not flow only from the competition for gain but also from the underlying fact that the seller must always seek to call forth new and differentiated needs of the lured customer. In order to find a source of income which is not yet exhausted, and to find a function which cannot readily be displaced, it is necessary to specialize in one's services. This process promotes differentiation, refinement, and the enrichment of the public's needs, which obviously must lead to growing personal differences within this public.

All this forms the transition to the individualization of mental and psychic traits which the city occasions in proportion to its size. There is a whole series of obvious causes underlying this process. First, one must meet the difficulty of asserting his own personality within the dimensions of metropolitan life. Where the quantitative increase in importance and the expense of energy reach their limits, one seizes upon qualitative differentiation in order somehow to attract the attention of the social circle by playing upon its sensitivity for differences. Finally, man is tempted to adopt the most tendentious peculiarities, that is, the specifically metropolitan extravagances of mannerism, caprice, and preciousness. Now, the meaning of these extravagances does not at all lie in the contents of such behavior, but rather in its form of "being different," of standing out in a striking manner and thereby attracting attention. For many character types, ultimately the only means of saving for themselves some modicum of self-esteem and the sense of filling a position is indirect, through the awareness of others. In the same sense a seemingly insignificant factor is operating, the cumulative effects of which are, however, still noticeable. I refer to the brevity and scarcity of the inter-human contacts granted to the metropolitan man, as compared with social intercourse in the small town. The temptation to appear "to the point," to appear concentrated and strikingly characteristic, lies much closer to the individual in brief metropolitan contacts than in an atmosphere in which frequent and prolonged association assures the personality of an unambiguous image of himself in the eyes of the other.

The most profound reason, however, why the metropolis conduces to the urge for the most individual personal existence—no matter whether justified and successful—appears to me to be the following: the development of modern culture is characterized by the preponderance of what one may call the "objective spirit" over the "subjective spirit." This is to say, in language as well as in law, in the technique of production as well as in art, in science as well as in the objects of the domestic environment, there is embodied a sum of spirit. The individual in his intellectual development follows the growth of this spirit very imperfectly and at an ever increasing distance. If, for instance, we view the immense culture which for the last hundred years has been embodied in things and in knowledge, in institutions and in comforts, and if we compare all this with the cultural progress of the individual during the same period—at least in high status groups—a frightful disproportion in growth between the two becomes evident. Indeed, at some points we notice a retrogression in the culture of the individual with reference to spirituality, delicacy, and idealism. This discrepancy results essentially from the growing division of labor. For the division of labor demands from the individual an ever more one-sided accomplishment, and the greatest advance in a one-sided pursuit only too frequently means dearth to the personality of the individual. In any case, he can cope less and less with the overgrowth of objective culture. The individual is reduced to a negligible quantity, perhaps less in his consciousness than in his practice and in the totality of his obscure emotional states that are derived from this practice. The individual has become a mere cog in an enormous organization of things and powers which tear from his hands all progress, spirituality, and value in order to transform them from their subjective form into the form of a purely objective life. It needs merely to be pointed out that the metropolis is the genuine arena of this culture which outgrows all personal life. Here in buildings and educational institutions, in the wonders and comforts of space-conquering technology, in the formations of community life, and in the visible institutions of the state, is offered such an overwhelming fullness of crystallized and impersonalized spirit that the personality, so to speak, cannot maintain itself under its impact. On the one hand, life is made infinitely easy for the personality in that stimulations, interests, uses of time and consciousness are offered to it from all sides. They carry the person as if in a stream, and one needs hardly to swim for oneself. On the other hand, however, life is composed more and more of these impersonal contents and offerings which tend to displace the genuine personal colorations and incomparabilities. This results in the individual's summoning the utmost in uniqueness and particularization, in order to preserve his most personal core. He has to exaggerate this personal element in order to remain audible even to himself. The atrophy of individual culture through the hypertrophy of objective culture is one reason for the bitter hatred which the preachers of the most extreme individualism, above all Nietzsche, harbor against the metropolis. But it is, indeed, also a reason why these preachers are so passionately loved in the metropolis and why they appear to the metropolitan man as the prophets and saviors of his most unsatisfied yearnings. . . .

The Mission of the City*

Lewis Mumford

In taking form, the ancient city brought together many scattered organs of the common life, and within its walls promoted their interaction and fusion. The common functions that the city served were important; but the common purposes that emerged through quickened methods of communication and co-operation were even more significant. The city mediated between the cosmic order, revealed by the astronomer priests, and the unifying enterprises of kingship. The first took form within the temple and its sacred compound, the second within the citadel and the bounding city wall. By polarizing hitherto untapped human aspirations and drawing them together in a central political and religious nucleus, the city was able to cope with the immense generative abundance of neolithic culture.

By means of the order so established, large bodies of men were for the first time brought into effective co-operation. Organized in disciplined work groups, deployed by central command, the original urban populations in Mesopotamia, Egypt, and the Indus Valley controlled flood, repaired storm damage, stored water, remodelled the landscape, built up a great water network for communication and transportation, and filled the urban reservoirs with human energy available for other collective enterprises. In time, the rulers of the city created an internal fabric of order and justice that gave to the mixed populations of cities, by conscious effort, some of the moral stability and mutual aid of the village. Within the theater of the city new dramas of life were enacted.

But against these improvements we must set the darker contributions of urban civilization: war, slavery, vocational over-specialization, and in many places, a persistent orientation toward death. These institutions and activities, forming a 'negative symbiosis,' have accompanied the city through most of its history, and remain today in markedly brutal form, without their original religious sanctions, as the greatest threat to further human development. Both the positive and the negative aspects of the ancient city have been handed on, in some degree, to every later urban structure.

Through its concentration of physical and cultural power,

* Lewis Mumford, *The City in History* (New York: Harcourt, Brace & World, Inc., 1961), pp. 568–576. © 1961, by Lewis Mumford. Reprinted by permission of Harcourt, Brace & World, Inc.

Lewis Mumford is the author of numerous articles on city planning, the history of the city, and the role of the city in social life.

the city heightened the tempo of human intercourse and translated its products into forms that could be stored and reproduced. Through its monuments, written records, and orderly habits of association, the city enlarged the scope of all human activities, extending them backwards and forwards in time. By means of its storage facilities (buildings, vaults, archives, monuments, tablets, books), the city became capable of transmitting a complex culture from generation to generation, for it marshalled together not only the physical means but the human agents needed to pass on and enlarge this heritage. That remains the greatest of the city's gifts. As compared with the complex human order of the city, our present ingenious electronic mechanisms for storing and transmitting information are crude and limited.

From the original urban integration of shrine, citadel, village, workshop, and market, all later forms of the city have, in some measure, taken their physical structure and their institutional patterns. Many parts of this fabric are still essential to effective human association, not least those that sprang originally from the shrine and the village. Without the active participation of the primary group, in family and neighborhood, it is doubtful if the elementary moral loyalties—respect for the neighbor and reverence for life—can be handed on, without savage lapses, from the old to the young.

At the other extreme, it is doubtful, too, whether those multifarious co-operations that do not lend themselves to abstraction and symbolization can continue to flourish without the city, for only a small part of the contents of life can be put on the record. Without the superposition of many different human activities, many levels of experience, within a limited urban area, where they are constantly on tap, too large a portion of life would be restricted to record-keeping. The wider the area of communication and the greater the number of participants, the more need there is for providing numerous accessible permanent centers for face-to-face intercourse and frequent meetings at every human level.

The recovery of the essential activities and values that first were incorporated in the ancient cities, above all those of Greece, is accordingly a primary condition for the further development of the city in our time. Our elaborate rituals of mechanization cannot take the place of the human dialogue, the drama, the living circle of mates and associates, the society of friends. These sustain the growth and reproduction of human culture, and without them the whole elaborate structure becomes meaningless—indeed actively hostile to the purposes of life.

Today the physical dimensions and the human scope of the city have changed; and most of the city's internal functions and structures must be recast to promote effectively the larger purposes that shall be served: the unification of man's inner and outer life, and the progressive unification of mankind itself. The city's active role in future is to bring to the highest pitch of development the variety and individuality of regions, cultures, personalities. These are complementary purposes: their alternative is the current mechanical grinding down of both the landscape and the human personality. Without the city modern man would have no effective defenses against those mechanical collectives that, even now, are ready to make all veritably human life superfluous, except to perform a few subservient functions that the machine has not yet mastered.

Ours is an age in which the increasingly automatic processes of production and urban expansion have displaced the human goals they are supposed to serve. Quantitative production has become, for our mass-minded contemporaries, the only imperative goal: they value quantification without qualification. In physical energy, in industrial productivity, in invention, in knowledge, in population the same vacuous expansions and explosions prevail. As these activities increase in volume and in tempo, they move further and further away from any humanly desirable objectives. As a result, mankind is threatened with far more formidable inundations than ancient man learned to cope with. To save himself he must turn his attention to the means of controlling, directing, organizing, and subordinating to his own biological functions and cultural purposes the insensate forces that would, by their very superabundance, undermine his life. He must curb them and even eliminate them completely when, as in the case of nuclear and bacterial weapons, they threaten his very existence.

Now it is not a river valley, but the whole planet, that must be brought under human control: not an unmanageable flood of water, but even more alarming and malign explosions of energy that might disrupt the entire ecological system on which man's own life and welfare depends. The prime need of our age is to contrive channels for excessive energies and impetuous vitalities that have departed from organic norms and limits: cultural flood control in every field calls for the erection of embankments, dams, reservoirs, to even out the flow and spread it into the final receptacles, the cities and regions, the groups, families, and personalities, who will be able to utilize this energy for their own growth and development. If we were prepared to restore the habitability of the earth and cultivate the empty spaces in the human soul, we should not be so preoccupied with sterile escapist projects for exploring inter-planetary space, or with even more rigorously dehumanized policies based on the strategy of wholesale collective extermination. It is time to come back to earth and confront life in all its organic fecundity, diversity, and creativity, instead of taking refuge in the under-dimensioned world of Post-historic Man.

Modern man, unfortunately, has still to conquer the dangerous aberrations that took institutional form in the cities of the Bronze Age and gave a destructive destination to our highest achievements. Like the rulers of the Bronze Age, we still regard power as the chief manifestation of divinity, or if not that, the main agent of human development. But 'absolute power,' like 'absolute weapons,' belongs to the same magico-religious scheme as ritual human sacrifice. Such power destroys the symbiotic co-operation of man with all other aspects of nature, and of men with other men. Living organisms can use only limited amounts of energy. 'Too much' or 'too little' is equally fatal to organic existence. Organisms, societies, human persons, not least, cities, are delicate devices for regulating energy and putting it to the service of life.

The chief function of the city is to convert power into form, energy into culture, dead matter into the living symbols of art, biological reproduction into social creativity. The positive functions of the city cannot be performed without creating new institutional arrangements, capable of coping with the vast energies modern man now commands: arrangements just as bold as those that originally transformed the overgrown village and its stronghold into the nucleated, highly organized city.

These necessary changes could hardly be envisaged, were it not for the fact that the negative institutions that accompanied the rise of the city have for the last four centuries been falling into decay, and seemed until recently to be ready to drop into limbo. . . . slavery, forced labor, legalized expropriation, class monopoly of knowledge, have been giving way to free labor, social security, universal literacy, free education, open access to knowledge, and the beginnings of universal leisure, such as is necessary for wide participation in political duties. If vast masses of people in Asia, Africa, and South America still live under primitive conditions and depressing poverty, even the ruthless colonialism of the nineteenth century brought to these peoples the ideas that would release them. 'The heart of darkness,' from Livingstone on to Schweitzer, was pierced by a shaft of light.

In short, the oppressive conditions that limited the development of cities throughout history have begun to disappear. Property, caste, even vocational specialization have—through the graded income tax and the 'managerial revolution'—lost most of their hereditary fixations. What Alexis de Tocqueville observed a century ago is now more true than ever: the history of the last eight hundred years is the history of the progressive equalization of classes. This change holds equally of capitalist and communist systems, in a fashion that might have shocked Karl Marx, but would not have surprised John Stuart Mill. For the latter foresaw the conditions of dynamic equilibrium under which the advances of the machine economy might at last be turned to positive human advantage. Until but yesterday, then, it seemed that the negative symbiosis that accompanied the rise of the city was doomed. The task of the emerging city was to give an ideal form to these radically superior conditions of life.

Unfortunately, the evil institutions that accompanied the

rise of the ancient city have been resurrected and magnified in our own time: so the ultimate issue is in doubt. Totalitarian rulers have reappeared, sometimes elevated, like Hitler, into deities, or mummified in Pharaoh-fashion after death, for worship, like Lenin and Stalin. Their methods of coercion and terrorism surpass the vilest records of ancient rulers, and the hoary practice of exterminating whole urban populations has even been exercised by the elected leaders of democratic states, wielding powers of instantaneous destruction once reserved to the gods. Everywhere secret knowledge has put an end to effective criticism and democratic control; and the emancipation from manual labor has brought about a new kind of enslavement: abject dependence upon the machine. The monstrous gods of the ancient world have all reappeared, hugely magnified, demanding total human sacrifice. To appease their super-Moloch in the Nuclear Temples, whole nations stand ready, supinely, to throw their children into his fiery furnace.

If these demoralizing tendencies continue, the forces that are now at work will prove uncontrollable and deadly; for the powers man now commands must, unless they are detached from their ancient ties to the citadel, and devoted to human ends, lead from their present state of paranoid suspicion and hatred to a final frenzy of destruction. On the other hand, if the main negative institutions of civilization continue to crumble—that is, if the passing convulsions of totalitarianism mark in fact the death-throes of the old order—is it likely that war will escape the same fate? War was one of the 'lethal genes' transmitted by the city from century to century, always doing damage but never yet widely enough to bring civilization itself to an end. That period of tolerance is now over. If civilization does not eliminate war as an open possibility, our nuclear agents will destroy civilization—and possibly exterminate mankind. The vast village populations that were once reservoirs of life will eventually perish with those of the cities.

Should the forces of life, on the other hand, rally together, we shall stand on the verge of a new urban implosion. When cities were first founded, an old Egyptian scribe tells us, the mission of the founder was to "put the gods in their shrines." The task of the coming city is not essentially different: its mission is to put the highest concerns of man at the center of all his activities: to unite the scattered fragments of the human personality, turning artificially dismembered men—bureaucrats, specialists, 'experts,' depersonalized agents—into complete human beings, repairing the damage that has been done by vocational separation, by social segregation, by the over-cultivation of a favored function, by tribalisms and nationalisms, by the absence of organic partnerships and ideal purposes.

Before modern man can gain control over the forces that now threaten his very existence, he must resume possession of himself. This sets the chief mission for the city of the future: that of creating a visible regional and civic structure, designed to make man at home with his deeper self and his larger world, attached to images of human nurture and love.

We must now conceive the city, accordingly, not primarily as a place of business or government, but as an essential organ for expressing and actualizing the new human personality—that of 'One World Man.' The old separation of man and nature, of townsman and countryman, of Greek and barbarian, of citizen and foreigner, can no longer be maintained: for communication, the entire planet is becoming a village; and as a result, the smallest neighborhood or precinct must be planned as a working model of the larger world. Now it is not the will of a single deified ruler, but the individual and corporate will of its citizens, aiming at self-knowledge, self-government, and self-actualization, that must be embodied in the city. Not industry but education will be the center of their activities; and every process and function will be evaluated and approved just to the extent that it furthers human development, whilst the city itself provides a vivid theater for the spontaneous encounters and challenges and embraces of daily life.

. . . the city has undergone many changes during the last five thousand years; and further changes are doubtless in store. But the innovations that beckon urgently are not in the extension and perfection of physical equipment: still less in multiplying automatic electronic devices for dispersing into formless sub-urban dust the remaining organs of culture. Just the contrary: significant improvements will come only through applying art and thought to the city's central human concerns, with a fresh dedication to the cosmic and ecological processes that enfold all being. We must restore to the city the maternal, life-nurturing functions, the autonomous activities, the symbiotic associations that have long been neglected or suppressed. For the city should be an organ of love; and the best economy of cities is the care and culture of men.

The city first took form as the home of a god: a place where eternal values were represented and divine possibilities revealed. Though the symbols have changed the realities behind them remain. We know now, as never before, that the undisclosed potentialities of life reach far beyond the proud algebraics of contemporary science; and their promises for the further transformations of man are as enchanting as they are inexhaustible. Without the religious perspectives fostered by the city, it is doubtful if more than a small part of man's capacities for living and learning could have developed. Man grows in the image of his gods, and up to the measure they have set. The mixture of divinity, power, and personality that brought the ancient city into existence must be weighed out anew in terms of the ideology and the culture of our own time, and poured into fresh civic, regional, and planetary molds. In order to defeat the insensate forces that now threaten civilization from within, we must transcend the original frustrations and negations that have dogged the city throughout its history. Otherwise the sterile gods of power, unrestrained by organic limits or human goals, will remake man in their own faceless image and bring human history to an end.

The final mission of the city is to further man's conscious participation in the cosmic and the historic process. Through its own complex and enduring structure, the city vastly augments man's ability to interpret these processes and take an active, formative part in them, so that every phase of the drama it stages shall have, to the highest degree possible, the illumination of consciousness, the stamp of purpose, the color of love. That magnification of all the dimensions of life, through emotional communion, rational communication, technological mastery, and above all, dramatic representation, has been the supreme office of the city in history. And it remains the chief reason for the city's continued existence.

Are Cities Dead?*

Robert Moses

I picked up a New York City paper one morning recently and was appalled by the space and emphasis given to an obscure assistant professor with no record of administration, who, enjoying a foundation grant and speaking for a regional civic organization, prophesied imminent chaos and the early disintegration of our metropolis. He maintained that there are 1467 municipal agencies, fiercely independent, viciously uncoordinated, and shamelessly spending taxpayers' money in frantic insanity.

These counsels of despair come just as the Congress plans a Department of Urban Affairs of Cabinet rank. If the new Secretary begins by believing that American cities are doomed in spite of the increasingly rapid shift from rural to urban centers, he will accomplish little. If emphasis

* Robert Moses, "Are Cities Dead?" *The Atlantic Monthly*, 209 (January 1962), 55–58. Reprinted by permission.

Robert Moses is currently President of the New York World's Fair 1964–1965 Corporation. He has held many planning positions in the New York City and State governments.

is on anything but local initiative, the effect will be zero, and we shall have merely elevated a bureau to an expensive department and put another bureaucrat in orbit. Anyway, if we are to have a new Secretary, let us see that he believes in cities.

There are plenty of things that are wrong with our cities. These things should not be slurred over or forgotten. There are many failures which should be appraised. But why exaggerate? Why imply that the faults are beyond redemption? Why minimize notable evidence of progress? Why ignore the remarkable people and achievements which make our big cities the powerful magnets they are?

One of the most-quoted Jeremiahs who inveigh against the condition of our cities is Lewis Mumford, author of *The City in History*. He is widely acclaimed in the academic world. I object to these Jeremiahs primarily because they attempt to poison a rising generation of ordinarily optimistic young Americans. There is another good reason for deprecating this school of thought: those who undermine the very foundations and *raison d'être* of cities, and not merely the incidental mistakes of individuals, make municipal administration increasingly unattractive and relegate it finally to the lowest politics and the poorest talent.

Suppose we were to ask some of our best and most ambitious mayors, battling valiantly for limited, immediate objectives, whether concentrations of population are beyond improvement, whether the *raison d'être* of the metropolis is gone, and whether their plans for redevelopment are essentially futile. I mean men like Lee of New Haven, Dilworth of Philadelphia, Miriani of Detroit, and former Mayor Morrison of New Orleans. Are the citizens who believe in such men now to be told that their trust has been betrayed?

There is, indeed, much wrong with cities—big and little—but the answer is not to abandon or completely to rebuild them on abstract principles. Only on paper can you disperse concentrations of population and create small urban stars with planned satellites around them. In the course of many years devoted to reclamation of water front, manufacturing of topsoil to cover thousands of acres of new parks, buying and preserving large areas of natural woodlands and shores in advance of the realtor and subdivider, planting thousands of trees along parkways and expressways, building hundreds of playgrounds, planning cultural centers in place of decaying tenements, tightening zoning and building laws, restricting billboards, opposing entrenched power companies and other utility corporations to keep the basic natural public resources inalienable, and stopping water pollution, I never caught a glimpse of the breast beaters who are now touted as pundits in this field. I saw none of them in our long battle to establish eleven thousand acres of Jamaica Bay within New York City as a permanent, protected, unspoiled natural game refuge. Is

Jamaica Bay a symbol of urban rot, or is it just too small and obscure to attract the attention of the critics?

Recently, a number of planners and civic leaders in New York wrote a letter to the press advocating the conversion to a park of the whole of Welfare Island, a wedge in the East River presently occupied by hospitals. I tried this twenty-five years ago, before new hospitals and a bridge on the wrong side of the river were built, but the hospital commissioner poured abuse on me and was supported by the then mayor. It is too late now, because of the huge investment in modern institutions and vehicular access. Meanwhile, we have built adequate parks on Randall's and Ward's islands a little way up the East River and a pedestrian bridge to Ward's, which the paper planners never mention. . . .

The physical beauties of a city can, no doubt, be exaggerated, but no balanced observer will ignore them. Europeans coming to New York City for the first time are ecstatic about the view of lower Manhattan in the early morning from a great liner as it passes through upper New York Bay; mid-Manhattan seen from the Triborough Bridge at sundown; the jeweled diadem spread before the jet flyer at night; the clean gossamer cobwebs of its suspension bridges; the successive bustle and tomblike silences of its streets; the fantastic daring, imagination, and aspiration of its builders. Visitors are, of course, aware of New York's congested traffic, but is the slowdown any worse than that in London or Paris?

Admittedly, the gasoline motor has provided us with problems which did not exist in ancient Rome. But the jaundiced eye of the city historian sees no signs of achievement and progress. He is obsessed with the harlotry and the decline and fall of Rome and Babylon, and the beams and motes blot out Jones Beach.

Here is one example of this counsel of despair:

"Such form as the metropolis achieves is crowd-form: the swarming bathing beach by the sea or the body of spectators in the boxing arena or the football stadium. With the increase of private motor cars, the streets and avenues become parking lots, and to move traffic at all, vast expressways gouge through the city and increase the demand for further parking lots and garages. In the act of making the core of the metropolis accessible, the planners of congestion have already almost made it uninhabitable. . . .

"We must restore to the city the maternal, life-nurturing functions, the autonomous activities, the symbiotic associations that have long been neglected or suppressed. For the city should be an organ of love; and the best economy of cities is the care and culture of men."

Nowhere does the author even remotely tell us how these "symbiotic associations" can be revived and encouraged or where he would start with this renaissance.

As to housing, we read many similar grotesque misstatements. For example, Mumford says: "Stuyvesant Town was built by a private insurance company with generous aid by the State: but its residential density of 393 per acre remains that of a slum. Despite its inner open spaces, this housing would require eighty additional acres to provide the park and playground space now regarded as desirable, nineteen more than the entire project without buildings."

Here are the facts. The state had nothing to do with this project. It is not a slum in any sense. It is not overpopulated. New York City and the Metropolitan Life Insurance Company substituted for filthy tenements excellent, modern, low-rental housing with plenty of light and air and views all around on less than 20 per cent land coverage. Everyone familiar with housing and recreation knows that no such huge additional space as eighty acres is needed for parks and playgrounds in a project totaling seventy-two acres.

Similar distortions appear in dicta regarding traffic.

"In the interest of an unimpeded traffic flow highway engineers produce vast clover leaves even in low density areas with limited cross traffic, where there is no reason whatever why the arterial flow should not be occasionally halted as in a city street."

Every competent engineer knows that halting through traffic at a clover leaf would produce strangulation and is the negation of all accepted standards for limited-access highways.

The prosperous suburbanite is as proud of his ranch home as the owner of the most gracious villa of Tuscany. In the suburbs the hiker finds the long brown path leading wherever he chooses, by day, in filtered sunlight, or by evening, in the midst of the rhythmic orchestration of tree frogs. The little identical suburban boxes of average people, which differ only in color and planting, represent a measure of success unheard of by hundreds of millions on other continents. Small plots reflect not merely the rapacity of realtors but the caution of owners who do not want too much grass to cut and snow to shovel—details too intimate for the historians.

The real-estate subdivisions east of the city are not all there is to Long Island. The South Shore is my home. It is still mostly unspoiled, well protected, and largely in public ownership. Those of us who work at the problems that critics chatter about go down to the sea in cars and ships for respite, to fish, swim, soak up sun, and refresh our spirits, and in off seasons to wander in the anonymous enveloping ocean mist. Our fog appears, not stealing in on cat feet, but as a ghostly emanation of the sea, in silence punctuated only by the muffled bell and intermittent warning of the buoys along the hidden channels. Here we knit up the ravell'd sleave of care. Who are these pundits to say we have neglected our problems or that others might solve them better?

The cultures, amenities, and attractions of cities, suburbs, exurbs, and open country are manifestly different but complement each other. The sanest, best-balanced people are those who spend part of the year in each area and do not stay continuously under urban pressure. In that way they get the best of the city and of the more or less open spaces. A shack nearby or shelter in some vast wilderness will shortly be within the reach of most families.

In Mr. Mumford's recent gloom book, Baron Haussmann, a giant among planners, who saved Paris and turned it into a modern city, is contemptuously dismissed as a bulldozer and sadistic wrecker of fine old neighborhoods.

Here is some further pontification:

"To keep the advantages first discovered in the closed city, we must create a more porous pattern, richer in both social and esthetic variety. Residential densities of about one hundred people per net acre, exclusive of streets and sidewalks, will provide usable private gardens and encourage small public inner parks for meeting and relaxing. This can be achieved without erecting the sterile, space-mangling high-rise slabs that now grimly parade, in both Europe and America, as the ultimate contribution of 'modern' architecture."

Can anyone possibly believe that garden apartments housing over one hundred persons an acre are uncivilized and that small public inner parks have not been repeatedly considered and found wholly unworkable?

To sum up, let me ask the Gamaliels of the city a few pointed questions.

By what practical and acceptable means would they limit the growth of population?

How would they reduce the output of cars, and if they could, what would take the place of the car as an employer of workers or as a means of transport in a motorized civilization?

If more cars are inevitable, must there not be roads for them to run on? If so, they must be built somewhere, and built in accordance with modern design. Where? This is a motor age, and the motorcar spells mobility.

Is the present distinction between parkways, landscaped limited-access expressways, boulevards, ordinary highways, and city streets unscientific? If so, what do the critics propose as a substitute?

Is mass commuter railroad transportation the sole and entire answer to urban street congestion? Is conflict between rubber and rails in fact irrepressible? Are there not practical combinations of public, quasi-public, and private financing which can solve the riddle? And what of the people who prefer cars and car pools and find them more comfortable, faster, and even cheaper than rails?

If a family likes present city life, should it be forced to live according to avant-garde architectural formulas? Do most professional planners in fact know what people think and want? The incredible affection of slum dwellers for the old neighborhood and their stubborn unwillingness to move are the despair of experts. The forensic medicine men who perform the autopsies on cities condemn these uncooperative families to hell and imply that they could be transplanted painlessly to New Delhi, Canberra, Brasilia, and Utopia. We do not smoke such opium. We have to live with our problems.

Is it a mark of genius to exhibit lofty indifference to population growth, contempt for invested capital, budgets, and taxes; to be oblivious to the need of the average citizen to make a living and to his preferences, immediate concerns, and troubles?

What do the critics of cities offer as a substitute for the highly taxed central city core which supports the surrounding, quieter, less densely settled, and less exploited segments of the municipal pie? Have they an alternative to real-estate taxes?

Pending responsible answers to these questions, those of us who have work to do and obstacles to overcome, who cannot hide in ivory towers writing encyclopedic theses, whose usefulness is measured by results, must carry on.

The Limits of Utilitarianism[*]

John Ely Burchard

. . . Big cities are bound to pose some disadvantages for their occupants. With imagination and courage and a little more generosity they could pose many fewer than they do. But still there will be prices

* John Ely Burchard, "The Limitations of Utilitarianism as a Basis for Determining Urban Joy," in *Man and the Modern City*, ed. Elizabeth Geen, Jeanne R. Lowe, Kenneth Walker (Pittsburgh: University of Pittsburgh Press, 1963), pp. 18–24. Reprinted by permission.
John Ely Burchard is Dean of the School of Humanities and Social Science at Massachusetts Institute of Technology.

to pay for the advantages, and many people find the prices too high. For most of them the answer probably is that they really do not care much about variety of choice and have no unusual yearnings. But some are just too depressed by the details of daily urban life to accept them as a price for the high moments the metropolis alone can provide. They propose solutions in communities of "human scale," say of 50,000. I always find this a little amusing and also puzzling. Where are these humane communities? Are Brockton and Fitchburg, Massachusetts, Cumberland and Hagerstown, Maryland, more humane than Rome or Paris—or for that matter, really, than New York or Chicago?

Let me be quite dogmatic about this. A city of 50,000 people using modern technology and the American economy resourcefully can manage a good, comfortable, safe, unexciting life for all its citizens. If this is all that anybody wants, we can have it; and there is no sense today in anything being bigger for most, perhaps all, of the technical economic reasons for the big city have disappeared. Let me remind you what such a group can do. It can support a satisfactory medical system for most ordinary patients but cannot deal with exceptional problems or advanced medical research. It can support a school of the size that Mr. Conant regards as critical and thus can take care of all but its most gifted; but where are these few to go when every other city is also 50,000 people? It can support a good supermarket which can purvey all the foods necessary for survival and in good quality and even a few highly popular and more interesting things, but hardly ripe cheeses, octopus tentacles, vintage wines, or ortolans. Through the highway system and decentralized industry all its citizens can work profitably somewhere within reach of their automobiles and without ever going downtown at all. It can support a comfortable movie house, though the house cannot afford many controversial or even foreign-language films. It can support a florist, but the span of the flowers will be limited to roses, carnations, philodendrons, and orchids, except that there may be poinsettias at Christmas and Bermuda lilies at Easter. It can have a suitable array of denominational churches though no very distinguished individual preacher. All its housing can be decent and in nominal variety of size and shape. It can be smog free. Its children may be able to cross streets safely. It can have hot and cold running water and sanitary plumbing in every house. It may have no important crime whatever. It can have trees and lawns and flowers in the gardens but not a fountain or a statue by Henry Moore. It can have birds. It can be quiet to sleep in at night until it falls under the approach lane of some new airport.

But it cannot have a significant museum or art gallery, or important art in the streets; it cannot have a symphony orchestra, or any theater beyond that of amateur dramatics. It cannot have its own first-class newspaper, a rich collection of library books, a brilliant park, a center for good jazz, a meaningful zoo or botanical garden, an opera company, not even on tour, a single first-class place at which to eat unless it is on a highway and lots of transients hear about it, whereupon the citizens cannot get into it any more. It should be noted that not many residents of Vienne eat at the Pyramide.

If such a community works hard at having any one of these greater experiences it may by specialization achieve it, become notorious thereby, and like Oberammergau be destroyed as a community. But most of the time it will have none of them. Of course it will have plenty of television sets and hi fi equipment, and all these cultural experiences I have been talking about can be conveyed by electronics these days—or can they? Our big cities are gradually declining to the dead level of the 50,000 town without shedding any of their metropolitan disadvantages. We are not going to have the little places that Wordsworth mourned the passing of a hundred years ago; Amenia would not be much except for Manhattan; and our problem is not that of arresting the metropolis but of making it justify itself.

The big metropolis can make all the greater joys possible. That is because it presents the statistical probability that within its boundaries there are enough potential customers for each experience which may be caviar to the general. We have to remember that most experiences are caviar, even professional football. The Green Bay Packers could not stay in business on the Green Bay audience, enthusiastic and chauvinistic as it is.

Now if the big metropolis is just an accumulation of contiguous communities of 50,000 as described above, if it does not maximize the opportunity for diversity, then it really has no reason to exist at all. Its disadvantages are so great that the sooner it is destroyed the better. Living near Manhattan is meaningless if you never visit any of the foci of Manhattan's culture and excitement. Can the active metropolis be planned for and the meaningless aggregation prevented by concrete measures?

The physical beauty, the amenities of variety, can be planned and designed, but they will not be built unless the public wants to pay for them. The cultural variety of a center of art or science cannot be maintained by the planners if the public is apathetic. Even the desecration of neglect cannot be prevented by the planners. This does not mean that there is not much that can and should be done by planners. It is pitiful that we have to spend so much money and especially so much human skill on missiles and early-warning systems while being willing to spend so little on urban analysis. It is a pity that planning does not seem to be able to apply the powerful modern tools of Operations, Network, and Systems Analysis. A great deal of imagination would pay off here, even though we know that the results of such analyses might be very hard to explain to the people who finally control what is done in the city. Beyond that, we can hope that we do not continue to muff the opportunities of urban redevelopment. We can hope that public urban transport will be at least as attractive to future Presidents as transcontinental highways. We can hope that contemporary architects will be more sensitive to the inhuman scale of their large projects. We can hope that they will become more sensitive to the work of others around them, past and present, as sensitive to the man-made landscape as they often are to nature. We can hope that in fixing up some of the manifest technical defects of the great cities we do not destroy the main reasons for their existence. We need, it seems to me, to cherish with great care all the personality our cities have left; to work very hard to recover what we may have ignored; to be very suspicious of benign causes which are anti-urbane. We need to work very hard, each of us, for the special joys that we would like to see survive in the city. The theater, for example, is almost dead in Baltimore and Boston and everywhere except New York, not by conspiracy but through lack of patronage. We need to worry much more about the "useless" things than we do about the "useful" things; to guard the air and the trees and the flowers and the birds and their metaphoric and more elusive counterparts in the realm of the spirit; to look upon the loss of an orchestra or an opera company or a resident theater as a calamity as great as the removal of a shoe factory to some other region where wages and taxes are lower. . . .

The most humane cities would perhaps be produced by a set of urban dictators, each benign, each of good taste, each of quite different but complex tastes, so that each city had a good and special flavor. Then citizens might much prefer one city to another and would have the freedom to settle or move. The dictators would have to be local and that would not be easy in a country where only the federal government seems to be able to supply funds. Anyway, not enough dictators are benign and anyway we don't want them, benign or not, even if we could select them democratically. In the end we are happily saddled with democracy and will have to do the best we can. But we will not do that best if we continue to let the forces of applied science continue to be guided only by economics. It is symbolically significant that engineers generally consider economics to be the only essential social science. But . . . there is a calculus of humanity as well as a calculus of economics. We use only the latter. . . .

In the end the humane city will depend not just upon the skill or power of the planners but upon how eager the people are for joy; and this in the end depends on how they define joy and how much they will pay for it. It is not for planners to define joy for others, but planners might offer more opportunities for joy and see if these are embraced. That would be quite a lot more than most of them are doing now.

The Farm and the City*

National Resources Committee

In looking at the urban problem . . . we consider it not as the concern of the city alone, but as a problem of the farmer as well, in that it is a problem of all the American Nation. From the point of view of the highest and best use of our national resources, our urban communities are potential assets of great value, and we must consider from the point of view of the national welfare how they may be most effectively aided in their development. In the short-time run, there may be clashes of interest between urban and rural populations, competing types of production, differing demands in consumption, different hours and wages, differing standards of living, and different ways of life. But in the long run and from the over-all point of view, their interests are mutual, reciprocal, interdependent.

They both face with the same bewilderment the enormous complexity of modern life and the whirl of change that surrounds us. They both face the struggle with the grim problems precipitated by modern technology, not merely mechanical in nature but reaching into social and political phases of wide-ranging significance. Modern civilization forces new ways of life—alike in the city and in the country. It releases new forces and produces new forms that affect in many important ways the family, the school, the market place, the church, and the government. The impact of new forces and the necessary introduction of new ways of life are at once the opportunity and the burden both of city and country. The broadening and organization of educational facilities, the readjustment in recreation and leisure time activities, the organization of cultural and spiritual as well as economic forces—all these present problems which are common to the city dweller and those who live on the farm. The endless types of readjustment required under modern conditions present more points of likeness than of difference between urban and rural communities. Their common problem is not merely one of differing degrees of population density, or manner of occupation as appears superficially, but that of orderly and wholesome life. It is indeed this community of interest, this common struggle for enduring satisfaction and security under modern conditions, this common adventure in pioneering on the frontiers of a new social world, that makes the bonds that unite the American people in an indissoluble union.

* Urbanism Committee, *Our Cities*, report to the National Resources Committee (Washington, D.C.: U.S. Government Printing Office, 1937), pp. 5–32.

Urban and rural communities have many economic problems in common. They have in common a decline in general ownership of or equity in land and dwellings. In our farming communities, farm ownership or equity in the hands of those who till the soil is declining, and in the larger cities especially the percentage of home ownership has reached its peak or is going down. In some of the more congested areas ownership of homes has almost disappeared. Both have the problem of inadequate living conditions. Cities have the problem of the slum, while in the rural communities there are wide ranges of habitations less picturesquely named, but far below any reasonable minimum standard of human living. Both have the problem of order, health, welfare, education, and the maintenance of democratic participation in the communal life.

Mechanization has produced great factories, and technology has greatly aided the output of the soil. But an indirect consequence has been the dominance of the machine over the ways of life in cities, while the machine in the country has increased the yield of farms yet diminished in many respects the value of its produce. In consequence, the man on the farm and the man in the city alike look with mingled admiration and fear at the machine which at the same time has increased their power and diminished their security.

The farm and the city have in common the problem of dealing successfully with large units of industrial organization. The farmer encounters this problem whether he buys or sells—in buying effectively what he consumes and in selling effectively what he produces for the consumption of others. Whichever way he turns, the farmer faces the industrial giants of modern America—producers and sellers of machines and merchandise, against whom he must match his wits and his economic power. The laborer in the city likewise confronts, in his struggle for wages, hours and working conditions, and parity of purchasing power, organized units of vast strength. The small business man is likewise embattled. The farmer has often learned the value of associations adapted to his way of life, and the laborer and small businessman the value of associations adapted to their way of life. Through these organizations they maintain themselves against other organizations, and often glean some gains, sometimes by one group at the expense of another, without advantage to the national welfare.

Yet, viewing the whole field, it is clear that there are large numbers of farmers and large numbers of city workers whose share in our magical civilization is spelled out in terms of daily life that is drab in color and sad in tone. The crowded poverty of the one may match the lonely poverty of the other—alike cut off from the rich inheritance of the richest of modern nations.

3
Suburbia: Values in Transition

The suburbs are essentially a post-World War II phenomenon. Until 1940, successive censuses showed consistent population increases in the city proper. Then came the long-sustained upward sweep in personal income which characterized the forties and fifties. The desire for space, apparently latent in almost all city dwellers, was translated into a massive outward migration. People enjoyed better incomes, they bought automobiles, and the resulting move to the suburbs meant that population growth in many central cities slowed appreciably. Some cities—San Francisco for example—actually declined in population between 1950 and 1960.

What caused this movement? Was there a conscious effort by urban residents to escape from the problems of the city, and to enjoy a rural atmosphere? Or was the underlying cause more prosaic—namely, that the newcomers could not be housed in the already densely settled city core, so that they were forced into the suburb? Perhaps both influences operated, and will continue to operate to produce what critics of the result call, with colorful invective, "slurbs."

The American intellectual's traditional suspicion of the city has undergone a transformation in the past twenty or thirty years. When there was a clear-cut distinction between the city and the farm, the intellectual generally turned on the city as the source of evil in society. But as the automobile broke down the older urban-rural distinctions, and as the city began to spread over the countryside, the intellectual transferred his allegiance to the city and began to defend it as the source of culture, the fount of knowledge, and the seedbed of social advance. Perhaps the most vocal of the new critics was Sinclair Lewis, whose *Main Street* became a classic indictment of the stultifying effect of the small town. Now the metropolis—particularly New York, and most particularly Manhattan—became the haven of the painter, the writer, the composer; and the small town, the former repository of civic virtue, became anathema to the new critics. H. L. Mencken summed up the case against the small town in his "The Sahara of the Bozart," a piercing diatribe against the semi-rural South, whose former glory had been precisely that it had preserved the cultural tradition against the brutalizing influence of Northern industrialism.

Given the new concept of the central city as the cradle of the struggling creative artist, the rise of the suburb could be viewed only as a threat to cultural advancement. And one of the strongest current defenses of the central city is that it houses the theaters, the art galleries, the museums, and the concert halls, which provide the city with its claim to intellectual respectability.

The authors of the following selections present a diversity of viewpoints on Suburbia. Some of them see the suburbs as a profoundly divisive force in American life; others see them as essentially unifying in character. But all of them are deeply concerned with the problems created through the interaction of this new way of life with older institutions—the family, the church, the school.

Paul Ylvisaker does not share the accepted view of the suburbs as an undesirable by-product of the automobile. Instead, he views them as a logical development in the spread of a national urban culture, as one more step in the historical process of breaking down the barriers between the city and the countryside. Moreover, he argues that suburbanization is desirable, and he implies that the current critics of the development are looking backward: "With inhibiting nostalgia, we have called the resulting form Suburbia, implying that we think metamorphosis is reversible and suggesting a dependence on the City of the Past which does not or will not for long exist. There is very little 'sub' about this new urbia! It's the prototype of the urban form which will dominate the life of our children."

A more widespread attitude is represented by William H. Whyte's comment on the "anti-city." To Whyte, the suburbs represent a completely new attitude toward city life; they perform, or fail to perform, functions other than the purely residential. Does this make them more or less like the cities of history? Without directly answering this question, David Riesman digs deeply into the attitudes, the expectations, and the mores of the suburbanite. Riesman views the leisure, cultural, and political activities of the suburbs and demonstrates their pervasive influence on the nation as a whole. One may regard the suburbs with the essential optimism of Ylvisaker or with the rather more pessimistic attitude of Whyte, but, as Riesman demonstrates, the suburbs cannot be ignored.

Riesman remarks that the suburbs seem to be breaking down the differences between different elements of America through a process of "homogenization." Because of the decentralizing impact of the suburbs, Riesman argues, life is becoming aimless and dull. Gibson Winter, in the final selection, would certainly agree that a certain aimlessness pervades modern life, but he does not dismiss the result as "homogenization." By tracing the impact of the suburbs on the church as an institution, Winter makes it clear that he views the suburbs primarily as a divisive factor in the fabric of American society. He argues that, by providing a mechanism for the attempt to preserve similarities in neighborhoods, they ultimately separate the blue-collar central-city dweller from the white-collar suburbanite and thus cut away one of the roots of a vital church—its appeal to all classes of society. Both Riesman and Winter might agree that the suburbs represent a reaction to industrialism. But to Riesman the suburbs carry the process of democratization one step further, for good or bad, while Winter feels they tend to create a stratified society.

None of these authors considers the question of why the move to the suburbs has taken place. It remains for Raymond Vernon to point out the underlying economic forces that have produced higher rates of population growth in the peripheral areas. He notes that because of the relationship between jobs and population, the pull of the suburbs is exerted first on industry and then on people. Vernon analyzes job opportunities in the suburb and the central city and draws some conclusions about their relative future populations.

The Shape of the Future*
Paul N. Ylvisaker

The next generation—accelerating the work of the present —will all but obliterate the historic image of the City, and complete the

* Paul N. Ylvisaker, "The Shape of the Future: Urban Life," address at the New School for Social Research, New York, October 26, 1961. Reprinted by permission. Paul N. Ylvisaker is Director of the Public Affairs Program of the Ford Foundation.

metamorphosis by which a radically new urban creature is being evolved.

What shape the future will give to this new form of urban life has already become visible enough to describe with some assurance. What it will do to the substance of urban life, and how that in turn will shape the human beings who live it, I can only guess. My guess will be no better than the hunches I go on when raising my own children to live in this future. Often these hunches go awry, and more often than not, my advice is argued down. But my children—and the urban future of which we're also parents—will probably be the fonder of the Old Man for trying. At least they will know he cared; and what's more lovable, he was usually wrong.

In that mood of gaily bringing up father, permit me my parental share of fallible prophecy and unheeded advice.

> This is the City that is being obliterated:
> (1) The City of unrelieved residential density, distinguishable boundaries, and slow-changing form;
> (2) The City capable of being defined and governed by a single and static plan.
> What the future is creating is:
> (1) A national urban culture, spreading amoeba-like over open land, plastic—seemingly shapeless—in its form, fluid at its boundaries, and in its cellular structure capable of infinite reproduction.
> (2) An urban way of life so intricate in its design and interdependencies that it will be extremely resistant and in some respects immune to frontal efforts to plan and order it.

This is an esoteric set of propositions to have to explain, let alone defend. They relate to the outer and inner dimensions of urban life, the physical shell and the essential character. Let me begin with the easier and more obvious: the radical change in urban form which the emerging future is building around us.

This metamorphosis began when technology and steadily rising income broke the constraining force of distance, crumbled the walls of the historic City, and deposited the City's substance upon the surrounding open land.*

With inhibiting nostalgia, we have called the resulting form Suburbia, implying that we think metamorphosis is reversible and suggesting a dependence on the City of the Past which does not or will not

---

* That's the way a biologist might put it; a mathematician would date the change from the time we began doubling our urban population while halving our urban densities.

for long exist. There is very little "sub" about this new urbia; it's the prototype of the urban form which will dominate the life of our children.

Difficult as it may be for a Manhattanite to accept (and I'll relent in a moment to say why he may never fully have to) the areas of new urban growth do not inherently need much or many of what we call the downtown. At this early stage of development, yes. But less and less. Already, the population of the new growth areas has a numerical and political edge over the old city. The margin will grow rapidly, and when agriculture finally loses its control over state governments, the mantle will fall on the children of Sprawl.

Politically, not sub-urbia but super-urbia. It is the central city that becomes subordinate; no longer the matriarch, but the aging and dependent mother in the new urban household.

Not only politically but economically. . . . There is still a vital symbiotic relationship between central business district and the periphery. But it will not be long before the new growth areas—these first and second generation disciples of the Los Angeles doctrine of how to develop, despoil (choose your own word) open land—will learn how to replicate most if not all the traditionally unique advantages of the old urban core. Every year, whole chunks of the central city's uniquenesses are being pulled into the periphery by the centrifugal processes of sub-urban invention. Incubating enterprises can flourish elsewhere than in the downtown lofts; look for them now in university professors' garages a hundred miles out, or in the pleasant shades of those new monasteries of the mind called research and development laboratories, which have re-treated to the gracious solace of the Stanfords, the Princetons, the Chapel Hills of the far countryside. The fascinations and tribulations of com-muter rail traffic are leaping headlines to those who still make the long haul from main line suburbs to the downtown; but these are a dwindling few compared to those who live and work beyond the boundaries of the old city. These latter travel to work by bits and pieces of major and minor roadway, not going to, nor coming from, but round and outside and at right angles to the older city. They couldn't care less when the rails and their riders cry ouch.

The cultural role and dominance of the old city? Manhattan, yes. But even then I wonder how far off Broadway the theatre of the future is likely to migrate. Shakespeare has by now reached Connecticut; Philadelphia's outside citizens, at least in the summer, already have ten times as many places to watch plays in the suburbs as they do downtown; and thanks to TV, the Play-of-the-Week decentralized more drama in two years than Manhattan had concentrated in twice that time.

This sounds like a savage attack on the Old City and a romance with the new. It is not. It is a statement of developing fact that most of the U.S. already knows, lives with and seems to prefer. But recognition of the fact has strangely been missing in the world of city planning. Why? Quite simply because those whose attachments are to the old order are the ones who have done most of the hiring of planners and most of the writing on urban problems: central business districts in decline; urban universities caught in the deteriorating gray areas; mayors plagued by a dwindling tax base; real estate operators crying a departing market; urban historians mourning a lost civilization.

Understandably, these partisans of the Old Order have resorted to hope. But hope alone makes a poor program of action, especially when it fails to accord with fact. The fact is, people are not going to return to the Old City in the numbers they have left; nor are industries; nor are shopping facilities; nor are commuters; nor none of the lost departed. The reasons for their going are too basic to be erased by a wish and a prayer. In the case of industry seeking land for horizontal layout and plant expansion, these reasons proceed from physical necessity; in the case of people searching for modern housing, elbow-room and freedom of choice, these reasons proceed from virtue; in the case of service establishments seeking a market, these reasons make good economics.

What in the long run is there to staunch this hemorrhaging of the old city? Not much. The supply of urbanizable land in the U.S. is so large that to this next generation it might as well be infinite. Automotive and air transportation make every part of this continent accessible; even if you are emotionally tied to Manhattan, you don't have to live there; from the Midwest, from California, from Florida, it's only a quick jet ride away. Within the present embrace of existing metropolitan areas— in the pockets of land which have been leapfrogged by the first rush of the bulldozer—there is at least another generation's space for ranch-house development.

On the drafting boards of new technology, there is at least another generation's propulsion toward the metropolitan periphery and the open space beyond. None of the new gadgetry or product development I know of is designed to reinstate the dense living patterns of the older city; electronics have a built-in penchant for urban expanse. Even Professor Vernon's concentrated world of the face-to-face is being plucked at by centrifugal forces; an Ad man I live with in the rural interior of New Jersey has cut his ties with Madison Avenue to the minimum of a couple of weekly visits—thanks to an electronic device clipped to his belt, he can potter in his garden while awaiting the unpredictable and unscheduled call which economists have told us would chain him physically to the downtown.

And in the minds of men, there is at least a generation more of the deep urge to flee the old city. Its housing is obsolescent and expensive to maintain; the new apartments are either too high in price or too low in status; you can get culture a lot more cheaply and conveniently by television than you can on Broadway; and the stigma of the slum is a dark shadow that will haunt and drive at least another generation of Whites and Negroes alike to the symbolic sanctuary of open land.

Not to mention the matter of defense. To the extent anyone is taking this matter seriously, the logic of dispersal is compelling. The old city is too easy a target.

Crying the demise of the centralized city in the midst of a booming Manhattan may seem foolhardy; I still think the prediction is accurate. We will spill out onto the land for another generation at least. Manhattan will survive longer than most; an exception, but a changing and misleading one. Already its downtown is an island of the old order in a flooding sea of the new; it is a Potemkin Village which obscures the view of the gray and green realities immediately beyond. It is not a model for the core cities of our 200 metropolitan areas; it is more a rival, siphoning off much of the economic and social potential of the Philadelphias, the Bostons, and even the Chicagos. It is sustained by the very forces that are contributing to urban dispersion throughout the country.

I would pause in this argument to concede that our society is not yet ready to accept this imminent future gladly as its permanent urban environment. Like Hamlet, we are soliloquizing—mournfully but still impotently—while events move swiftly on and around us. To be or not to be a sprawled urban civilization . . . to debate but not to decide.

I sense that as a nation—not merely as Manhattanites—we are uncertain to the point of bad conscience over having bowed thus far to the powerful forces of dispersion. Sprawl is a bad word in just about everyone's dictionary; so is suburbia; and significantly, no one has come forward to suggest a favorable name for the urban developments lately taking place. Even among the emerging majority of people who have chosen this new form, you won't find many rising publicly to boast about it. It's like being newly rich—it may feel good but it doesn't look good. These days, a Book-of-the-Month Club's circulation and income automatically awaits the author who makes a public confessional about the crack in the picture window. . . .

Arguing from analogy, one could make a persuasive case for the conservative point of view that in destroying the historic city at present speed we are recklessly uncoiling the mainspring of our civilization and dissipating the compressed power of the City aimlessly over an unready countryside.

But I don't think either the analogy or our soliloquy is influencing events; as in the case of Hamlet, our inability to decide and our unwillingness to leave the injured spirit of the past is making us even more certainly the victim of the present and inviting the worst consequences of an unsettled future. . . .

Beyond generalities, there are two specifics which need

doing: One is a thought job. The City has not just grown bigger than its boundaries—it has outgrown the concept and vocabulary of the city itself. The distinction, at least in this country, has been blotted out between agricultural and urban life; television, the automobile, and the agricultural revolution have taken care of that. Geographical distinctions are also fading; what we call the City today is to all intents and purposes the same as the nation. And in another generation or two—if we can survive the savagery of this latter-day and I think last-ditch stand of nationalism— urban society will dissolve into world society.

But each of these fading separatenesses are still being dealt with on separate assumptions and policy criteria. It shows in both our academic and real-world behavior; one of the obsolescences most relevant here is the separate way we go about national planning and urban planning. One is largely economic; the other largely physical. Neither translates very well into the other's language. Economists deal with orderly aggregates, which somehow never achieve the reality of urban form; and as I've tried to point out earlier, urban form and policy never quite seem to survive the tests of national aggregates.

It's about time we did try at least to develop a unified field theory. I'm not very hopeful that we'll ever achieve one; after all, our physical scientists aren't doing so well on that one either. But the search, with the confrontation of methods, assumptions and objectives, is one that might help narrow the rate of our urban lag. . . .

The Anti-City*

William H. Whyte, Jr.

Sub-urban (what an apposite word) conveys to many people merely an extension of the city in an enlargement of its boundaries. When we speak of "urbanization," we tend to think of the city as sprawling, or oozing, over the landscape. But actually it is not the city that is spreading; it is suburbia. We would do well to keep the distinction in mind. There

* William H. Whyte, Jr., *Man and the Modern City* (Pittsburgh, Pennsylvania: University of Pittsburgh Press, 1963), pp. 46–50. Reprinted by permission.
William H. Whyte, Jr., is the author of several well-known books, including *The Organization Man*.

is a pitfall in the term "urbanization," for it implies the spread, not only of the city, but also of the city's values.

It is true that the city and suburb together make up the metropolitan area. The two are alike in more ways, perhaps, than they are different. Yet there are profound differences in the values each emphasizes, and to speak of suburbia as part of the greater city can obscure these distinctions. Geographically speaking, the distinction is difficult to make. Wrestling with the job of defining the city, my colleagues at *Fortune* magazine and I finally threw up our hands. We decided the city was, simply, what was within the city limits. This may seem grossly mechanical, but as a working definition it is not without some merit. However, in three important ways, I suggest, the city and the suburb represent antithetical values. They might be posed thus: mixture versus homogeneity; concentration versus dispersion; specialization versus the middle range.

Think of the city and the way its activities are combined in a small area; think of the tremendously varied ethnic, social, and economic groups it brings into juxtaposition. Then compare this complexity with the relative homogeneity of the suburb, with the dominant pattern, more and more, of a series of suburbs, each catering to a particular group differentiated by income and age. This is true to such an extent that a child in some suburbs may hardly ever see a Negro, a poor person, or, for that matter, anyone over fifty.

The concentration that is the hallmark of the city is often equated with congestion. Some people . . . think that to get rid of congestion we should get rid of concentration, too. But concentration, which is the reason for the city's being, existed long before the special kind of congestion caused by modern means of transportation. Suburbia, by contrast, represents dispersion. The term is relative, of course. The best-planned suburbs do not sprawl; they have a cohesion that makes them far better, economically and aesthetically, than the usual agglomeration of subdivisions. Basically, however, suburbia and concentration are disparate concepts, and those who look for a better order of things through the creation of "regional cities" are asking for a contradiction in terms.

The city and specialization are inextricable. Most highly specialized activities, or services, flourish best at the center of things where they can draw on a huge area and still be near the center of its traffic. When we speak of "urbanity," we are often referring to the characteristic specialization of the city. It is the natural habitat of the specialty shop, the one-of-a-kind restaurant; suburbia on the other hand is the habitat of such institutions of the mode as Sears Roebuck and Howard Johnson (I am not being invidious; Howard Johnson restaurants are superb in their function. I am stressing compatibilities). So, too, is the city the great breeding ground of enterprise. In the later flush of success, a firm may move out to a suburban location, but, in its formative years a firm is vitally dependent on the city's low-rent loft and specialized labor.

The inclination to suburban values can be discerned in the current image of what is wrong with the city. All of us would agree on many aspects of this image, whether we really like cities or detest them. Most of us, sensibly, do not like noise, dirt, slums, jammed traffic, street gangs, and the host of other ills that seem to make the city a destroyer. But at the same time we must recognize how inextricably many of these ills are interwoven with the ancient strengths of the city. This is what makes our efforts to rebuild the city so very difficult, and yet so demanding and so fascinating. The conventional image of what is wrong with the city and the prescriptions that it implies do not acknowledge this double-sidedness. Instead we are led to believe that we can easily excise the bad features without upsetting the dynamic interplay of forces.

Take traffic congestion for example. While we hear a great deal about traffic "strangulation" and about overcrowding, we hear very little about the necessity for concentration. Indeed, one could gather that the easy way to clear up the problem is to have everybody go somewhere else. It should be acknowledged that congestion and concentration do not have to be synonymous. We can have a heavy concentration of activities and at the same time a traffic flow that is not hopelessly choked. Theoretically, it is much easier simply to do away with the concentration and spread things out. But this is tackling the city, not on its own terms, but on the alien ones of suburbia. The popular image of what is wrong with the city is, to put it another way, what is right with suburbia. . . .

The present day conflict between the city and suburbia is not a new phenomenon. Long before there were suburbs there was a rural-urban conflict. A persistent theme in utopian literature has been the basic immorality of cities and the coupling of the good life with the rural virtues. What makes the conflict so pointed today is not the change in the city but in the rest of our environment. City life, almost because it has not changed much, has more and more become a mockery of the American dream. The norm of middle class aspiration is suburbia, and as our middle class has expanded the distance between the city and the consensus of the good life has grown. Look at the advertisements of happy families drinking beer, washing the car, or tinkering with hobbies; or take the *Saturday Evening Post* covers with their pictures of humorous incidents. Rarely is there a city in the background. In the pictorial representation of the American Dream the *mise en scene* is suburbia. Ideologically, as well as physically, no dialect jokes, no racial characteristics mar the picture. All that is behind us; it is *similarity* that is celebrated, often with deliberate moral overtones. . . .

Suburban Attitudes*

David Riesman

. . . for millions of suburbanites, their post-World War II experience has been prosperous and open far beyond their depression-born expectations. For them, the suburbs have been one vast supermarket, abundantly and conveniently stocked with approved yet often variegated choices. The children are less of a worry there than on city streets; the neighbors often more friendly than those city folk who "keep themselves to themselves"; life in general is more relaxed. The confidence such people often have that things will continue to go well for them is revealed in the story told one journalist in a Southern California suburb where employment depends on nearby defense plants. When he asked people what would happen to them in case of a depression or cancellation of defense contracts, they answered: "Why then the government will stockpile cars." Life on credit has worked out well for many such home owners, allowing them to have their children young and in circumstances far better than those in which they themselves grew up. Whatever the outsider might say about the risks blithely taken, with no allowance made for personal or social setbacks, or about the anemic quality of the relaxed life or its complacency, he would have to admit that such first-generation suburbanites have found the taste of abundance pleasant and, for the younger ones with wages rising faster than prices, not notably problematic.

Revolt against industrialism

This subjective attitude does not, however, alter the fact that, among such suburban dwellers and in general in our society, we are witnessing a tremendous but tacit revolt against industrialism. It is a very different sort of revolt from either that of the machine smashers of the early nineteenth century or that of the various anti-industrial sects—socialist, anarchist, agrarian, etc.—of an earlier day. Large manufacturing industry is increasingly moving to the luxury side of the "dual economy," and backbreaking toil and harsh physical conditions are vanishing (except in industrialized farming and the service trades) with the coming of electricity, full employment, unions, and personnel men. But the luxury, which is often used to make the work more gregarious and less of an

* David Riesman, "The Suburban Dislocation," *The Annals of the American Academy of Political and Social Science*, 314 (November 1957), 129–142.
David Riesman is Professor of Sociology at the University of Chicago.

effort, is seldom used to make it less monotonous. Naturally, men treat their work as delinquents treat school though schools are less likely than plants to pioneer the partial truancy of the four-day week, escaping and sabotaging when they can. Managers and foremen try in vain to restore the "old school spirit" to their employees and, failing, seek through automation and quality control to make up for the deliquescence of the "instinct of workmanship" once so painfully built into the labor force. Observers of factory life have repeatedly pointed out that status within the plant is no longer gained by hard work and craftsmanship, but rather by one's consumer skills outside. Men dream, not of rising in the factory, but of starting a small business such as a motel, gas station, or TV repair shop in the shabby and open-shop underside of our dual economy. For youngsters from subsistence farms, for hillbillies, and Southern Negroes, a Detroit or Gary factory is still glamorous or at least a liberation from drastic poverty and insecurity; but for second- and third-generation factory workers, it no longer holds much meaning other than as a (hopefully temporary) source of funds and fringe benefits.

To be sure, there is a new industrialism of electronics, plastics, aviation, and so on, which retains a certain appeal that the older industries have so largely lost. However, the new firms, increasingly located in suburbs or where people want to live: California, and the Southwest and Florida, speed the movement out of heavy industry and merge factory and suburban life. But we see in these industries precisely the form that the revolt against industrialism has taken today, namely to partially incorporate the "enemy" so that industrialism is not compartmentalized but rather, in muted form, spreads into all parts of the culture. This is, of course, what happens in so many social struggles: One defeats the enemy by becoming more like him.

Let me pursue this further by looking at what is happening to the older form of industrial and commercial metropolis. When, a few years ago, I studied interviews done with several hundred college seniors at twenty representative universities, asking them what they would like or expect to be doing in fifteen years, I was struck by the fact that the great majority planned to live in the suburbs. They expected to be married, and in describing their prospective spouses they hoped for what we might call station-wagon types: educated, companionable, civic-minded, and profoundly domestic. There were few who recognized some incompatibility between focus on suburban life and focus on big-city ambitions (for instance, a senior who wanted to go into advertising, yet not live in or near New York). They were—with some exceptions especially among the Southerners—willing to sacrifice the heights of achievement, though not the plateaus of the luxury economy, in favor of their goals of suburban domesticity and peace. Those who hailed originally from the suburbs suffered from no disenchantment and wanted to return to them—often to the same one—while both city-bred and small-town boys also preferred the suburbs. I assume that some of the latter in an earlier day would have wanted to leave Main Street behind and make their mark in the big city, whatever lingering agrarian fears and suspicions of it they still harbored. The city today, for many, spells crime, dirt, and race tensions, more than it does culture and opportunity. While some people still escape from the small town to the city, even more people are escaping from the city to the suburbs. . . .

Suburban way of life

This life, as just indicated, is increasingly focused on the suburbs which, since World War II, have grown so in quantity as to change their quality. For, although upper-class and upper-middle-class people have lived in the suburbs of our great cities since the 1880's or earlier, the cities before World War II still retained their hegemony: They engrossed commercial, industrial, and cultural power. The city represented the division and specialization not only of labor but of attitude and opinion: By discovering like-minded people in the city, one developed a new style, a new little magazine, a new architecture. The city, that is, provided a "critical mass" which made possible new combinations —criminal and fantastic ones as well as stimulating and productive ones. Today, however, with the continual loss to the suburbs of the elite and the enterprising, the cities remain big enough for juveniles to form delinquent subcultures, but barely differentiated enough to support cultural and educational activities at a level appropriate to our abundant economy. The elite, moreover, tend to associate with like-income neighbors rather than with like-minded civic leaders, thus dispersing their potential for leadership beyond township boundaries. Ironically, these people sometimes choose to live in communities which might be almost too manageable if millions of others did not simultaneously make the same choice.

Indeed, the suburbs are no longer simply bedroom communities but increasingly absorb the energies of the men as well as the women and children. The men, that is, are not simply being good providers while still attached to the values of the industrial system: They are seekers after the good life in the suburbs on their own account. Early marriage and the rise in the birth rate are so many rivulets of individual, only barely self-conscious protest against the values inherited from industrialism and the low-birth-rate middle-class metropolis—so many decisions to prefer companionship in the present to some distant goal, and so many mortgages of the future in the benevolent shadow of the luxury economy and its escalator of slow inflation, promotion, and protection. Whereas men once identified themselves with commerce and industry— with its power, its abstractions, its achievements—and forced women to remain identified with domesticity—save for those women who broke through the barrier and became man-imitating career girls—now, as many observers have pointed out, a growing homogenization of roles is occurring. Women take jobs to support the suburban menage periodically while men take part in its work (do-it-yourself), its civic activities (Parent-Teachers Association, and so on), and its spirit. Rather than delegating religion to their womenfolk, men go to church in increasing numbers, occasionally as in an earlier day to be respectable or to climb socially, and occasionally out of a genuine religious call, but more typically because the church, like the high school and the country club, has become a center for the family as a social and civic unit. . . .

Our Center for the Study of Leisure has been conducting studies of limited scope in several Chicago suburbs in an effort, *inter alia*, to see what happens to people who leave the city for the suburbs in terms of new commitments and new demands. We have also done a very inconclusive study of how people in the city spend their week ends. We have the impression that the suburbanite, tied to his house as the doctor is to his practice, may actually be less likely to take off for a week end in the country than the urban dweller whose janitor can look after his apartment and even the cat. Indeed, it is the city people, freed by industrialism from long hours of grinding work, who (along, of course, with an ample supply of untied suburbanites) make up a large proportion of the outboard population of our lakes and rivers and of the thirty-five million fishermen—more than twice the number of those urban sportsmen, the bowlers. Although air-conditioning makes even the most humid and dirty city potentially habitable, people can't wait to leave town on week ends and during the summer, even though in many parts of the country it means spewing the city into the countryside and fighting with like-minded crowds for space on roads, lakes, and at motels.

As I have indicated, I believe that snobbery and imitation of the rich play a declining part in this exodus to the suburbs and that the quiet revolt against the city and industrialism plays an increasing part. I would argue that there is often less "front" in the new suburbs than in equivalent sections of a metropolis, and less pressure for a lace-curtain life concealing back-stage scrimping and meanness than there once was. People do not usually learn the idea of a garden suburb either from British models or Mumford or Clarence Stern: The idea, in its uncomplicated forms, is an omnipresent dream, carrying overtones of the Bible, peasant life and folk imagery. The urban wish for contact with nature has been crystallized for many Americans around the habits of the British gentry and their middle-class imitators. But, more modest than the aspidistra-lovers of the London suburbs, we prefer not to give fancy names to our own "villas" but to let this dumb show be done for us by the realtors. In the Chicago area, for instance, a great many suburbs have either "Park" or "Forest" in their names, and two of them have both! Furthermore, social mobility means that many, perhaps most urban dwellers will have suburban relatives or friends. The mass production of suburbs, especially in the postwar years, has made them accessible to almost everyone. Only in the rural and impoverished parts of the South and Great Plains farming regions are we likely to find many people who do not know anybody who lives in a suburb and have never had occasion to visit one. Beyond that, the vicarious socialization of Americans into the experiences of consumption they are about to have is the continuous task of the mass media. Many of these, and at a variety of income levels, are devoted to expounding the suburban way of life directly in ads and features; other media are indirect vehicles for suburban styles in the homes pictured in stories, the sport shirts worn, and the idols of consumption portrayed. The whole American ethos, which once revolved about the dialectic of pure country versus wicked but exciting city, seems to me now aerated by the suburban outlook. This produces an homogenization of both city and country, but without full integration.

While on the whole the lower-middle- and middle-income suburbs sponsor the relaxed life, there is one area where they impose an imperative which many city dwellers have not met, namely that of having some sort of garden—less as a cultural amenity than as a minimum contribution to civic decency: A kind of compulsory outdoor housekeeping. Indeed, in the study of gardening in two Chicago suburbs conducted by our Center for the Study of Leisure we gained the impression that garden clubs were not extremely active in either one (though we have found very active and prestigeful clubs on the North Shore); garden clubs are much more characteristic of older communities, where they represent a familiar activity of some of the established families, rather than of the new suburbs, where gardening must compete with many other hobbies and activities, both outdoor and indoor. We found in Fairlawn, a new developer's suburb, for example, that to many housewives the garden was simply one more chore. It represented neither a contrast with the asphalt jungle of the city, nor a pleasure in growing things, nor a rage for order. It was rather a tax imposed by neighborhood consciousness—the neighbors often being interpreted as more concerned and censorious than they, for the most part, were. Thus we find that many people who have moved newly to the suburbs to escape the city come without awareness of the constraints they will find—or mistakenly interpret—in the suburb. Like the appointment in Samara, they meet pressures they had thought to leave behind, though altered in form and impact.

One of these pressures, already adverted to, is the metropolis itself; its traffic, its ethnic minorities, and its tax rates tend to catch up with them. The waves of succession within the city proper do not halt at its boundaries, and many old and established suburbs are finding themselves cut in two by freeways and by the new kinds of people they bring. In this situation, some of the old kinds of people are among those tempted to become exurbanites, putting the ever-approaching city another few miles away and hoping to solve the dilemma of distance versus intimacy by a superhighway.

However, in this quandary the emphasis on superhighways —and on supercars which require them—takes on much of the lunatic quality of an arms race. As highways get bigger and better, they invite more cars, destroy what undeveloped and unschematized country (or central city) remains, and require still more highways in an unending spiral.

People have been drilled by industrialism in the values of efficiency—narrowly defined in terms of speed, performance, and a kind of streamlined look (what Jacques Barzun has referred to as "America's Romance with Practicality"). Thus even when they flee from the cities and the style of life industrialism has brought about, they cannot change the style of thought which sees the solution to ribbon developments in stretching them still further until our East and West coasts threaten to become continuous roadside slums.

What is true of the planning, or lack of it, of our road-centered culture as a whole is also true of domestic architecture. Efficiency here is less stark—and consequently often less attractive—since it must compete with traditional definitions of a suburban free-standing home. But, as many architects have pointed out, the interiors are highly modern in the sense of mechanization. Indeed, one reason why husbands have been willing to become domesticated is that they have been promoted from dishwashers to operators of dishwashers. Similarly, they use power mowers to give crew cuts to handkerchief-sized lawns and pierce their wives' and neighbors' ears with the screams of high-fidelity music. The open plan of the very newest ranch-style homes puts the TV set on a swivel in the center. Here it can be seen from all parts of the house so that urban news, fashions, gossip, and jokes can circulate in the home throughout the daily cycle of the members of the family. But all these improvements are bought at the expense of space for the individual whose bedroom in the suburban development is often smaller than in city tenements. This is especially true, as Albert Roland of *Household* magazine has pointed out to me, of the newest suburban homes. These have both a family room and a living room. The latter, like the old parlor, is used only for state occasions; the family room is big enough for games, the TV, an inside barbecue, and general clutter.

Nor does the lawn or backyard provide a bounteous free space in most of the new developments. In comparison with the size and cost of the house, plots are small (much as they have traditionally been in midwestern cities where people wanted to avoid the row house but not to be too far from their next-door neighbors). Moreover, the fact that there is both a front and a backyard—the latter being, in many developments, the "family room" and the former the "parlor"—means that what space there is becomes divided. And just as the homes have no interstitial spaces, no nooks and crannies, so the lots have no texture taken individually or together. I keep asking myself what the lots will look like when the explosion of our population doubles the numbers in the suburban hegira without, in all probability, increasing proportionately the services that our new expectations crave. Will houses and lots get smaller when people can no longer spread further afield? People have been moving to the suburbs in many cases in pursuit of an inchoate dream of spaciousness. They have looked for a release from urban tensions, from crowded and ugly schools, from indoors. And ordinarily this release has more than compensated for losses in urban qualities which are difficult to sense or describe—qualities of possibility, often, rather than of actual use. What will occur when the urban qualities have been dissipated, while the suburban ones elude all but the rich?

Such questions assume, as I have here been doing, that Americans have ceased being socially inventive outside the corporate or military spheres. They assume that we will not discover the governmental or voluntary channels either to give many people alternative satisfactions to large families or to create forms of life and livelihood appropriate to another age of population expansion—this time with no frontiers left. Certainly, there is now a kind of private inventiveness in the suburbs among people who, having lost "the track of generations" and traditional standards of judgment and taste, are somehow managing, with ambivalent aid from the media, to create new forms and styles. The leaders of Park Forest and several other new communities, surrounded by others as green as they, often managed to develop some communal decencies and controls; in that sense, the town-meeting spirit is far from moribund. It is easy to see the negative and ironical features of the suburbs—harder to see emergent crystallizations.

But one trouble is that the suburbs, like the families within them, can scarcely control their own immediate environs, let alone the larger metropolitan and national orbits that impinge on them and decide their eventual atmosphere. And here is where the suburbanites' immense liking for Ike is portentous. It expresses the wish of so many of the college seniors mentioned above that civics and the Community Chest replace politics; it expresses the hope, built into the very structure of credit and the additive-extrapolative style of thought, that nothing serious will occur, that everything will go on as before. And it expresses this hope, of course, at the very moment when private decisions—irresponsibly influenced—to buy or not to buy, to propagate or not to propagate store up our destinies (quite apart from the similar activities of the rest of our small planet). In interviews done in Chicago suburbs by Louis Harris before the 1956 elections, he asked potential voters how they felt about a part-time, golf-playing president. Many were indignant, saying they would play golf too if they had such problems—though when asked to name serious problems facing the country, they could often get no further than high taxes. Plainly, Ike's complacencies mirrored and supported their own (Eisenhower, of course, like most anyone in Washington, is far less complacent than these constituencies), and their defenses against untoward apprehension were too great to allow thought for the morrow.

In the days of Lincoln Steffens and later, people emphasized the "shame of the cities," and in the 1920's major novelists emphasized the constraints of small-town and occasionally of small-suburban life. Today, the comparable worry, in the books dealing with the suburbs, is conformity—*Point of No Return*, with its concern for place and competition, strikes a somewhat older note; writers point to the uniformity of the ranch style, the ever-present television antennae, the lamp, if not the crack, in the picture window—which usually provides a view of the nearly treeless street, the cars, and someone else's picture window. Actually, uniformity and conformity are quite different matters as Georg Simmel has observed in his essay on "Fashion." The former may dictate to men only in inessentials, whereas the latter involves some psychological mechanism. And the conformity of the new suburbs is, in some important ways, far less stringent than that of the old; if it is not quite the case that "anything goes," lots of things do go which once would, if known, have brought ostracism. If one does not seek to force the new suburbanite back across the ethnic tracks he has just crossed, he is quite tolerant, even bland. If he is political at all—rather than parochially civic-minded, tending to a "garden" which includes the local schools and waterworks—he is apt to be an Eisenhower Republican, seldom informed, rarely angry, and only spasmodically partisan.

No, what is missing in suburbia, even where the quality of life has not overtly deteriorated, is not the result of claustrophobic conformity to others' sanctions. Rather, there would seem to be an aimlessness, a pervasive low-keyed unpleasure. This cannot be described in terms of traditional sorrows but is one on which many observers of the American scene and the American visage have commented, notably Erich Fromm in *The Sane Society* and the Goodmans in *Communitas*. For millions of people, work no longer provides a central focus for life; and the breadwinner is no longer the chief protagonist in the family saga—just as Saturday night no longer provides a central focus for festivity. In fact, the decentralization of leisure in the suburbs is not only spatial but temporal, as evenings from Thursday through Sunday are oriented to play rather than work and are not individually accented or collectively celebrated.

The Suburban Captivity
of the Churches*

Gibson Winter

The major denominations of Protestantism are gradually becoming metropolitan in character; nevertheless, Protestant memberships are still more rural than would be expected in view of the growing concentration of people in the metropolis. A report for 1953 indicated that only 46 per cent of Protestant strength was in metropolitan areas, although 56 per cent of the total population resided in these areas at the time. In view of the traditionally rural character of Protestantism, this is a reasonable showing. Certain denominations are, of course, markedly urban, whereas several large denominations continue to be primarily rural. In general, the churches have prospered in the course of urbanization, and are still growing.

A brief indication of recent religious growth may suggest the mental climate that pervades the churches. In the 1958 yearbook, contributions to most of the major bodies showed a gain of 11 per cent over the preceding year. Despite inflation, this is a notable gain. Church membership was 62 per cent of total population in 1956 as compared to 49 per cent in 1940. Opinion polls of attendance at church by adults indicated that 41 per cent of the respondents attended in the week preceding the interview in 1939 as compared to 51 per cent in 1957. Construction of new church buildings reflects somewhat more closely the state of the economy; however, comparing the lush years of 1928 and 1956, expenditures on new building show roughly a 400 per cent increase by 1956. These figures give some hint of the increase in religious interest.

The metropolitan problem of the churches is not a failure in organizational growth; the present rate of metropolitan expansion among the churches should soon bring their religious constituencies into line with general population trends. Metropolitan churches are confronted with a dilemma between organizational expansion and responsibility for the central city—at least, this is the superficial way in which the problem emerges. Satellite areas, as indicated above, are growing rapidly; the churches are capitalizing on this growth with an unprecedented expansion;

* Gibson Winter, *The Suburban Captivity of the Churches* (New York: Doubleday & Co., Inc., 1961), pp. 29–37. Copyright © 1961 by Gibson Winter. Reprinted by permission of Doubleday & Co., Inc.

Gibson Winter is a member of the faculty of the Chicago Divinity School, University of Chicago.

simultaneously, however, the churches are losing contact with the central city areas—at least, this is true of the major denominations of White Protestantism. The metropolitan schism is present within the life of Protestantism: Negro and sectarian churches are multiplying in the central cities, but they are not in a position to come to grips with the social disorganization of the central city areas; for the most part they are small, inadequately staffed churches; ethnic churches are losing their ethnic traditions and their constituencies are moving to middle-class areas; the major White denominations are concentrated on the periphery of the city; the central city churches of these denominations recruit more than 50 per cent of their memberships from a great distance; these central city churches, meanwhile, lose members while satellite churches grow. Protestantism divides along racial lines and between blue-color and white-color populations. The major denominations, whose membership includes from 80 to 90 per cent of all Protestants, are being alienated from the peoples and problems of the central cities; the White branches of the major denominations are aligned with the middle-class, suburban side of the social-class and racial schism.

The schism in Protestantism is also reflected in the mixed attitudes of religious leaders toward metropolitan needs. Denominational leaders have watched the new residential areas surrounding the central cities with greedy eyes. These are largely middle- and upper-class residential areas; they have adequate resources for constructing church buildings; their residents are responsive to religious programs; in fact, denominational leaders call these "high potential areas,"—and they do not mean potential for prayer. In recent decades almost exclusive attention has been given to establishing churches in suburban areas. Denominations have joined forces for the development of new churches through federations and councils of churches; they have set up planning staffs for cooperative church extension, usually called comity. Although comity programs for church extension vary considerably, all of them attempt to allocate new residential areas to different denominations in order to avoid duplication in expenditure and prevent over-churching of particular areas. Comity, to use a phrase from H. Paul Douglass, is a combination of ecclesiastical eugenics and planned parenthood. The growing co-operation on comity is an index of the extent to which organizational growth has been central to denominational concerns: the satellite areas have increased the demand for churches; denominational co-operation has attended to this demand.

Concentration on satellite areas is perfectly understandable in terms of the organizational interests of the denominations; central city areas, particularly the inner zones of the central city, confront the churches with innumerable problems; in fact, congregations have been retreating from these areas for decades, and only a few churches have been able to remain active in these parts of the cities. The central city is littered with decaying church buildings in areas of rapid population change. It has been difficult to obtain pastors for these churches; in fact, change of pastorate is almost an annual phenomenon. In recent years, however, the denominations have become aware that they were losing touch with central city areas, and that greed for growth was driving them to the outer zones of the central city. Programs of church extension have strengthened the major denominations in the satellite areas, but at the risk of losing touch with the heart of the metropolis. Policies of church extension, therefore, are arousing the anxieties of some farsighted denominational leaders: on the one hand, they are committed to a policy of extension on the growing perimeter of the cities; on the other, they sense that this policy is disengaging the churches from the center of the metropolis; since the whole central city is deteriorating rapidly, the net effect is to alienate the churches from the central cities.

Denominational leaders are troubled with problems even more serious than the schism between the central city and satellite areas. The preceding discussion has focused on this schism in the ministry to the city, but the alienation from metropolitan life runs much deeper, for the identification of congregational life with neighborhoods also means insulation from metropolitan concerns. At a meeting of City Churchmen of the United Church of Christ in 1958, John Osman said, "Religion today is challenged to create an urban civilization. . . . Religion has abandoned the city and left its redemption to business and industry. . . . Only religion can regenerate our cities by making them a place for spiritual growth." At the same meeting, Truman B. Douglass said, "Not only has American Protestantism failed to penetrate the culture of modern cities, it has largely refused to take that culture seriously, and it has withdrawn from the task of relating the Christian faith to the problems and needs of human beings in contemporary urban society." These statements reflect a profound concern with the alienation of the churches from urban culture—the religious betrayal of the metropolis—and express the views of a prophetic minority in the churches.

The tension between the churches' responsibility for metropolitan life and their desire for suburban growth revealed itself at a meeting of Methodist leaders in 1959. John Wicklein of the New York *Times* headlined his report of the meeting with this statement: "The Methodist Church, the largest Protestant denomination in the country, is dying out in the cities." His report also contains an observation made at this meeting by a Methodist leader: "In Boston five churches died in ten years, leaving only five surviving in the inner city."

At this Methodist meeting, concern focused on the schism between central city and satellite areas; disengagement of Protestant churches from the central city is the most obvious and manifest form of alienation from metropolitan life, since the heart of the metropolis continues to be a significant center of population, a pivot of political power. The central city is the area which suffers most radically from the disorganizing effects of urban life; it is the area of most pressing personal and social need and the scene of repeated defeats for the churches. Every venture in the inner city involves exorbitant cost in personnel and money, with little hope of return in new members or funds. Every advance toward the satellite areas, on the other hand, promises unlimited return with minimal outlay. The organizational extension of Protestantism has followed the line of least resistance; church extension, thus, runs counter to the metropolitan responsibility of Protestantism, since it threatens to alienate the major White denominations from the central city areas. Denominations cannot continue their organizational growth without sacrificing their moral and religious responsibility to the total metropolitan area or to about one half of the metropolitan population. This is the dilemma which has faced Protestantism; its roots, however, lie deeper than the mistaken strategy of denominational leaders.

The metropolis has become an interdependent whole without adequate internal processes of communication to provide stability and direction. The most obvious symptom of this internal breakdown is the lack of political coherence in the metropolitan area—a void which has the most serious consequences for every aspect of metropolitan life, from park planning to police protection. The problem of the churches is that their strength centers in the fabric of a local community, for both parochial and congregational forms of religious organization emerged as expressions of cohesive, local communities in the villages of feudal Europe and in the local enclaves of medieval cities. When metropolitan changes practically dissolved neighborhood communities, the churches were left without any communal fabric to sustain their congregational life. Meanwhile, the breakdown of communication in the metropolitan area had created a search for insulated neighborhoods; hence, the neighborhoods in which the churches vested their basic unit of organization—parish or congregation—became the scene of a struggle for insulation. Segregation became the path to stability. While the metropolis needed new channels of communication, the more homogeneous communities on the fringe of the city were struggling to break communication with other groups in the metropolis. These citadels became dungeons for congregational and parochial life. The churches entered a period of suburban captivity, deserted the central city and aligned themselves with the status panic, becoming mere refuges for the fleeing middle classes. The churches, which should have facilitated communication, became instruments to block it.

The exodus from the central city reveals the struggle of middle-class people to fabricate some semblance of common life through a religious congregation. This struggle is a tragic story in the history of the Christian ministry to the metropolis, since it led to the unchurching of blue-collar people and the provision of ministry almost exclusively on the basis of power to pay—a ministry which was becoming increasingly costly in training and paraphernalia. The struggle for stability led to an uprooting of the congregations, since the emerging middle classes, which carried the weight of the Protestant population, were moving nearer and nearer to the edge of the city. The very dependence of congregational and parochial life upon a fabric of cohesive community made them vulnerable to the suburban captivity, for here at least they could find some semblance of common life to sustain their rituals. Nevertheless, the relationship of the major denominations to the middle classes was a two-way street, for the middle classes used the congregation as a platform upon which to build a sense of belonging and tradition, even as the major denominations used the middle classes as a pool for recruitment. In this way the exodus from the central city and the concentration on suburban growth were both products of the peculiar needs of the middle classes and the particular vulnerability of the major denominations in the changing metropolis.

The activity of the congregations of the major denominations and their appalling superficiality have often been noted by foreign observers; these visitors from afar look wistfully at church activities and budgets but stand aghast before the spiritual emptiness of these associations. This strange combination of vitality and emptiness can be understood in the light of the peculiar coalition between the major denominations and the emerging middle class. A wholly new style of religious life emerged in this coalition; in fact, the constellation of forces at work in the metropolis gave birth to the organization church. The bond between the organization church and the particular interests and needs of the white-collar ranks can be discerned, but the real problem remains as to whether this fabricated community can serve as a platform for a mission to the metropolis or must be abandoned for a renewed church.

The breakdown of local community meant the dissolution of the fabric which had made sense of congregational life, for without this communal fabric the congregation met in a vacuum, no longer a fellowship representing the community from which it was called. Assembled from no real community and witnessing to none, it merely contemplated its own budget. The same thing happened to the parish, for the parochial form had represented a geographical area in which economic, political, and communal interests intersected. When the residential area became a place for social and economic insulation, the parish became a highly segregated community which could barely survive the rapid population changes to which most metropolitan neighborhoods were subject. In either case, the breakdown of local community gave rise to an organization church as a substitute form of community. The principal difficulty lay in the fact that the organization church was neither a community of faith nor a truly universal form of organization which could bring together the conflicting and estranged elements in the metropolis, for the organization was anchored in a segregated context rather than a ministry. The organization church can be a platform for a mission and an appropriate form for reconciling diverse elements in the metropolis only insofar as it can be freed from the shackles of local enclaves. This is the real problem confronting Protestantism in the metropolis. The solution of this problem can pave the way for the churches to renew their ministry to the metropolis and ultimately to reopen communication in the metropolitan area.

This verdict—the essentially optimistic view that major denominations have a working base from which to launch a mission to the whole metropolis and to halt their flight into middle-class enclaves—has some warrant in recent developments among the churches. On May 1, 1960, Protestants, Catholics, and Jews joined together for a Conference on Problems of Housing in the Chicago Metropolitan Area. It was an historic occasion both because these groups have had relatively little communication and because they joined forces in confronting one of the most difficult problems in a metropolitan area. This interfaith venture into metropolitan communication over crucial problems of metropolitan community may come to nothing, but it is at least a straw in the wind. The great religious faiths which have emerged on the American scene are powerful forces for communication and renewal when they begin to look toward human needs in contemporary life. They can be vehicles of reconciliation and communication, even as the organization churches can provide the base for a totally new form of ministry to the metropolitan area. This is the promise of the churches in the metropolis, though at the moment no more than promise, since these same churches are largely preoccupied with organizational interests. . . .

The Economic Function of the Suburb*

Raymond Vernon

. . . in the past half century urban areas of the United States have grown much faster than the nation as a whole. But during this time, the area of fastest population growth in the typical large metropolis appears to have lain in a ring surrounding the city center—a ring whose distance from the center has tended to increase as the city has grown. The great mushrooming of suburbs after World War II carried on this long term trend at an accelerated tempo, perhaps as a reaction to the prior fifteen-year interruption occasioned by depression and war.

The shift in populations from city to suburb carried with it an inevitable shift in certain kinds of jobs. One may readily assume, for instance, that jobs in the retail trades and in household service lines followed the drift of households to the suburbs. But solid figures measuring the long-term shift in jobs between the periphery and the center of the large metropolitan areas are only available with respect to manufacturing employment. We shall begin, then, by exploring the movement of jobs for this sector of the nation's economy.

Manufacturing employment over the past half century has tended to grow at the periphery of the larger urban areas at a faster rate than at the center. The trend toward an outward redistribution of manufacturing jobs has been gradual but persistent, and it has characterized the overwhelming majority of the major metropolitan areas. By 1955, manufacturing jobs in the centers of those areas were no longer a major element. In New York City, for instance, only 24 per cent of the total jobs were reported in manufacturing whereas the ring counties reported 39 per cent of their jobs in the manufacturing category.

To understand these shifts, we must first of all explore the differences in function between these two portions of the large urban area. A clue to some of these differences is offered by the fact that for large metropolitan areas, the manufacturing plants in the core of the area tend to be smaller than those located at the periphery. Part of this differ-

* Raymond Vernon, "Production and Distribution in the Large Metropolis," *The Annals of the American Academy of Political and Social Science*, 314 (November 1957), 21–26.
Raymond Vernon is Professor of International Trade and Investment at Harvard University and was Director of the New York Metropolitan Regional Study.

ence is due, of course, to the fact that the industries of the core differ in character from those of the ring. But part of the relationship is due also to the fact that even within any given industry the firms in the center are smaller than those at the periphery. . . . What accounts for the pronounced shifts that have been taking place between the core and the ring within such areas? One element in the outward shift has been the movement of small firms graduating to larger size in some given industry. Numerous analyses have been conducted on the subject of plant migration, covering a number of areas and varying circumstances. All the surveys are vulnerable, of course, in the sense that they have sought to classify and categorize a decision-making process—a process culminating in a decision to move—which at best is complex, obscure, and highly subjective in character. What is more, since the firms involved were usually interviewed after they had made the decision, their reasons before the fact and their rationalizations after the fact are probably hopelessly intertwined.

Yet the studies are astonishingly consistent in one respect. They show that in a high percentage of cases the triggering factor which led manufacturing firms to move away from the center of metropolitan regions was that they were running out of existing space at their central location. Second in importance was a variety of other asserted problems: high labor costs, high taxes, traffic congestion, onerous city fire and health ordinances, local graft, and so on. But none of these problems appears to have had primacy over the space problem.

The decision to move, then, appears superficially to be associated with growth. And this is precisely what one would expect if the hypotheses outlined earlier have any validity. For the growth of firms, according to our reasoning, reduces their reliance on otherwise indivisible inputs of labor and capital, such as a few hours' work on electrical wiring or the part-time use of a metal-stamping machine. At some stage in the firm's growth, it is in a position to take on these indivisible elements at a unit cost which compares favorably with the sub-contractors' price. What is more, the growth of a firm probably reduces the level of its uncertainty as well, allowing it to plan its space, inventory, and labor needs with a surer hand and with less concern for violent fluctuations in these needs. As a result, the special pull of the center of the urban complex is greatly weakened.

As the outward movement of growing firms has progressed, the small firms which have sprung up to fill the resulting vacuum have not been sufficient to allow the growth of manufacturing employment at the center of our large metropolitan areas to keep pace with the growth of the ring; indeed, of late, there has even been an absolute decline in manufacturing jobs at the center of many large metropolitan areas. This has been due in part, no doubt, to the fact that the truck has displaced the dray horse; interplant hauling, therefore, may now take place in a wider area. But there is a strong probability that it has been due also to the fact that the periphery of many of these urban areas, having developed their own industrial complexes, can now provide many of the "external economies" once available primarily at the center. In short, fractional transportation and service facilities and the easy availability of added space, materials, and labor, so indispensable in some industries for the small firm competing with larger rivals, now are available over wider geographical areas.

The shift of the small manufacturing firm probably has not been the only factor contributing to the net outward movement of manufacturing jobs in metropolitan areas. The changing technical requirements of large firms also have added to the drift. Over the past half-century the tendency of large firms in many lines of manufacture has been to move from "batch" production to continuous production. Such a shift characteristically involves a basic change in the flow of materials inside the factory. In general, the shift consists of bringing the materials in a regular flow to fixed stations at which machines and labor are located; it reduces the movement of labor and the use of movable machines in the plant. Since it is ordinarily easier to engineer a continuous flow of materials in a single-level plant than in multi-story structures, this development has encouraged a preference for horizontal layouts in large plants. As a result, large establishments tend to avoid cramped sites more than they did in the past; the overwhelming preference is for open sites where horizontal expansion in any direction is relatively unimpeded.

The slack at the center of large metropolitan areas created by the shifting locus of manufacturing jobs has been taken up in part by jobs of other types. Data which might afford a long-term perspective of this process cannot be had readily, but recent figures for the New York metropolitan region illustrate the trend. From 1947 to 1955, for instance, while manufacturing jobs in New York City fell by 42,000, the number of jobs in finance, insurance, and real estate increased by 28,000.

Some of the reasons for the attraction of business services to the center are suggested by our discussion of the location of manufacturing establishments. It is a small step from the proposition that "unstandardized" manufacturing operations are attracted to the core of our urban areas to an understanding of the core's attraction for such business services as central offices, advertising agencies, law firms, commercial banks, and certain types of salesrooms. Some of these services, like the manufacturing establishments just discussed, have the need to gather up a heterogeneous and constantly changing mix of unstandardized "inputs." For the central office, these "inputs" consist of the counsel of lawyers and bankers, the gossip of the trade, the advice of advertising agencies and management firms, the major negotiated decisions of large suppliers or large customers; a varied, unstandardized mix requiring face-to-face confrontation with a wide variety of other entities. For the advertising agency or the publishing firm, one adds the materials obtained from free-lance writers and artists, the layouts of printers, and so on.

As we already intimated in our earlier discussion regarding manufacturing firms, it is the unstandardized nature not only of the inputs but also of the outputs which pulls the service industries toward the urban core. Purveyors of advertising space or high-style clothing, diamond merchants, and art dealers offer products which are unstandardized in character and which require face-to-face communication. The buyer of all these services or products will wish to see them and engage in comparative shopping before making a purchase. The seller whose service or product cannot be shopped at minimum cost to the buyer will be handicapped in the market, and his handicap will increase in proportion as the product is unstandardized. . . .

part two

The Physical Environment: Alternative Patterns

Much of the following material is critical of the city. In general, the line of inquiry is set by the contrasting views of the metropolis that were examined in Part One. As we saw there, the older attitude, in which the rural virtues point up the city's vices, has given way to the expression of hostility toward the suburb rather than the city. Now the question confronting us seems to be: Will the American intellectual rescue the urban way of life by supplying planners, architects, and economists with a philosophy that will fuse acceptance of increasing urbanization with preservation of the individual flavor of rural life? There is a plethora of piecemeal practical suggestions for dealing with the physical aspects of the urban problem. But there is no underlying synthesis, no urban science, which unifies the suggested programs so that their advocates can operate within a generally accepted framework. This may be pleasing to the intellectual, who is thus reassured that his role in the urbanization process is as yet unfinished. But it is a source of deep concern to the planner, the land economist, the traffic engineer; for it means that they must continue to meet real problems in a theoretical vacuum.

4

Urban Design

part two

The Physica
Alternative Patterns

Architecture is the means by which urban design is expressed. But urban design is more than architecture, for without some underlying concept of the purpose of the city, design is impossible. Thus, each of the writers in this chapter favors a different approach to urban design, depending on his concept of the function of the metropolis.

To Frank Lloyd Wright, the metropolis no longer serves a valuable purpose for the individual and therefore "the city, as we know it today, is to die." It simply is not feasible, Wright tells us, for men to live in close proximity in a world in which machines have become dominant. So far, architecture has attempted to compromise with the machine by giving us machine-like cities, but this compromise is doomed to failure. Only after the city has been completely transformed into a machine will architecture again make a vital contribution: "This, *the only possible ideal machine* seen as a *city*, will be invaded at ten o'clock, abandoned at four, for three days of the week. The other four days of the week will be devoted to the more or less joyful matter of living elsewhere under conditions natural to man." The new architecture will be neither an architecture of the city nor the suburb as we know them, but of some nonurban form.

Kevin Lynch here engages in no philosophical speculations about the functions of the city. Instead, he offers a variety of basic design shapes, and comments at length on the advantages and special features of each. There

90

is no necessity to seek *the* design, Lynch seems to say. Simply decide what it is you wish your city to do—the design follows readily enough.

City design is architecture to many architects. They argue that if one designs a collection of buildings appropriately, many civic problems will be solved. Jane Jacobs, however, opposes the idea that the approach to proper city design lies through architecture: "To approach a city, or even a city neighborhood, as if it were a larger architectural problem, capable of being given order by converting it into a disciplined work of art, is to make the mistake of attempting to substitute art for life." Those who engage in this sort of urban design are "taxidermists," observes Mrs. Jacobs. Her approach to urban design is based on the conviction that it is both desirable and possible to have a mixture of land uses—residential, commercial, and perhaps some light industry—so as to provide neighborhood diversity, color, and life. As an example of the kind of urban design she has in mind, consider her description of life on Hudson Street, with its built-in mechanisms for preventing the kind of social disorganization to be explored more fully in a later chapter.

Muted support for Mrs. Jacobs' criticisms of sterile design comes from Lewis Mumford. But Mumford emphatically disagrees with her concept of the goal of urban design as the production of neighborhoods with diverse land uses. "Chaos," says Mumford. The real problem, he says, is that modern designers lack a satisfactory and all-embracing concept of the modern city. Find this, and you have the criteria for good design. But note that Mumford does not tell us what the saving "multidimensional image of the city" is to be.

The City as Machine*

Frank Lloyd Wright

Is the city a natural triumph of the herd instinct over humanity, and therefore a temporal necessity as a hang-over from the infancy of the race, to be outgrown as humanity grows?

*Frank Lloyd Wright, *The Future of Architecture* (New York: Horizon Press, 1953), pp. 165–175. Copyright 1953 by Horizon Press, Inc. Reprinted by permission. Frank Lloyd Wright was one of America's foremost architects.

Or is the city only a persistent form of social disease eventuating in the fate all cities have met?

Civilization always seemed to need the city. The city expressed, contained, and tried to conserve what the flower of the civilization that built it most cherished, although it was always infested with the worst elements of society as a wharf is infested with rats. So the city may be said to have served civilization. But the civilizations that built the city invariably died with it. Did the civilizations themselves die *of it?*

Acceleration invariably preceded such decay.

Acceleration in some form usually occurs just before decline and while this acceleration may not be the cause of death it is a dangerous symptom. A temperature of 104 in the veins and arteries of any human being would be regarded as acceleration dangerous to life.

In the streets and avenues of the city acceleration due to the skyscraper is similarly dangerous to any life the city may have left, even though we yet fail to see the danger.

I believe the city, as we know it today, is to die.

We are witnessing the acceleration that precedes dissolution.

Our modern civilization, however, may not only survive the city but may profit by it; probably the death of the city is to be the greatest service the machine will ultimately render the human being if, by means of it, man conquers. If the machine conquers, it is conceivable that man will again remain to perish with his city, because the city, like all minions of the machine, has grown up in man's image—minus only the living impetus that is man. The city is itself only man-the-machine—the deadly shadow of sentient man.

But now comes a shallow philosophy accepting machinery, in itself, as prophetic. Philosophers draw plans, picture, and prophesy a future city, more desirable, they say, than the pig-pile now in travail, their pictures reducing everything to a mean height—geometrically spaced.

In order to preserve air and passage, this future city relegates the human individual as a unit or factor to pigeonhole 337611, block F, avenue A, street No. 127. And there is nothing at which to wink an eye that could distinguish No. 337611 from No. 337610 or 27643, bureau D, intersection 118 and 119.

Thus is the sentient individual factor—the citizen—appropriately disposed of in the cavernous recesses of a mechanistic system appropriate to man's ultimate extinction.

This future city may be valuable and utilitarian along a line of march toward the ultimate triumph of the machine over man and may be accomplished before the turn finally comes.

To me it is dire prophecy. Skull and crossbones symbolize a similar fate. Let us prefer to prophesy, finally, the triumph of man over the machine. . . .

What built the cities that, invariably, have died? Necessity.

With that necessity gone, only dogged tradition that is another name for *habit* can keep the city alive, tradition that has the vitality of inertia and the power of the ball and chain.

Necessity built the city when we had no swift, universal means of transportation and had no means of communication except by various direct personal contacts. Then the city became naturally the great meeting-place, the grand concourse, the immediate source of wealth and power in human intercourse. Only by congregating thus, the vaster the congregation the better, could the better fruits of human living then be had.

In that day the real life of the city lay in the stress of individual ties and the variety of contacts. The electric spark of curiosity and surprise was alive in the street, in public buildings, in the home.

Government the city had—fashions and fads. But the salt and savor of individual wit, taste and character made the city a festival of life: a carnival as compared with any city today.

And architecture then reflected this livelier human condition as it now reflects the machine. Nor had the common denominator then arrived in the reckoning.

The common denominator has arrived with the machine in Usonia. Machine prophecy such as we have just referred to shows, if nothing else, that we are to deal with machinery considered as common-denominator salvation and in its most dangerous form here among us and deal with it soon, before it has finally to deal with our posterity as dominator. To deny virtue to the common denominator or to deny virtue to its eventual emancipator the machine would be absurd. But the eventual city the common denominator will build with its machines will not only be greatly different from the olden city or the city of today; it will be vastly different from the new machine-city of machine-prophecy as we see it outlined by Le Corbusier and his school.

What once made the city the great and powerful human interest that it was is now preparing the reaction that will drive the city somewhere, into something else. The human element in the civic equation may already be seen drifting or pushed—going in several different directions.

Congestion was no unmixed human evil until electricity, electrical intercommunication, motorcars, the telephone and publicity came; add to these the airship when it lays away its wings and becomes a self-contained mechanical unit.

Accepting all these, everything changes.

Organic consequences of these changes, unperceived at first, now appear. Freedom of human reach and movement, therefore the human *horizon* as a sphere of *action* is, in a single decade, immeasurably widened by new service rendered by the machine. Horizontality has received an impetus that widens human activities immeasurably.

Therefore such need for concentration as originally built the city is really nearing an end. But these new facilities—of movement—gifts to us of the machine, have, for a time, only intensified the old activity.

We are really witnessing an inevitable collision between mechanistic factors. The struggle is on. Additional human pressure, thus caused, thoughtlessly finds release by piling high into the air. The thoughtless human tendency in any emergency is to stand still, or to run away. We do—stay right there and pile up, or run away from the collision, to live to fight again some other day. To meet this human trait of staying right where we are, the skyscraper was born and . . . has become a tyranny. But the skyscraper will serve, equally well, those who are to run away, because probably the tall building has its real future in the country. But the skyscraper is now the landlord's ruse to hold the profits not only of concentration but of super-concentration: in the skyscraper itself we see the commercial expedient that enables the landlord to exploit the city to the limit, and exploit it by ordinance. . . .

Only when the city becomes purely and simply utilitarian, will it have the order that is beauty, and the simplicity which the machine, in competent hands, may very well render as human benefit. That event may well be left to the machine.

This, *the only possible ideal machine* seen as a *city*, will be invaded at ten o'clock, abandoned at four, for three days of the week. The other four days of the week will be devoted to the more or less joyful matter of living elsewhere under conditions natural to man. The dividing lines between town and country are even now gradually disappearing as conditions are reversing themselves. The country absorbs the life of the city as the city shrinks to the utilitarian purpose that now alone justifies its existence. Even that concentration for utilitarian purposes we have just admitted may be first to go, as the result of impending decentralization of industry. It will soon become unnecessary to concentrate in masses for any purpose whatsoever. The individual unit, in more sympathetic grouping on the ground, will grow stronger in the hard-earned freedom gained at first by that element of the city not prostitute to the machine. Henry Ford stated this idea in his plan for the development of Muscle Shoals.

Even the small town is too large. It will gradually merge into the general non-urban development. Ruralism as distinguished from urbanism is American, and truly democratic. . . .

The Pattern of the Metropolis*

Kevin Lynch

The critical aspects of metropolitan form

There are at least three vital factors in our judging the adequacy of the form of the metropolis, once its total size is known. The first of all is the magnitude and pattern of both the structural density (the ratio of floor space in buildings to the area of the site) and the structural condition (the state of obsolescence or repair). These aspects can be illustrated on a map by plotting the locations of the various classes of density ranging from high concentration to wide dispersion, and the various classes of structural condition ranging from poor to excellent. Density and condition provide a fundamental index of the physical resources an urban region possesses.

A second factor is the capacity, type, and pattern of the facilities for the circulation of persons, roads, railways, airlines, transit systems, and pathways of all sorts. Circulation and intercommunication perhaps constitute the most essential function of a city, and the free movement of persons happens to be the most difficult kind of circulation to achieve, the service most susceptible to malfunction in large urban areas.

The third factor that makes up the spatial pattern of a city is the location of fixed activities that draw on or serve large portions of the population, such as large department stores, factories, office and government buildings, warehouses, colleges, hospitals, theatres, parks, and museums. The spatial pattern of a city is made up of the location of fixed activities as well as the patterns of circulation and physical structure. However, the distribution of locally based activities, such as residence, local shopping, neighborhood services, elementary and high schools, is for our purpose sufficiently indicated by mapping the density of people or of buildings. Hence, if we have already specified structural density and the circulation system, the remaining critical fact at the metropolitan scale is the location of the city-wide activities which interact with large portions of the whole.

* Kevin Lynch, "The Pattern of the Metropolis," in *The Future Metropolis*, ed. Kevin Lynch (New York: George Braziller, Inc., 1961). Reprinted by permission of the publisher, George Braziller, Inc.
Kevin Lynch is Associate Professor of City Planning at The Massachusetts Institute of Technology.

When we come to analyze any one of these three elements of spatial pattern, we find that the most significant features of such patterns are the grain (the degree of intimacy with which the various elements such as stores and residences are related), the focal organization (the interrelation of the nodes of concentration and interchange as contrasted with the general background), and the accessibility (the general proximity in terms of time of all points in the region to a given kind of activity or facility). In this sense, one might judge that from every point the accessibility to drugstores was low, uneven, or uniformly high, or that it varied in some regular way, for example, high at the center and low at the periphery of the region. All three aspects of pattern (focal organization, grain, and accessibility) can be mapped, and the latter two can be treated quantitatively if desired.

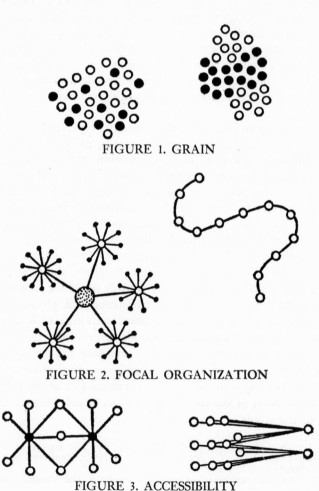

FIGURE 1. GRAIN

FIGURE 2. FOCAL ORGANIZATION

FIGURE 3. ACCESSIBILITY

It is often said that the metropolis today is deficient as a living environment. It has suffered from uncontrolled development, from too rapid growth and change, from obsolescence and instability. Circulation is congested, requiring substantial time and a major effort. Accessibility is uneven, particularly to open rural land. The use of facilities is unbalanced, and they become increasingly obsolete. Residential segregation according to social groups seems to be growing, while the choice of residence for the individual remains restricted and unsatisfactory. The pattern of activities is unstable, and running costs are high. Visually, the city is characterless and confused, as well as noisy and uncomfortable.

Yet the metropolis has tremendous economic and social advantages that override its problems and induce millions to bear with the discomforts. Rather than dwindle or collapse, it is more likely to become the normal human habitat. If so, the question then is, what particular patterns can best realize the potential of metropolitan life?

The dispersed sheet

One alternative is to allow the present growth at the periphery to proceed to its logical conclusion but at a more rapid pace. Let new growth occur at the lowest densities practicable, with substantial interstices of open land kept in reserve. Let older sections be rebuilt at much lower densities, so that the metropolitan region would rapidly spread over a vast continuous tract, perhaps coextensive with adjacent metropolitan regions. At the low densities of the outer suburbs, a metropolis of twenty million might require a circle of land one hundred miles in diameter.

The old center and most subcenters could be dissolved, allowing city-wide activities to disperse throughout the region, with a fine grain. Factories, offices, museums, universities, hospitals would appear everywhere in the suburban landscape. The low density and the dispersion of activities would depend on and allow circulation in individual vehicles, as well as a substantial use of distant symbolic communication such as telephone, television, mail, coded messages. Accessibility to rural land would become unnecessary, since outdoor recreational facilities would be plentiful and close at hand. The permanent low-density residence would displace the summer cottage.

The system of flow, concerned solely with individual land (and perhaps air) vehicles, should be highly dispersed in a continuous grid designed for an even movement in all directions. There would be no outstanding nodal points, no major terminals. Since different densities or activities would therefore be associated in a very fine grain, the physical pattern similarly might encourage a balanced cross-section of the population at any given point. Work place and residence might be adjacent or

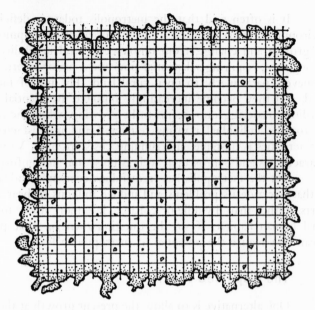

FIGURE 4. THE DISPERSED SHEET

miles apart. Automatic factories and intensive food production might be dispersed throughout the region.

Frank Lloyd Wright dreamed of such a world in his Broad-acre City. It is this pattern toward which cities like Los Angeles appear to be moving, although they are hampered and corrupted by the vestiges of older city forms. Such a pattern might not only raise flexibility, local participation, personal comfort, and independence to a maximum, but also go far toward solving traffic congestion through the total dispersion and balancing of loads. Its cost would be high, however, and distances remain long. Accessibility would be good, given high speeds of travel and low terminal times (convenient parking, rapid starting); at the very least it would be evenly distributed. Thus communication in the sense of purposeful trips ("I am going out to buy a fur coat") might not be hindered, but spontaneous or accidental communication ("Oh, look at that fur coat in the window!"), which is one of the advantages of present city life, might be impaired by the lack of concentration.

Although such a pattern would require massive movements of the population and the extensive abandonment of equipment at the beginning, in the end it might promote population stability and the conservation of resources, since all areas would be favored alike. It gives no promise, however, of heightening the sense of political identity in the metropolitan community nor of producing a visually vivid and well-knit image of environment. Moreover, the choice of the type of residence would be restricted, although the choice of facility to be patronized (churches, stores, etc.) might be sufficiently wide.

The galaxy of settlements

We might follow a slightly different tack while at the same time encouraging dispersion. Instead of guiding growth into an even distribution, let development be bunched into relatively small units, each with an internal peak of density and each separated from the next by a zone of low or zero structural density. Depending on the transport system, this separation might be as great as several miles. The ground occupied by the whole metropolis would increase proportionately; even if the interspaces were of minimum size, the linear dimensions of the metropolis would increase from thirty to fifty percent.

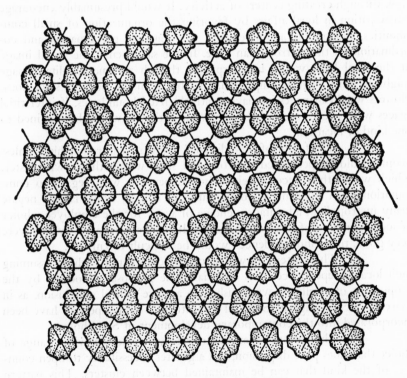

FIGURE 5. THE GALAXY

City-wide activities could also be concentrated at the density peak within each urban cluster, thus forming an over-all system of centers, each of which would be relatively equal in importance to any of the others. Such a metropolitan pattern may be called an "urban galaxy." The centers might be balanced in composition or they might vary by specializing in a type of activity, so that one might be a cultural center, another a financial center.

The system of flow would also be dispersed but would converge locally at the center of each cluster. It might be organized in a triangular grid, which provides such a series of foci while maintaining an easy flow in all directions over the total area. Since median densities remain low, while the centers of activity are divided into relatively small units, the individual vehicle must be the major mode of transportation, but some supplementary public transportation such as buses or aircraft running from center to center would now be feasible.

While it retains many of the advantages of the dispersed sheet, such as comfort, independence, and stability, this scheme probably enhances general communication, and certainly spontaneous communication, through creating centers of activity. It would presumably encourage participation in local affairs by favoring the organization of small communities, though this might equally work against participation and coordination on the metropolitan scale. In the same sense, the visual image at the local level would be sharpened, though the metropolitan image might be only slightly improved. Flexibility might be lost, since local clusters would of necessity have relatively fixed boundaries, if interstitial spaces were preserved, and the city-wide activities would be confined to one kind of location.

The factor of time-distance might remain rather high, unless people could be persuaded to work and shop within their own cluster, which would then become relatively independent with regard to commutation. Such independent communities, of course, would largely negate many metropolitan advantages: choice of work for the employee, choice of social contacts, of services, and so on. If the transportation system were very good, then "independence" would be difficult to enforce.

This pattern, however, can be considered without assuming such local independence. It is essentially the proposal advocated by the proponents of satellite towns, pushed to a more radical conclusion, as in Clarence Stein's diagram. Some of its features would appear to have been incorporated into the contemporary development of Stockholm.

The pattern of an urban galaxy provides a wider range of choice than does pure dispersion, and a greater accessibility to open country, of the kind that can be maintained between clusters. This pattern has a somewhat parochial complexion and lacks the opportunities for intensive, spontaneous communication and for the very specialized activities that might exist in larger centers. Local centers, too, might develop a monotonous similarity, unless they were given some specific individuality. That might not be easy, however, since central activities tend to support and depend on one another (wholesaling and entertainment, government and business services, headquarters offices and shopping). A compromise would be the satellite proposal proper: a swarm of such unit clusters around an older metropolitan mass.

The core city

There are those who, enamored with the advantages of concentration, favor a completely opposite policy that would set median structural densities fairly high, perhaps at 1.0 instead of 0.1; in other words, let there be as much interior floor space in buildings as there is total ground area in the city, instead of only one-tenth as much. If we consider the open land that must be set aside for streets, parks, and other such uses, this means in practice the construction of elevator apartments instead of one-family houses. The metropolis would then be packed into one continuous body, with a very intensive peak of density and activity at its center. A metropolis of twenty million could be put within a circle ten miles in radius, under the building practice normal today.

FIGURE 6. THE CORE

Parts of the city might even become "solid," with a continuous occupation of space in three dimensions and a cubical grid of transportation lines. (The full application of this plan could cram a metropolis within a surprisingly small compass: twenty million people, with generous spacing, could be accommodated within a cube less than three miles on a side.) Most probably there would be a fine grain of specialized activities, all at high intensity, so that apartments would occur over factories, or there might also be stores on upper levels. The system of flow would necessarily be highly specialized, sorting each kind of traffic into its own channel. Such a city would depend almost entirely on public transport, rather than individual vehicles, or on devices that facilitated pedestrian movement, such as moving sidewalks or flying belts. Accessibility would be very high, both to special activities and to the open country at the edges of the city. Each family might have a second house for weekends; these would be widely dispersed throughout the countryside and used regularly three or four days during the week, or even longer, by mothers and their young children. The city itself, then, would evolve into a place for periodic gathering. Some of the great European cities, such as Paris or Moscow, which are currently building large numbers of high-density housing as compact extensions to their peripheries, are approximating this pattern without its more radical features.

Such a pattern would have an effect on living quite different from that of the previous solutions. Spontaneous communication would be high, so high that it might become necessary to impede it so as to preserve privacy. Accessibility would be excellent and time-distance low, although the channels might be crowded. The high density might increase discomfort because of noise or poor climate, although these problems could perhaps be met by the invention of new technical devices. As with the previous patterns, the choice of habitat would be restricted to a single general type within the city proper, although the population could enjoy a strong contrast on weekends or holidays. The nearness of open country and the many kinds of special services should on the whole extend individual choice. Once established, the pattern should be stable, since each point would be a highly favored location. However, a very great dislocation of people and equipment, in this country, at least, would be required to achieve this pattern.

Such a metropolis would indeed produce a vivid image and would contribute to a strong sense of the community as a whole. Individual participation, on the other hand, might be very difficult. It is not clear how running costs would be affected; perhaps they would be lower because of the more efficient use of services and transportation, but initial costs would undoubtedly be very high. The segregation of social groups, as far as physical disposition can influence it, might be discouraged, although there is a level of density above which intercommunication among people begins to decline again. Certainly this solution is a highly rigid and unadaptable one in which change of function could be brought about only by a costly rearrangement.

The urban star

A fourth proposal would retain the dominant core without so drastic a reversion to the compact city. Present densities would be kept, or perhaps revised upward a little, while low-density development at the outer fringe would no longer be allowed. Tongues of open land would be incorporated into the metropolitan area to produce a density pattern that is star-shaped in the central region and linear at the fringes. These lines of dense development along the radials might in time extend to other metropolitan centers, thus becoming linear cities between the main centers. The dominant core, however, would remain, surrounded by a series of secondary centers distributed along the main radials. At moderate densities (less than the core pattern, and more than the sheet), the radial arms of a metropolis of comparable size might extend for fifty miles from its own center.

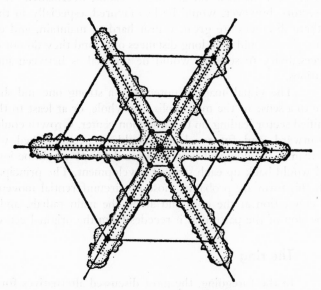

FIGURE 7. THE STAR

The metropolitan center of the star pattern would again contain the most intensive types of city-wide activity. Elsewhere, either in the subcenters or in linear formations along the main radials—whichever proved the more suitable—these activities would be carried on at a less intense level. The system of flow would logically be organized on the same radial pattern, with supplementary concentric rings. An efficient public transportation system of high capacity could operate along the main radials, whereas the ring roads could accommodate public transit of lower intensity. To some degree, travel by individual vehicles, although discouraged for centrally bound flows, would be practicable in other directions.

This pattern is a rationalization of the manner in which metropolitan areas were developing till the individual vehicle became the usual means of travel. It is the form the city of Copenhagen has adopted as its pattern for future growth. . . . This form retains the central core with its advantages of rapid communication and specialized services yet permits the location of other kinds of major activities. Lower residential densities are also possible. Individual choice should be fairly wide, both in regard to living habitat, access to services, and access to open land—this land lies directly behind each tongue of development, even at the core, and leads continuously outward to rural land.

Movement along a sector would be fairly fast and efficient, although terminals at the core might continue to be congested and, with continued growth, the main radials might become overloaded. Movement between sectors, however, would be less favored, especially in the outer regions; there distances are great, transit hard to maintain, and channels costly, since they would span long distances over land they do not directly serve. Accessibility to services would be unequal as between inner and outer locations.

The visual image is potentially a strong one and should be conducive to a sense of the metropolis as a whole, or at least to the sense of one unified sector leading up to a common center. Growth could occur radially outward, and future change could be accomplished with less difficulty than in the compact pattern, since densities would be lower and open land would back up each strip of development. The principal problems with this form are probably those of circumferential movement, of potential congestion at the core and along the main radials, and of the wide dispersion of the pattern as it recedes from the original center.

The ring

In the foregoing, the most discussed alternatives for metropolitan growth have been given in a highly simplified form. Other possibilities certainly exist—e.g., the compact high-density core pattern might be turned inside out, producing a doughnut-like form. In this case the center would be kept open, or at very low density, while high densities and special activities surround it, like the rim of a wheel. The principal channels of the flow system would then be a series of annular rings serving the high-intensity rim, supplemented by a set of feeder radials that would converge at the empty center. In fact, this is essentially a linear system, but one that circles back on itself and is bypassed by the "spokes" crossing the "hub." This system is well-adapted to public transportation, both on the ring roads and the cross radials, while individual vehicles might be used for circulation outside the rim.

Densities within the rim would have to be rather high, while those beyond the rim could be low. A system of weekend houses might also be effectively employed here. The central area could either be kept quite open or devoted to special uses at low densities. City-wide activities could be spotted round the rim in a series of intense centers, supplemented by linear patterns along the annular roadways. There would be no single dominant center but rather a limited number of strong centers (an aristocracy rather than a monarchy). These centers might also be specialized in regard to activity—finance, government, culture, etc.

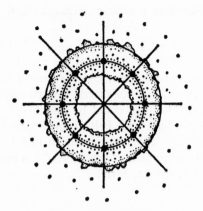

FIGURE 8. THE RING

This pseudo-linear form, like the radial tongues of the star plan, has the linear advantages: a high accessibility, both to services and to open land; a wide choice of habitat and location of activities; and a good foundation for efficient public transit. Congestion at any single center is avoided, yet there is a high concentration. In contrast to the galaxy or satellite form, the variety and strong character inherent in the specialized centers would have some hope of survival because of the relatively close proximity of these centers.

The visual image would be strong (though perhaps a little confusing because of its circularity), producing a particularly clear impression of the centers around the rim, in contrast to the central openness, and of their successive interconnections. The whole metropolis would seem more nearly like one community. One of the most difficult problems would be that of growth, since much development beyond the rim would soon blur the contour and require a new transportation system. A second concentric ring might be developed beyond the first, but it would negate some of the advantages of the first ring and would demand massive initiative by the central government to undertake its development. Another difficulty would be that of control. How can the belts of open land or the accessible center be kept free of building? Even if this problem were solved satisfactorily, a dilemma is also likely to arise in regard to the size of the ring: should it be small enough for the major centers to be in close proximity to one another or big enough to allow all the residences and other local activities to be related to it?

One classic example of this form exists, although on a very large scale—the ring of specialized Dutch cities that surround a central area of agricultural land, Haarlem, Amsterdam, Utrecht, Rotterdam, The Hague, and Leiden. This general pattern is now being rationalized and preserved as a matter of national policy in the Netherlands. In our own country, the San Francisco Bay region appears to be developing in this same direction.

The ring tends to be rather rigid and unadaptable as a form. It would require an extreme reshaping of the present metropolis, particularly with regard to transportation and the central business district; but it might dovetail with an observable trend toward emptying and abandoning the central areas. The plan could be modified by retaining a single major center, separated by a wide belt of open space from all other city-wide activities to be disposed along the rim. It may be noted that this use of open land in concentric belts ("green belts") is exactly opposite to its use as radial tongues in the star form. . . .

A City Is Not a Work of Art*

Jane Jacobs

When we deal with cities we are dealing with life at its most complex and intense. Because this is so, there is a basic esthetic limitation on what can be done with cities: *A city cannot be a work of art.*

We need art, in the arrangements of cities as well as in the other realms of life, to help explain life to us, to show us meanings, to illuminate the relationship between the life that each of us embodies and the life outside us. We need art most, perhaps, to reassure us of our own humanity. However, although art and life are interwoven, they are not the same things. Confusion between them is, in part, why efforts at city design are so disappointing. It is important, in arriving at better design strategies and tactics, to clear up this confusion.

Art has its own peculiar forms of order, and they are rigorous. Artists, whatever their medium, *make selections* from the abounding materials of life, and organize these selections into works that are under the control of the artist. To be sure, the artist has a sense that the demands of the work (i.e., of the selections of material he has made) control him. The rather miraculous result of this process—if the selectivity, the

* Jane Jacobs, *The Death and Life of Great American Cities* (New York: Random House, 1961), pp. 372–376, 50–54. Copyright © 1961 by Jane Jacobs. Reprinted by permission of Random House Inc., New York, and Jonathan Cape Ltd., London.
Jane Jacobs is consultant to *Architectural Forum* magazine.

organization and the control are consistent within themselves—can be art. But the essence of this process is disciplined, highly discriminatory selectivity *from* life. In relation to the inclusiveness and the literally endless intricacy of life, art is arbitrary, symbolic and abstracted. That is its value and the source of its own kind of order and coherence.

To approach a city, or even a city neighborhood, as if it were a larger architectural problem, capable of being given order by converting it into a disciplined work of art, is to make the mistake of attempting to substitute art for life.

The results of such profound confusion between art and life are neither life nor art. They are taxidermy. In its place, taxidermy can be a useful and decent craft. However, it goes too far when the specimens put on display are exhibitions of dead, stuffed cities.

Like all attempts at art which get far away from the truth and which lose respect for what they deal with, this craft of city taxidermy becomes, in the hands of its master practitioners, continually more picky and precious. This is the only form of advance possible to it.

All this is a life-killing (and art-killing) misuse of art. The results impoverish life instead of enriching it.

To be sure, it is possible for the creation of art not to be so individualistic a process as it usually is in our society.

Under certain circumstances, the creation of art can apparently be done by general, and in effect anonymous, consensus. For instance, in a closed society, a technologically hampered society, or an arrested society, either hard necessity or tradition and custom can enforce on everyone a disciplined selectivity of purposes and materials, a discipline by consensus on what those materials demand of their organizers, and a disciplined control over the forms thereby created. Such societies can produce villages, and maybe even their own kinds of cities, which look to us like works of art in their physical totality.

But this is not the case with us. For us, such societies may be interesting to ponder; and we may regard their harmonious works with admiration or a kind of nostalgia, and wonder wistfully why we can't be like that.

We can't be like that because the limitations on possibilities and the strictures on individuals in such societies extend much beyond the materials and conceptions used in creating works of art from the grist of everyday life. The limitations and strictures extend into *every* realm of opportunity (including intellectual opportunity) and into relationships among people themselves. These limitations and strictures would seem to us an unnecessary and intolerable stultification of life. For all our conformity, we are too adventurous, inquisitive, egoistic and competitive to be a harmonious society of artists by consensus, and, what is more, we place a high value upon the very traits that prevent us from being so. Nor is this the constructive use we make of cities or the reason we find them valuable: to embody tradition or to express (and freeze) harmonious consensus.

Nineteenth-century Utopians, with their rejection of urbanized society, and with their inheritance of eighteenth-century romanticism about the nobility and simplicity of "natural" or primitive man, were much attracted to the idea of simple environments that were works of art by harmonious consensus. To get back to this condition has been one of the hopes incorporated in our tradition of Utopian reform.

This futile (and deeply reactionary) hope tinctured the Utopianism of the Garden City planning movement too and, at least ideologically, somewhat gentled its more dominant theme of harmony and order imposed and frozen by authoritarian planning.

The hope for an eventual, simple environment formed of art by consensus—or rather, a ghostly vestige of that hope—has continued to flit through Garden City planning theory when it has kept itself pure from Radiant City and City Beautiful planning. Thus, as late as the 1930's, Lewis Mumford in *The Culture of Cities* gave an importance, which would be puzzling indeed in the absence of this tradition, to pursuits like basket weaving, pottery making and blacksmithing in the planned communities he envisioned for us. As late as the 1950's, Clarence Stein, the leading American Garden City planner, on the occasion of receiving the American Institute of Architects' gold medal for his contributions to architectural progress, was casting about for some object which might suitably be created by harmonious consensus in the ideal communities he envisioned. He suggested that citizens could be allowed to build a nursery school, of course with their own hands. But the gist of Stein's message was that, aside from the conceded nursery school, the complete physical environment of a community and all the arrangements that comprise it must be in the total, absolute and unchallenged control of the project's architects.

This is, of course, no different from the Radiant City and City Beautiful assumptions. These always were primarily architectural design cults, rather than cults of social reform.

Indirectly through the Utopian tradition, and directly through the more realistic doctrine of art by imposition, modern city planning has been burdened from its beginnings with the unsuitable aim of converting cities into disciplined works of art.

Like the housers who face a blank if they try to think what to do besides income-sorting projects, or the highwaymen who face a blank if they try to think what to do besides accommodate more cars, just so, architects who venture into city design often face a blank in trying to create visual order in cities except by substituting the order of art for the very different order of life. They cannot do anything else much.

They cannot develop alternate tactics, for they lack a strategy for design that will help cities.

Instead of attempting to substitute art for life, city designers should return to a strategy ennobling both to art and to life: a strategy of illuminating and clarifying life and helping to explain to us its meanings and order—in this case, helping to illuminate, clarify and explain the order of cities.

We are constantly being told simple-minded lies about order in cities, talked down to in effect, assured that duplication represents order. It is the easiest thing in the world to seize hold of a few forms, give them a regimented regularity, and try to palm this off in the name of order. However, simple regimented regularity and significant systems of functional order are seldom coincident in this world.

To see complex systems of functional order as order, and not as chaos, takes understanding. The leaves dropping from the trees in the autumn, the interior of an airplane engine, the entrails of a dissected rabbit, the city desk of a newspaper, all appear to be chaos if they are seen without comprehension. Once they are understood as systems of order, they actually *look* different.

Because we use cities, and therefore have experience with them, most of us already possess a good groundwork for understanding and appreciating their order. Some of our trouble in comprehending it, and much of the unpleasant chaotic effect, comes from lack of enough visual reinforcements to underscore the functional order, and, worse still, from unnecessary visual contradictions.

It is fruitless, however, to search for some dramatic key element or kingpin which, if made clear, will clarify all. No single element in a city is, in truth, the kingpin or the key. The mixture itself is kingpin, and its mutual support is the order.

When city designers and planners try to find a design device that will express, in clear and easy fashion, the "skeleton" of city structure (expressways and promenades are current favorites for this purpose), they are on fundamentally the wrong track. A city is not put together like a mammal or a steel frame building—or even like a honeycomb or a coral. A city's very *structure* consists of mixture of uses, and we get closest to its structural secrets when we deal with the conditions that generate diversity.

Under the seeming disorder of the old city, wherever the old city is working successfully, is a marvelous order for maintaining the safety of the streets and the freedom of the city. It is a complex order. Its essence is intricacy of sidewalk use, bringing with it a constant succession of eyes. This order is all composed of movement and change, and although it is life, not art, we may fancifully call it the art form of the city and liken it to the dance—not to a simple-minded precision dance with everyone kicking up at the same time, twirling in unison and bowing off en masse, but to an intricate ballet in which the individual dancers and ensembles all have distinctive parts which miraculously reinforce each other and compose an orderly whole. The ballet of the good city sidewalk never repeats itself from place to place, and in any one place is always replete with new improvisations.

The stretch of Hudson Street where I live is each day the scene of an intricate sidewalk ballet. I make my own first entrance into it a little after eight when I put out the garbage can, surely a prosaic occupation, but I enjoy my part, my little clang, as the droves of junior high school students walk by the center of the stage dropping candy wrappers. (How do they eat so much candy so early in the morning?)

While I sweep up the wrappers I watch the other rituals of morning: Mr. Halpert unlocking the laundry's handcart from its mooring to a cellar door, Joe Cornacchia's son-in-law stacking out the empty crates from the delicatessen, the barber bringing out his sidewalk folding chair, Mr. Goldstein arranging the coils of wire which proclaim the hardware store is open, the wife of the tenement's superintendent depositing her chunky three-year-old with a toy mandolin on the stoop, the vantage point from which he is learning the English his mother cannot speak. Now the primary children, heading for St. Luke's, dribble through to the south; the children for St. Veronica's cross, heading to the west, and the children for P.S. 41, heading toward the east. Two new entrances are being made from the wings: well-dressed and even elegant women and men with brief cases emerge from doorways and side streets. Most of these are heading for the bus and subways, but some hover on the curbs, stopping taxis which have miraculously appeared at the right moment, for the taxis are part of a wider morning ritual: having dropped passengers from midtown in the downtown financial district, they are now bringing downtowners up to midtown. Simultaneously, numbers of women in housedresses have emerged and as they crisscross with one another they pause for quick conversations that sound with either laughter or joint indignation, never, it seems, anything between. It is time for me to hurry to work too, and I exchange my ritual farewell with Mr. Lofaro, the short, thick-bodied, white-aproned fruit man who stands outside his doorway a little up the street, his arms folded, his feet planted, looking solid as earth itself. We nod; we each glance quickly up and down the street, then look back to each other and smile. We have done this many a morning for more than ten years, and we both know what it means: All is well.

The heart-of-the-day ballet I seldom see, because part of the nature of it is that working people who live there, like me, are mostly gone, filling the roles of strangers on other sidewalks. But from days off, I know enough of it to know that it becomes more and more intricate.

Longshoremen who are not working that day gather at the White Horse or the Ideal or the International for beer and conversation. The executives and business lunchers from the industries just to the west throng the Dorgene restaurant and the Lion's Head coffee house; meat-market workers and communications scientists fill the bakery lunchroom. Character dancers come on, a strange old man with strings of old shoes over his shoulders, motor-scooter riders with big beards and girl friends who bounce on the back of the scooters and wear their hair long in front of their faces as well as behind, drunks who follow the advice of the Hat Council and are always turned out in hats, but not hats the Council would approve. Mr. Lacey, the locksmith, shuts up his shop for a while and goes to exchange the time of day with Mr. Slube at the cigar store. Mr. Koochagian, the tailor, waters the luxuriant jungle of plants in his window, gives them a critical look from the outside, accepts a compliment on them from two passers-by, fingers the leaves on the plane tree in front of our house with a thoughtful gardener's appraisal, and crosses the street for a bite at the Ideal where he can keep an eye on customers and wigwag across the message that he is coming. The baby carriages come out, and clusters of everyone from toddlers with dolls to teen-agers with homework gather at the stoops.

When I get home after work, the ballet is reaching its crescendo. This is the time of roller skates and stilts and tricycles, and games in the lee of the stoop with bottletops and plastic cowboys; this is the time of bundles and packages, zigzagging from the drug store to the fruit stand and back over to the butcher's; this is the time when teen-agers, all dressed up, are pausing to ask if their slips show or their collars look right; this is the time when beautiful girls get out of MG's; this is the time when the fire engines go through; this is the time when anybody you know around Hudson Street will go by.

As darkness thickens and Mr. Halpert moors the laundry cart to the cellar door again, the ballet goes on under lights, eddying back and forth but intensifying at the bright spotlight pools of Joe's sidewalk pizza dispensary, the bars, the delicatessen, the restaurant and the drug store. The night workers stop now at the delicatessen, to pick up salami and a container of milk. Things have settled down for the evening but the street and its ballet have not come to a stop.

I know the deep night ballet and its seasons best from waking long after midnight to tend a baby and, sitting in the dark, seeing the shadows and hearing the sounds of the sidewalk. Mostly it is a sound like infinitely pattering snatches of party conversation and, about three in the morning, singing, very good singing. Sometimes there is sharpness and anger or sad, sad weeping, or a flurry of search for a string of beads broken. One night a young man came roaring along, bellowing terrible language at two girls whom he had apparently picked up and who were disappointing him. Doors opened, a wary semicircle formed around him, not too close, until the police came. Out came the heads, too, along Hudson Street, offering opinion, "Drunk . . . Crazy . . . A wild kid from the suburbs."*

Deep in the night, I am almost unaware how many people are on the street unless something calls them together, like the bagpipe. Who the piper was and why he favored our street I have no idea. The bagpipe just skirled out in the February night, and as if it were a signal the random, dwindled movements of the sidewalk took on direction. Swiftly, quietly, almost magically a little crowd was there, a crowd that evolved into a circle with a Highland fling inside it. The crowd could be seen on the shadowy sidewalk, the dancers could be seen, but the bagpiper himself was almost invisible because his bravura was all in his music. He was a very little man in a plain brown overcoat. When he finished and vanished, the dancers and watchers applauded, and applause came from the galleries too, half a dozen of the hundred windows on Hudson Street. Then the windows closed, and the little crowd dissolved into the random movements of the night street.

The strangers on Hudson Street, the allies whose eyes help us natives keep the peace of the street, are so many that they always seem to be different people from one day to the next. That does not matter. Whether they are so many always-different people as they seem to be, I do not know. Likely they are. When Jimmy Rogan fell through a plate-glass window (he was separating some scuffling friends) and almost lost his arm, a stranger in an old T shirt emerged from the Ideal bar, swiftly applied an expert tourniquet and, according to the hospital's emergency staff, saved Jimmy's life. Nobody remembered seeing the man before and no one has seen him since. The hospital was called in this way: a woman sitting on the steps next to the accident ran over to the bus stop, wordlessly snatched the dime from the hand of a stranger who was waiting with his fifteen-cent fare ready, and raced into the Ideal's phone booth. The stranger raced after her to offer the nickel too. Nobody remembered seeing him before, and no one has seen him since. When you see the same stranger three or four times on Hudson Street, you begin to nod. This is almost getting to be an acquaintance, a public acquaintance, of course.

I have made the daily ballet of Hudson Street sound more frenetic than it is, because writing it telescopes it. In real life, it is not that way. In real life, to be sure, something is always going on, the ballet is never at a halt, but the general effect is peaceful and the general tenor even leisurely. People who know well such animated city streets will know how it is. I am afraid people who do not will always have it a little wrong in their heads—like the old prints of rhinoceroses made from travelers' descriptions of rhinoceroses.

* He turned out to be a wild kid from the suburbs. Sometimes, on Hudson Street, we are tempted to believe the suburbs must be a difficult place to bring up children.

On Hudson Street, the same as in the North End of Boston or in any other animated neighborhoods of great cities, we are not innately more competent at keeping the sidewalks safe than are the people who try to live off the hostile truce of Turf in a blind-eyed city. We are the lucky possessors of a city order that makes it relatively simple to keep the peace because there are plenty of eyes on the street. But there is nothing simple about that order itself, or the bewildering number of components that go into it. Most of those components are specialized in one way or another. They unite in their joint effect upon the sidewalk, which is not specialized in the least. That is its strength.

The Design of the City*

Lewis Mumford

Nobody can be satisfied with the form of the city today. Neither as a working mechanism, as a social medium, nor as a work of art does the city fulfill the high hopes that modern civilization has called forth—or even meet our reasonable demands. Yet the mechanical processes of fabricating urban structures have never before been carried to a higher point: the energies even a small city now commands would have roused the envy of an Egyptian Pharaoh in the Pyramid Age. And there are moments in approaching New York, Philadelphia or San Francisco by car when, if the light is right and the distant masses of the buildings are sufficiently far away, a new form of urban splendor, more dazzling than that of Venice or Florence, seems to have been achieved.

Too soon one realizes that the city as a whole, when one approaches it closer, does not have more than a residue of this promised form in an occasional patch of good building. For the rest, the play of light and shade, of haze and color, has provided for the mobile eye a pleasure that will not bear closer architectural investigation. The illusion fades in the presence of the car-choked street, the blank glassy buildings, the glare of competitive architectural advertisements, the studied monotony of high-rise slabs in urban renewal projects: in short, new

* Lewis Mumford, "The Future of the City," *Architectural Record*, 132 (October 1962), 121–128. Excerpted from the article "The Disappearing City," Part I of the five-part series by Lewis Mumford. Copyright 1962 by F. W. Dodge Corporation, a McGraw-Hill Company, with all rights reserved.

buildings and new quarters that lack any esthetic identity and any human appeal except that of superficial sanitary decency and bare mechanical order.

In all the big cities of America, the process of urban rebuilding is now proceeding at a rapid rate, as a result of putting both the financial and legal powers of the state at the service of the private investor and builder. But both architecturally and socially the resulting forms have been so devoid of character and individuality that the most sordid quarters, if they have been enriched over the years by human intercourse and human choice, suddenly seem precious even in their ugliness, even in their disorder.

Whatever people made of their cities in the past, they expressed a visible unity that bound together, in ever more complex form, the cumulative life of the community: the face and form of the city still recorded that which was desirable, memorable, admirable. Today a rigid mechanical order takes the place of social diversity, and endless assembly-line urban units automatically expand the physical structure of the city while destroying the contents and meaning of city life. The paradox of this period of rapid "urbanization" is that the city itself is being effaced. Minds still operating under an obsolete 19th century ideology of unremitting physical expansion oddly hail this outcome as "progress."

The time has come to reconsider the whole process of urban design. We must ask ourselves what changes are necessary if the city is again to become architecturally expressive, and economically workable, without our having to sacrifice its proper life to the mechanical means for keeping that life going. The architect's problem is again to make the city visually "imageable"—to use Kevin Lynch's term. Admittedly neither the architect nor the planner can produce, solely out of his professional skill, the conditions necessary for building and rebuilding adequate urban communities; but their own conscious reorientation on these matters is a necessary part of a wider transformation in which many other groups, professions and institutions must in the end participate.

The multiplication and expansion of cities which took place in the 19th century in all industrial countries occurred at a moment when the great city builders of the past—the kings and princes, the bishops and the guilds—were all stepping out of the picture; and the traditions that had guided them, instead of being modified and improved, were recklessly discarded by both municipal authorities and business enterprisers.

Genuine improvements took place indeed in the internal organization of cities during the 19th century: the first substantial improvements since the introduction of drains, piped drinking water, and water closets into the cities and palaces of Sumer, Crete and Rome. But the new organs of sanitation, hygiene and communication had little effect on the visible city, while the improvements of transportation by railroad, elevated railroad and trolley car brought in visual disorder and noise and, in the case of railroad cuts and marshalling yards, disrupted urban space as recklessly as expressways and parking lots do today. In both the underground and the above-ground city, these new gains in mechanical efficiency were mainly formless, apart from occasional by-products like a handsome railroad station or a bridge.

In consequence, the great mass of metropolitan buildings since the 19th century has been disorganized and formless, even when it has professed to be mechanically efficient. Almost until today, dreams of improvement were either cast into archaic, medieval, classic or renascence molds, unchanged except in scale, or into purely industrial terms of mechanical innovations, collective "Crystal Palaces," such as H. G. Wells pictured in his scientific romances, and even Ebenezer Howard first proposed for a garden city shopping mall. In America, despite the City Beautiful movement of the Nineties, urban progress is still identified with high buildings, wide avenues, long vistas: the higher, the wider, the longer, the better.

Current suggestions for further urban improvement still tend to fall automatically into a purely mechanical mold: gouging new expressways into the city, multiplying skyscrapers, providing moving sidewalks, building garages and underground shelters, projecting linear Roadtowns, or covering the entire area with a metal and plastic dome to make possible total control of urban weather—on the glib theory that uniform conditions are "ideal" ones. So long as the main human functions and purposes of the city are ignored, these subsidiary processes tend to dominate the architect's imagination. All the more because the resulting fragments of urbanoid tissue can be produced anywhere, at a profit, in limitless quantities. We are now witnessing the climax of this process. . . .

. . . formless urbanization, which is both dynamic and destructive, has become almost universal. Though it utilizes one kind of structure in metropolitan renewal projects and a slightly different kind in suburbia, the two types have basically the same defect. They have been built by people who lack historical or sociological insight into the nature of the city, considered as anything but the largest number of consumers that can be brought together in the most accessible manufacturing and marketing area.

If this theory were an adequate one, it would be hard to account for the general exodus that has been taking place from the center of big cities for the last generation or more: and even harder to account for the fact that suburbs continue to spread relentlessly around every big metropolis, forming ever-widening belts of population at low residential density per acre, ever further removed from the jobs and cultural opportunities that big cities are by their bigness supposed to make more accessible. In both cases, cities, villages and countryside, once distinct entities with individuality and identity, have become homogenized masses. Therewith one of the main functions of architecture, to symbolize and express the social idea, has disappeared.

During the last generation an immense amount of literature on cities has belatedly appeared, mostly economic and social analysis of a limited kind, dealing with the subsidiary and peripheral aspects of urban life. Most of these studies have been entirely lacking in concrete architectural understanding and historical perspective. Though they emphasize dynamic processes and technological change, they quaintly assume that the very processes of change now under observation are themselves unchanging; that is, that they may be neither retarded, halted nor redirected nor brought within a more complex pattern that would reflect more central human needs and would alter their seeming importance.

For the exponents of aimless dynamism, the only method of controlling the urban processes now visible is to hasten them and widen their province. Those who favor this automatic dynamism treat the resultant confusions and frustrations as the very essence of city life, and cheerfully write off the accompanying increase in nervous tensions, violence, crime and health-depleting sedatives, tranquillizers and atmospheric poisons.

The effect of this literature has been, no doubt, to clarify the economic and technical processes that are actually at work in Western urban society. But that clarification, though it may help the municipal administrator in performing his daily routines and making such plans as can be derived from five-year projections, has so far only served to reinforce and speed up the disruptive processes that are now in operation. From the standpoint of the architect and the city planning, such analysis would be useful only if it were attached to a formative idea of the city; and such an idea of the city is precisely what is lacking.

"Idea" comes from the original Greek term for "image." Current proposals for city improvement are so imageless that city planning schools in America, for the last half-generation, have been turning out mainly administrators, statisticians, economists, traffic experts. For lack of an image of the modern city, contemporary "experts" covertly fall back on already obsolete clichés, such as Le Corbusier's Voisin plan for Paris. Following the humanly functionless plans and the purposeless processes that are now producing total urban disintegration, they emerge, like the sociologist Jean Gottmann, with the abstract concept of "Megalopolis" —the last word in imageless urban amorphousness. And unfortunately, people who have no insight into the purposes of urban life have already begun to talk of this abstraction as the new "form" of the city.

The emptiness and sterility of so much that now goes under the rubric of modern city design is now being widely felt. Hence the interest that has been awakened by books like Jane Jacobs' *The Death and*

Life of Great American Cities, with its keen appreciation of some of the more intimate aspects of urban life, and with its contrasting criticism, largely deserved, of radical human deficiencies in the standardized, high-rise, "urban renewal" projects.

But unfortunately Mrs. Jacobs, despite her healthy reaction against bad design, has, to match her phobia about open spaces, an almost pathological aversion to good urban design. In order to avoid officious municipal demolition and regulation, she would return to Victorian *laissez faire;* in order to overcome regimentation, she would invite chaos. Mrs. Jacobs has made a sentimental private utopia out of a very special case—a few streets in a little urban backwater—a special neighborhood of New York that happily retained its historical identity longer than any other area except Brooklyn Heights. In any large sense, she lacks an image of the modern city. Her new model is only the old muddle from which less whimsical planners are belatedly trying to escape.

The fact is that 20th century planning still lacks a fresh multi-dimensional image of the city, partly because we have not discussed and sorted out the true values, functions and purposes of modern culture from many pseudo-values and apparently automatic processes that promise power or profit to those who promote them.

What has passed for a fresh image of the city turns out to be two forms of anti-city. One of these is a multiplication of standard, de-individualized high-rise structures, almost identical in form, whether they enclose offices, factories, administrative headquarters or family apartments, set in the midst of a spaghetti tangle of traffic arteries, expressways, parking lots and garages. The other is the complementary but opposite image of urban scatter and romantic seclusion often called suburban, though it has in fact broken away from such order as the 19th century suburb had actually achieved, and even lacks such formal coherence as Frank Lloyd Wright proposed to give it in his plans for Broadacre City. As an agent of human interaction and cooperation, as a stage for the social drama, the city is rapidly sinking out of sight.

If either the architect or the planner is to do better in the future, he must understand the historical forces that produced the original miscarriage of the city, and the contemporary pressures that have brought about this retreat and revolt.

5

Planning

The next two chapters deal in very specific terms with the issues raised about man's development in the urban surroundings. This transition from a discussion of the broader issues is a relatively painless one, because the authors indicate their underlying value assumptions.

The problems of planning are many and diverse, but they can be traced ultimately to one of two major themes, which serve to unify the selections in this chapter: the internal development of cities, and the expansion of cities at their peripheries. City growth is manifested in two ways: through internal changes, the slow process by which settlement replaces vacant land, and neighborhoods develop, grow, and decay into slums; and through external growth, the expansion of city boundaries as transportation arteries, suburbs, and shopping centers replace farm lands.

Planning meets the challenge of internal growth through urban renewal, and this is the theme of the first group of writers. In general, they are united in a common desire to do something about the problems of the modern city and its inhabitants, and in a common belief that some ultimately beneficial action is possible. Even Representative Alger is a proponent of a limited program of action—though of a non-governmental nature. However, the similarity of this group of writers extends no further, and each strikes out on his own in advocating a means of urban salvation. Most favor planning, but questions of "how" and "for what" provoke a diversity of answers.

The overriding need, says John Dyckman, is for planning on a national basis. Dyckman's proposal is couched in terms of urban renewal, but his comments apply to the more general problems of planning. His fundamental criticism of current planning in the urban framework is that its tools and techniques are utilized only in bits and pieces by means of a myriad of local programs and that the development of adequate planning requires that it be done on a national basis. Only then, says Dyckman, will we be able to weave the various threads of national policy together into some coherent pattern. Only then will we be able to deal intelligently with such problems as the relative importance of public as contrasted to private resources in planning, or make urban renewal relate effectively to other government programs. Dyckman's many-sided analysis is summed up in his major recommendation, the creation of a cabinet level post for "urbiculture."

Henry Churchill, taking direct issue with Dyckman, argues that city planning is, or should be, synonymous with physical design and should not be concerned with slum clearance or the fiscal productivity of property located in blighted areas. Presumably, Churchill would not agree with Representative Alger either, since Alger's alternative to urban renewal is simply that local supervision and action be substituted for federal supervision and support. But Churchill is somewhat ambivalent on the precise nature of planning. When he says, "City planning is not a part of the Miltonic moral order," he seems to disown the esthetic element in planning stressed heavily by some of the writers in the preceding chapter. Churchill clearly favors an open-ended approach to a definition of planning when he suggests that it should provide surroundings in which "anything can happen."

Generally speaking, an intense desire to be rational characterizes the planner. Yet Representative Alger criticizes urban renewal precisely for its alleged lack of rationality. Alger contends that it is basically irrational to involve the government in the process of city growth and change through urban-renewal efforts when, left to itself, the marketplace would accomplish the task and would avoid the painful experiences of displacing the individual as well.

The second major theme in this examination of the planning process in American urbiculture centers on the rapid and ever increasing encroachment of the growing metropolitan centers on peripheral agricultural lands. Professor Higbee touches on this problem and notes also that the capital gains resulting from such encroachment often accrue to individuals who are not really farmers at all. Not the least intriguing of Higbee's comments is his suggestion that the farm areas surrounding the metropolis be regarded as reservoirs of space for future needs, and he sets out some specific proposals for implementing this concept of the farm as space.

Marion Clawson's information on the use of land has stimulating implications. Are cities more efficient users of land than farms? If small cities use land less efficiently than large cities, what are the implications for public policy? If metropolitan city growth has had the effect of increasing the amount of land in agricultural use, what happens to the arguments of those who raise alarms over urban encroachment?

A perennial solution to the urban sprawl problem has been the creation of "garden cities." This concept of land use, the brainchild of Ebenezer Howard, is described by Lewis Mumford in his review of Howard's book *Garden Cities of Tomorrow.* Are Howard's ideas valid today, given the pace of urban growth? Or should they be regarded as an interesting but somewhat dated approach to the planning process in its urban-rural phase?

National Planning for Urban Renewal*

John Dyckman

The American professional planning movement has long been catholic in its allegiances. Planners not only have worked for private as well as public clients, but also have welcomed the call from all levels of government. The ranks of professional planning societies include regional and national as well as city planners. Many of their members move freely back and forth across these boundaries, ready to move in the direction that political and economic circumstances lead.

For this last group, the trail of moves reflects shifting national programs and shifting sponsorship of planning. In the thirties bright young planners cut their teeth in public works such as the T.V.A., in the Greenbelts of the Rural Resettlement Administration, or in the National Resources Planning Board staffs. After World War II and the passage of the 1949 Housing Act there was a rush into local-housing and redevelopment authorities. Since the "reassessment" of the 1954 Housing

* John Dyckman, "National Planning for Urban Renewal: The Paper Moon in the Cardboard Sky," *Journal of the American Institute of Planners,* 26 (February 1960), 49–59. Reprinted by permission.
    John Dyckman is Chairman of the Center for Planning and Development Research, and Professor of City and Regional Planning at the University of California, Berkeley.

Act there has been a discernible drift toward local renewal coordinator's offices, and downtown business associations.

These bureaucratic migrations have had an impermanent ideological imprint. For ten years planners have worked in housing and redevelopment programs with only the mistiest view of the national planning horizons. Programs have floundered and have been jacked up with new local programs, accompanied by fresh exhortations to local governments and businessmen. The shift from the redevelopment of 1949 to the renewal of 1954 was brought about in some measure by the realization of the scope of the redevelopment and clearance repercussions and the staggering scale of costs. But five years of living with renewal have only extended the realization of the enormity of the task to many other groups, and deepened it for the planners. . . .

Despite a sizable planning apparatus and a wide variety of well-established economic controls, there is virtually no national planning in the United States. If the planners of the urban renewal of individual cities were even momentarily attentive to the renewal of all our cities, they would not fail to see this. The periodic struggle between the Treasury and the Federal Reserve for "tighter" or "cheaper" money has diverted attention from the possible role of monetary policy in achieving planned objectives of the economy. . . .

Tax policies—particularly the division of taxing powers by governmental level—could scarcely be more of a handicap for local governments embarking on ambitious renewal programs. The clamor for Federal aid to meet local service deficiencies arises in large part because the federal government has a stranglehold on the most flexible and politically acceptable tax, the graduated income tax. Urban renewal, to succeed, must provide rental housing on attractive terms. But the tax that the federal government dominates, the income tax, allows deductions for interest payments and other costs of home-ownership, while granting no relief to renters.

Only government spending on renewal can be said to be planned, and then only the expenditure itself is planned; there is no planning of the total outcome, or performance. Agencies charged with administering programs may even resist the programs. The idea that there might be a national plan for urban renewal—or for housing—seems never to have attracted much interest. There have been programs offered by pro-housing forces, a loose lobby, but no administration interest comparable to that expressed in the ill-fated Brannan Plan for agriculture. When spending goes up, it is most often in response to pressure brought to bear on the Congress to increase special appropriations. The relation between this spending and any administration "plan" may be remote.

Under our constitutional division of powers, it is rare when any administration has such concerted congressional support that it is free to "plan," in the sense that socialist bloc countries can plan. But the line between planning and leadership in any free society, whatever the formal structure of government, is thin. And the principal responsibility of government in our time is leadership. The failure to plan has become a symptom of a failure in political leadership. . . .

An example of what national planning documents might be like was provided by the 1958 *Project Report IV* of the Rockefeller series, which undertook to blueprint how we might, by 1967, achieve "an unprecedented degree of well-being for our citizens while making an increasing contribution to the world economic progress which is indispensable for a lasting peace." If it had issued from governmental sources, this would have the unmistakable status of an outline for a "ten year plan."

The important part played by renewal expenditures in this plan is made plain by the weight given to public works in general, and the renewal program in particular. The report, for example, calls for minimum increases of 216 per cent in public works, 185 per cent in education and school building, 166.5 per cent in hospital and health facilities, 219 per cent in roads, 208 per cent in water and sewage-disposal facilities, and 571.4 per cent in urban renewal outlays from 1957 to 1967. The recommended rate of increase in renewal spending in the "high growth" model was 1,000 per cent, a tenfold increase from 700 million dollars per year to 7 billion dollars by 1967. . . .

In the Rockefeller Brothers Fund Report urban renewal is integrated into a structure of national objectives and thereby is brought closer to the stature of a plan than in any other document, public or private. The programmed investment in renewal and public works is aimed at (a) stimulating growth of national product at a higher rate, (b) securing anticyclical action by government, and (c) remedying deficiencies in public services. All these might have independent status as national objectives. Here an attempt is made to bring them together and to achieve them by a coherent program. This process is essential to national planning. . . .

Despite the widespread enthusiasm for urban renewal, the new concept of renewal is integrated into national policy even less fully than is housing. While there is no long-range housing plan for the United States, there is at least a continuing expectation of an annual housing bill. But no one has yet—at least not in official circles—totaled up the implications of a national extension of local renewal activities. Without such understanding, the development of a renewal movement has all the efficacy of tilting at windmills.

At the request of A.C.T.I.O.N., Reginald Isaacs and I, assisted by Peter Senn, undertook to estimate the capital requirements of a national urban renewal and development program which would achieve for all cities the level of development investment which appears in the typical renewal plan or local general plan. Our estimates, which were built on the fragile foundation of the "typical" case were admittedly crude.

Nevertheless, care was taken to insure they would be conservative. A development target date of 1970 was set arbitrarily.

Using that date, and applying prorata the findings of our case city, we calculated a national urban renewal and development bill of over 100 billion dollars per year, totaling more than a trillion dollars for the twelve years 1958–1970. Viewed alone, these figures appear staggering. The present annual rate of *all* investment, government and private, is less than 100 billion per year. But if urban renewal in its global economic sense were a seriously undertaken national policy, part of the planning task would become that of identifying the degree to which such objectives could be approached. Indeed, a closer look at the components of national investment suggests that the spending levels are not beyond reach *if* some major reallocations are made. And there is nothing sacred about the 1970 target date.

But even by 1970, given uninterrupted growth of the economy, national output may begin to approach a level which would make renewal at least arithmetically possible. Gross national product, in 1958 prices, will be close to 650 billion dollars under the most conservative growth assumptions. With product so large, relatively modest shifts in allocation could make available enormous resources for renewal. Two allocations would be particularly important. First, public works expenditure. This item must rise to a level of about 27 to 30 billion dollars in 1958 prices by 1970, or about double the 1958 expenditure. It can do this easily, if the proportion of military spending to total government spending is reduced approximately to its 1941 level, and if total government spending as a share of national product remains at least as high as 20 per cent. Second, the share of private investment in gross national product must be maintained at a high level—at least as high as that achieved in the period 1948 to 1950. If these conditions were met, and if income should grow as expected, a 12-year investment total of close to 1,400 billion dollars might be forthcoming. Out of such investment, urban renewal approximating that dreamed of by local administrations could be fashioned.

Many changes would, of course, be wrought in the economy. Construction, which reached an annual level of 52 billion dollars at the end of 1958, would have to be expanded by 50 per cent. There would be no chance to reduce the present ratio of long-term debt to gross national product; debt might even expand somewhat. State and local debt would rise particularly rapidly. The ratio of debt to assessed valuation in the short run would be at least doubled for many cities. Taxes would increase as a share of household income, even though total government spending did not increase as a share of gross national product, owing to the greater state and local role in renewal spending, and the dependence of state and local governments on nonbusiness taxes.

Certainly, renewal of this order is a far cry from the present outlook of urban renewal. It is estimated that some 500 cities now have renewal programs. If these cities were to carry out their programs as presently planned, Federal funds of at least the scale of 3 billion a year would be needed. Under existing legislation, only about one-tenth this much will be spent by the federal government for renewal in 1960. The Rockefeller Report talks of federal renewal contributions of 7 billion a year by 1967. Our estimate is based on a higher ratio of private to public funds than that in the Rockefeller Report, but even in the more conservative estimate, an enormous increase in present federal contributions would be required. The 254 projects now under way in various stages with H.H.F.A. assistance total over one billion dollars, and they are admittedly a small drop in the renewal bucket. . . .

The Congress of the United States continues to appropriate money not only for housing and urban renewal, but also for local planning of these programs. Through the H.H.F.A. the administration makes planning advances to local communities for community facilities planning, and through Section 701 of the Housing Act, makes available assistance on a matching basis for local general plan studies which could conceivably serve as the required basis for a workable program. Thus the law requires local planning as a condition of qualification for federal renewal assistance, and permits sizable assistance to localities for the preparation of plans of both the general plan and specific community works programming variety. The implication is inescapable that the Congressional intention is to encourage local planning. The conclusion is equally inescapable that no provision has been made for incorporating the consequences of these local planning efforts into a set of national plans or policies.

The federal government may do individual works programming on a long-term basis. The national highway program is a good illustration of such activity. But the idea that anybody at a national level should look at all the local plans, attempt to coordinate them, and even ultimately assign priorities both to activities and to geographic areas, seems to be politically unattractive.

There is unmistakably a core of government short-range policy planning. Such planning, developed around monetary policy, was undoubtedly implicit in the administration attack on the 1959 housing appropriation. There are many other policies, some stated, some unstated, which bear directly on the possibility of achieving urban renewal in the United States today. If the Congress insists on passing or advancing renewal legislation, and if the administration, in one or another guise, supports local renewal programs, it is incumbent on some national agency to draw attention to the *national* planning prospects of renewal.

The decisions which must be faced at such a level are easily specified. Many of the specifics arise from the need for clarification of potential public and private roles in renewal. First there is the question, how much public spending? Is there a limit to the role of government in an enterprise economy which is measurable and can be made an operational distinction? If the government's share in gross national product could be allowed to expand to twice its present level (from 25 per cent to 50 per cent), the problem of renewal incentive might be greatly simplified. Most free-enterprise economists, however, would contend that this development would be incompatible with private capitalism. But what are the limits of compatibility? Are they, as some economists suggest, at about 25 per cent?

The arithmetic of our A.C.T.I.O.N. study demonstrates that if the government spending limits are to be held somewhere below 25 per cent of national product, a new decision burden is thrown upon government—that of deciding how to allocate government expenditures when the total expenditure is small compared to competing claims. At a 20 per cent government-spending level, we found that renewal ran headlong into the competition of military and space-age programs. Should these be retarded in order to make way for renewal? What should the apportionment of public funds between these programs be?

If we seek to achieve renewal by greater public participation in the process, what will happen to the present structure of assets in our communities? In our case city program, we found that the private stake in renewal and development was about seven-eighths of the total. Similar balances are observable nationally as well as in specific communities. If seven dollars in private investment are required for every dollar of public investment, urban renewal is overwhelmingly a reinvestment in *private* assets. Relatively greater government participation in the program, then, must mean either increased government subsidy to private holdings, or must mean government purchase or other appropriation of these assets. Our society has not been successful in finding devices for completely reconciling private gain with some independently determined view of the public good. There is virtually no meaning in renewal if it is interpreted as simply the sum of private objectives. The global definition of urban renewal now in vogue forces this issue upon policy makers.

Private spending, particularly for capital goods, has been one of the most unstable elements in the national economy. It is particularly sensitive to long-range prospects, as well as to the short-run opportunities. If we want renewal on present private-ownership terms, our government must find a way to insure that private investment in new construction will reach a level of about seventy billions per year by 1970. (The 1958 level was about 60 per cent of this amount.)

Not only must we have public planning for private investment programs, but we must have public planning for private consumption as well. For if consumers do not vote with their dollars for the products, public and private, made available to them in these renewal programs, the incentives for further production of these goods and services will disappear. If the consumers who can spend money on housing do not choose to do so, there will be little momentum for continuing to pile up better—and more expensive—housing. Similar forces affect public transit, public utilities, and even education. Moreover, consumers may be reluctant to buy houses unless the costs of related household durables place these within their reach. The task of financial manipulation and incentive management is extremely complex, but no more so than that which was required in wartime. As in wartime, it may develop that nonmonetary incentives come to play a role almost as important as that of the monetary incentives.

Urban renewal for all cities is a campaign which would require national mobilization and national planning. It may further require hard choices of a national government. Its cost is little more than the cost of all defense spending programs which are programmed for the ten to twelve years ahead. While it is unrealistic to expect that all armament spending will melt away, there is hope that world peace may gather momentum. If it should, it is well to remember that the mobilization for urban renewal would require little greater drain on our national resources than that which we have willingly undertaken in arms spending.

The most direct approach to the planning of urban renewal would be one which utilized existing controls. In the earlier part of this paper we mentioned three important classes of such controls: (1) money; (2) taxation; (3) government works and other spending programs. Though these controls clearly exist, it is difficult in our present governmental framework to utilize them for planning effectuation. But it is even more difficult to achieve coherent policy determination and planning at the federal level.

One reason, of course, is that while Congress makes laws, and even appropriations, it does so on a short-run basis only. Furthermore, the continually changing composition of the Congress makes long-run continuity difficult to achieve. Nevertheless, no new Congress sweeps entirely clean. And there are a number of programs which have such general support that they have enjoyed Congressional favor and immunity from budget slashing for long periods of time. Conceivably, urban renewal could rise to such a status.

More difficult is the task of preventing a Congress from passing legislation which offsets the purposes of other legislation. That is, the Congress is under no constraint to be consistent, except that constraint imposed by presidential veto. But the president and his administration can go far towards achieving consistency in emphasis, if they are clear on their own goals and pursue them consistently. The individual agencies charged with special works programs do tend to have some continuity, and that continuity takes the form of long-range programs or even plans. The great task today in the organization of federal planning is the reconciliation of these agency objectives, and the coordination of their individual efforts.

The most nearly coordinative agency, because of its global outlook, is the Council of Economic Advisors. Its view could be long range; its concerns are with finance and fiscal policies which often dominate the effectuation of individual programs. So far, there is little evidence that the Council has paid much attention to urban renewal as a national objective. On the contrary, there is every evidence that the Council sees as a major priority the battle against inflation, even if it should slow down present renewal programs.

Public works, which would be the skeleton, though not the flesh, of proposed renewal, are planned in a general way by the Bureau of the Budget. That is, the Bureau performs a compilation of long-range works programs, and reviews certain project reports, for example multipurpose water projects. The president's coordinator of public works planning has the task of a more general coordination of state and local programs with federal works. (This is the office whose clear-cut planning criteria were stated earlier.) But the main attention to public works, at least in the Bureau of the Budget and in the Council of Economic Advisors, in recent years has been focused on their potential inflationary impact. There is no evidence of a long-run program which expresses works scheduling in terms of national objectives to be realized. The Department of Health, Education, and Welfare comes closer to this in its periodic evaluation of our educational needs. Real federal planning would provide for some agency which would express in program terms the magnitude of undertakings necessary to meet all our national needs—or at least those for which government has been given responsibility. . . .

Creation of a cabinet post in urbiculture might generate pressure within the executive branch for leadership in declaring urban renewal and development a high-priority issue. Congress might affirm a policy of renewal by passing further legislation. But the existence of policies is not enough for national planning. Policies do not lead directly to programs unless they are stated hierarchically. The various programming devices needed to convert policies into programs await executive formulation.

Such programming ordinarily starts with a measurement of long-term need, followed by long-range plans for meeting the need, the arrangement of the plans in a tentative sequence of programs, and finally, the preparation of budget requirements which can be used in the weighing of short-term priority claims leading to actual immediate allocations. The amount of "deficiency" revealed by the initial stock-taking measurements, along with the time perspective developed and the general priority accorded renewal, will greatly influence the pace of programs that will be chosen. But these essential first steps—which almost got under way with the President's Advisory Committee on Housing and Renewal in 1953—have never been completed. They must be carried out by an advisory agency directly responsible to the executive, and with full political responsibility, if urban renewal is not to be a convenient local political mirage, hopelessly beyond the reach of most communities.

Instead of Urban Renewal*

Bruce Alger

1. How is need determined?
2. Where does the money come from?
3. Who gets the money?

How is need determined? . . . I have never heard a liberal member of Congress suggest that federal subsidies should be made available unless a need for them can be demonstrated. Differences of opinion on this subject center entirely on the question of what constitutes need.

I have tried to find out how the Housing and Home Finance Agency satisfies itself about need before it makes any financial commitment on behalf of the federal government. This is not easy to do.

One point is certain. HHFA has not promulgated any criteria or standards to which all communities must conform. Instead, it seems to be relying almost entirely on the provision of law which requires that, before federal urban renewal aid is made available to any community, the local governing body must make a finding that aid is needed.

The law has been so administered by the Housing and Home Finance Agency that many communities which did not require aid have been receiving it. . . .

One very interesting example of . . . excess is to be found in the accounting procedures which have been prescribed in the Urban Renewal Manual. These procedures use technical terms such as "gross project cost" and "net project cost"—terms which are well known to accountants. But the manual suggests items for inclusion in these costs which are completely foreign to sound economics.

By definition, gross project cost includes all the costs which are charged against a project. With respect to federal urban renewal projects, the manual either permits or requires that expenses be included in gross project cost which no private enterprise project could afford.

A proportionate share of all the expenses of a local public agency can be charged to gross project cost. In most communities the legally established local public agency has no funds with which to undertake projects. It can borrow from the federal government 100 per cent

* Bruce Alger, "Bulldozers and Boondoggles: A Congressman Unmasks Urban Renewal," *Human Events* (April 1963), pp. 5–7.
Bruce Alger is a Republican Congressman from Texas.

of the money it needs to put itself in business. It can also borrow additional money from the federal government, without security, for preliminary studies and for the formulation of an urban renewal plan. A proportionate share of all that is borrowed becomes part of the gross project cost for each project.

Again without security, the local public agency, after its urban renewal plan has been approved, can borrow the money required to purchase, clear the property, install site improvements and make arrangements for the resale of the land. While these terms sound similar to those used by private enterprise, the costs involved are frequently far in excess of what any private enterprise project could afford.

The item of land acquisition offers some excellent illustrations of the amount of some of the excesses. In New York City on the first ten urban renewal projects for which statistics became available, properties bought by condemnation averaged 155 per cent of fair market price. . . .

In states where vast amounts of federal urban renewal funds are flowing, slight changes in state laws could eliminate the need for federal funds and could remove the justification for local claims of the necessity for federal assistance. A case in point is New York City. My evidence is a report prepared by a special committee on tax policies organized by the Citizens Housing and Planning Council of New York, Inc. The report says:

> These data show that under the present real property tax system, after making full allowance for some $75 million in exempt properties, these projects will produce a net tax gain of $5 million a year, sufficient to repay the city's costs in 6 years and all public costs in 18 years. If the net taxes could be dedicated to a special land-acquisition fund, the title I program could be made self-liquidating.

Let me make the point that instead of sending out agents of the federal government trying to get cities to take federal funds, we should be passing legislation that no project which is capable of self-liquidation should receive federal aid. This will put pressure on the states to enact their own laws to make such projects self-liquidating.

The Housing and Home Finance Agency has failed not only to make certain that federal aid was needed, but also to determine the extent of need.

Proof of this is to be found in the answer to a single question. How many projects can any one community undertake?

There is no limit on the number of projects for which any locality can get aid.

Likewise, there is no limit on the amount of money a city can spend on a single project. . . .

Where does the money come from? My second question becomes particularly embarrassing to liberals. Their philosophy on this point is well set and widely publicized. They are in favor of using the power of taxation to take away from those who have in order to help those in need. They become terribly embarrassed when in urban renewal they discover that the officially established policy of the federal government is to do exactly the opposite. The liberals, who have had their way without limit in the establishment of this program, are taking money away from the poor states and pouring it into the great centers of population and wealth.

Of the 50 states, 34 pay more than they receive for urban renewal. Among these states are Mississippi, Montana, New Mexico, South Carolina, South Dakota, Vermont, West Virginia and Wyoming—all small states with less than average wealth. Among the states which receive more than they contribute are New York, Connecticut, Massachusetts, New Jersey and Pennsylvania—the centers of population and wealth. . . .

My contention that urban renewal is being financed by taking from the poor to benefit the rich is supported also by figures based on family incomes. The facts are that reservations of urban renewal funds totalling $1.85 billion were made for 254 cities where the average household income was above the US average, while $400 million was committed for 172 cities where average household income was below the US average. In other words, for each $1 reserved for cities with above-average incomes per household, less than 22 cents was reserved for low-income cities.

Who gets the money? My third question is equally embarrassing to devotees of the liberal philosophy, since their record of performance is incompatible with their views.

The liberal philosophy is reflected in the National Housing Policy which was established by the Congress in the Housing Act of 1949, whereby the money is to be used to provide a decent home and a suitable living environment for every American family. Almost everyone joins the liberal in his concern for human need.

The performance of the federal government in trying to meet this need is a totally different thing. Billions of dollars have been spent and more billions are committed to activities that have little or no relation to stated government policy.

Do the American families who are not now living in decent, safe and sanitary housing get the money?

Not so that you can notice it. Many families in project areas get forced out of their homes and neighborhoods without even enough money to pay their relocation expenses.

Homeowners in project areas are paid fair value for their homes. But how is fair value determined? On appraisal techniques designed for federal use and not for the special circumstances frequently found in slums, some homeowners in slum areas who have had to purchase their homes at inflated prices in order to get a place to live, have received from the government less than the actual price they paid for the property. . . .

But that is not the full story of where the money goes. Let me illustrate by returning to the Eastwick project in Philadelphia. I have already said that close to a million dollars was spent on planning that project. This money went to the planners, engineers, appraisers, architects, economists and other experts who made studies and developed plans for the project. Then a federal loan of $78,593,273 was approved with which to undertake the project. This money was spent to acquire the property in the area, provide fill and utility improvements which were needed and to put the project in shape for its intended new uses. This money went largely to contractors. They are very happy with this kind of urban renewal.

When all the work was done and the land was offered for sale, the principal redeveloper was a large corporation interested in promoting use of its construction materials more than promoting housing for people. It has been responsible for constructing and placing on the market houses not much different in price from other houses which were built without any federal subsidy.

Eastwick has been no bonanza for families who have bought homes in the project area. But it has been a fine thing for the redeveloper. That company has received the following specific financial benefits from its participation in the project:

First. A writedown on the land which it purchased in the project area.

Second. An opportunity to make a market for its building materials and to demonstrate their use.

Third. A special form of mortgage insurance from the Federal Housing Administration designed to permit minimum equity investment in the project.

Fourth. A guarantee from the Federal National Mortgage Association to purchase the mortgages already insured by FHA on such a basis that the redeveloper is almost completely protected against financial loss on the project.

Do these facts demonstrate who gets the money? Do they suggest how far from its stated purpose the urban renewal program has been allowed to drift? Do they indicate the extent of the deceit which is being practiced on the poor people who have been told that the program is for them? . . .

In all fairness to those in need of better housing, I am not justified in indicting federal urban renewal unless I am prepared to offer a positive alternative. That is what I propose to do.

The answer lies simply in the use of the police powers of the community to enforce local codes of public safety and health. In communities throughout the country, such action has served as a spur to community development through private enterprise.

How does a city get started on its own? In my opinion one excellent answer already exists in the community development program now being promoted by the Chamber of Commerce of the United States. That program is now being demonstrated successfully in a number of communities. It allows faster, lower cost and more efficient community development than is possible with federally-subsidized urban renewal. Most important, it involves neither the use of eminent domain nor federal subsidy with its inevitable controls.

Another program of local self-help is outlined in an interesting little booklet, *Blueprint for Neighborhood Conservation*, published by the National Association of Real Estate Boards.

Here are the steps it outlines for community improvement without federal aid:

First. Establish realistic ordinances specifying health, safety and sanitary standards for housing. Rehabilitate the substandard housing, at the expense of the property owners, through firm enforcement of these ordinances.

Second. Demolish those slum structures which are unfit for rehabilitation, at the expense of property owners, again through firm enforcement of city ordinances.

Third. Establish systematic public improvements to schools, streets, parks, sewers and to such municipal services as refuse collection, traffic and other facilities.

Fourth. Establish more livable, attractive and convenient neighborhood environment by replanning, rezoning and replanting cleared and long vacant sites and by closing or widening streets.

Fifth. Acquire and remove structures and uses of land which might delay, obstruct or hinder carrying out the program.

Sixth. Attract investment in new construction as well as in rehabilitation and modernization by the application of specific federal income tax incentives.

Seventh. Elicit the cooperation of local financing institutions to secure credit facilities for property owners' participation in the conservation program. Most banks and lending institutions can offer loans or monthly payment plans, or credit may be secured under the FHA section 220 mortgage insurance program and the FHA title I program for insurance of home repair loans.

Eighth. Improve credit facilities for your city through federal insurance of municipal neighborhood conservation bonds on the basis of an insurance premium, so that these bonds will be readily marketable at favorable interest rates.

In Gadsden, Alabama, it is my understanding that no right of eminent domain was used in redeveloping a rundown area. Neither did this city have a proper housing code or proper enforcement. City teams talked to owners about rehabilitation. When the owners refused to clean up the slumlike property, the city teams went directly to the property tenants. Each tenant was asked if he wanted a new home in a nearby residential development to be built with FHA financing under section 221. When most tenants signed up the realtors, builders, mortgage men and bankers went to work. A lovely new development was completed. The tenants moved into the new homes. The old shacks were left vacant. The owners then agreed to cooperate.

Take Charlotte, North Carolina, for example. As of today 12,000 residences have been rehabilitated—10,000 bathrooms were added. Two thousand buildings could not be saved and were demolished, at the owner's expense. Meanwhile the city did its part by paving 65 miles of streets, adding street lights and providing playgrounds, parks and other needed improvements. Two thousand families were relocated in privately owned homes, rehabilitated or new. Two thousand new private housing units were built—all of this without federal aid. Note also the financial impact with increased revenue to the city. There are expenses but urban renewal also generates revenue.

The New Orleans story is much the same, so is the Los Angeles story and the others—each without federal aid. In fact, the cases where there was no federal aid involved suggest that the other areas getting federal aid could have done it on their own.

In all these cases there is no politics as such, as far as whether it was Republican or Democrat. These people decided they would do the job locally, and they did the job. There is the same story in each of them.

To conclude, urban renewal and housing can be solved in one sentence: Local problems can be solved locally with each locality solving the problem in its own way, without any federal participation whatsoever.

New Tendencies
in Planning*
Henry S. Churchill

The absurd process of tearing things down before there is any economic demand for replacement is more and more being brought into question. So too the wisdom of "the big plan" which will "rebuild the area" and "capture the imagination" is being questioned—or at least the wisdom of trying to put such plans into effect all at once is being questioned, since they do not seem to capture the imagination of investment capital.

Investment capital has indeed found occasional use for Urban Renewal, but not quite according to the intent of the framers of the laws. Large corporations wanting to get hold of a site on which to put a building, influential individuals looking for a good deal, and even Educational Institutions seeking to expand, have been able, in complaisant jurisdictions, to get the local powers to use Eminent Domain for their special benefit, forcing a reluctant owner to sell regardless of whether or not there were well considered and pressing plans for Renewal. This pernicious practice has not yet been sanctified by the courts, probably because the cost of carrying a case to at least the highest State court is far in excess of what a small owner can afford.

We are, we always have been, a slogan-happy nation. In 1945 our population curve was going to drop, to everyone's dismay; in 1962 it is going to rise like an anti-missile missile. In 1945 our builders were not taking care of Large Families; in 1962 we are all out to house the Silver Hairs among the Gold. . . . The Comprehensive Plans for cities today are being based on today's current data. There can be no objection to such procedure, for there is no other data available. The difficulty is of another sort. If there is insufficient data, or data which is reasonably unreliable by its nature, then plans which must rely on such data for their chief support ought not be formulated.

Nor are population data the only weak link in Comprehensive Planning. Land-use patterns are in part based on industrial growth forecasts; the trends for Central Business Districts, for suburban commer-

* Henry S. Churchill, *The City Is the People* (New York: W. W. Norton, Inc., 1962), pp. 198–202. Copyright 1945, © 1962 by Henry S. Churchill. Reprinted by permission of W. W. Norton & Company, Inc.
Henry S. Churchill was a practising architect.

cial needs and for supersonic highways are likewise based on guesses about the future economic state of the nation.

It follows that most Comprehensive Planning is wishful thinking. Even if the forecasts should prove to be largely correct, as well they might, there are no controls by which the distribution of people and land can be made to conform to the Plan. The Plan is therefore considered "flexible," and subject to revision to fit the facts as they evolve over the years. This, of course, is what has always happened. Plans are made and parts are carried out. Then the Plan drops out of sight and life goes on until someone thinks there ought to be another plan.

It would be instructive to dig up these old plans. They are not hard to find, they exist in the cellars of City Halls, in library stacks, in the files of architectural magazines.

Some cities have had three or even four officially proposed plans. They are instructive because nearly always they show a lot of things that fortunately were never done. They also, of course, show what the city was like before a lot of things were done, and some of the things that were done were excellent, for which the citizens should be duly grateful. Also some proposals seem perennial; they appear on all the plans and are never carried out. It would be interesting to know why.

The makers of Comprehensive Plans look forward wishfully, but they do not look back critically. It seems to me they should. There are lessons to be learned. The successes and failures of previous plans represent, in a very large measure, what is the true relation of planning theory to practice, of planning ideas to public and political acceptability. An analysis of the whys and wherefores of the success or failure of these plans should serve many purposes. This would require research into old newspaper files and other contemporary sources.

It is necessary to look back in order to go forward. Besides providing reference points as to direction, hindsight teaches many lessons. In the *Journal of the American Institute of Planners* for August 1961 Dr. William L. C. Wheaton points out that "Half a century ago, American literature offered amazingly bold visions of an egalitarian society of the future. Henry George's *Progress and Poverty*, Edward Bellamy's *Looking Backward*, and Herbert Croly's *Promise of American Life* may be cited as examples of utopian concepts that stirred the nation, set broad political movements into motion, excited the popular imagination. Today we seem largely fearful of the future, committed to lesser goals, afraid of 1984."

We would do well, I think, to review this aspect of prophecy along with the purely city-planning concepts of the past. For the works referred to are concerned with people and their future, and, as Wheaton phrased it, an egalitarian society. This too was the concern of Ebenezer Howard and his precursors and his followers—both in England and in the United States. The planning literature of today (this is a debased use of the word "literature") is concerned almost entirely with statistical averages and with statistics as "science." This leads away from the difficulties of reality into as fanciful a realm as was ever inhabited by theological scholiasts.

It is a paradox that the idea of planning for the average always results in authoritarian controls for enforcement by the few. This has been no less true of theological presumption than of political utopianism; indeed it is the moral of the myth of Procrustes. To make everyone average in order to fit an Average of any kind requires authority to cut down or stretch out. (Remember too, it is always *your* average, not the other fellow's.) People are of various sizes, and they have various needs, interests, desires, hates and loves. They are irrational, intuitive; they like sex, money, fun. They do not all want the same thing, particularly when they are told they should have it.

It would seem therefore that cities should be designed not for the average but for the extremes. That takes a lot of imagination as well as a lot of trouble.

Nobody should have to live in an unsanitary slum. But that is an economic problem which could be solved by purely economic action. It has little to do with city planning. It has been our efforts to redress economic wrong by "city planning" that have gotten us into such a mess of political and ethical difficulties. The mixing of physical development with social purpose has resulted in economic exploitation and political deals in which the social purpose has been lost. Worse, some ancient protections of the pursuit of happiness have gone down the drain or been seriously weakened.

What is now needed is a return to a direct and singular approach to city planning. City planning is not slum clearance (social service) nor fiscal solvency (tax reform) nor the achievement of a righteous goal (honest government). City planning is the production of physical order and amenity—a three-dimensional frame for the multitude of activities of people. What goes on within the frame may be chaotic, ordered, brightly lit, lewdly conceived, dourly preached. City planning is not a part of the Miltonic moral order.

Yet is has a by-product of importance for the spirit of man. It may, indeed it is likely to, produce esthetic betterment. With our increasing awareness of our surroundings, with increased leisure to look, pleasantness has become an asset. Not the least of the attractions of the shopping centers is their visual appeal—not just the visual appeal of formal, organized "beauty" but the fortuitous appeal of movement, lights, displayed merchandise, squawk-boxes and radio, an ambient, in other words, rather than a studied design.

There are "projects," too, that will perhaps—if they are built —create pleasant spaces without being frigid and empty. That will be fine.

In the meantime we must take care not to lose our places of real life—our Times Squares and Piccadilly Circuses, our neon-lighted Main streets and our seething Oxford streets. If we can keep these (and their counterparts in all cities and towns) great civic creations will appear in due course, although we cannot command them. We may not even recognize them. Our grandchildren will admire them and praise us, as we admire and praise the works of the past. There is always another generation snapping at our heels. Beauty, like the city, is always in process. So perhaps the chief purpose, though not the objective, of city planning, should be to provide a setting in which anything can happen. The objective should be that, within this setting, the creative genius of the few can find a way to benefit the many.

The Farm as Space*

Edward Higbee

The process of human glaciation, by which productive cropland is buried beneath an avalanche of shingles and concrete, is beginning to arouse some concern among professional agriculturists. In just the past fifteen years an area equal to one twentieth of all the productive cropland in the United States has been removed from the plow by advancing urbanization. This is because approximately half the acres of tillable soil in this country are located in and around growing metropolitan areas. At that rate another 150 years would find us cropping mountain sides, marshes, and other areas that for the moment are unsuitable, in order to make up for the loss of one half the present cultivated land. It will be expensive to reclaim what are now considered wastelands. We have already had a taste of this sort of thing in some of the Western states, where the Federal Government and private landowners have together invested as much as $5000 per acre to bring desert lands into irrigation. . . .

For the moment a better technology is more than making up for the shrinkage of agricultural space. Otherwise, of course, a food

* Edward Higbee, *The Squeeze: Cities without Space* (New York: William Morrow & Co., Inc., 1960), pp. 166–189. Copyright © 1960 by Edward Higbee. Reprinted by permission of William Morrow & Co., Inc., New York, and Cassell & Co., Ltd., London.
Edward Higbee is Professor of Geography at the University of Delaware.

pinch would have developed already. Every state has examples of increased production by fewer farmers on less land. In Delaware in 1945 there were 9296 farms. When the last census was taken in 1954, there were 6297. In 1945 there were 923,000 acres of land in farms. Recently farm economist William McDaniel estimated the total is down to 800,000 acres. However, a productivity index which stood at 100 in 1946 had increased to 159 in 1958. As long as a technological revolution can compensate for the cannibalism of farm land by metropolitan sprawl, the American city will have a full stomach, but it had better not press its luck too far. There is a point at which the farm will vanish. According to one of the best contemporary standards the limit at which a farm ceases to qualify as such is reached when it drops below three acres in size. This is the point-of-no-return established in 1959 by the Farm Bureau of Caroline County, Maryland, when it refused to qualify aspirants for its annual Farm Beauty Queen Contest if the old homestead had shrunk beyond that limit.

Economically the farmer should be the last person to give a hoot about the extinction of the farm on the urban fringe. Except for whatever sentimental ties he must sever, no happier fortune could befall the plowman than to be approached by a realtor willing to pay him more for his land than he could earn by working it a lifetime. The sudden golden shower of capital gains that attends the transmutation of cornfields into speculative real estate has caused nearly every farmer on the urban fringe to put out the welcome mat for the bulldozer. Of course the shrewdest husbandmen hold out as long as possible inasmuch as the last acreage to go into developments usually brings the fattest price. Understandably, most farmers do not want to be spared this delicious fate. When Fairfax County, Virginia, recently tried to limit suburban sprawl in outlying agricultural districts by raising the minimum area of house lots to three acres, the local farmers blew their tops. They contended that the new ordinance would force them to stay in farming whereas otherwise they might have a fling at real estate. They challenged the legality of the zoning ordinance in the courts and defeated it. They argued that most homeowners could not afford three acres of land at house-lot prices and that therefore the zoning ordinance deprived them of customers and a chance to sell their land in smaller pieces at maximum prices. The judge agreed and invalidated the county's restrictions.

Most farmers on the urban fringe, even if they had not wanted to sell their land to an advancing suburbia, are eventually persuaded by a series of events to change their minds. Slowly they are overwhelmed by an endless rise of taxes to help defray the mounting costs of new schools and roads, as well as the wages of the inevitable bureaucracy that comes with urbanization. In the country the many duties of local administration are usually carried on by senior citizens without salary or for nominal stipends. As long as a place is truly rural, the population remains relatively stable and schools built by one generation may accommodate the next with slight additions. The tax base is adequate to support simple services without much of an annual increase.

The advent of suburbia changes that. In the absence of industry there is nothing else upon which to hang the burden of heavier civic expenses; so tax assessors hit the farms on the assumption that if one of them sold for a high price to a subdivider, then they are all worth a mint of money. This sounds reasonable but the fallacy is that the expanding community, no matter how fast it grew, could not use all the land at once even if every farmer were willing to sell. But the assessors are hungry and they are often under the pressure of land speculators with political influence to put the squeeze on operating farms so that owners will sell quicker at bargain prices.

The premature expulsion of the farmer from the edge of the city via the tax-pressure route commonly creates a belt of idle land which grows into unsightly weeds and brush between advancing city construction and the outer rim of operating farms. This desolate no man's zone is composed of the slaughtered carcasses of farms which, as it were, hang on the hook in cold storage awaiting the slicers and cutters who will hack out pieces for the retail trade. No genuine farmer could afford to hold high-tax land even if he were cropping it, but the land butchers are able to hold it in complete idleness because that is their business and they have the capital to buy today for sales that may not take place until five or ten years hence. They are well-financed professionals who understand the beauties of land-value appreciation under population pressure and are prepared to invest in them. They know that space in the path of growth increases in value faster than money in the bank; and they are favored further by the fact that their profits, in contrast to ordinary income, will be taxed as capital gains. The farmer is financially unprepared to play in this big league; when he sells he makes a nice profit, but not the kind of killing that would otherwise be possible. When the stakes are really high, City Hall or the County Court House may step in to take care of its own during the final ripening period when land values make their fantastic final spurt.

Generally, it is while land between an advancing suburbia and the belt of retreating farms is ripening in the hands of professional land wolves that the future shape of a growing settlement is determined. The design they create is seldom drawn for the ultimate utility and convenience of tomorrow's community or for preservation of landscape beauty and function. During this crucial stage, when there are fortunes to be made or lost, energy is not wasted on silly byplay. That can come later with the promotion blurbs appealing to prospective homeowners after the main battle has been fought behind the scenes. In fact rational master plans are seldom possible, even if some operators wanted them, because many individual speculators are involved and each is restrained or pushed by his own clientele, associates, and political connections. It is during this interim period between liquidation of the farm and the arrival of the bulldozer that the hottest jockeying for licenses, permits, and special zoning concessions goes on. It is no small wonder that a functional design does not emerge, but rather a patchwork compromise by which the influential get the commercial sites and the multi-family dwelling permits, while the weak find themselves holding low-value single-family residential land which they may have to sell at little profit, if not a loss. In the course of this melee the mistakes are born that breed future suburban-renewal projects before even the first ranch house, supermarket, or dual-lane highway is built on what used to be a peaceful field of clover. . . .

In his use of land the farmer harvests a crop, plows under the useless aftermath, and starts afresh with each new seeding. He repeats this cycle over and over, year after year. If he is an intelligent man he learns from this experience and his techniques improve as time goes by. To the agriculturist land is a renewable resource, capable of restored fertility and ever better crops. He does not plant for permanence but for the season, and he expects that each new effort will eventually be superseded by another even better. The farm is an enormous blackboard upon which the operator continuously draws and erases patterns of use. Its function is to be neutral—constantly subject to change and improvement under increasingly better management.

The city uses land differently. What it plants it cannot plow under except at a sacrifice. Buildings and streets are not crops to be harvested but useful facilities to be preserved with care, and utilized where they stand decade after decade. Though a city may learn from experience how to make better use of land, only in the most exceptional circumstances can it afford to apply this knowledge by tearing down and starting over. If it learns anything that is widely applicable, it is how to plan the future consumption of virgin space so as to avoid the mistakes of the past. A growing city which cannot learn from its own experience how to utilize newly acquired farm lands more appropriately than in the past is destined to consume this irreplaceable resource to the ever-increasing expense and dissatisfaction of its citizens. It is difficult for the American city to adopt such an attitude of self-criticism toward its own growth because throughout our history the conquest of space has been glorified. Almost invariably it has been considered an obstacle to be overcome rather than a limited asset to be handled with thrift. . . .

From the standpoint of the greatest good for the greatest number of American citizens at this particular moment in the nation's development, the most important function of the farm on the urban fringe is as a reservoir of space which eventually will be urbanized. Unless a growing community regards the farms on its periphery as the most important raw material out of which its future will be molded and treats them accordingly, there can be no sensible policy for the eventual allocation of their space to urban uses. If a community must first misuse land, create congestion, license inefficiency, and promote dissatisfaction before it is shocked into seeing the importance of rational space allocation, there can be no hope. We shall have to live with folly if we are not wise enough to prevent it, and this will become a permanent drag on our economy and a constant irritation to our daily living. That we have muddled through in the past will not comfort us in the future. Effective urban renewal is already far beyond the financial means of our economy; yet the speed-up in population growth and metropolitan expansion has only begun. The deluge is yet to come and we have only a sieve to bale out the boat. . . .

. . . The dream boat of state is wrecked upon the shoals of reality. The abstract idea, that the development of space in metropolitan areas should be guided, sounds nice, but a community can do very little without controls. There are strict limits to a community's authority over landowners and what they should do with their real estate. This is as it should be for, otherwise, the very ownership of property would be a delusion. It would be clearly unethical and illegal for a public authority to permit one farmer to sell his land for great profit to real-estate developers and to deny this right to his neighbors on the assumption that their acres should be conserved as open space until the community approved conversion to other uses. This would be an arbitrary and a discriminatory exercise of police power out of keeping with constitutional guarantees. . . .

. . . If communities want to plan their growth and dictate the way space should be used when it passes from farm to city, then they will have to do more than pass ordinances. They will have to gain control of the land. To get control they will have to buy it just as any individual would. Cities do not normally engage heavily in the real-estate business but they will have to if the pattern of their future growth is to be rational. Planning without control is idle dreaming. There are several ways by which a community could purchase control. It could buy land on the open market when it is in farms and hold it until it is ripe for development. It could then sell its holdings with restrictions in the deeds so that developers would have to build whatever the community would have planned for that particular space. This approach would be impossible for most cities or counties. They are already in debt for current needs and could scarcely find funds to invest in properties they could not use or sell for twenty years.

William H. Whyte, Jr., one of the authors of *The Exploding Metropolis*, has proposed that communities purchase "development easements" from farmers on the urban fringe. By the sale of such easements farmers would surrender the right to use their land for anything but agriculture. Space would then lose its speculative value because developers would scarcely care to collect cornfields and pastures if that were all the land could be used for. Possibly only farmers, who want to continue farming on their present properties, would be interested in forfeiting development privileges. Many estate owners who are harried by mounting taxation might sell such easements if their preference were to live on their properties indefinitely rather than to sell them for a profit. Local real-estate taxes would certainly be lower on farms and estates stripped of their speculative prospects because their market values would be comparatively low.

The "development easement" idea is a good one and a farmer who would sell such rights need not necessarily be a financial dim wit. Either he could charge a high price for parting with the speculative value of his land or he could afford practically to give away development rights if he were to reserve an option to repurchase them for a nominal fee at any future time the community should decide that his farm space were needed for urban development. By these devices a community could be protected against premature and disorganized expansion. It would gain control of its own future growth pattern because it could specify the uses to which the land might be put when it eventually released the rights which it had held in trust. The farmer would not be chased away until his land was urgently needed and meanwhile he would enjoy low taxes. Also the farm community could not be infiltrated and split up by other types of land uses if all farmers in the vicinity were to make similar sales of development rights simultaneously. Obviously the time for a community to buy development rights is not when the land is almost ripe for urbanization but when that day is twenty, fifty, or a hundred years away. The more remote the prospect, the easier and cheaper it should be to acquire them.

There are other ways to skin the cat. A community could establish a revolving fund with which it would purchase farms on the urban fringe. Once they were in legal possession, then restrictions could be written into deeds that any change of use would have to conform to the development plans of the community. With these restrictions recorded the land could then be resold immediately into private hands for farming or speculation. Such a program would be senseless unless the community had a comprehensive plan for its future expansion. Another device would be for private citizens to establish a corporation either for profit or as a non-profit foundation which would acquire farms and sell them with restrictions in their deeds that would conform to uses designated in a community's master plan. By processing properties in such ways as these relatively little capital would need to be tied up at any particular moment. Also, the chances are that while farms are in the temporary possession of the processing agency they could be rented so as to return a reasonable interest on the invested capital. . . .

The capital-gains tax on real estate is the logical source of the funds with which communities either might buy space for future public needs or acquire land temporarily in order to write development restrictions into deeds. These capital-gains taxes, which can amount to as much as twenty-five per cent of profits made on real-estate transactions, are now collected by the Federal Government as though they were ordinary revenue. Capital gains on real estate are actually the product of local community growth and should properly be collected by the community which created them rather than by the Federal Government. Either that or the Federal Government should return these revenues to the communities which produced them with the proviso that they be used only for planning and for the acquisition of land. They should be spent to buy space for future roads, parks, reservoir areas, school sites, airports, disposal areas, and other public facilities. These funds should also be available to buy development rights from landowners.

Revolving funds built up out of capital-gains taxes on real estate could be used to buy and sell land in order to amend deeds so that they would conform to master plans for future growth. The capital-gains tax on real estate should be regarded not as revenue but as a vital instrument with which to obtain control over the way a community grows. . . .

Urban Land Use*

Marion Clawson

1. The available data are ill-suited to any economic analysis of urban land use. A few sample data relate rather closely to land actually used; but these are mostly for political, not economic, cities, and the sample is small. Census data conform neither to the concept of land actually used for urban purposes nor to the concept of land withdrawn by the city from any other land use, although they are nearer the latter than the former. Census data are available for incorporated cities as legal entities, but these are sometimes artificial in terms of economic activity, and are in any case affected by the accidents of history. Some data are available for larger urban groupings as economic entities (urbanized areas). The SMA's† include all the population and economic activity centered around the larger cities; but to do so they must also include vast areas of nonurban land uses, thus distorting the whole land use picture.

* Marion Clawson, et al., Land For the Future (Baltimore: Resources for the Future and The Johns Hopkins University Press, 1960), pp. 94–95, 122–123. Reprinted by permission.
Marion Clawson is Director of Land Use and Management for Resources for the Future, Inc.
† SMA is a U.S. Census term designating county-wide areas with a central city of 50,000 or more population.

2. The average density of land use, and hence the area required for any given population, depends to a great extent upon the size of the city. Small cities are more lavish than large cities in their use of land; this is natural, and from their point of view, logical. But there are great variations in this relationship between size of city and land use. . . .

3. Within all incorporated cities of 2,500 population and over, cities of less than 25,000 contain at least half of the land. These small cities and other still smaller towns, both incorporated and unincorporated, use perhaps as much as three-fourths of all land withdrawn from other uses. Some of these small towns and cities are satellites to larger cities, but many are independent. These are the cities whose large use of land would seem to offer the greatest opportunity for intensive study. On the other hand, both the incentive to more intensive land use and the social and governmental mechanisms whereby it might be brought about operate against more frugal use of land in small cities.

4. Although the data are inadequate, there seems good reason to believe that there is much idle land within city boundaries; studies of sample cities would indicate that the idle land averages one-third or more of the total. Some idle land available for expansion or new uses is desirable, but it appears that the amount now idle is far in excess of a reasonable amount, and that great economies could be achieved in its better use. On the other hand, much of the land is ill-suited to use, primarily because of the size of holdings into which it has been divided. For some of it, titles are fouled up and thus its value is further reduced.

5. All incorporated cities of 2,500 and over report 13 million acres within their borders. An estimate of total area within urban places is perhaps ½ to 1 million acres larger; this takes account of the urban population outside of incorporated cities. There are nearly 14,000 "places" of less than 2,500 persons, that are classed by the Census as rural; they average less than 800 persons each. The total area of land in them is unknown but probably is in the rough magnitude of 10 million acres. However, it is more than likely that the area is included in the statistics of surrounding land uses—forestry, grazing, agriculture, etc. All of these figures represent more than area used, but somewhat less than area withdrawn from other uses. Bearing in mind the data's limitations and imperfectly defined relationships, it is still possible to make a very rough estimate of the area occupied by all urban population as that term is defined by Census:

> withdrawn area: 17 million acres
> used area: 11 million acres

In recent years, many people with different professional and interest backgrounds have been disturbed at urban growth and its encroachment upon agricultural land. Most people have recognized that the total areas involved until now are small compared with the total area of agricultural land, and that no immediate shortage of agricultural land is in prospect. Some, however, have been disturbed about the immediate effects. Many have been much concerned about the long-run effects upon our ability to produce the crops we need, and most people have been concerned over the disturbance that urban expansion creates in the rural community. Some have written or spoken as though the city were a sinister thing, reaching out to strangle and engulf the rural area and its people.

In our view, much of this writing has been exaggerated. In the first place, most people are confused as to the nature of the force that is operative. It is not city growth, as such, that creates the problem, but population growth. Had the population growth of the last twenty or fifty years occurred without any major increase in city population—had it, in short, taken place in open country—the area required for site purposes would have been far larger. If it is use of land we are concerned about, the city is far more efficient than the open country: the larger the city, the less land is required for a given population increase. If we must have high rates of population increase and if our objective is to minimize the area of land needed for site purposes, then the city is the best place to put the extra people. This does *not* say that the cities that have arisen are the best that could be devised, or that the resulting pattern of land use within the cities has been perfect.

In the second place, most cries of alarm over urban expansion have been superficial in their level of economic analysis. The direct shift of land is from farm to urban use. But what are the indirect influences and results? American agriculture today is market-oriented and market-limited. The volume of agricultural output is definitely limited by available markets, and the quantity of resources used in agricultural production is also limited by market demand for agricultural products. There is much land in the United States, physically capable of being farmed, that is not farmed. In the southern Coastal Plain alone there are 36 million acres of good potential cropland. As nonfarm populations grow, they constitute an increased demand for agricultural products, and this stimulates the use of land for agricultural purposes. It is true that, with present-day transportation methods and costs, the stimulus to land development is less local than it once would have been. Nevertheless, a considerable part of agriculture in the northeastern third of the nation has been directly affected by city demand within the region for fresh milk and other products produced locally. It should be recalled that Bogue found that the area in farms in the SMA's *increased* as urban population rose. He thought this was an "apparent impossibility," but we wish to suggest that this increase in farm area near cities was neither impossible nor unexpected. Rather, it was, at least in large part, a reaction to the stimulus of nearby increased demand for farm products.

In the third place, the discussion of the effects of urban expansion into rural areas ignores the technological, economic, and cultural complex of the present and recent past. . . . An agricultural revolution has taken place in the United States in the past forty years or so. If the total population of the United States today were 100 million, as it was at the time of the First World War, the area in crops would be *less* by at least 100 million acres. The growth of cities over the past generation has kept infinitely more land in agricultural production than it has taken out of it.

Urban expansion poses many serious land use and other problems; but solution is not facilitated by misunderstanding the nature of the problems and the facts that produce them.

The Garden City of Ebenezer Howard*

Lewis Mumford

At the beginning of the twentieth century two great new inventions took form before our eyes: the aeroplane and the Garden City, both harbingers of a new age: the first gave man wings and the second promised him a better dwelling-place when he came down to earth. Both inventions had originally been conceived by that brilliant, many-sided technician, Leonardo da Vinci; for he not merely studied the flight of birds to good purpose but proposed to abate the congestion and squalor of Milan by building a group of ten cities of five thousand houses, limited to thirty thousand inhabitants each, cities which, in another place, he proposed to design with a complete separation of pedestrian and horse traffic, and with gardens attached to a municipal irrigation system.

Ebenezer Howard was not influenced even at second hand by Leonardo, whose notebooks were not yet available in English; instead, he was in the tradition of a group of early nineteenth-century writers: Spence, the land reformer, who sought the nationalization of land; James

* Lewis Mumford, "The Garden City Idea and Modern Planning," introductory essay to *Garden Cities of Tomorrow* by Ebenezer Howard (London: Faber and Faber, Ltd., 1946), pp. 29–36. Reprinted by permission of the publishers.

Buckingham, who had published a plan for a model industrial town in 1848; Edward Gibbon Wakefield, who had pointed out the necessity for a more systematic plan of colonization for distant lands; and not least, two critical thinkers who were nearer at hand, Henry George and Peter Kropotkin. The work of these men gave substance to Howard's own intuitions and beliefs; but no little stimulus came to him from his visit to America, where he had before him the constant spectacle of new communities being laid out every year on new land, and he was impressed by the possibility of a fresh start.

Had Howard been a mere dreamer this book might have remained an object of curious discussion, like Edgard Chambless's *Roadtown*, which gave to the physical utilities of planning the priority that Howard, a far better sociologist, gave to social and economic arrangements. But Howard was a practical idealist, like the Rochdale co-operators before him; and he utilized the widespread interest in his idea to gather support for the planning and building of an experimental Garden City.

Howard's initiatives in the Garden City paralleled the Wright Brothers'. I emphasize this parallelism because it points to a functional relationship that has too often been overlooked even by those who have advocated the Garden City; for if the aeroplane, in its present or conceivable future forms, is to be anything but a menace to health and sanity and safety, and if it is to become as much a part of our daily life as the motor-car now is, it will be so only after the Garden City, with its wide belt of open land, has become the dominant urban form. . . .

Howard's prime contribution was to outline the nature of a balanced community and to show what steps were necessary, in an ill-organized and disoriented society, to bring it into existence. On one side was the overgrown and over-congested metropolis penalized in its health by its slums, and in its efficiency by ill-sorted and misplaced industries, given to extravagant wastes in time and energy and money merely to transport its goods and people over distances that had been expanded for no good human purpose, desolate in its lack of social facilities, though possessing, in its central institutions, the chief organized forms of social life. The continued growth of centres like London, Paris, and Berlin, and their imitators lower down in the urban scale, had not resulted in any commensurate gains in social life. Hence the increase of population and wealth in our big centres had paradoxically resulted in destitution, and no small part of the city's income was concerned with alleviating this destitution by costly measures of sanitation and slum clearance.

The country, on the other hand, was equally impoverished: emptied out of its more able and enterprising spirits by the very growth of big cities. Here were fresh air, sunlight, pleasant vistas, quiet nights, all scarce commodities in the big cities; but on the other hand, there was another sort of destitution, a dearth of human companionship and of cooperative effort. Agriculture, having lost much of its local market, was a declining occupation, and life in a country town was as mean, illiberal, and dismal as life in a metropolitan slum. Nor would decentralization of single industries into the open country help matters here: for if man is to live a balanced life, capable of calling out all his faculties and bringing them to perfection, he must live in a community that fully sustains them. What was needed, Howard saw—as Kropotkin at the same time proclaimed—was a marriage of town and country, of rustic health and sanity and activity and urban knowledge, urban technical facility, urban political co-operation. The instrument of that marriage was the Garden City.

Here again I must utter a warning against those who mistake Howard's programme for one of breaking down the distinction of town and country and turning them into an amorphous suburban mass. The reader who has the patience to follow Howard's argument will see that he had no such end in mind; indeed, the whole project is an attempt to guard against its happening.

For the Garden City, as conceived by Howard, is not a loose indefinite sprawl of individual houses with immense open spaces over the whole landscape: it is rather a compact, rigorously confined urban grouping. Of the total tract to be included in the domain of the Garden City, one thousand acres, at the centre, were to be occupied by the city itself; and five thousand acres formed an agricultural green belt. Thirty thousand people were to live on those thousand acres; 30 per gross acre as compared with 57 per gross acre in the present congested, park-destitute county of London. Parks were provided within the Garden City on the basis of a little more than nine acres per thousand; well above the four acres suggested in the new plan for London, but not so much higher than the six that Westminster normally boasts. It may be argued that Howard's town-density is greater than would be generally acceptable; he cannot be accused of being an advocate of urban sprawl.

Where then did Howard's originality lie? Not in special details, but in his characteristic synthesis; in particular these proposals: the provision of a permanent belt of open land, to be used for agriculture as an integral part of the city; the use of this land to limit the physical spread of the city from within, or encroachments from urban development not under control at the perimeter; the permanent ownership and control of the entire urban tract by the municipality itself and its disposition by means of leases into private hands; the limitation of population to the number originally planned for the area; the reservation for the community of the unearned increment from the growth and prosperity of the city, up to the limits of growth fixed; the moving into the new urban area of industries capable of supporting the greater part of its population; the provision for founding new communities as soon as the existing land and social facilities are occupied.

In short, Howard attacked the whole problem of the city's development, not merely its physical growth but the interrelationship of urban functions within the community and the integration of urban and rural patterns, for the vitalizing of urban life on one hand and the intellectual and social improvement of rural life on the other.

In treating rural and urban improvement as a single problem, Howard was far in advance of his age; and he was a better diagnostician of urban decay than many of our own contemporaries. His Garden City was not only an attempt to relieve the congestion of the big city, and by so doing lower the land values and prepare the way for metropolitan reconstruction: it was equally an attempt to do away with that inevitable correlate of metropolitan congestion, the suburban dormitory, whose open plan and nearer access to the country are only temporary, and whose lack of an industrial population and a working base make it one of the most unreal environments ever created for man: a preposterous middle-class counterpart to the courtly inanities of those absolute monarchs who, at Versailles or Nymphenburg, contrived for themselves a disconnected play-world of their own. *The Garden City, as Howard defined it, is not a suburb but the antithesis of a suburb: not a more rural retreat, but a more integrated foundation for an effective urban life.*

Howard saw that there was no solution of the city's problems within the existing framework of municipal administration, because one of its greatest problems was the lack of economic and social and political relation to the surrounding countryside: here his vision was far clearer than the vision of those municipal reformers and those housing experts who have let themselves become absorbed in some single aspect of urban development and have forgotten the larger situation of which the narrow problem they have chosen to solve is but a part. What Howard said about the relation of town and country within the Garden City area is equally applicable to the entire business of city and regional planning: the administrative unit that is created must be capable of embracing both the urban and the rural aspects of the region.

Not the least part of Howard's conception was his emphasis upon the *grouping* of Garden Cities; he realized that the advantages of a single city would be multiplied by the creation of 'town-clusters,' groups or constellations of such cities. But with his resolute sense of the practical, he first proposed to make an experimental demonstration with a single Garden City. Unlike many bold dreamers, he not merely helped to bring Letchworth into existence; but in time he founded a second city, Welwyn. Meanwhile the ideas Howard had expounded were to become the common property of planners all over the world and were to influence the planning of Hilversum in the Netherlands, Ernst May's satellite communities in Frankfort-am-Main, and Wright and Stein's Radburn. . . .

6

The Automobile and Its Consequences

In a number of the previous selections, peripheral comments have been made concerning the changes brought about in the American cityscape by the automobile. At first, the privately owned automobile was the means by which the average citizen attained an appreciation of the spaciousness of his country. At one time it seemed as if national prosperity owed a great deal to the automobile; economists often point out that mass production of the automobile, and the concurrent national program of road construction which enhanced its utilization, had a doubly stimulating effect on employment in the twenties. Furthermore, by extending the range over which individuals could travel in a given period of time, the automobile directly influenced the amount of land area contained in cities. Cities settled before the advent of the automobile tend to be smaller in size and more intensely developed than cities that grew to maturity after the appearance of the automobile. The automobile, not the relative supply of land, has helped make the newer cities of the West more spacious than their older Eastern and Middlewestern counterparts.

There were other effects of the widespread use of the automobile, some not so favorable. Indeed, as the following selections indicate, nothing is more fashionable today than to heap abuse on the horseless carriage. Edward Higbee's amusing vignette opens this chapter and serves to dramatize the enormous changes which the advent of the automobile brought about—especially for city dwellers.

In spite of the criticisms of it, one can easily see why the automobile became enormously popular. It was relatively cheap and therefore available to most jobholders. It opened up American cities, particularly those whose growth came mainly after the large-scale use of the automobile in transportation, in a way entirely unknown to the older cities of Europe and Asia. The difference was that the newer American cities could make much more liberal use of land than had cities of the past. Streets and highways designed to accommodate the passenger car were themselves more spacious than the narrow streets of medieval cities or of cities designed to accommodate horse-drawn vehicles. Furthermore, the wider accessibility brought about by the automobile meant that American cities covered a larger area. This extension of the time-distance span of the individual also made possible the rapid growth of suburban America; and as dwellings moved outward from the city core, commercial operations followed—so that the shopping center, the suburban medical complex, the myriad of conveniences that go to make suburban life possible, if sometimes complicated, are outgrowths of the automobile.

Robert Heilbroner takes an essentially optimistic view of the impact of the automobile on American life, and his major concern is that city planners not attempt to turn back the clock. The auto is here to stay, he says; we are not going to replace it with other methods of transportation, and we had better learn to live with this fact. "However dangerous, foolish, expensive, troublesome and inconvenient the car may be, all these demerits are far overshadowed by one consideration: the automobile has become indispensable."

Indispensable or not, Gilbert Burck presents a strong and detailed case in favor of substituting mass transportation as the means of moving large numbers of people within the city for what he feels is a dangerous and unnecessary reliance on the private automobile. Burck does not ignore the difficulties involved; the mass transportation he envisages is not the sometime thing that is presented to commuters in many of our major cities today. But, he argues, if we stop subsidizing the owner of the private motor car by providing him with tax-free roadways, and if we start supplementing user taxes on gasoline and excise taxes with toll charges, the mass-transportation system needed will be developed. The technology is there, says Burck; and if the urban-transportation market is allowed to operate as a free market should, we can unchoke our cities.

No one could disagree more with Burck than J. M. Roche, who says emphatically that congestion is not the result of the automobile, but stems from too few highways and insufficient parking areas. Any mass-transportation system designed to serve downtown commuters will not unchoke our cities, argues Roche, because downtown commuter traffic represents only a small portion of the problem. In fact, he says, if given a free choice, the public will choose the automobile over other forms of transportation, as it has done in the past.

Considerable support for Burck's position is provided by the majority report of the Senate Committee on Banking and Currency on the proposed Mass Transportation Act of 1962—although the committee also recognizes that lack of adequate earnings on invested capital imperils the continued health of the existing mass-transit systems and makes their expansion impossible. This is the point seized on by the House Committee on Banking and Currency in its minority report on the same bill. The authors of the minority report insist that the Act would really represent subsidies to public agencies. They say that in the large metropolitan centers, where mass transportation already exists, the larger proportion is privately owned and operated; and they imply that earnings must be adequate, or these private concerns would close their doors.

Turnabout*

Edward Higbee

Many years ago, on summer evenings, people who lived in a red-brick apartment house on Thompson Street, south of Washington Square in New York City, looked out of their windows onto the cobblestones below. There they saw a steady procession of horse-drawn wagons and carriages cluttering the streets. The cursing of the drivers with reins and whips in hand and the jostling of the traffic made the people who looked down from their windows a little sad to think that a horse must live such a hard existence. Today all that is changed. There are only a few horse-drawn vehicles left, and only a few horses to pull them. Consequently life is a little better for those beasts. People are more considerate; they admire the mild-mannered mares and geldings as relics of the past. On Thompson Street the apartments in the red-brick building have been vacated by their human occupants. Stairways have been replaced with ramps while bedrooms and parlors have been converted into stables. This is where some of the last weary dray horses of New York come at night. Following the ramps they walk up into the dingy building to get their oats, hay, and a night's rest. On warm summer evenings, when it is stuffy inside, some of the old nags stick their heads out of the windows and look down on the streets below. There, like the human tenants of old, they see a steady procession of traffic cluttering the streets. They hear what they may suspect is cursing above the din of motors and they are a little sad to think that people live such a hard existence.

* Edward Higbee, The Squeeze—Cities without Space (New York: William Morrow & Co., Inc., 1960), p. 220–221. Copyright © 1960 by Edward Higbee. Reprinted by permission of William Morrow & Co., Inc., New York, and Cassell & Co. Ltd., London.

Halfway to the Moon on Wheels*

Robert L. Heilbroner

From the earth to the moon it is 238,000 miles as the rocket flies; to the sun it is some 92½ million more. Out to the very rim of the solar system it is nearly 4 billion miles; once around the system itself is about 22 billion miles. That gives some indication of what *seven hundred billion* miles means, particularly if you can imagine such a distance being folded up inside a container as small as the map of the United States.

Yet 700 billion is the mileage clocked last year by the American people as they drove their 70 million cars, trucks, buses, jeeps, ice-cream wagons, bookmobiles and hot-rods to work and to play, on missions of life and of death—or just around the block looking for a parking space.

The statistics of the automobile are all astronomical. If you take the favorite statistician's device and put our cars bumper-to-bumper, you get a string of vehicles that would itself reach halfway to the moon. If you take the amount of money laid out for the purchase and operation of our automobile armada you get a sum larger than the combined national incomes of Canada and Mexico. Or if you simply take the amount of love and hate, care and carelessness, pride and perspiration evoked by the Car, you get something which, however unmeasurable, is nonetheless recognizable as an integral part of our national character.

Yet all these images at best only indicate in a vague way the most important fact about the car. This is the truly astonishing degree to which it has imposed its stamp on the society which created it. Having set out to do no more than make a practical machine for moving people and things about, the auto manufacturers set in motion a device which quite literally revolutionized our environment. In a single generation the automobile evolved from an extravagant plaything which Woodrow Wilson singled out as an example of the "arrogance of wealth," to a ubiquitous possession in which, as Will Rogers quipped in the 'thirties, we would be the first people in history able to ride to the poorhouse.

We are all aware in a general way of this pervasive "auto-mobilization" of the economy. Yet it is a curious fact that when we pic-

* Robert L. Heilbroner, "Halfway to the Moon on Wheels," *Petroleum Today* (Spring 1960), pp. 1–4.

Robert L. Heilbroner is the author of several well-known books dealing with economics and economic policy, including *The Worldly Philosophers*.

ture the economic implications of the car, we almost always think on much too small a scale. . . .

There is perhaps only one evolutionary step left—to put our cities on wheels. It is a step we have already begun to take: our trailers, if grouped together, would form America's sixth largest city, with a population of 1,850,000.

Meanwhile, the mobile dollar is forcing a change which cuts even deeper into our economic pattern of life. This is the new channels into which it is directing the distribution of goods.

Trucking is of course the prime example. Today rail transport has become the great bulk cargo carrier; air transport flies in the small, high value stuff; truck transport moves all the rest. Fifty-nine thousand fleets of trucks—counting only fleets with ten trucks and up—shuttle 76 per cent of the nation's total freight tonnage.

But aside from the trucking revolution, the car itself is imposing its imperious demands on merchandising. If you want to sell goods these days you have to put them where you can get *to* them by car, and preferably where you can get *at* them without even leaving your car. Thus the shopping centers, mushrooming at the crossroads, are steadily displacing the traditional downtown areas as the nation's favored retail locations. And thus, too, the "drive-in" is taking the place of the retail counter itself. In ancient times merchants humbly spread their merchandise before the potentate lounging in his palanquin; in modern times as we make bank deposits, borrow and return books, order groceries, view movies and eat pizza pies without having to leave our mechanized palanquins, we seem to be recapturing the languor, if not quite the splendor, of the antique potentate.

Yet these reflections on the impact of the automobile still fail to do justice to its quintessential contribution to our lives. This is its gift of mobility itself—not mobility as a dollar-spreading device or as a mechanical substitute for personal movement, but as a direct enhancement of life, as an enlargement of life's boundaries and opportunities. This is so enormous, so radical a transformation that its effect can no longer be measured or appreciated by mere figures. It is nothing less than the unshackling of the age-old bonds of *locality;* it is the grant of geographic choice and economic freedom on a hitherto unimagined scale.

We can do no more than point in the general direction of the changes which mobility has wrought. We see it in the breakdown of the old factory town where workers perforce dwelt in the shadow of the mills and plants: today seven out of ten workers drive their cars regularly to work—and are thereby free to live in residential rather than industrial areas. We see it in the proliferation of suburban life, a development impossible without mass automotive transportation. We see it in the great currents of internal migration, in which one family in every five changes its address each year in search of a better job, a better home. What this has meant, not alone in terms of wider economic horizons, but in terms of wider life horizons is incalculable. . . .

[There] are real costs to be taken into account when we seek to assess the impact of the automobile on our lives. Yet they are at most a large discount and not a cancellation of the gain which automobiles have brought. However dangerous, foolish, expensive, troublesome and inconvenient the car may be, all these demerits are far overshadowed by one consideration: The automobile has become indispensable.

Every indication points to the conclusion that it will become even more inseparable from our way of life. Our automotive flotilla grows steadily; by 1975 it will number 111 million vehicles. The web of transportation is growing more complex, more all-encompassing; the pace and reach of our automotive mobility is increasing yearly.

What ultimate effects, good and bad, this growing automobilization of our economy may bring, no one can clearly foresee. What is certain, however, is that the progressive dependence of our economy on the car will pose two major problems over the coming years.

One of these is traffic congestion, particularly in urban areas. There is no easy solution to this problem, for more is involved than difficult questions of traffic engineering. At least as important is the "financial engineering" which sets the pace and determines the limits of our highway program. Today that financial approach is far from constructive in many respects. On the one hand, we tend to restrict highway construction to those funds raised by highway taxes and tolls—even though our road network brings vast economic benefits to non-motorists as well. On the other hand, the federal government sidetracks 40 cents out of every dollar received in special taxes on the motorist into the Treasury's General Fund—while in many states also we allow as much as 20 to 30 per cent of highway revenues to be used for non-road purposes.

Thus to some extent we use our highway traffic as a means of generating general fund revenue but we fail to view the highway system itself as a general national asset on which non-highway revenues may legitimately be expended. In other words, we are still looking at our road system as something which can be viewed apart from the economy as a whole rather than as the foundation for our economy on wheels.

Equally important as an adequate supply of highway space is a second problem—the assurance of adequate and economical supplies of fuel. . . .

Neither the proper means of financing our needed highway system nor the best methods for encouraging the maximum flow of oil are easy matters to decide. Without a doubt these will remain matters of legitimate debate for many years. But what may help to sharpen and clarify this debate is to bring into the foreground the main problem at issue. This is our economy on wheels itself. Neither highway building nor oil production are any longer—if ever they were—parochial questions which concern only those whose interests are immediately at stake. Behind the continuing debate looms an ever more pressing reality. This is to keep the wheels of our automotive economy rolling.

How to Unchoke Our Cities*

Gilbert Burck

A city is a place where people get together to get things done, and a basic problem of the city has always been to keep people from crowding so much that they can't get things done. The crowding is not necessarily the result of too many citizens; a small city can be more congested than a large one. "Crowding" means that the citizens have arranged something—usually their traffic—stupidly. Today what complicates and multiplies the age-old problem of urban congestion, of course, is the motorcar. The U.S. automobile population is still growing much faster than the U.S. human population—and a rolling motorcar uses nine times as much space as a human being takes up in a public conveyance, while a parked car takes up as much space as an office. Thus many a city has found its downtown streets clogged although its daytime human population is no larger than what it handled comfortably decades ago. Thus, too, many a city has seen its most rewarding residents and its most remunerative factories escaping the congestion by moving to the suburbs. And thus many a city, though it may seem more crowded than ever, has found itself in, or threatened by, a "progressive" disintegration, with its central business district (C.B.D.) declining, its blighted areas expanding, and its mass transportation going bankrupt or being abandoned.

For two generations Americans have averted their eyes from what the automobile has done to their cities. Most metropolitan areas, at heavy and increasing cost, have dealt only with those traffic problems pressing enough to demand immediate action. This temporizing approach is no longer good enough. Obviously the automobile is here to stay (in much greater numbers than at present); and an overwhelming majority of

---

* Gilbert Burck, "How to Unchoke Our Cities," *Fortune*, 63 (May 1961), 119–126. Reprinted by Special Permission; © 1961 Time Inc.
Gilbert Burck is a member of the Board of Editors of *Fortune* magazine.

Americans of the next fifty years are going to live in metropolitan areas. Unless Americans snap out of the despair with which they have regarded traffic congestion, their urban habitats will be less and less worthy of a society with a reputation for social efficiency. . . .

Many specific public questions relating to traffic turn around one basic issue: can mass public-transport systems (trains, buses, subways) be preserved and extended, or should they be allowed to continue their decline until the private car becomes virtually the sole means of personal transport in and around cities. Detroit, which created the motor age, and Los Angeles, which grew up in it, are still dedicated to the latter "solution," which will demand more and more freeways and produce more and more sprawling decentralization. Cities with geographically restricted cores, such as New York and Philadelphia, now realize that they simply haven't enough room to let everybody travel by private car; belatedly, they are trying to save commuter and rapid-transit services. Most municipalities don't know what to do. . . .

. . . An army of special interests, ranging from professional uplifters and high-powered realtors to dedicated idealists, is drumming up support for its pet cures. Some would go on constructing freeways ad infinitum, while others are plumping for massive federal aid to rapid transit and commuter trains. A number of planners seem to believe that the federal government should adopt a master plan and assume all responsibility for determining land use and allocating the country's transportation resources. What most have in common, besides a tropism for the federal till, is the assumption that the consumer cannot be relied on to choose his own mode of transport.

But a nation tending to spend more on personal transportation than on housing needs nothing less than it needs massive federal subsidies to transportation. And despite all the recent authoritarian assaults on the American consumer's good sense and taste, he generally makes the correct choice when subjected to the discipline of the market and confronted with the true cost of alternatives. The trouble is that the American consumer, in deciding between private and mass transportation, has for years and years been presented with a market heavily rigged in favor of using his own car in city traffic. How the market is rigged and whether it can be unrigged, and the probable role of public transport, are the concern of this article, which takes the view that public policy should move to a more precise correlation of user charges and user benefits. Specifically, let the consumer himself choose the way he wants to ride, but let him pay for his rides. Let his roads be financed not out of general tax funds, but by definite user charges. Let these charges be large enough to pay back the full investment in the facilities he uses. And let them be levied so that, as nearly as possible, he is always confronted with the true cost of his choice when he makes it.

Whether the vehicle owner pays all the costs of the facilities he uses is at least debatable. Last year federal, state, and local governments collected nearly $10 billion in tolls and other "user taxes" (fuel taxes, fees, vehicle excise taxes); and they spent a grand total of $10.7 billion (including $979 million in interest and debt retirement) on building and operating the nation's roads and streets. Autos, moreover, create expensive parking, congestion, and safety problems for which the owners may not be proportionately assessed in the reckoning of total expenses. Above all, those who use cars in cities do not pay taxes on the land occupied by the thoroughfares. Vast acreages of immensely expensive land are now being requisitioned for expressways, and cities are forfeiting taxes on them and so in effect subsidizing the vehicle owners.

It is true that car owners in the cities and their environs do not get a fair split of total expenditures. Although they pay about half of all the user taxes, only about a third of total capital outlays on roads finds its way to city streets and freeways. Philadelphia estimates it spends some $50 a year more per auto than it takes in, Milwaukee $90. The main reason is that rural areas are heavily overrepresented in the legislatures of many states, and the urban areas are consistently shortchanged in the allocation of state money.

But this is a minor example of what is wrong with the present tax system. Most so-called user taxes are collected as gas and excise taxes and fees, and only 5 per cent as tolls. Only 5 per cent of user taxes, in other words, confront users with their costs where and when those costs occur. It is as if a railroad charged a passenger only 5 per cent of his fare and billed the tax collector of the community where the passenger lives for the rest.

Metropolitan-area highways or "freeways," because they are toll free, have often rigged the market against rail and rapid-transit lines and their commuters. Take, for example, the case of the Port of New York Authority, which owns and operates two excellent tunnel systems and the great George Washington Bridge across the Hudson River between New Jersey and Manhattan. All these facilities charge tolls. The catch is that the Port Authority was never assigned responsibility for anything except the crossings and the immediate access facilities. Although bridge and tunnel tolls were high enough to earn handsome sums, the earnings were probably not high enough to pay for the freeways and other facilities that New York and New Jersey had to build to make the bridges and tunnels profitable. So the general taxpayers picked up the tab and subsidized highway vehicles.

Partly because of the competition of the tax-free tunnels and bridge, the commutation traffic of the New Jersey railroads, whose taxes are inordinately high, began to decline steeply. Today only a few more people cross the Hudson than in 1928, but a vastly greater portion of the region's resources are being used to carry them across than in 1928. The old rail ferries across the Hudson were admittedly slow and technically obsolete, and a genuine economic demand doubtless existed for new highway crossings. But the public demand for the road crossings might have been much smaller than it was if the users had been confronted with all their costs. And there might have been a genuine demand for a new commuter rail crossing to replace the ferries. The Port Authority is finally making amends by offering to buy and rehabilitate the bankrupt Hudson & Manhattan Railroad, which connects lower and midtown Manhattan with New Jersey; it has been asked to pledge up to 10 per cent of its annual "surplus" to aid commuter service around New York.

Adam Smith himself described the toll road as an incomparably equitable method of raising a tax; and toll systems, many people are belatedly realizing, can put urban highways on a sound economic basis by charging the motorist for what he uses when he uses it. Tolls should have been, and still should be, substituted for gas and other so-called user taxes in metropolitan areas where the cost of building expressways is mounting astronomically. . . . This cost goes more and more to subsidize rush-hour traffic. A selective toll system, or one that levies high toll during rush hours and over expensive and popular roads can make for a much more efficient use of a community's transportation plant by diverting consumers from unessential rush-hour trips, or to less crowded roads, or to mass transportation.

And toll systems, which are commonly objected to as cumbersome and time-consuming, need not be so. Professor William Vickrey of Columbia University, a pioneer in the movement for what he calls the economic pricing of road services, has shown how cars can be recorded electronically by roadside "interrogators" that would pass the information on to processing centers, which in turn would bill the driver at convenient intervals. Vickrey argues plausibly that the system would be very cheap compared to the capital otherwise needed to build enough highways to handle peak traffic.

Unfortunately for the U.S., its $41-billion, 41,000-mile interstate highway and "defense" system has been set up largely as a toll-free network—even though many new metropolitan-area freeways are being built under the program. The official reason for this decision was that only a few more than 8,500 miles of the system can expect enough traffic to pay for themselves as toll roads—which obviously is less a reason for eliminating tolls than evidence of the fact there is no genuine demand for most of the new highways. To many, the system looks like one of the biggest boondoggles in history.

It will of course take an act of Congress to change the highway-construction law. But cities can still do a lot to price their road space rationally. One of the most glaring of all urban subsidies to the motorist is the common practice of letting him park on busy arteries of traffic. Busy streets are for running, not parking. The most effective and economically equitable way of alleviating urban congestion is to forbid street parking (and enforce the regulations) where traffic is heavy, and to let market demand set prices for off-street parking lots and garages. This policy can create a few problems, but they are not insoluble. By experimenting a little, any city can adjust the demand for its street and parking space to the supply thereof. Attempts to do this are often howled down by special interests and pressure groups, which fear that somehow people will be deterred from shopping downtown. What really deters customers is congestion. And congestion is simply what happens when the demand for street and parking space is greater than the supply.

Partly because the urban transportation market is rigged and may not be unrigged easily, there is a growing tendency to help mass transportation hang on to a share of the market. Two wrongs don't make a right, particularly in economics, but when the alternative is the destruction of useful and necessary service, a countervailing wrong, if temporary, can be defended as the lesser of two evils.

The great majority of rapid-transit lines are now municipally owned, and some have kept fares down for political reasons, and so rely on liberal drafts from the general tax fund. Gaining ground, moreover, is the doctrine that privately owned mass transit should be relieved of property taxes and other payments into the general fund, and that this abatement should not be, as it so often is, stigmatized by the brand of subsidy. Rail and transit lines occupy valuable city land, but freeways of equivalent capacity occupy more. If highway users pay no taxes on this land, commuter trains cannot be expected to pay property taxes on rights-of-way. Abatement of such taxes will create some trouble for town and city tax authorities, but these taxes bulk relatively small.

Rail commuter lines still carry more than 220 million people a year, and taxes allocable to their operations range up to 20 cents of every revenue dollar. In many instances this represents the difference between loss and profit. As a transportation factory the commuting train is technically the cheapest way of moving a passenger from here to there, and mass-transit advocates love to point out that a single track can carry 40,000 or more people an hour past a given point, or twenty times as many as a single-lane highway. But these days the commuting train frequently has serious disadvantages. Its terminals are often badly located, and its tracks often go to the wrong places. And like all factories, the train must be used a fair amount of the time or overhead and capital costs will more than offset its potentially high output per employee-hour. Because commuting railroads, together with other mass-transportation devices, have lost nearly all their weekend and off-peak business, they are like expensive, efficient factories that have to run at forced blast about twenty hours a week and lie nearly idle the rest of the time. The Illinois Central, for example, is burdened with rush-hour loads as heavy as any in the 1920's, yet it is carrying half as many commuters as it did in the 1920's.

But the commuter train has not been able to capitalize on all its inherent advantages. Technology has advanced to the point where a 1,000-passenger train can be operated almost automatically, with perhaps two men; yet the so-called full-crew laws compel such a train to carry at least five. Railroads are also regulated as if they were still monopolies against which the public must be protected, and consequently the "public interest"—usually the special interests of a few petitioners—prevents them from readily experimenting with schedules, dropping costly off-peak runs, and otherwise exercising the prerogatives of management. Given freedom, management might well get rid of more ill-located commuter operations than it has. But given freedom and tax equity, says one prominent Chicago railroad man, many a well-located commutation line can offer better and faster service, increase its business, reduce its fares, and even make a little money in the bargain. Since nearly every railroad has to adopt the poorest possible posture when asking for rate increases, most of his colleagues might quibble with him publicly, but few would dispute him privately. Surely the commuter train should be operated at maximum efficiency before it asks for special favors; if it were, it might not need them. . . .

There is no question that efforts to restore mass transportation will have hard going. In 1946 Americans made about 24 billion local trips by public carriers. Last year they made 11 billion—half by bus and the rest by commuter train, trolley, taxi, and rail transit (subway, elevated, off-street and surface rail lines). By contrast, in 1946 Americans made about 25 billion trips by private car, and last year they made about 50 billion in the metropolitan areas alone. Walter S. Douglas of Parsons, Brinckerhoff, Quade & Douglas, the engineering firm largely responsible for designing the Bay Area system, believes the private car will continue to handle the metropolitan-area base load. The job of the modern mass rail carrier, he says, is largely one of serving the highly concentrated flow of commuters, who are the cause of most metropolitan traffic congestion.

Decentralization and suburbanization of both living and work, so vividly illustrated by Los Angeles and Detroit, are among the reasons why mass transport has declined relatively. Until the motorcar became popular, American cities spread outward along the main commuting and streetcar lines. Growth was largely residential, most industrial and commercial activity stayed downtown, and trips of consequence took people no farther than downtown and back. But the motorcar enabled millions of people who otherwise would have been forced to live in the cities to move into the suburbs and own a house and a piece of land. After they moved out, companies also began moving out, and the C.B.D. in many a metropolitan area virtually stopped growing. Some experts feel that any attempt to force people back to unpopular mass transportation might hasten the decentralization process, although on this point there is no agreement and possibly no way of proof.

At all events, a large percentage of metropolitan-area trips occur to and fro within the cities, in and around the suburban areas, and between one suburban area and another. The "scatteration" of these trips, combined with relatively low population density where many occur, precludes economic train operation and in many areas will not even support bus lines. As hours of work decline, moreover, recreation travel becomes steadily more important and American families on pleasure bent pile into their cars, they don't take to buses and trains. . . .

That public transportation will eventually return to its own is self-evident. So long as the U.S. population keeps on increasing at anything like its current rate, the day is bound to come when whole regions of the country will be so densely populated that some kind of mass transport, if it didn't then exist, would have to be invented. Meantime it has a good chance to play an important part in rationalizing the nation's transportation plant by handling peak traffic that would otherwise require a staggering investment in expressways. But to be successful, it must be wanted by the consumer. He will want it if he is presented with a reasonably unrigged choice, and if mass transportation itself comes up with a product that will once again make its advantages attractive to him.

The Public Prefers the Automobile*

J. M. Roche

The pioneers in the automobile business saw clearly that their future depended on getting motorists out of the mud. We today must see with equal clarity the need to get them out of the muddle.

* J. M. Roche, "The Public Prefers the Automobile," *Highway Highlights* (August–September 1962), pp. 6–7. Published by the National Highway Users Conference.

J. M. Roche is a vice president of one of the major automobile manufacturing firms and is Secretary-Treasurer of the National Highway Users Conference.

Economic indicators suggest that prospects are bright for an expanding automotive market—"bigger pie." Population is growing. The gross national product and disposable income are rising. And people are increasingly dependent upon personal transportation. These and other factors support the prediction that by 1970 the number of motor vehicles in the United States will increase about one-third—to almost 100 million.

Right now, we appear to be well launched toward that altitude. However, this is a prediction—not a promise. Like all forecasts, it must be qualified by important "ifs."

One of these is: the market will expand greatly *if* we achieve the better environment for driving that is necessary to maintain the automobile's utility and appeal at a high level. Failing in this, we might well find much of the future's greater purchasing power diverted from automobiles to competing goods and services.

Among the many factors in the highway traffic environment, none is more critical than safety. Most people accept moderate risks as part of a full life, but none want to "live dangerously" to such an extent that disaster is probable.

We must help assure that in the years ahead people have no cause to regard driving as not worth the risk. Today, most people, although concerned about traffic accidents, do regard driving as relatively safe. It certainly is—and mile for mile of travel it is becoming more so every year. But this is no basis for complacency.

A marked increase in the accident toll—or in alarmist propaganda—could well arouse public anxiety that would depress automobile sales and use. Many people are now reluctant to drive on holiday weekends after exposure to scare-type publicity. This is just a sample of what could develop on a broader scale.

Beyond this, growing concern over traffic hazards could provoke drastic control measures. Carried to unwarranted extremes, these could make driving less convenient, less enjoyable and much more expensive.

A case in point is the growing effort in some quarters to impose Federal regulation on automotive safety features—on the false premise that the industry is indifferent to the safety of its products. It takes little imagination to picture the kind of an automobile that would come from the drawing boards of bureaucracy.

The vast roadbuilding program now under way will do much to provide a still safer environment for automobiles. Interstate freeways, for example, are more than twice as safe as roads lacking their modern design features. However, it would be a serious mistake to look upon this as a cure-all. Roads, like cars, can be designed with progressively greater built-in safety, but they cannot be made foolproof. . . .

It is clearly imperative that we give active support to effective measures for congestion relief. Chief among these are: modern traffic engineering to increase the capacity of existing streets and highways; adequate off-street parking facilities in business districts; and extensive freeway networks in metropolitan areas.

The potential impact of congestion on the average person's opinion of the automobile's merits is not the only concern we have.

The traffic problem in cities is being used as a springboard for a massive campaign of anti-automobile and anti-freeway propaganda by certain rail transit interests and urban planners.

The theme of this campaign is that "excessive" use of automobiles is blighting cities and that more urban freeways and downtown parking facilities will only make the situation worse. The solution proposed is greater reliance on mass transportation by rail. Measures advocated include a cutback in urban freeway construction, a ban on cars in central districts of cities, special tolls to discourage downtown auto travel and use of motorist taxes to subsidize mass transit.

Obviously, people in cities need mass transportation as well as cars. However, this campaign rejects the principle of a balanced urban transportation system by treating the problem as a transit versus automobile issue. This is a grossly distorted approach that ignores some important facts.

It ignores the fact that downtown commuting, although important, is a relatively small portion of all urban travel. The bulk of transportation needs in cities can only be met with an adequate highway network for efficient travel by car, truck and bus.

It ignores the fact that dispersion of population and economic activity into suburban areas make it impossible for rail transportation along a few narrow corridors to serve the majority.

It ignores the fact that congestion means insufficient highways and parking facilities—not "too many cars." As these facilities become more adequate, it will become increasingly clear that the motor car and the metropolis can be quite compatible.

It ignores the fact that freeway construction, far from blighting cities, is contributing importantly to their rejuvenation.

And, above all, it ignores the right of the people to make a free choice of travel modes. It arrogantly suggests that people be told what is best and most efficient for them and compelled to take it whether they like it or not.

For many years, the public has been increasingly demonstrating its preference for the automobile for most urban area travel. In fact, for many people travel by car is virtually essential as well as more pleasant and convenient. One factual measure of this is the trend in urban mass transportation patronage. From a peacetime peak of more than 17 billion passengers in 1926, volume declined almost 50 per cent by 1960—despite a 57 per cent increase in urban population during this period.

Clearly, people are not in a mood to have this trend reversed by arbitrary measures to get them out of their cars. However, this does not justify dismissing the anti-automobile and anti-freeway campaign as an impotent force. Misguided minorities have put over unsound and unpopular measures before. They could well achieve some success in this case. In fact, they are already getting their way or coming close to it in some cities.

It is therefore important that there be vigorous opposition to this reactionary movement. There are two ways to do so. One is to refute fallacious arguments against automobile use in cities. The other is to support urban traffic measures that will better accommodate the automobile.

Such action need not and should not involve an anti-mass transit position. An adequate, balanced urban transportation system must include good mass transit. However, it seems clear that rail service, as a major component, is practicable only in those few large metropolitan areas where it already exists. For most cities, the best answer appears to be primary reliance on buses. These can provide rapid commuter service on freeways and have the important merit of flexibility to meet shifting demands.

It was heartening to note that the President's message to Congress on transportation emphasized the need for a balanced system of urban transportation and recognized the important role of highways. It is to be hoped that whatever legislative and administrative action is taken to implement the President's recommendations will be in full accord with this concept.

The Mass Transit Bill—Pro*

Senate Committee on Banking and Currency

The committee believes that there is no doubt about the critical need for action on the urban transportation problems in our Na-

* Senate Committee on Banking and Currency, Majority Report, from Committee Report 1852, submitted to the Senate on August 7, 1962, to accompany S. 3615, the proposed Urban Mass Transportation Act of 1962.

tion's cities. Every citizen who commutes to work is aware of the serious impact of inadequate and overcrowded existing facilities and the necessity for immediate action to improve and expand transportation systems.

The problem derives both from the rapidly increasing concentration of people and vehicles in the metropolitan and other urban areas of the Nation and from a rapid decline and deterioration of mass transportation services and facilities in those areas. The decline in mass transportation service has coincided with the decline in riders, which has taken place primarily during off-peak hours. This decline in passengers and the corresponding reduction in revenues, coupled with rising costs, has imperiled the ability of mass transport carriers to continue providing adequate rush-hour service. The loss, deterioration, and curtailment of such service has many profound adverse effects on the community. It deprives many people of an essential service either because they are too young, too old, or too poor to drive, and, in many cases, because many families have two members who must work but have only one car. It also increases street and highway congestion, accentuates downtown parking problems, and lowers the values of residential property, to mention just some of the ill effects on the community.

Efficient and economical mass transportation service is essential to the people who live in and around our urban centers. Unfortunately, it is not now available in many places, and the present conditions will grow worse in the years ahead unless prompt action is taken. The movement of families away from concentrated built-up areas into scattered suburban patterns and the shift to the use of private automobiles for commuting to and from work has taken many passengers away from public transportation.

In the last decade the number of private motor vehicles on the streets has been increasing faster than the population. The availability and convenience of this mode of transportation has put it into strong competition with mass transportation. Moreover, by filling up available street space, the increased automobile traffic has prevented the efficient and rapid operation of surface mass transit vehicles which use the same rights-of-way.

It is clear from these present and expected future trends that a balanced urban transportation system, utilizing both highways and transit, is essential to help shape as well as serve future urban growth and to achieve optimum efficiency, economy, and effectiveness in meeting the transportation needs of the urban area.

One of the factors contributing to the deterioration of mass transit service in many areas is the inability of the system to maintain an adequate level of capital investment in new facilities and equipment. Despite the tremendous growth of our cities and the future outlook for an even more intensive concentration of our people in and around urban areas, capital investment in urban transportation systems has declined rather than increased.

Many private bus, transit, and rail carriers are finding it extremely difficult to meet operating expenses of existing facilities and almost prohibitive to finance new capital improvements to meet expansion requirements. Caught in the squeeze of rising capital and operating costs, and declining patronage, many private bus and rail carriers must resort to raising fares, trimming service, and deferring maintenance—which simply drives away more riders and accelerates the downward spiral.

According to the American Transit Association, these declines in riding, with their resulting serious financial impact, have caused the sale or abandonment of many transit companies in recent years. The committee was informed that since the beginning of 1954, a total of 211 transit companies have been sold, and an additional 152 have been abandoned.

One regrettable consequence of this trend is that many communities have abandoned mass transit rights-of-way which are now urgently needed by an expanded population, but which can be redeemed or replaced only at heavy cost.

The heavy cost of acquiring new rights-of-way through congested city areas may suggest the abandonment of all efforts to provide adequate mass transportation facilities for the central business districts of our cities in favor of complete reliance on business developments in the suburbs. However, any objective appraisal of the needs of our cities will show this to be a wholly unrealistic and impractical approach.

There is a new and emerging concept of the downtown which sees the basic purpose of downtown as providing those unusual and unique services and goods which cannot be economically supported in suburban locations. It should mean for all of the people in the area access to a more diverse and livelier life through improved employment opportunities and shopping facilities, through the cultural institutions of the area, and through numerous opportunities for amusement and entertainment. Many of these functions and opportunities will not be carried out and will not be available unless they can survive in the core of the city.

The bulk of the population increase is occurring and will continue to occur in the outlying portions of the metropolitan areas. The population of the suburbs and the resulting commuter traffic are increasing much too fast for the central cities to cope with anything but a small fraction of it.

With proper planning, mass transit as well as highways can be as great a boon to the suburbs as to the central city. It can be a vital tool to help curb suburban sprawl, and help provide better patterns of suburban development.

It would be a mistake to conclude that mass transportation is a problem of concern only to larger areas. The larger cities usually command more national publicity. The American Transit Association estimates that there are about 60 cities of 25,000 population or more which have no public transportation service at all. Many of our smaller cities and towns are experiencing rapid rates of growth, and they are beginning to taste the first bitter fruits of traffic congestion. Testimony before the committee showed that, growing rapidly or not, these cities and towns all have a sizeable portion of their residents who have been seriously inconvenienced by the loss of public transportation service.

The proposed Federal program is designed to help assist in the solution of mass transportation problems wherever they occur, in large cities or in small ones, and the committee believes the legislation can be extremely beneficial to both, but at the same time the committee recognizes that areas having the most critical needs, considering density of population and other factors, should have priority.

When State or local governments begin searching for an answer to traffic problems, they are faced with the overwhelmingly powerful economic fact that in many cases they need put up only 10 percent of the cost for a highway solution, whereas they must bear 100 percent of the cost of a transit solution, whether it involves improving a rail line, buying a new fleet of buses, providing fringe area parking, or establishing a downtown distributor system. Obviously this situation is not conducive to the establishment of a balanced urban transportation system, utilizing transit where it is logically needed and using a highway where it is logically needed.

There are, of course, a number of other reasons why this problem involves a considerable measure of Federal responsibility.

For one thing, the problem of providing adequate urban mass transportation service has long ago spilled over the boundaries of many local political jurisdictions. In fact, it has spilled over a good many State boundaries.

Traffic congestion also adds to the cost of moving interstate freight through metropolitan areas, because trucks have to compete for clogged street space with the automobile. Trucks are faced with incessant stops and starts, which are not only time consuming but extremely expensive.

Public safety is another factor to be considered when reviewing problems of traffic congestion. In some cities, traffic, during peak hours, has become so dense that it is extremely costly to provide a police force sufficiently large to unsnarl traffic congestion and to direct an efficient ingress and egress on urban arteries.

And, last but not least, an incalculable number of man-hours are lost by our people—from family life, from work, from recreation —because of having to commute through traffic congestion.

It is for these reasons that the leadership and financial assistance of the Federal Government is needed now to encourage solutions that are forward looking and generally applicable to urban areas regardless of size.

The Mass Transit Bill—Con*

House Committee on Banking and Currency

This is not a mass transportation bill at all. Its basic policy is erroneous. It seeks to establish as its fundamental policy that it is a Federal responsibility to subsidize public transportation in communities or places of 2,500 or more in population. We reject that policy as nonsense. . . .

The Housing Agency in a memorandum under date of June 6, 1962 [said] . . .

"It is not the intention of this bill to provide assistance for all public transportation, and we would have no objection to the insertion in the bill of definitions of these two terms. We would suggest the following language, to be inserted as new paragraphs in section 10(b) of this bill:

"(4) the term *urban area* means any area that includes a municipality or other built-up place of more than 2,500 inhabitants, and is appropriate, in the judgment of the Administrator, for a public transportation system to serve communities or others in the locality, taking into consideration the local patterns and trends of urban growth;

"(5) the term *mass transportation* means public transportation by bus or rail, or by other public conveyances moving over prescribed routes."

The subcommittee did not accept these proposed amendments of the Housing Agency. In our opinion, the real reason the com-

* House Committee on Banking and Currency, Minority Report, from Committee Report 1961, submitted to the House on July 3, 1962, to accompany H.R. 11158, the proposed Urban Mass Transportation Act of 1962.

mittee did not do so is that no one relished the prospect of trying to defend on the floor of the House a provision spelling out the fact that communities as small as 2,500 in population were eligible for assistance under this proposed new subsidy-grant program. Now that the Housing Administrator has made clear that a community of 2,500 or more in population is an urban area, as he would interpret this undefined term, the Congress must face up to this fundamental policy decision.

It is a fact that whatever breaking point the Congress might set, if it approves the bill, as to size of community eligible for the subsidy assistance, it will be making an arbitrary decision. Even with the 2,500 population standard, the 54.1 million people comprising our rural population will be denied any benefits under this subsidy program. Their participation under the program will be the dubious privilege of helping subsidize the public transportation costs of the 125.3 million people living in approximately 6,000 communities of over 2,500 population.

It is a fact, according to the 1960 U.S. census, that there were only 24 metropolitan areas in the United States which had populations in excess of 1 million people. In our opinion, this fact alone raises serious question as to the validity of the claim that subsidization of mass transit facilities is a Federal responsibility. Should all of the taxpayers of the Nation be called upon to provide Federal subsidy benefits for these relatively few areas where the problem of congestion is most acute?

It is a fact that it is cheaper to ride mass transit than it is to operate a private automobile in going to and from work. For instance, a 15-cent fare on the New York City rapid transportation system is good for a 25-mile ride. Such a fare would not even pay the cost of gas alone for such a ride in a private automobile. This suggests that there are other powerful factors than the economic factor which enter into the decision of an individual as to whether he will or will not use mass transit facilities.

It is a fact that approximately 55 percent of the traffic on a mass transit system is carried in but 20 percent of the 24 hours in a day; namely, the morning rush hours going to work and the late afternoon rush hours going home. The resulting peaks and valleys in use of capacity at different times of the day make crowding inevitable at rush hours. And of course the passengers "grouse—and make their contribution to the overall image of the awful transit problem."

It is alleged to be a fact that the fare box will not pay operating costs and debt service on debt issued to maintain and improve mass transit systems. That seems strange to us since 94 percent of the mass transit systems in the country are privately owned and privately operated.

part three

Social Issues in Urban Life

The preceding discussions—on design; on architecture as a stimulus to the good, and perhaps beautiful, life; on the relative merits of urban renewal and the private-market approaches to real-estate development; and on mass transportation—have one common element: they affect people directly. Decisions about urbanization have to take place within a human framework, since this is basically what urbanization is—the closer grouping of individuals. It follows that the real conflicts in values are not those concerned with the abstract beauty of one city plan, one style of architecture, one kind of transportation system. Rather, they are conflicts over what happens to people in the urban culture when a particular plan is put into practice; how their lives are shaped; and what the costs are in human terms.

These conflicts are approached in the next three chapters through discussions of housing (particularly slums and their role in social organization and disorganization) and of race (particularly the Negro). But the issues are not raised merely to arouse passionate reactions against slum housing, segregation, overcrowding, crime, and disease. Once again, the focus is on methods of coping with these issues within the metropolis. The authors present significant, if widely divergent, solutions to these problems, and they present their solutions in concrete terms rather than allowing them to remain at the level of abstraction.

7

Housing

Faced with the diversity and mobility of the housing market, and the intricate heterogeneity of the housing industry, the planner and the urban-renewal-agency staffs have an extremely delicate and complex task.

The first set of articles discusses the housing needs of the country in the immediate future. Catherine Bauer Wurster estimates that during the 1960s about 2 million new houses will be needed annually. Since just over 1.4 million new houses were built in the most active year so far in this decade (the biggest housing year in history, 1959, saw the construction of only 1.5 million units), Mrs. Wurster's suggestions for some specific programs to attain the desired rate of construction attain critical importance.

There are more basic issues, though. Implicit in the forecast of annual construction needs is the assumption that homeownership is a good thing in itself and should be encouraged. But how far in the direction of 100 per cent homeownership do we want to go? From a nation of renters in the early thirties, when roughly 30 per cent of all American families owned a house, we have become a nation of homeowners, so that today over 60 per cent of all families own their homes. And Nathan Glazer comments that the rental units presently available are so unsatisfactory that it is surprising to find so many people who prefer to rent. But there are some indications that an even larger proportion of the population may occupy rental units in the years to come, not through necessity but out of preference. Elderly couples whose children have departed find the joys of suburban living stale compared with the comparatively carefree existence of the apartment dweller—carefree especially in comparison with the time spent by suburbanites maintaining yards. In addition, the emergence of a larger proportion of younger couples who rent while on their way up the economic ladder may stimulate this type of occupancy.

However, as Michael Harrington reminds us, for large segments of the population, these considerations simply do not apply; to the poverty-stricken American, for instance, the issue of rental versus ownership is completely meaningless. Harrington calls for action on a wide scale to eliminate slums, slum psychology, and the attendant social costs. A key element in his proposal is a revised and expanded public-housing program.

Since its inception, public housing has provoked controversy. Those who oppose public housing—notably, Representative Gwinn and Senator Thurmond—contend that it is the entering wedge of socialism or worse. Furthermore, Senator Thurmond opposes certain details of the program. Specifically, he argues, public-housing legislation does not provide low-rent housing; rather, it establishes income levels which cut off the lowest income groups from occupancy. In addition, he says, private industry is capable of providing the necessary low-cost housing.

The final selection deals with the housing industry. Here the basic questions are: How efficient is the housing industry in providing attractive housing at prices consumers can afford? Does the way in which the housing industry is organized handicap its performance? What implications do new technological developments have for the future of housing?

Gurney Breckenfeld describes some of the trends in materials and techniques which offer promising possibilities for the immediate future (though Glazer and Mrs. Wurster have pointed to some of the difficulties standing in the way of the adoption of these new methods and materials). A step in the direction of recognizing the importance of technological change was taken in the 1960 housing act when FHA insurance coverage was extended to houses built using some new techniques, but this provision has unfortunately not been utilized by builders and lenders.

Breckenfeld's emphasis on the technological aspects of the housing industry indirectly raises another issue, however. To what extent have the newer techniques in management and finance permitted a more efficient industry to develop? A glance at almost any current tract-house-building operation provides the answer. Through mass merchandising of housing—a feature of the industry only in the post-World War II period—the builder and developer can take advantage of production methods that were formerly restricted to factory operations. With the advent of the tract house, the assembly line came to the construction industry. Instead of the product's being moved past stationary workers, however, the workers moved past a stationary product. Gangs of cement pourers, carpenters, plumbers, roofers, cabinet finishers, plasterers, electricians, and painters move from house to house in the modern tract. The necessary materials are scheduled with the same precision as in the most advanced missile factory. When completed, the houses are marketed by the same sales devices that are used to market cars, refrigerators, and other mass-produced products. Many observers profess to be alarmed by these developments; but if efficiency is defined as the lowering of costs relative to output, then the past decade and a half has been a period of tremendous strides in the housing industry. Can these same techniques be exploited in the next ten years to provide still more housing at lower costs? Or have the present limits of mass merchandising been reached pending further technological breakthroughs?

Housing: A Wider Range of Choice *

Catherine Bauer Wurster

. . . There will have to be about ten million additional homes in the United States by 1970, and there ought to be up to ten million more to replace seriously substandard dwellings and the large number normally lost for other reasons. Still another ten million or so will need some degree of improvement. Two million dwellings per year is about 40 per cent higher than the record output in 1950 and over 60 per cent more than the annual average for the decade. But this volume, plus rehabilitation and services, is well within the prospective capacity of the construction industry. Indeed, the pending flood of new job-seekers calls for a 20 per cent rise in total employment by 1970, and the

* Catherine Bauer Wurster, "Framework for an Urban Society," in The Report of the President's Commission on National Goals, *Goals for Americans* (Englewood Cliffs, N.J.: Prentice-Hall, 1960), pp. 234–237. © 1960 by The American Assembly. Reprinted by permission of Prentice-Hall, Inc., publisher.
Catherine Bauer Wurster is Professor of City and Regional Planning at the University of California, Berkeley.

Labor Department counts on an increase in construction opportunities "much faster" than 20 per cent, as a major source of additional jobs.

This rate of construction cannot be achieved if the market for new housing remains limited to the top 30 to 40 per cent of the population (less in high-density development), with a tiny volume of public housing (2½ per cent of new construction in 1959) at the bottom. Construction costs have risen faster than incomes. High interest rates have further reduced the market. Under typical present conditions for a house with FHA-insured mortgage, a two per cent lower interest rate would mean about 25 per cent lower monthly payments, which would add about 15 per cent of all American families to the potential market, getting well down into the middle-income group.

Together, the new dwellings and the present supply of good or adequate homes must somehow meet the urgent needs of the poor, the aged and minorities—millions of whom will be forcibly displaced from their present quarters—as well as middle and upper-income white families. The homes must be varied enough to fit big and small households with differing incomes, tastes and living habits. A suitable choice of homes must be located within reasonable distance of local employment centers. And the housing supply in any locality should permit enough vacancies at all price levels to insure adequate choice and mobility, without exploitation.

This does not mean that a large proportion of the low-income households will necessarily need heavily-subsidized new housing. In central cities, and even to some extent outside, there is a big supply of moderate-quality older homes which could be made available, with modest grants and some rehabilitation where necessary, *if* there were enough vacancies to free up the market, encourage normal mobility, and permit the "filtering" process to operate effectively. This would require a great deal of middle-income construction, however, which is impossible with present costs and financial terms. Ample means must be available to provide new subsidized housing for displaced families (although not solely in large publicly-owned projects), wherever this seems to be the only immediate solution. Slum clearance operations which merely force the occupants into other slums are indefensible.

Cooperatives and other forms of non-speculative enterprise which have proven successful for both middle-income and subsidized housing in northern Europe should be further encouraged, and new sources of equity and mortgage funds should be sought out. Big redevelopment projects currently sponsored by the aluminum industry, in the hope of expanding outlets for its enormous productive capacity, exemplify an entirely new kind of housing enterprise which may have wide potential significance. The airplane industry is likewise scrutinizing the possibilities in the housing field.

The upward drive of 18 million Negroes and other minorities must sooner or later mean federal action against discrimination in federally aided housing, as predicted and supported by the Commission on Race and Housing, an unofficial but nationally representative body. Laws against discrimination are already being enacted by city and state governments in the North. In the meantime there must be concerted public, private and individual efforts to give minority families more freedom of choice in housing and neighborhoods, particularly in outlying areas. This will not only ease the transition but also avert the ghetto trend in central cities and help solve the housing problems of everyone.

In the housing field the general goals are much clearer than the specific means. What we need primarily is responsible programming of local requirements, with a period of systematic but flexible experimentation. Working principles for the next decade are here proposed:

(1) Public agencies must set over-all goals, then provide assistance and incentives to private enterprise to carry out as much of the program as possible on their own initiative, with full encouragement for innovations. This is already beginning to happen in renewal programs.

(2) Future housing requirements, to insure a balanced inventory in both central and outlying areas and to meet the needs of displaced families, must be determined by local agencies on a metropolitan-wide and city-wide basis. This is an extension of the "workable program" principle, a condition of federal renewal aid since 1954. More refined techniques of housing market and needs analysis will be essential.

(3) Better coordination and greater flexibility are required in all federal and state programs related to housing, to meet the full range of local needs. Public policies have enhanced the disjointed, over-specialized, and generally inflexible character of the housing market, whether in standardized suburbia or in standardized public housing. Inducements rather than rigid controls are necessary, particularly to encourage responsible local programming of needs.

(4) To expand the effective market for new and improved housing, and the range of consumer housing choice, will be a major challenge to industry, finance, architects, researchers, and to housing, renewal and planning agencies, with federal leadership and assistance required.

Since there are no clear-cut answers as yet to many of the problems involved, programs must be designed to encourage local and private experiment instead of stifling it. Measures should include the following:

(a) A long-term nation-wide program of technological and design research, including systematic field experiment and public education, to lower construction costs, remove restrictive obstacles, and tackle rehabilitation. Substantial federal funds would be supplemented from other sources, and all kinds of industrial, academic and local agencies should be utilized, under broad federal leadership.

(b) An experimental program of federal financial assistance to localities, for new housing or rehabilitation which appears to be needed as part of a locally determined program. The program would be limited to five years, with maximum freedom to provide mortgage insurance, low-interest loans, annual or capital grants or other aid. These aids would be offered to both private builders and public agencies, but only on the firm condition of complete cost-accounting, for purposes of comparative analysis. Substantial funds should be made available, and a thorough report should be made to Congress and the public at the end of the period, to provide a basis for permanent legislation. This program would be used in part to encourage co-operative and other forms of non-speculative enterprise, to tap new sources of equity and mortgage funds, and also to facilitate technological and design experiments. All the regular federal programs for housing assistance should be continued, however, during the period of experiment.

(c) Legal and administrative action against racial discrimination, particularly in publicly-assisted housing. Pending federal action on a nation-wide basis, federal policies should fully support state and local laws, and should offer financial inducements for "open occupancy" housing, particularly in suburban areas. . . .

Housing and the Consumer*

Nathan Glazer

. . . There has always been considerable public apathy over housing. Since the amelioration of the post-war crisis in housing, caused by fifteen years of very little building of new housing, the public at large has been relatively quiescent, taking what it is given, and with hardly much of a grumble. When the public is queried over what it wants in housing, . . . it evinces no sharp demands differing greatly from what it gets. It wants nothing that a little more money for each family would not get it: an extra bathroom or bedroom, a few more trees, even more and newer kitchen equipment. One cannot expect an aroused public opinion on housing when all the public wants is another bedroom or half-bath in the split-level. This is not the stuff of which revolutions—even housing revolutions—are made.

And this should not surprise us too much. What people want is determined by their experience and by what they have known. What they have known since the war has been one thing almost exclusively: the one-family, detached house with small bedrooms, built of light materials, with fine kitchens and bathrooms, on a rather bare lot. When people think of what they would like, they think of improved versions of this. Since 1947, single-family houses have composed four-fifths of all starts; since 1955, 90 per cent of all starts. Rental housing in multiple units—not to speak of other alternatives to the universal ranch or split-level—have been so scarce that it would require a great act of imagination, or the experience of travel and living in certain European cities, to conceive of different possibilities. When one is informed . . . that at least 70 per cent of Americans prefer to own, one is surprised that perhaps as much as 30 per cent might prefer to rent. For the rental space of which Americans have experience is often decrepit, if it is available at all, while new rental space is undersized, and generally either for the very rich or the totally impoverished. In addition, government lending policies make buying economically very attractive. In sum, often the only way to get even minimal housing is to buy. And most studies show that people seem to

* Nathan Glazer, *The Consumption of Housing and the Urban Community* (New York: ACTION, Inc., May 1959), pp. 5–10. Policy Background Paper No. 3, from the Newark Conference on the ACTION program for the American city. Reprinted with permission, and through the courtesy of ACTION, Inc. This paper was written in response to comments by four other experts in the field.

Nathan Glazer, a consulting editor for Random House, is Professor of Sociology at the University of California, Berkeley.

prefer what their experience makes familiar, and what they have today dominates their ideas of what they would like to have.

Under these circumstances, it is reasonable to ask again: Just what is the problem about consumer satisfaction with housing, if any?

. . . While it is true the consumer engages in no *massive* action of dissatisfaction, he does evince dissatisfaction in other ways. There is, to begin with, his great volatility: the large number who move. Twenty per cent of Americans, we are informed, move every year; over a period of five years, 50 to 60 per cent move; over 10 years, 75 per cent. Now a good deal of this movement has nothing to do with housing dissatisfaction: one-third is movement between communities, based largely on the need to follow jobs, or the search for better jobs. Of the remaining two-thirds, part is involuntary, based on the destruction of houses by public improvements or other causes, part is based on a sharp increase of income or a sharp decrease of income, part is based on changes in the size of households by births, marriages, and deaths. But a good two-thirds of this huge volume of movement is related to dissatisfaction with housing.

And, we are informed from an analysis of surveys, people are dissatisfied with primarily two things: one is the amount of space they have (and we have seen how the amount of space has dropped greatly in the past half-century, though there has been an upturn in the size of new dwellings in recent years); and they are dissatisfied with their neighborhoods. The building industry can take no comfort from the nature of their dissatisfaction, for it turns out that they are dissatisfied with even new houses, which have all the initial temporary advantages of being new. "Of 1949–50 homebuyers interviewed several months after their purchase, 36 per cent wanted more rooms than they had in their new homes, 55 per cent wanted larger rooms. . . ."

Nor is there much satisfaction to be found in the fact that renters are more mobile than owners, and somewhat more dissatisfied. For the gap between the volatility of renters and owners is steadily declining. During the 1930's, renters moved ten times as frequently as owners; today, they move less than twice as frequently. There are many reasons for this: that there is less rental space than there used to be; that it is easier to buy and sell houses owing to government-sponsored financing arrangements. And yet part of the reason may also be that the bloom is wearing off the new, single-family, detached house, and that certain disadvantages are beginning to weigh heavily on the American family.

Great as the present-day mobility of Americans is, there is reason to believe it may become even greater. And yet it is great enough today so that everyone feels skittish about the future of even brand-new neighborhoods of brand-new houses: builders, lending agencies, mortgage insurers, the people moving in. The fears over neighborhood stability are such as to suggest that the builders, bankers and insurers know what the economist proves so devastatingly in this study: people are not getting much for their money, and if they don't know it now, they may know it later when the first blush of newness wears off the exterior and the machinery.

So despite the general passivity of the American housing consumer as far as political pressure or very real vocal demands go, the home-building industry does have some cause for concern with the state of consumer satisfaction. Naturally, this concern is very much like the concern of any business with its market: which way is the wind shifting? But while the concern is an economic one, and the crisis, if it were to come, would be expressed in a decline in values . . . it would be caused not by a change in consumer *income*, but by a change in consumer *taste*. Conceivably there may be a crisis caused by a drop in income, but even on the economic level so many changes have occurred in home-owning and home-building that it is hard to imagine quite the kind of thing that happened in 1929. One of the differences is that very large numbers of people have invested in their homes not much more than the equivalent of rent, and consequently are free to express a change in taste rather easily. Their home does not represent their "life-savings," as it so often did in 1929, and does not tie them down as much. Then too, society is very different in its class structure, and contains much larger numbers of the professional and well-educated element who . . . move around most often and most easily. And then too, and perhaps most important, . . . taste, fashion, the forging of a distinct and individual life, *means* much more to more people, and to people further down on the income scale, than it ever has in America before. Under these circumstances, it is easy for things to change very rapidly. Not that everyone can indulge his taste, of course. Many millions of people must take what they can get, and must hold on to what they have been sold. These are the poor and, even more so, the new Negro city-dwellers. But there is a vast market of the prosperous and the nearly prosperous, which has been growing steadily since the war, and which has been engaged in exploring, and refining, and developing its tastes. . . .

. . . There [seem] to be two large causes of consumer dissatisfaction leading to the search for a different house: one [is] lack of space; the other [is] dissatisfaction with neighborhood. The studies on which these conclusions are based were generally in older neighborhoods, and when people voice dissatisfaction with their neighborhood, they refer to what we know as blight, and they very often refer, too, to the movement into their neighborhood of low-income and minority families who have become a major element of the city populations of the North and West and who will become an ever larger part of these city populations. But the dissatisfaction with neighborhood, while it expresses itself today largely in terms of dissatisfaction with old neighborhoods, represents a more general concern with environment: and just as [there may be] a potential consumer dissatisfaction with the new houses with which Americans have been provided in such great numbers, [there may *also* be] the possibility of the development of consumer dissatisfaction with the new neighborhoods with which they have been provided. Too, the builder and the building industry is concerned with the house, and wonders how the changing winds of taste will affect that; but another group of expert city planners have been concerned about the new neighborhoods, and how shifts of taste will affect that. The planner's view of the picture has to be larger than that of the consumer, who looks for a single house in a given neighborhood. It has to be larger than that of the developer who thinks of a group of houses that takes advantage of, or tries to create, a certain neighborhood. The city planners see whole communities, whole groups of communities, entire urban regions. They are concerned over the fact that the multiplication of single-family homes on large lots over mile upon mile of open country does not by itself create stable and satisfying neighborhoods. They wonder how vast areas containing people of one income level and without industry will support schools and other necessary community facilities and services. They wonder how this enormous movement (heavily underwritten by government) to the outskirts of cities and outside city boundaries will affect the ability of central cities to maintain their existing huge investments in facilities, facilities which still serve everyone in the metropolis. They worry over the quality of life in areas in which residential streets are laid out, and in which shopping centers are planned, but in which everything else that in the past has lent interest and excitement and enrichment to life is left to come later, to "just happen," in effect. At that point, schools and hospitals and libraries and museums (if one ever gets that far) are painfully and slowly brought in by people already burdened with the heavy expenses of raising young children, paying for and furnishing houses, maintaining automobiles, and paying for and equipping a whole new set of communal necessities.

Consumer satisfaction with housing, the planners know, does not begin and end with a house. A house is part of a neighborhood, and is carefully selected in terms of avoiding certain kinds of neighborhoods and choosing others. Very largely, in recent years, the choice has had to be blind, because one has bought the raw house, on the raw lot, surrounded by other houses, and one has had to hope that the new neighborhood would turn out well, would be the kind one vaguely felt one wanted. So the city planner looks ahead, too, to a time not very far off when the newness wears off, when some kind of total neighborhood has come into being, and wonders how satisfied the consumer will be then with his choice.

We have, then, two very different perspectives on consumer satisfaction with housing.

We have the perspective of the immediate present, in which we find that the consumer, if not overjoyed with what he has is generally willing to accept what builders, with government help, have provided him. Real crisis and dissatisfaction exist only in concentrated areas: in particular, in the older sections of big cities which are now, and will be for many years, reception centers for hundreds of thousands of low-income families, principally migrating Negroes and Puerto Ricans, and where the old inhabitants and the new settlers are both dissatisfied.

But then there is the perspective of the future in which everything is only potential, but which it would be naive to see only as a simple extrapolation of the past. As we have emphasized before, this is an exceedingly rich country. Industrial societies are incredibly productive. Great cities can be rebuilt in relatively few years and changes of taste could lead to radical and massive reconstruction. And this is also a country in which the creation of a style of life becomes something in which larger and larger numbers of Americans participate as problems of sheer economic survival recede in consciousness and reality. A crisis in housing, if it were to come, would not . . . be a simple economic crisis in which the total volume of demand failed radically, or in which economic necessity imposed a heavy demand for one kind of housing rather than another. This of course may come about. But what is more likely is the kind of thing that is happening in the automobile industry where the impact of a massive change of taste, apparently, is as important as the impact of the total volume of demand. Indeed, in automobiles, and in housing, too, taste which was once dependent on and a simple function of economic demand (the rich could have tastes, and the poor got what they could), taste now itself becomes an independent factor, affecting the kind of demand and the total volume of demand.

Houses, as we all know, are far more complicated than automobiles. They cannot easily be made on assembly lines, vastly greater numbers of producers and suppliers are involved, they are decisively affected by their environment, and they are produced for local markets. Yet the recent developments in the automobile industry are instructive to our understanding of the consumer in general. Probably no industry has spent more on consumer research than the automobile industry. These researches very likely showed no general dissatisfaction with the American car. But when a new alternative was offered—the small foreign car, expressing a very different taste—it turned out that very large numbers of Americans were interested. Yet there was no way of knowing this in advance.

Now fortunately for the stability of the building industry,

while one can export European cars, one cannot export comfortable and reasonable apartments, let us say, along with an interesting urban environment. And so the dominant style of American housing will not be presented to American consumers with the same dramatic contrast to it unless the investors, government, the community and the producers themselves imaginatively provide the alternative.

But there is a more general point to be learned from the automobile experience. That point relates to our understanding of the American consumer. As soon as we use such a term, we tend to forget the enormous size of the American population and its enormous variety. We tend to forget that what 10 per cent of Americans want provides us with a market greater than that of all of Canada. What 20 per cent of Americans want provides us with a market greater than all of England or France. And yet we focus on "the American consumer." He wants a single-family house, which he may buy, where he may garden, where his children may have play space, where he may be intimately involved with his neighbors. Indeed, he does—but perhaps only 50 or 60 or 70 per cent want that. Perhaps others want to be able to live in a clean and efficient and varied city. Perhaps others are willing to give up space for the advantage of being closer to the city. Perhaps others will take less elaborate kitchen and laundry equipment and even less elaborate bathrooms for a larger bedroom or living room, or an additional tree. There is enormous range even in the existing wants of Americans, a range which makes it possible to provide, at a profit, a far greater range of housing alternatives than is at present provided for Americans. The range of taste, which at present is barely suggested by the offerings on the market, probably will grow even wider, even greater.

At present, there are two great areas of deficiency, if we look at the American Consumer and what he wants, and what is provided to him.

One area is that of the low-income family—namely the Negro and Puerto Rican city dwellers. They want the houses that other Americans have, but owing to poverty and racial restrictions cannot get them. Then there are those who *don't* want the housing that Americans are being provided with so lavishly, and who cannot find what they do want except at great expense of money and ingenuity. The solutions to these two great deficiencies are linked: when the low-income city dwellers of different race find it possible to move outside the blighted ghettos of the central city and those who want an urban life find it possible to move back into the central city, the range of consumer satisfaction with housing will be much greater than it is today. At that time, both kinds of neighborhoods, those provided by the suburbs and those provided by the city, will be able to offer a greater range of satisfaction to the American consumer.

The Role of Public Housing*

Michael Harrington

In 1949 the Housing Act authorized the construction of 810,000 new units of low-cost housing over a four-year period. Twelve years later, in 1961, the AFL-CIO proposed that the new housing law should provide for 400,000 units—in order to complete the total projected in 1949. The Kennedy Administration asked for 100,000 new units.

This has been one of the greatest single domestic scandals of postwar America. The statistics have all been nicely calculated; everyone knows the dimension of the problem; and articles appear regularly, predicting the next catastrophe that will come from inaction. But nothing is done to attack the basic problem, and poor housing remains one of the most important facts about the other America. This is where the nation builds the environment of the culture of poverty.

So it was that the 1960 census (these are preliminary figures) reported that 15.6 million of the 58,000,000 occupied dwelling units in the United States were substandard. This represented 27 per cent of the nation's total housing supply. Of these, some 3,000,000 were shacks, hovels, and tenements. Another 8.3 million units were "deteriorating," and 4.3 million units were structurally sound but lacking some or all of the essential plumbing facilities. In addition, these figures do not take account of "sound" housing that is terribly overcrowded.

As the AFL-CIO Civil Rights Department put it, "It seems, therefore, certain that 30 per cent of American families are living in substandard homes today." For those interested in historical echoes, that amounts to one third of a nation that is ill housed.

Perhaps a more dramatic statement of the problem was made by Charles L. Farris, the president of the National Association of Housing Officials: at the end of the fifties there were more Americans living in slums than on farms.

These figures apply only to the "old" slums, the obvious tenements and the broken-down houses. But the new public housing projects themselves have become a major problem. Many of them have become income ghettos, centers for juvenile gangs, modern poor farms where social disintegration is institutionalized. In addition, the destruction

* Reprinted with permission of The Macmillan Company from *The Other America* by Michael Harrington (New York: The Macmillan Company, 1962), pp. 139–157. Copyright 1962 by Michael Harrington.

Michael Harrington is a member of the editorial board of the political journal *Dissent* and a participant in Fund for the Republic studies.

of old slum neighborhoods for public housing or Title I programs has resulted in mass evictions. The new public housing did not provide enough units for those who had been driven out to make way for improvement. The projects thus created new slums and intensified the pressures within the old slums, particularly for minority groups.

This grim inventory could be continued indefinitely, yet that would be to miss a major point about America's slums. The problem of housing is not simply a physical matter. In 1950, for instance, the Census defined "dilapidation" as occurring when "a dwelling unit is run down or neglected, or is of inadequate original construction so that it does not provide adequate shelter or protection against the elements or it endangers the safety of the occupants." Such a definition has a bureaucratic neatness to it, but it misses the very essence of what a slum is.

A slum is not merely an area of decrepit buildings. It is a social fact. There are neighborhoods in which housing is run-down, yet the people do not exhibit the hopelessness of the other Americans. Usually, these places have a vital community life around a national culture or a religion. In New York City, Chinatown is an obvious example. Where the slum becomes truly pernicious is when it becomes the environment of the culture of poverty, a spiritual and personal reality for its inhabitants as well as an area of dilapidation. This is when the slum becomes the breeding ground of crime, of vice, the creator of people who are lost to themselves and to society.

Thus, there are in the United States old slums where the buildings are miserable and decayed; and there are new slums in which the culture of poverty has been imported into modern housing projects. Both are parts of the other America.

First, take the obvious slum of tenements and hovels. The most important fact about these places in the sixties is that they are the environment of pessimism and of hopelessness.

Indeed, there is a sense in which the "old" slums are new. There once was a slum in American society that was a melting pot, a way station, a goad to talent. It was the result of the massive European immigration in the late nineteenth and early twentieth centuries. That flood of human vitality came to an end after World War I when the nation established quota systems, but the tradition of the ethnic groups survived for a generation. Symbolically, the tenements in which these newcomers lived had been built for them and had not been trickled down after the middle class found them inadequate. The neighborhoods were dense and the housing was inadequate, yet the people were not defeated by their environment. There was community; there was aspiration.

In most cities in the United States, it is still possible to take a bus or subway into this part of the American past. The Kerry Patch, the Ghetto, Little Italy, and other ethnic slums remain. Yet, like archaeo-logical remnants of some dead culture, they are being buried under the new metropolis. Yet, even today, there is still a unique feeling of life in the remains of the old ethnic slums. The crowding gives rise to a lusty richness of existence. The children swarm on the streets throughout the day and into the early evening, but they rarely form themselves into violent gangs. If the neighborhood is strident, it is vital, too; if it is dotted with the signs of the Old Country, it is a way station to the new land as well. . . .

Where the ethnic slum once stood, in the "old" slum neigh-borhood, there is a new type of slum. Its citizens are the internal migrants, the Negroes, the poor whites from the farms, the Puerto Ricans. They join the failures from the old ethnic culture and form an entirely differ-ent kind of neighborhood. For many of them, the crucial problem is color, and this makes the ghetto walls higher than they have ever been. All of them arrive at a time of housing shortage (when the public housing program was first proposed in the thirties, around a quarter of the slum units were vacant), and thus it is harder to escape even when income rises. But, above all, these people do not participate in the culture of aspiration that was the vitality of the ethnic slum.

Most of the examples in this section are from New York, which is hardly a typical American city. It is more of a melting pot; it has more multiple dwellings (the euphemism for tenement); and there are other important differences. Yet the New York transition is being re-peated in various ways across the nation. In Chicago, an important ele-ment is the Negro; in St. Louis, the white sharecropper; in Los Angeles, the Mexican-American. But in each case the internal migrant joins with the traditionalists and failures from the ethnic slum.

When you leave the subway at the Marcy Street stop in Williamsburg, the first thing you notice is a Spanish record playing, Spanish titles on the movie marquee, Spanish shops along the street. But then, next to these signs of the Puerto Rican migrants, there are the shops with Hebrew lettering in the window. And down the street there is the center for the remnants of an old German community. There is "integra-tion" here—some of the tenements house Negroes, Puerto Ricans, and whites—but it is the integration of poverty, of rootless transients, of dis-integration.

As a young priest at Holy Trinity sees his parish, it is made up of people on relief and of workers with low-paying jobs, many of them in the garment industry. There are three or four children to a family (the most typical family in the American culture of poverty has seven or more members), but those who stayed behind in the German community have not produced much of a neighborhood social life. There are few clubs, and the church is the center of what community life there is. The people, the priest continues, are very worried because a Title I project is moving into the area and will uproot them.

Down the street, at a community center, a social worker has a different perspective. For him the large fact is that 6,000 people have moved out in the recent past. The poor among them have gone to other slums, the better off to the suburbs. (In every slum in New York there is a group of people who have fairly decent incomes but who stay behind out of attachment to a neighborhood, a school, a church.) Since 1955 there has been a steady influx of Negroes and Puerto Ricans, and all this movement has produced an environment of social disintegration and with it violent gangs like the Phantom Lords and the Hell Burners. There is a low-cost housing project near by, but the natural leaders have been evicted because their income rose too quickly for the legal maximum. . . .

The current American answer to the problem of the slum is the low-cost housing project. The theory behind this approach contains at least the beginnings of an attack upon the culture of poverty: a public commitment to create a new environment for human beings.

But the practice has lagged far behind the intention. The concerned citizen, as noted earlier, sees that tenement eyesores have been torn down, and he is satisfied. He does not understand that the number of units that have been built do not equal the number that have been destroyed in clearing the project sites. In New York in 1954, for instance, there was one unit for every 7.1 eligible new families; in 1956, one for every 10.4 eligible new families. And these figures are roughly typical of the nation as a whole.

In some areas people who have priority for getting low-cost housing do not take advantage of it. Some refuse to go in because of their reputation for violence or because of their interracial character. Some are on the fly and fear any contact with the public authorities— and not necessarily because of crime; perhaps because of marriage irregularities, for instance. Still another group, according to Tom Wolfe of New York's Hudson Guild, simply do not know about the opportunity. Long-time citizens of the other America, they assume that there is no real hope, that no one is going to help them, and they vanish. That is one reason why over half of the people displaced by projects in the United States are listed on the records as "address unknown."

So, first of all, there is not enough public housing to go around. But there are some hundreds of thousands of people who have gone into projects recently, and their experience is perhaps even more significant than that of those who were simply displaced. . . .

Most public housing, even at its best, fails to solve the problem of the slum and, above all, the problem of slum psychology. In some cases the gains appear minimal, for one must balance the physical improvement (and, hopefully, the consequent improvement in health) against the new forms of alienation and, at the extreme, of violence. But, perhaps most crucial, the housing policy of America has sought the integration of the poor with the poor—which is to say, the segregation of the other Americans from the society at large.

For some people the failures of public housing are cited as an argument against national involvement in this problem. This is a disastrous and wrongheaded deduction.

With all that has been said about the inadequacies of the housing projects, it is clear that only one agency in America is capable of eradicating both the slum and slum psychology from this land: the Federal Government. Time and time again, private builders have demonstrated that they are utterly incapable of doing anything. If the Federal Government deserts the field, that would be tantamount to a decision to enlarge the slums of America. A new determination and imagination are needed, not a retreat.

The cost of an all-out attack upon the slums is measurable. In 1955 Joseph P. McMurray, then State Housing Commissioner of New York (and now chairman of the Federal Home Loan Bank), testified before the House Subcommittee on Housing. He estimated that it would take $125,000,000,000 of public and private investment to end slums within twenty-five years. This, he said, would require a combined program five times larger than the current Government commitment. Clearly, this is an expensive business; clearly it is not beyond the bounds of possibility.

In 1961, Leon Keyserling, former chairman of the President's Council of Economic Advisers, calculated that a serious attack upon the problem would require about two million units a year for the next four years. Of these, 1.2 million would be privately financed housing for upper-middle-income families; about 500,000 would be provided for lower-middle-income families (with some kind of Government subsidies); and about 300,000 homes a year would be brought into the reach of low-income families, including the aging, through joint Federal and local contributions.

Predictably, the plans put forward by Washington as the sixties began fell far short of these appraisals. The Kennedy Administration proposed funds for 100,000 new low-income public-housing units (this would mean that the United States would still be short of the goals projected in 1949 for a four-year period!), and subsidies that would provide for about 75,000 middle-income housing units.

Second, under the present setup, it is the poor who are victimized by urban renewal. In 1959 Charles Abrams told a Senate Committee that the public housing program had become "tattered, perverted and shrunk . . . little more than an adjunct of the publicly subsidized private urban renewal program. This urban renewal program too, while it does help the cities to get rid of slums, has developed into a device for displacing the poor from their footholds to make way for higher rental dwellings which those displaced cannot afford. Thus, the lowest-income family remains the forgotten family, though it is still the most home-needy in the American family circle."

If these problems of financing are not solved, if America does not have the will to eradicate the slum in its midst, then no amount of imagination will deal with the situation. But if the will were there, if the money were appropriated, then there is a crying need for new directions in public housing.

Public housing must be conceived of as something more than improved physical shelter with heat and plumbing. It must be seen as an important organism for the creation of community life in the cities. First and foremost, public housing should avoid segregating the poor off in some corner of the metropolis. That is the "modern poor-farm mentality," as one critic described it. The projects and subsidized homes should be located as parts of neighborhoods, so that income groups, races, and cultures will mingle.

Many housing experts have already laid down some fairly obvious principles for accomplishing these ends. (The vision is not lacking; only the will.) For example, Charles L. Farris of St. Louis has proposed specific steps: low-cost and middle-income units should be interspersed, and there should be an attempt to integrate public housing with existing and vital neighborhoods. There should be a limit on building size (Farris suggests eight families) so as to avoid the creation of an impersonal, bureaucratic environment. And the private individual housing that still exists should become the focus of a campaign for rehabilitation.

Private ownership is one of the great myths of American life—for more than half the people do not, and cannot, own their homes. In 1959 Charles Abrams estimated that an annual income of over $6,000 was required before an American family could seriously think of buying a home. In 1957, for instance, less than 6 per cent of the families who purchased new homes under the FHA had incomes under $4,200. In other words, the upper half of the population benefited from this program to the extent of 94 per cent of the housing, while those who most desperately needed it shared 6 per cent of the total.

It would be magnificent if America were to make home ownership a goal of national policy. As it is today, the poor are completely excluded from this possibility, and even the great middle third of the income pyramid have considerable difficulties.

Where projects are undertaken (and it must be emphasized that the reference is not to huge high-rise ghettos, but to a new kind of public housing) there must be an adequate budget for social work. You cannot take people out of an old-fashioned slum, where reality has been giving them a grim, distorted education for years, place them in a project, and expect them to exhibit all kinds of gentle, middle-class virtues. This transition is a crucial moment. If the people are left to themselves, then the chances are that they will import the culture of poverty into the public housing. If they are helped, if there is real effort to forge neighborhood communities, this need not happen.

Many of the public-housing administrators are sincere and imaginative public servants, but they have been frustrated at every turn by the inadequacy of funds and by the fact that the nation has yet to make a real commitment to build a human environment.

And the cost? The point has already been made, but it deserves repeating: we already pay an inordinately high price for poverty in the United States. Misery generates social chaos, and it takes money just to police it, just to keep it from becoming so explosive that it will disturb the tranquillity of the better off. In cold cash-and-carry terms, there would be a long-range pay-off if slums were abolished in the United States. In human terms, such an action would mean that millions of people would be returned to the society and enabled to make their personal contribution.

At this writing, one must sadly report that it does not seem likely that there will be an adequate crusade to end the misery of the millions of Americans who live in substandard housing. The figures have all been tabulated; the reports are in; and the direction of human advance is clear. But, as the sixties open, there is not yet the political will to get at the root of the problem.

So the new form of the old slums will continue; the inadequacies and tragedies of our past public housing policy will remain with us; and that tenacious organism, the culture of poverty, will settle down comfortably in our urban rot.

In Opposition to Public Housing*

I Ralph W. Gwinn

I am in unqualified opposition to public housing bills which forsake freedom and resort to the compulsions of the authoritarian governments to house the people. I propose to show that such public-housing schemes are fraudulent in their promises to the poor and ruinous to our free economy that alone can build houses and cure society of its slums. Besides, government housing brings political corruption by the exchange of tenants' votes for low rents. It leads in the nature of things to government bribery of investors and must lead, as the sad experience of Europe proved, to state socialism, totally contradictory to everything which we think of as American freedom and American self-government.

Now, who are the low-income or poor families involved? Which political party will select them and vote them and their dependents in on the deal is not disclosed. In fact, one of the neatest deceptions used to build public emotional support is to advertise that it is a gift to the poor or the low-income families.

The casual workers, the unskilled and the unemployable, the sick, the aged, and low-paid workers do not get into public housing because, even with tax exemption and subsidies, Government housing rents are too high for them. The American Legion told a joint committee of the House and Senate that many of the disabled veterans who had really low incomes could not get into public-housing projects. In my district when they tried to make the over-income tenants move, so the space could be rented to low-income veterans, the tenants went to court, and the court upheld them. The proportion of truly destitute families that get into public-housing projects is very low in every city.

Unfortunate citizens cannot pay operating and maintenance costs which are too high in Government housing. If public housing could give us additional houses above the rate now being built, which it cannot, or if it could give us cheaper housing, which it cannot, or if it could build and operate houses at a profit which it never does, even then the only justification for it would be to help the really poor and needy. Instead they are turned away and favored tenants who can pay higher rents to the Government landlord are chosen. . . .

* Ralph W. Gwinn, "Public Housing—Disastrous Here and Abroad," speech made on the floor of the House of Representatives, June 4, 1948.
Ralph W. Gwinn was a Republican Representative from New York (1945–1959).

Public housing was used as the central highway on which Socialist cabinets and parliaments and dictators rode to power in Europe. Votes of the tenants organized by the Socialists and Communists, always in goodly numbers in the public-housing projects, were delivered to the candidates who promised more public housing.

Appropriations of billions out of the taxpayer's money means vast immediate deductions from the private funds which taxpaying workers, contractors, and owners are now using to meet the housing need by voluntary building. Loaded down with prohibitive taxation fewer citizens can afford to become home owners.

When a political party which runs the Government controls house construction, it bids up the price of carpenters, bricklayers, nails, lumber, plumbing, and land, and all materials and workers and credit beyond the reach of private persons. Whatever the cost is, the taxpayer is lashed into paying it.

Some people point to the building of national roads as an argument that government can do business better than a voluntary free society. But, post roads, harbors, and rivers are specifically listed as a proper enterprise of a constitutional government. Houses are not. Roads, for example, are all taxed by the consent of the governed, because all citizens use the roads. All benefit. All pay the same price for stamps at the post office. All are treated alike, an impossibility in Government housing. That is one reason why the Constitution did not include housing as a proper function of our Government.

It is so easy to go socialist. The taxpayers are too weak, scattered, and confused to organize and do anything about it. Besides, under the socialist scheme of things, those with property to tax are in the minority.

The public-housing advocates employ an old trick. They have learned how to induce private investors to finance their Socialist schemes. The Government offers to guarantee income and capital if it is loaned to public housing.

With the Government guaranteeing their interest and principal, they have achieved Government security for their capital and joined a continuous WPA for investors. Capital goes on the dole.

In this manner, no bloody revolution is necessary to take over private property. The most powerful forces in the free economy meekly surrender without a struggle.

When Government is the borrower, lenders are made to feel that if Government is not safe, nothing is. There is no risk under the sun which the taxpayers will not be compelled to make good. Finally, investors have no place to go but to the Government. It then makes its own terms for capital. The end is always the same.

If we give the public-housing agency the billions it asks for, we will be giving to government the small block of "stock" through which it can get control of the whole company.

Public housing is the greatest known build-up of political patronage. Mayors and other officials are hoping to add patronage to their pay rolls and votes for their party.

Government has almost unlimited choice of where to put its projects. It can find its "low-income families" anywhere, under the broad definition it uses. So practical politics is free to decide to put the Government houses where they will "do the most good"—that is, where a critical vote for Senator or Congressman or the electoral college is in doubt.

Government housing doubles the corruption of the voters beyond anything ever dreamed of under the old WPA. It will become the crucial but permanent governmental spending fund for propaganda, for votes, for re-election. It is the speeded-up version of the slogan "spend and spend, tax and tax, elect and elect."

In Opposition to Public Housing*

II Strom Thurmond

I am opposed to the public housing and urban renewal provisions of this bill.

I am informed that by the end of fiscal year 1960, more than 475,000 federally aided public housing units will be occupied by more than 2 million people; and in addition, 110,000 units which now are authorized will be under contract, but not occupied.

It is estimated by the public housing authority that there is an annual turnover of 30 per cent of the tenants in public housing. This means that, from units built and to be built without any additional legislation, there will be available approximately 180,000 units for occupancy by new tenants annually.

A study of this bill will reveal that no longer is it the pur-

* Strom Thurmond, "In Opposition to Public Housing," speech made on the floor of the Senate, February 5, 1959, during discussion of the Housing Act of 1959.
Strom Thurmond is the junior Senator from South Carolina.

pose of this program to provide low-rent housing for persons who cannot afford adequate housing built with funds from private sources. The original purpose of the bill has long since lapsed into oblivion. I am informed that the Public Housing Administration authorizes the construction of units at a maximum cost of up to $17,000 a unit. Although income requirements for tenancy in public housing have been most loosely administered in the past, this bill abolishes all pretense at providing housing solely for low-income tenants. It repeals the requirement for eviction of over-income tenants. It gives the housing authorities complete discretion in setting rents and income.

The continued extensions and degenerations of the public housing activities of the U.S. Government cause me to wonder whether we are adhering in principle to article VI of the Constitution of the Union of Soviet Socialist Republics, which reads as follows:

"Art. 6. The land, its mineral wealth, waters, forests, mills, factories, mines, rail, water and air transport, banks, communications, large state-organized agricultural enterprises (state farms, machine and tractor stations and the like), as well as municipal enterprises and the bulk of the dwelling houses in the cities and industrial localities are state property, that is, belong to the whole people." . . .

Our humanitarian instinct comprises one of our strongest national traits. I am motivated by as strong a humanitarian instinct as anyone in our country. I have real concern for those who are in dire economic circumstances and without decent and suitable living quarters. However, it is our very humanitarianism, admirable and worthy though it be, on which the complacency of the American people is founded. By using a subtle, sometimes even subliminal approach, our enemies have enlisted our unthinking support of causes apparently for the promotion of human rights, but which, when carefully examined, reveal an underlying advancement of collectivism, which is the gravest threat to our country today. We find ourselves even more vulnerable to plans for promoting the economic welfare of all, or a particular portion, of our people, at the instance of government. We are inclined to direct our exclusive attention to the purportedly noble purpose of the plan, but to ignore the threatened jeopardy to our individual liberty and the impracticality of utilizing the tool of government, in lieu of personal and private initiative.

After careful personal analysis of the public housing provision of S. 57, I can only see in this proposal a further involvement of our Government into private enterprise activities, an increased national debt, and another smashing victory for the insidious forces of socialism. In fact, the public housing program further proves the point that socialism is an inefficient and impractical philosophy. I can see no excuse for its continuation.

Private enterprise has also been tested in this country. Unlike socialism, however, it has proved itself by giving to our country a standard of living which, at its lowest ebb, is far superior to any other known to the world. Private enterprise can do and is doing the housing job at no cost to the taxpayer. I do not believe that the Government should be in the housing business or any other business unless two conditions are fully met.

First, the project must be something that is vitally needed. As I have pointed out, almost 600,000 units will be in existence without any further legislation on the subject, and this will accommodate approximately 180,000 family units annually. The second condition for the Government to get into business is that private enterprise is not willing to do the job. In this instance private enterprise is doing the job. We are undergoing at present a private housing boom. There is no slack in the building program. One but needs to examine the classified ads under real estate in any newspaper to see that not only new housing is available, but that there is also a surplus of adequate existing housing available at low cost.

The question of cost to the taxpayer is also extremely pertinent on this issue. There is involved in this bill a revival of about 10,000 units for which authority expired in June of 1958, an extension of the 35,000 units authorized for the current fiscal year until June of 1961, and an additional increment of 35,000 new units which will be open until July 1, 1963. This is an unjustifiable splurge on an unworkable program. The cost of the subsidies for these units will be astronomical. It is an insult to the already overburdened American taxpayer, and adds further to the debt obligations which his children will bear for years to come. . . .

Future of the Housing Industry*

Gurney Breckenfeld

Housing, sometimes described as "the industry capitalism forgot," is probably more maligned than it deserves.

* Gurney Breckenfeld, *Technological Changes and the Future of the Housing Industry* (New York: ACTION, Inc., May 1959), pp. 3–8. Policy Background Paper No. 2, from the Newark Conference on the ACTION program for the American city. Reprinted by permission, and through the courtesy of ACTION, Inc.
Gurney Breckenfeld is Managing Editor of *House and Home*.

Housing suffers from a plethora of problems, ranging from aesthetic controls to zoning straight jackets. But its chief ailment is not the shortcomings of the industry itself, or even its much-derided horse and buggy technology. The central trouble is restrictions and controls imposed on it from outside.

These form a web of interlocking and mutually supporting restraints that resist change—or at least make change so troublesome and costly that only the bravest and richest dare innovate. And even they usually find they must innovate gently.

So home building is still only on the threshold of taking full advantage of 20th Century methods—technological, managerial, fiscal, design and distribution—the methods that have produced such hallmarks of this era as autos and superhighways, airplanes and rockets, television and washer-dryers, frozen foods and throw-away paper hankies.

"The system of construction and mortgage finance, the basis of building regulation and inspection, and the organization of the design profession itself all show anachronistic allegiance to the notion that houses are and will continue to be assembled at the site by skilled craftsmen under the direction of contractors who have estimated what it will cost them to buy materials from local distributors and have them put into place according to drawings and specifications."*

Moreover, most producers of housing materials are either small or very remote from the final house. None so far has justified research on the whole complex problem of house building. No single element of this much fractionated industry can bring new channels of distribution and building teams into being unaided. Neither can any single element take the risk of being the first to make a major change in how it does business.

"Codes, zoning and subdivision controls all tend to be one-sided, concentrating on community protection without noticing that [this may also produce] unnecessary and often unwise restrictions on sound and appropriate development ideas."

Finally, the federal government itself has propped up this old order by setting up a system of housing aids that requires consumer financing before a house can be built. The effect is to make the archaic inefficiencies in housing palatable for the moment, by postponing for 30 years the time when we must pay for them.

This old order, this localism, is the major roadblock to better housing, to better living standards in the U.S.

Considering the handicaps under which the housing industry struggles, it has been doing "a reasonably good job—in some instances a very good job indeed. Yet the average man has become con-

* This quotation, like all others in this paper not otherwise identified, comes from *Design and the Production of Houses*, by Burnham Kelly (New York: McGraw-Hill Book Co., Inc., 1959).

vinced that the industry is obsolete and almost stubborn in its refusal to seek its own salvation." People suspect they are not getting their money's worth for housing any more. So consumers grow more and more tight-fisted with their housing dollars. To put it another way, the consumer demands less than he can get, gets less than he used to for what he pays, and spends less for housing than for autos, TV sets and amusements.

These are not complaints to be met by more tinkering with tomorrow's house, by better sales campaigns or new styling. "Fundamental improvements are called for!"

Fortunately, the trend is now away from "localism." It is a trend that is inevitable and irreversible.

Mass production of at least the component parts of tomorrow's house will be compelled by (1) that old bugaboo of housing —high cost and (2) a looming labor shortage.

Mass production cannot operate without mass markets for identical assembled products. Already, much of today's house is mass produced. Doors, windows, hardware, wall panels and other parts are more and more cut, stamped, shaped, assembled and even finished in the factory. The newest trend, best exemplified by packaged kitchens, is for factory-production of components—big pieces instead of little parts.

Even so, the basic character of today's house, notably its shell, is just about what it was 50 years ago. The industry cannot go much further towards changing it by making only minor adjustments here and there, disturbing as little as possible the comfortable status quo of local officials, local regulations, local financing, local materials distribution and local construction.

The time must come soon when gradual changes build up to a point where conventional resistance fades away and there is a sudden snapover to "an entirely new industrial situation in which stereotypes are abandoned and standards undergo rapid and radical transformation."

How do we get there? Largely by exploiting the potentials of innovation. Quality housing will come faster if production and design and management ingenuity are freed to a degree comparable with other industries. This will, of course, take teamwork.

Consider what freedom from localism's Lilliputian ties has done for the technology of housing's often overlooked competitor, the trailer. Trailer production is wholly divorced from a local site, and thus from local officialdom. The trailer is efficient and cheap—and it has outsold the prefabricated house every year since World War II. In 1957, trailer production reached 140,000 units—well over 10% of the total of that year's housing starts. Yet nine out of ten trailers are fixed in place as permanent homes—more and more often in planned trailer parks (which qualify for FHA-insured mortgage loans). The trailer is wholly factory-built. The prefabricated house, putting it roughly, is about half factory built. The traditionally-built house gets only its myriad little parts from industrial production lines.

What is this industry—an industry poised on the edge of a revolution often predicted, but never reached?

The federal government, whose statistics are questionable but the best available, figures it at $16 billion a year, or about 4% of Gross National Product. The industry provides about 2½ million jobs, half on the site, half producing and distributing materials and equipment. Housing consumes about a third of the nation's lumber, two-thirds of its brick, four-fifths of its gypsum products. It is estimated that each new house sale generates at least $1,500 worth of retail sales in furnishings and equipment.

Thirty years ago it was a rare builder who built more than one house a year. Recent estimates are that 1% of the home builders now put up 33% of the new houses. And the largest 10% of builders put up more than 66%. Almost all experts agree the size of housing firms is still increasing. It may be that many future communities will go up in a single, planned Levitt-like operation. Nobody expects the builder of under 25 houses a year to disappear. There are too many little markets. But the really pint-sized producer (of less than four units) seems likely to account for a smaller and smaller share of the nation's new housing.

As any home buyer knows, prices of new homes are going up. The average 1956 house, for example, was priced 41% above the average 1950 house. But it was 25% bigger. And it has more built-in equipment, which is more costly than the shell. Indeed, when you consider how much more money goes into housekeeping equipment instead of the space to have servants do it, the much advertised decline in consumer spending for housing since 1900 seems to shrivel considerably.

Demand for new housing is, like the U.S. population, on the rise. More increase is in prospect in the years just ahead. And the late 60's, when the post-war baby crop will be marrying and producing its own offspring, may well push new housing to the magic 1.5 million-a-year figure. Demand for suburban family homes, the mainstay of the industry's present output, will increase. But the sharpest rise in demand is likely to come in demand for in-town rental units for young marrieds without school-age children and for couples (who will be living longer) whose children have grown. This will be particularly true if design is improved.

The next decade's prospect for a major step-up in housing output will create not just a change but a real need for new materials, designs and methods.

Amid sweeping generalizations about housing's backwardness, it's easy to overlook progress toward industrial methods that has already been made.

Even the typical site operation in housing is shifting away from handicraft. More of the house is factory-built. Field techniques use more power tools, sub-assemblies and pre-finished surfaces. These items cut costs. A prediction: "It is probable that any new material which does not reflect this trend to rationalized construction is foredoomed to failure." . . .

A major new trend in techniques is toward use of big-size components: to build a house of a few dozen or score parts instead of hundreds or thousands of little pieces. Stressed-skin wall panels are probably the No. 1 example. Prefabricators, particularly, use them often. In a stressed-skin panel, the covering is firmly bonded to the ribs so the covering carries a substantial part of the load and the overall efficiency of materials' use is high. This contrasts sharply with ordinary stud construction, where the outside sheathing and inside lath and plaster are dead load added to the other load the studs must carry.

Structural sandwiches are a logical extension of the stressed-skin principle. Here the surface materials carry most of the load. Ribs are replaced by a continuous lightweight core. It stabilizes the surfaces against buckling under compression, develops shear strength, provides insulation. Like stressed-skin building, the sandwich panel is adapted largely from the airplane. But unfortunately, it has found little actual use in housing so far. First, it departs so far from most building codes, it is hard to get permission. Second, the sandwich panel needs volume output to make costs competitive.

Trussed rafters, now common in prefabs and development homes, save much labor and so cut costs. So far, they have found little use in custom-built housing. They can be assembled quickly in jigs either in a factory or in the field, in good weather. They go up fast, permitting early closing in of the house. And they permit complete flexibility in interior layout.

Mechanical equipment has seen many of the most radical developments of assemblies. Yet the unit bathroom is not generally available, though there is "no inherent reason why the bath cannot be built like the kitchen. When codes permit, prefabbers and development builders are using preassembled plumbing stacks, to which the fixtures are attached in the field." Among accessories, prefab chimneys are growing more common, and, to a smaller degree, so are prefab fireplaces.

Thus efficient house production is taking two forms:

"1. *The development house* built by the operative builder, who combines a high degree of site work specialization with a maximum amount of precutting and a carefully scheduled delivery of packaged materials, and

"2. *The prefab house* built in a shop and sent in sections to the site to be assembled and finished on lots locally prepared." The prefabber operates with most success where labor shortages, site troubles or scattered small-scale demand make it hard to organize a big building operation in one place.

To the creeping evidences of technical change in housing must be added one with the really big potential: the invasion of housing markets by more and more giant corporations whose central interests are not housing.

More and more of the cost of houses is going to chemical companies, electric companies, appliance makers. And lately aluminum companies have been bidding for a much bigger share of the housing dollar. These are large and aggressive firms, well capitalized with big research and development staffs. They are not committed to existing channels of distribution, nor do they have any vested interest in propping up conventional code and labor arrangements. "If they were not ham-strung by the localisms involved in such channels and arrangements, they would be likely to explore far more fully the potentials of technology and to seek to give the consumer a higher sense of value for his money."

But even so, such concerns are destined to play a much bigger role in tomorrow's housing. For one thing, such companies are beginning to realize they cannot leave research and development of better uses for their products up to small fabricators and builders. And many have come to see housing as an untapped growth area, "one of the few remaining industrial frontiers." So many big materials producers are stepping up their efforts to bring out assemblies and components that "represent a real concern for the design of the final house." Some are riding hard on everything right through actual construction. "Such efforts will very soon bring about a significant change in the character of the housing industry."

The break-through into house design by outside fabricators is already being led by the appliance makers.

They start with two advantages. First, people want modern conveniences more than a romantic, old fashioned look—in these parts of their homes. Second, they are less encumbered than other materials makers by localisms. "They have brought about major changes in hous-ing design with minor resistance because they concern themselves pri-marily with simplifying by improving household tasks and services and very little with the architectural appearance of the living areas."

Today, refrigerators and radios have over 95% saturation in the U.S. housing market and electric washers, TV and irons have 85%. *Such gains come from major research, major investment, major merchandising effort.* General Electric spent four years and $90,000 before it accepted design of its Disposall for volume production. It spent 19 years and over $1 million more before it made a profit on the unit. "Where in the housing industry would this have been possible?" Now, GE markets a kitchen center complete with stove, dishwasher, sink, garbage grinder, clothes washer, dryer and related storage cabinets. It is designed to be free-standing or a room divider. It offers a single buy (with credit aid from GE), unified design, simple installation (a 230-volt electric line, one hot and one cold water pipe, one vent and a drain). Upshot: "a major area of house design is thus handled in one package from the appliance industry."

Indeed, appliance men are so active that industry spokesmen say they are selling the builders' houses for them. For their part, appliance men know about half their growth items go into houses, and that well-designed homes are their best showrooms.

Some of the men who are helping revolutionize the design of house components aren't architects at all.

Big builder William J. Levitt and his organization, for example, are primarily responsible for Plextone paint. Plextone is a sprayed on paint which, through texture and a splatter method of coagulating separate colors, provides both a textured surface and also conceals flaws in material beneath. Other firsts have been developed for Levitt houses. One is a hot-water oil-burning unit contained in a counter-high exposed cabinet which was added to the kitchen and given a stainless steel counter top. It was backed up to a fireplace, thus furnishing a unique exposed system for panel slab hot water heat. Levitt was among the first to use split bamboo for closet doors. Today it is common. Working with Johns-Mansville or Celotex Corporation, Levitt has developed several types of asbestos siding. Thus Levitt has been a major influence in developing new components for mass housing. Other builders have been only too happy to use the products he pioneered.

A second major force for change in housing is the trend toward larger-sized builders.

A big builder places big orders for supplies. Often, he can buy direct from a jobber or manufacturer, cutting out one layer of middleman profit. Big orders mean basic suppliers can use quantity methods. The big builder can afford research and more expert advertising and sales programs. He can afford much more overhead to deal with the tangled skein of local and FHA-VA regulations.

One major builder estimates that 40% of his house costs arise from planning, finding and assembling land, and dealing with local controls. The other 60% is split evenly between the cost of underground and community facilities and the structure itself. Only a big builder can afford such an overhead. But he can, and the public may benefit.

Big-scale land development, itself, is emerging as one of the most profit-laden enterprises in the nation's economy, and companies in this field may well have as good a chance as big producers to make a major breakthrough in technical innovation.

Large-scale land development usually means unincorporated territory. Thus "most of the limiting localisms can be avoided." And an organization that goes into land with enough money to wait and gradually harvest the profit in development would create a captive market for new building products. . . .

8

The Urban Melting Pot

In this set of two long selections, we return to a number of issues raised earlier, but here viewed from a somewhat different perspective. The problems of the central city versus the suburbs, the tasks and perplexities of urban renewal as a special part of the planning process, the housing issues—all these are re-examined in relation to the problems of minorities in American urban life.

The idea of America as a melting pot in which all races and cultures merged and fused is essentially based on the experience of Europeans who emigrated to this country in the late nineteenth and early twentieth centuries. Cultural differences were gradually submerged, and the newcomers were absorbed into the American fabric. The process took place mainly in the larger cities, so that the stereotype of America as a melting pot was actually drawn from what was taking place on the urban scene.

The inadequacy of this stereotype to portray the realities of present-day urban experience, or, indeed, to provide any valuable or refreshing insights into this experience, is the theme of this chapter. The earlier immigrants were not colored. Today's newcomers are. And for them the city has functioned not as a place in which they can lose their isolation and merge with the rest of society, but as a place where their apartness is intensified.

Dennis Clark underlines the plight of the Negro in the city by examining his position vis-a-vis each of the major immigrant groups from Europe who were successful in their struggle to attain the good life in America. By examining the mechanisms that operate to separate Negro and Pole, Negro and Italian, Negro and Jew, and Negro and native-born white, Clark throws the problem into sharp relief. In the process of describing the movement from immigrant to full-fledged member of the urban group, Clark provides us with the tools for analyzing the difference between immigrant relations and race relations. The melting pot dealt effectively with problems of immigrant relations. What will take its place in the field of race relations?

A further point embedded in Clark's conspectus is crucial in understanding the depth of feeling that has produced the recent pressure for equal rights on the part of the Negro. This is the desperation the Negro feels as he sees the melting-pot process work for all immigrants except himself. The door to the good life seems permanently closed to him alone of all the newcomers. If this feeling of alienation persists and spreads, the possibility of communication among the races diminishes. This feeling is the spring from which movements like the Black Muslims issue. It is this persistent failure of the melting pot to work in the case of the Negro which differentiates him from other non-Caucasian races. The Chinese have generally had access to the good things in American life. The Japanese are so caught up in the process of becoming westernized that observers have often commented that there seems to be more social distance between the Japanese older and younger generations than between the younger Japanese and their western counterparts. Yet the Japanese are the only racial group in America who, in the persons of those on the West Coast, have been subjected to full scale confinement in concentration camps. Repeated resistance to efforts by the Negro to be admitted to the club has been more damaging to his outlook than the one sharp wartime rebuff has been to the Japanese.

Robert Weaver gives strong expression to another view of the urban problem of the Negro. Dr. Weaver, a Negro himself, and Administrator of the Housing and Home Finance Agency (and mentioned as President Kennedy's choice for his projected cabinet post for urban affairs), argues that the urban problem is not solely a problem of Negro migration. "Cities which have few non-white migrants are experiencing the same problems—a fact suggesting that this is a class as well as a color phenomenon." Weaver also lays bare the role of government agencies in promoting the very things that produce the problems they have been set up to eliminate. He argues for mixed neighborhoods, but warns against exceeding the "tipping point" at which racial tensions become unbearable. His basic concern, however, is the preservation of the health and vitality of the central city. He does not want to eliminate the slum completely ("a certain amount of individual choice will dictate their perpetuation") or even to produce completely mixed neighborhoods, but he does advocate the judicious use of the urban renewal process as one means of making sure that the disadvantaged colored newcomer does not remain permanently disadvantaged.

Immigrant Enclaves in Our Cities*

Dennis Clark

. . . The formation of the residential group was a response of newly arrived immigrants to the confusion and strangeness of the nineteenth-century city. This ethnic enclave based upon language difference or foreign origin became a fixture of American urban areas. It was a form of social protection and expression and a testimony to the pluralist character of our national life. Little Italy, Irishtown, Chinatown—dozens of such immigrant clusters dotted the cities. These neighborhoods provided the setting for the drama of ethnic group life. They also conditioned the common attitude and expectations with regard to the family and residential life of ethnic groups within the larger urban society. In the last century, the ethnic neighborhoods almost always established a picture in the public mind of poor living conditions and social disorganization. For over a century this picture was transmitted to a nation dominated by rural, native-born citizens, who prided themselves on their isolation from "foreign" influences and whose virtues of self-reliance and stability contrasted with the disorders of the struggling urban immigrant groups.

Eventually the dynamic quality of our urban life began to dissolve the ethnic communities which had partitioned the larger cities. Foreign immigration on a large scale ceased, and the influence of cultural media hastened the assimilation of the immigrant worlds which had flourished for decades. Physical and social mobility quickened this trend. But the experience of the immigration period and the concentration of ethnic groups had left a strong imprint upon national opinion. The stereotypes

* Dennis Clark, *The Ghetto Game: Racial Conflicts in the City* (New York: Sheed & Ward, Inc., 1962), pp. 4–6, 109–111, 113–118, 121–133. © 1962 Sheed & Ward, Inc. Reprinted by permission.
Dennis Clark has been housing specialist for the Philadelphia Housing Authority.

with regard to the attitudes and practices of ethnic groups were a part of the general cultural outlook. They did not dissipate as the ethnic communities themselves waned in significance, for they were consecrated by tradition. They were given wider currency and more vivid outlines by their use in the mass media which grew up to serve the urban populations.

In addition, the fluidity of urban society created a great hunger for social status. Distinctions based on ethnic and racial characteristics became important instruments in the psychic game of status seeking. Thus, although rising educational levels have reduced the crudity of the prejudices and stereotypes inherited from the American immigration experience, that experience was too sustained and significant not to leave lasting impressions.

The persistence of racial and ethnic distinctions was helped by the fact that leadership in the industrial metropolis was not unitary but composed of a balance of contending groups reflecting the economic, ethnic and religious affiliations of the citizens. A wide diversity of leaders emerged in the political and civil life of the urban areas. In some an oligarchy of "old families" or political bosses became dominant, but their power was always conditioned by the presence of the disparate representatives of a variety of groups. Under these conditions, it was not wholly unnatural that racial groups should be set apart and cultivated as were the other urban population elements grouped around national origin, language or religion. . . .

The primary consideration of the relationship of foreign-language communities to non-white population is that the "immigrant" neighborhoods have usually been physically contiguous or in apposition to non-white concentrations. The Negro and the foreign-language immigrant shared the limitations of income that forced them both to accept the older housing in the areas close to the center of the city. For the Negro this condition was more enduring. He remained confined, often while a succession of foreign-born groups came and went through the old neighborhoods. This physical proximity is important. It meant that the two types of minority groups, racial and lingual, were often in competition for the same shabby tenements and back-street houses. The foreign-born groups were often accustomed from their European background to working within circumscribed physical conditions. Their diligence and ingenuity would be lavished upon tiny areas that, however poor they seemed by general American standards, still represented relative comfort and security for the immigrant. As the foreign-born groups thinned out, they tended to shrink their concentrations or yield territory to others. Growing Negro population often filled the abandoned Irish, Italian or Slavic areas. But in order for the Negro to gain access to the general channels of urban movement, he frequently had to overcome or somehow bypass a tradition-rooted core of immigrant residence. These immigrant communities served as barriers against Negro mobility for the rest of the city population.

Examples of such roadblocks to Negro movements could be seen in St. Louis around 1930, where Germans, Jews, Poles and Italians bordered the Negro district west of the Mississippi. "The Polish Principality" of Hamtramck in Detroit has for years been impenetrable by Negroes. The ethnic ghettos along Franklin Street in North Philadelphia have long prevented the eastward movement of Negroes.

The physical confrontation of the Negro and the white minority groups has been fraught with social factors that bedevilled the relationship. The foreign-born were often not sure of themselves at all in their new urban environment. Many were unused to democracy and its concepts of social and racial equality. Upon achieving some status in this new country, they felt they could not afford to have it undermined by mixing with the stigmatized non-white group. Although at times sensitive to discrimination themselves, they were in too precarious a social position to let this permit a softening in their own attitude toward the non-whites. The foreign-born groups were beset with many internal conflicts, and it was an easy response to direct hostility against the non-whites. The social conflicts and tensions accompanying the process of adjustment of the foreign-born to urban life tended to produce crime and delinquency, which sometimes became a behavior pattern within the groups. This turbulence became exceedingly dangerous when racial incidents took place.

To the tightly knit foreign-born groups the Negro was often a strange and dreadful creature. They would have less knowledge of him than even the native white American. He would not be another European like the rest of the minorities. He would not have the elaborate rituals and customs of the Europeans, but would seem to defy any cultural definition. As a competitor for jobs, space and facilities, he was a threat.

It is evident, then, that among the group antagonisms in American cities, the relationship between the Negro and the foreign-born presented special difficulties. "But this is all in the past. It was acted out in the early part of the century," some would say. This is too facile a judgment. The foreign-born communities have been tenacious. Some have thrived for generations. In addition to the foreign-born persons in these groups, the second- and third-generation offspring are often strongly identified with ethnic ties.

Even where they have lost numbers and vitality, immigrant areas have imparted an identity to a section of the city. This identity is significant. People are often more impressed by reputations than by realities. Negroes may shun an area for a long while because of the area's reputation for hostility, despite opportunities to enter it. . . .

The Poles. People with race relations experience contend that Polish neighborhoods are particularly resistant to racial change and are likely to react violently to incursions by non-whites. Areas of Polish immigrant or other Slavic concentration have been the scenes of some of the most notable outbursts of racial violence in Northern cities. Violence in Detroit is often ascribed to Polish elements, as were outbreaks in Cicero, Illinois, adjacent to Chicago.

The Poles are noted as a highly individualistic people, a people caught in historic contradictions. The history of the mother country may be very significant in explaining the Polish attitude toward group relationships in this country. Poland's shifting borders and political life have embraced a number of traditionally hostile ethnic and nationality groups. Within Poland there have been in modern times a variety of populations coexisting in uneasy polity. Lithuanians, Estonians, German-speaking elements, Ukrainians, White Russians, Jews and various Balkan strains have lived in Polish territory intermittently. The Poles have had a difficult time, to look at it from their viewpoint, with a long historical succession of fiery, separatist, unyielding, foreign-language and ethnic minorities. This accounts for some of the furious quality of Polish nationalism. With such a legacy of intergroup difficulty, it is not surprising that Poles did not come to the polyglot American city with a bland attitude toward minority neighbors in the New World. . . .

As a minority group the Poles have not fared as well in the American immigrant sweepstakes as others. . . . The second-generation Poles in the United States have actually a lower socio-economic status than the first generation. Poles have also remained in a position near the bottom of the "social distance scale," a device drawn up by social scientists to reflect prevalent ethnic preferences.

In terms of educational attainment, the Poles rank low among immigrant groups in this country. The Jews and Irish do well in increasing the level of school years completed between first and second generation. Italians and others complete fewer years in school. These factors would certainly have an influence upon the race relations of the group. Deprivation of social status would heighten the likelihood that Poles would feel a need for a scapegoat. The Negro would be present, and often in a position to compete with the Pole for jobs and other opportunities. The lower educational achievement of the Pole would increase the possibility of unthinking and pugnacious responses to racial change.

Because the percentage of Polish-born persons in the population will decrease rapidly in coming years, and because residential mobility will continue to erode the old Polish-occupied neighborhoods, the acuteness of the racial problem with respect to this group is likely to diminish. Since the Poles are a predominantly Roman Catholic group, the gradual but pervasive Catholic moral concern for the elimination of racial inequities will have an effect as the educational level of people of Polish background rises.

The Italians. Of all immigrant groups the Italians are most symbolic for the twentieth century of the great American experience of immigration. Of the major immigration groups, they were the last great wave to arrive from Europe in the tens of thousands. Their arrival was the denouement of the tremendous Atlantic migration. They seemed to enact the drama of building an urban ethnic world in American cities with a zestful enthusiasm. Numerically, the Italian-born are our largest foreign-born group. Their concentrations in the "Little Italys" in the various cities are still very much with us. The Italian neighborhoods are some of our most striking examples of ethnic aggregation today, if we omit Negro neighborhoods from consideration.

The Italian neighborhoods with their accompanying churches, fraternal lodges, Italian food shops and gregarious family life have not been confined to older large-city areas. Many smaller industrial towns in the East, fruit-growing areas on the West Coast and food-processing centers have strong Italian communities. We are most concerned, however, with the Italian-occupied areas adjoining Negro districts. These older neighborhoods usually derived their Italian character from the first waves of immigration from Southern Italy. Beginning in the 1880's and reaching its height in the early years of this century, the tide ebbed after World War I. The exhaustion of the Sicilian sulphur mines, the demise of feudal estates with political change, the great disaster of the blight of the grapevines, and the hope for a better life in America brought tens of thousands of Italians to our urban areas. At times, the immigrants were recruited for American industry by agents in Italy. Employment was found in railroad construction, the garment trades, the building trades and food industries.

With some assurance of steady income the Italian immigrant turned, characteristically, to the domestic world, the family sphere focused on the neighborhood. He found himself in second-rate residential areas or outright slums. The cohesiveness and energy of the Italian families was turned to making the areas tolerable. The immigrant families seemed incurably horticultural. Gardens were ingeniously worked into backyards, onto balconies and rooftops. The houses were colorfully refurbished with a kind of casual Italian grace and flair. It is true that these improvements were often only a cosmetic treatment of basically inadequate neighborhoods, but the neighborhoods became familiar, distinctive and alive. The vitality of the large Italian families was imparted to the neighborhoods in an informal but effective way. The Italian populations found their leaders in civic and political life and developed a morale and a distinct style of life which impregnated the local area.

One striking feature of the Italian residential blocks has been the housing improvements that have taken place under private initiative. The extensive engagement of Italians in building trades meant that the families usually had valuable skills available. The men could cut stone, lay brick and cement and do a great number of things by way of physical improvement of homes and shops. And, significantly, they could do these things themselves well enough to be proud of the results. Owing to the association of Negroes with shabby and deteriorated houses, the financial and emotional investment of the Italian householder was felt to be in jeopardy when Negroes encroached.

Also the Italian neighborhood has been steadily replenished by second- and third-generation offspring. Strong family ties induce a number of the younger families to stay within walking distance of parents and grandparents. The beloved "nona," the winemaking grandfather, the generous uncle or godparent are just too well-accepted and compatible to desert.

Large families in small houses mean that the young will seek the outdoors. In cities this means the street corner or some familiar sandwich shop. In the Italian neighborhoods the "pizza" shops and the soda fountain hangouts are the scenes for second- and third-generation street-corner society. It is in the relations of juvenile groups that antagonism between Negroes and white immigrant groups often flares up. . . . A further complication to the racial issue may be a Latin concept of personal honor which requires an injury to be avenged. This would increase the possibility of hostile exchange.

The Jews. Jewish people are wise in the ways of cities. They have for centuries been an urban people. Time after time they have seen racial antagonism mount in city streets. It is improbable, however, that they have ever encountered on such a large scale the kind of problem presented by the urbanization of the American Negro. The entire social life of the modern city is momentously different from that of the past. In the past, population movement was slow; today there is swift movement resulting in an almost random mixture of people from various backgrounds in metropolitan centers. In this setting the large Jewish populations of the major northern cities are involved in a very distinctive way in the nation's struggle to resolve the "American Dilemma" of race relations.

One of the places in which Negroes confront Jews is the corner store. In many of the great segregated districts the last outposts of white residence are the groceries, small dry-goods stores and pharmacies which are in many cases owned and operated as family businesses by modestly prosperous Jewish people. Because of their economic stake in these small businesses, the owners have frequently been reluctant to leave areas which have changed racially. In segregated neighborhoods where the earning power and standard of living are often depressed, these little stores fit intimately into neighborhood life. They are flexible enough to meet the irregular needs of informal local and family living. In overcrowded Negro districts the street-corner society which affords an outlet to the young centers around such small businesses.

In these circumstances the Jewish storekeeper is often the only white man many Negroes see on a regular basis. He is a person who gives service, but often he is also a family creditor to whom the grocery bill is owed. The amount of anti-Semitism that may grow out of this latter relationship is surprising. As the last white resident on the block in sections where existence is less than genteel, it is understandable that the small shopkeeper should at times feel the pressure of minority-group frustration and counter-prejudice.

A second "sphere of influence" in which Negroes and Jews interact is in those heavily Jewish neighborhoods that have begun to change racially. The sequence of migrations of minority groups through our cities has often placed Negroes next in line to Jews in social status and home-buying ability. Neighborhoods once forbidden to Jews have received substantial influxes of Jewish home owners. Because of geographical convenience or economic accessibility, these same neighborhoods are now attractive to non-white home buyers. The aspiring Negro sees in these areas the same virtues of middle-class respectability that Jewish families, fresh from the immigrant "Jewtowns," saw in them a generation ago. Perhaps there is also some basis for supposing that the "liberal" opinion prominent in big-city Jewish circles and the traditionally non-violent disposition of Jews exert an attraction on Negroes seeking a way out of segregated neighborhoods. . . .

The problem of a synagogue in a racially changing area should also be noted. Unlike many Christian denominations, the Jews do not proselytize. The synagogue congregation can not absorb incoming Negro families the way a correctly oriented Roman Catholic or a Congregational or Methodist Church can, and reduction in the congregation due to the removal of a Jewish family is likely to be permanent. If a sufficient proportion of the congregation migrates, it may be economically mandatory for the temple to follow. This is one reason for the growth of the "echo ghetto" in the suburbs. The old downtown congregation re-forms in the new area.

The third sphere in which Negroes and Jews are particularly linked is not so much physical as it is one of social psychology. The Negro and Jew are both members of a minority group that experienced a sour tolerance or actual ill-treatment on the American scene. This fact has brought forth a sort of kinship or practical affinity between Jews and

Negroes, based on their common concern for fair treatment and democratic rights. Hence Jewish and Negro organizations can usually be found working together for civil rights, fair employment, intergroup understanding and racial integration. Many Jewish groups devote more effort to bettering race relations than to any other object.

Opposite these factors facilitating contact between Negroes and Jews must be ranged certain social characteristics of each group which serve to produce a distressing tension between them. Despite the strong affinity that we have noted, there is a great cultural difference between the Jew and Negro. This is not just a difference between a group long urbanized and one of very recent agrarian background. It is a difference of cultural heritage and experience. Although the Negro folk culture had as a cardinal element a familiarity with and reverence for the Bible, and notably for the prophets and kings of Israel, there is a vast difference between the Jewish view of this heritage and the Negro folk view of it. The complexity of the unique Jewish tradition, heavy with history, stands in strong contrast to the youth and the directness of the American Negro orientation. This contrast is made most vivid when we compare the educational status of the two groups. American Jews have from the time of their immigration achieved an extraordinary educational eminence. In terms of formal schooling, they enjoy a top position among American ethnic groups. Negroes, on the other hand, are still struggling under the educational disabilities inflicted upon them by segregation and exploitation. In education Negroes and Jews are further apart than any of the other groups in the mainstream of American life.

In family life and in the incidence of crime Jew and Negro are also in vivid contrast. The ceremonial of the Jewish home has no parallel in highly variable Negro domestic life. The widely publicized crimes of some Negroes which glare from the pages of metropolitan newspapers have a bewildering effect on many Jewish citizens, who seem unable to comprehend that such things can exist. The American Jew, largely middle-class in thought and demeanor, is out of touch with the world of rejection, privation and violence to which the Negro has been assigned by current social forces.

The American Jew shares actively in the economic abundance that has been the nation's harvest for the last fifteen years. He walks with non-Jews as leader, organization man and laborer in the economic activities of the day. He inhabits suburbia and plays a vigorous role both as producer and consumer. The Negro, by contrast, is just beginning to emerge from an economic limbo. His family income, job status, savings and property ownership are all below the national average for whites, and nobody really knows how much of the recent progress of Negroes in these areas has been achieved at the expense of such sacrifices as the employment of mothers and the postponement of medical and educational needs.

In social organization we perceive once again a great disparity between Jew and Negro. Jews have an enviable apparatus of fraternal, charitable, and civic organizations manned by articulate and effective leaders. Negroes are still suffering from the paucity of leadership that has been a traditional characteristic of depressed ethnic groups arriving on the urban scene. Men like Martin Luther King are exceptional in any group. The ability of a group to train and consistently present skilled leadership is slow-growing. Leadership in effective force does not rise out of a vacuum; it must have preconditions of education, organized tradition, a degree of leisure and concourse with the elites of power and learning.

In addition to these social contrasts between Negro and Jew there is the difference in the commitment each group bears to ideals of community life. Whatever our predictions about the future, we must recognize that at present Negroes do most emphatically exist as a social group. As such, they seem to have largely renounced the ideal of racial solidarity in favor of a rather loosely constructed racial affiliation permitting full integration, when possible, into the general community. In this respect non-whites seem to have a somewhat unreserved commitment to the undifferentiated "liberal" egalitarian community. Jews, on the other hand, have a distinctive ideal of community life with deep religious implications. This historic ideal, which antedates by ages the "open community" concept, is operative today in the voluntary residential clustering around synagogues which produces heavily Jewish neighborhoods in our big cities. These two community ideals, that of the religiously based community and that of the open community based upon secular citizenship, are not mutually exclusive, but they can lead to divergent views on questions of intermarriage, community life and education which are of mutual concern to both Jews and Negroes.

An examination of the relationship between the Negro and the Jew in the light of the social factors mentioned above indicates that there is a considerable social gap between the two groups in spite of the bond of sympathy they share. One of the practical effects of this situation is that Jews are often placed under extreme pressures when they face up to racial issues. Often Jewish people solidly supporting liberal race relations practices and programs feel genuinely repelled by the social differences persisting in the Negro population when racial integration confronts them, and they are brought face to face with the contrasts between the great bulk of the newly urbanized Negro population and their own established middle class. Thus Jews do seem to have a special problem with respect to racial change.

Puerto Ricans. Although Puerto Rican migration to the

mainland has not brought about a great dispersion of Spanish-speaking people generally through the Eastern cities, it has resulted in strong Puerto-Rican concentrations in the old neighborhoods of Philadelphia, Chicago, Bridgeport and, above all, New York. The influx has thus placed the Puerto Ricans in some of the major urban centers which are today vast laboratories of social tension and racial change. Placed beside American Negroes or intermingled with them, the Puerto Ricans have been very confused in their racial attitudes. Their Hispanic background has endowed them with a rather casual attitude toward race. This attitude is subtle. In the mainland cities, the keen consciousness of race among the general population forces Puerto Ricans to question their own tradition in racial matters, and frequently to adopt a more decisive attitude towards racial differences in response to the mainland aberrations. But this is done with much inner confusion.

Racial distinctions in Puerto Rico are mild, but they are there. The Spanish terms of *el blanco* (white), *el indio* (dark skin with straight hair), *el grifo* (white coloring, but with hair or features of a negroid cast), *el bien triguena* (a fairer Negro) and the use of the term *el Negro* as a word of opprobrium reflect the differing values ascribed to racial visibility on the island. Within the Puerto Rican group, however, particularly in Puerto Rico, color is inconsequential in social relations. In families there will sometimes be a subtle feeling of status difference based on color between siblings, but this is seldom serious. On the mainland, this attitude of casual acceptance can suddenly become starkly challenged, and the emotional impact on family life and personal awareness can be tremendous.

The acute in-group feeling and loyalty in the Puerto Rican communities induces the Hispanos to reject the American Negro on double grounds; first as an outsider, and second as a symbol of and a target for racial discrimination with which it would be unwise to be identified. The Spanish-speaking Puerto Rican of dark color is fraternally treated—except, perhaps, on the mainland where there is question of intimate or permanent relationships—but the American Negro is an interloper, a threat, a puzzle. The fact that similar disabilities afflict both groups in many ways only heightens the Puerto Rican's resentment against the American Negro. Thus Puerto Ricans may resent appeals against prejudice and discrimination which link American Negroes and Hispanos.

Puerto Ricans in New York and elsewhere have been harbingers of racial change. In East Harlem, the Bronx and Brooklyn they have preceded Negro entries. Having the Puerto Ricans in the role of precursors has not noticeably slowed the classic white response of withdrawal upon Negro influx. In the mainland cities, the relations between American Negroes and Puerto Ricans have commonly been strained, with juvenile fights the most frequent expression of this antagonism. The tension seems greatest with respect to newly arrived Puerto Ricans. There is some moderation of hostility as the groups reside in the same area over a period of time. Small groups will become friends and establish ties casually in the second or third generation, but the barrier to intimate association will usually remain.

There is the old area competition between the two groups for jobs and housing. The Negro resents the arrival of the Puerto Rican to work for lower pay. Puerto Ricans who open small shops and stores accuse Negroes of being stupid or lazy because they have in the main been slow to build such businesses. Any advances made by Hispanos are subject to criticism by Negroes because the Puerto Rican, not born on the mainland and speaking a foreign language, is successful "at the expense of Negroes."

While Hispanos and Negroes may resent one another, their residential association is constantly enforced. The Puerto Ricans are recently arrived in the cities, and so are many Southern Negroes. Landlords are seldom capable of according the groups separate status, although the language factor may make property rental more difficult for the Hispanos. The distinction and separation is made at the insistence of the Puerto Ricans, who tend to choose dwellings removed from Negro occupancy, so far as this is possible in areas crowded by the adjacent groups.

Perhaps the chief factor separating the two groups, besides the consciousness of color, is a difference in attitudes about sex and the family. At the neighborhood level this is extremely important, for the residential world is a domestic one. The Hispano family is extended, proud, and has a careful code of behavior and relationships prescribed by long tradition. The Negro family is nuclear, weakened by many long-term influences and informal in its relationships. In the Puerto Rican family, the male has high status. In the Negro family, the woman has so often been breadwinner that she is the main figure. Puerto Ricans resent the easy approach to women that mainland Negroes may exhibit. For Puerto Ricans the woman is guarded by a protective supervision of attitudes and customs. Hence there is a subtle strategy of withdrawal among the Spanish-speaking families which evades advances by American Negroes, even though life may be proceeding on a friendly basis. The Negro, who may have encountered promiscuous contacts between Puerto Rican males and American Negro women, sees no reason why the compliment shouldn't be returned by Puerto Rican women, especially since many may be just as dark as he is.

There are other divergences in churches and in recreation. Some commentators state that integration of the mainland Negroes and Puerto Ricans is far away. The two groups will continue to share the worst of the housing supply, with the Puerto Rican frequently unable to escape identification with the Negro, although residential segregation of necessity will operate less precisely in the case of some Spanish-speaking because they are not readily identifiable as colored. The Puerto Rican will continue to be the "alter ego" of the mainland Negro in residential matters.

The Negro neighborhoods adjoining the white minority communities have an ambiguous set of attitudes toward their "distant neighbors." On the one hand, the immigrants are subject to some discrimination, as is the Negro. In some ways relationships may be casual and unprejudiced. Negroes may shop in the curbside Italian markets, or go to school with Puerto Ricans or realize that Jewish organizations are pro-integration. On the other hand, there will be a recognition that the immigrants do constitute a group by themselves, with their own exclusive clubs and programs, and the Negro will know that acquiring a house in the immigrant area will mean trouble.

For the Negro population the significance of the white immigrant as a member of a minority group tends to be obscured by the simple fact that the immigrant is white, thereby sharing the negative characteristics of the stereotyped white person so common in the thinking of Negroes. It is frequently observed by native Negroes, with some bitterness, that they are denied opportunities which the foreign-born can easily obtain. The resettlement of Hungarian refugees after the disorders in that country in 1956 aroused resentment in Negro circles. As they saw it, persons who had made no contribution to this country were fussed over by the government and resettled in good houses in good neighborhoods. Negroes couldn't occupy those same houses without bringing the scorching wrath of their fellow citizens down on their heads.

On succeeding some immigrant population in an area, Negroes often find that the housing is owned by a number of absentee landlords of the previous immigrant group. The Negro families may face rent gouging and other forms of exploitation, and their attitude toward the group represented by the landlords may become hostile. The activities of immigrant savings and loan societies which control property or immigrant fraternal groups who purchase property to keep it out of the hands of Negroes produce the same kind of negative reaction.

The Muslim and Black Nationalist groups which have been widely publicized in recent years are not averse to singling out Jews and other groups for special indictment in race relations. These Negro extremist cults do not represent any large segment of Negro opinion, but their arguments in this matter will usually be listened to with care by a great number of Negroes, who may be familiar with the racial thinking of white ethnic groups.

As the inquirer proceeds to the more educated levels of Negro life, however, he finds that the commitment of Negroes to tolerance and interracial fellowship offsets bad experiences. The informed and intelligent Negro seldom singles out particular white ethnic groups for criticism in racial matters, but tends to argue in terms of the white population as a whole.

Native Whites. Although we have concentrated our attention upon foreign-born groups in this chapter, it should not be inferred that cohesive, native-born neighborhoods are not a frequent source of trouble. The problems arising from neighborhoods with a high percentage of Appalachian mountaineers have been of considerable concern in some cities. Cities with a high home-ownership rate, where neighborhoods are stable and the population relatively settled, produce the phenomenon of entrenched "burghers," with practically no immigrant ties, who yet vigorously oppose racial change. Such areas are not nearly so troublesome as immigrant locales, but they indicate that it is not so much immigrant peculiarities as the fundamental sense of group cohesion which threatens social harmony in racial situations.

The population elements deriving from "the old immigration" of the early nineteenth century have, of course, been deeply enmeshed in the traditions of racial exclusion and restriction. Whatever our estimate of the reactions of new immigrant groups, we must not forget that these groups have been entering into an American stream of social opinion in which racism was a strong current. The upper-class and middle-class neighborhoods of the successful "old immigration" elements were the models for the newer arrivals.

There are forces at work in native-born neighborhoods that on occasion can produce agitated waves of racial feeling, although such areas seldom hold the same violence potential as immigrant communities. The insecurity of the "junior executive" suburb is an example. In a suburb of "organization man" families, the corporations that control the jobs of the breadwinners may transfer a household head to another city on short notice. Hence the home owners are extremely sensitive to anything which would make the selling of their houses more difficult. The presence of Negroes in the area is such a factor. This "junior executive" difficulty was thought to be one of the reasons why the suburban town of Deerfield, Illinois, reacted with hostility to a plan to erect a limited number of attractive homes for interracial occupancy nearby.

Another reaction in native-born "old immigration" areas in recent years has been the product of a decline into minority status on the part of formerly predominant groups. Old-line white Protestant communities in large cities, where the populations are increasingly Catholic and Negro, are beginning to display all the marks of minority psychology. They feel hemmed in, discriminated against, objects of the ill-will of the growing Negro and Catholic elements. Security and self-possessed assurance are beginning to wane under the impact of metropolitan population mobility and changes in the urban power structure. Even though many of the old-line neighborhoods and suburbs are not yet confronted with racial change, they have had to admit Jews, Italians and a variety of other formerly proscribed groups. Having been nudged this far, the old-line residents have begun to fear that the next step, racial change, is inevitable. This is a reaction that is not found among the hardier new immigrants, who are often ready to contest each street in their area.

The shifting population of the urban centers will alter the residential make-up in the central city areas. Only vestiges of the immigrant communities will remain. For some years yet, however, these communities will have a special significance for race relations. In most of the larger cities the municipal intergroup relations agencies have representation from the different ethnic groups on their boards or in staffs. This at least permits some communication with the groups so that when conflict situations or severe tensions arise, there can be consultation and the exertion of accepted leadership to avoid outbreaks or the continuation of hostility. Formal representation of ethnic groups on those civic bodies committed to peace and fair play increases the possibility that mutual respect will be maintained. The leadership of each group is loath to be stigmatized as irresponsible or incendiary in the eyes of the other group. Such a formula for civic peace in the diversified urban community can be effective if it is well administered and serviced with an adequate program of information, conference and involvement of representative opinion leaders. But if the formula is mere window-dressing, a coalition of ethnic leaders for mutual admiration and ego-gratification or for the sake of political display, then the city that permits such a fraud may find its peace broken and its minority group relations poisoned by antagonism.

The day of immigrant neighborhoods may be fading fast, but these areas have had a strategic significance in the last two decades in their effect upon non-white urban movement. They represent a notable interlude in intergroup relations. The lessons we can learn from them should not be readily forgotten.

Class, Race, and Urban Renewal*

Robert C. Weaver

Urban renewal has opened Pandora's Box in several fields. It has occasioned a fresh look at slums; it has given rise to renewed discussion of racial balance in neighborhoods; it has inspired new thought and approaches relative to the racial and class composition of schools in the central city; and of course it has intensified research in the fields of housing, city planning, and municipal government.

Since one of the principal objectives of urban renewal is to attract more middle-class families back into the central city and slow down the exodus of middle-class families from the inlying areas, much of the current discussion about color and class is oriented around these goals. There is, however, a tendency to treat current problems as though they were unique and devoid of historical precedents. Actually, this is not only untrue but dangerously misleading. As Oscar Handlin has most recently pointed out, the flight of older, middle-class families from proximity to the latest newcomers is as old as immigration. What is unique is not the human behavior but the physical limits of the city and the multiplicity of local governments.

Since in many American cities a principal wave of low-income migrants is composed of readily identifiable members of color minorities, there is a tendency to identify the problem as one of race alone. This is inaccurate and unfortunate. Cities which have few non-white migrants are experiencing the same problems—a fact suggesting that this is a class as well as a color phenomenon. Should further proof of this be required, the experiences of Chicago, Cleveland, Detroit, Cincinnati, and a score of other cities with Appalachian Mountain whites will provide convincing documentation.

Identification of the decline of central cities with the encroachment of non-whites (and in a few places Puerto Ricans) upon established middle-class neighborhoods reflects our consciousness of color. It does more. Such superficial analysis weakens our capacity to deal effectively with the problems of our cities. The color and class aspects of these problems are frequently intertwined but neither should be ignored. Any workable program must recognize both and learn to deal with each.

* Robert C. Weaver, "Class, Race and Urban Renewal," *Land Economics*, 36, No. 3 (August 1960), 245–251. Reprinted by permission.
Robert Weaver is Administrator of the Housing and Home Finance Agency.

On the other hand, it would be sheer sophistry to deny that, under existing demographic and ecological changes, long-standing racial attitudes, and the current economic forces which operate in the housing market, the arrival of increasing numbers of non-white families may, and often does, lead to the departure of previous middle-class whites. This long recognized phenomenon has recently been expressed in terms of a "tipping point" theory, which says that there is in any neighborhood a point at which whites will move out when the proportion of non-whites reaches a certain size.

Many factors are involved in the desertion of a neighborhood. First there is the economic climate. In a period of general prosperity transition is accelerated; the same occurs in a loose housing market. The location of the neighborhood involved is important, too. Factors tending to stabilize middle-class occupancy include proximity to, and identification with, institutional facilities, such as in the area around a university or college or around long-established religious facilities.

Access of minority and low-income families to a formerly white middle-class neighborhood is not always a consequence of whites' desertion of an area in the face of the encroachment of new user groups. Often it results from vacancies caused by the movement of earlier residents and failure of other middle-class whites to replace the former occupants. The cause of the desertion of such neighborhoods is usually the attractiveness of other areas: they may be suburban subdivisions or, as in the case of the East Side of Manhattan, a new prestige location in the central city. Once the vacancy rate becomes high, as it did in New York City's West Side, owners and property managers are happy to substitute new user groups rather than suffer greater losses.

The impact of newcomers on the housing market

From early days, middle-class Americans have wanted distance between themselves and the newcomer; that desire has been accentuated by two recent developments—the rise of prestige-laden, single-class, homogeneous suburban areas and the identification of color with a large number of low-income migrants. The recent concern of Americans with the quality of education has, of course, occasioned increasing emphasis upon good schools.

As long as there was ample space within the city limits and no effective modes of rapid transportation, most of the outward movement of middle-class families occurred within the city proper. The streetcar, automobile, and bus changed the situation, opening for housing development large areas of virgin land removed from the central city. The fact that estates of the wealthy were already located on such lands augmented their appeal to medium-income groups intent on upward social mobility. Real estate operators, developers, and land speculators, readily joined the commuting railroad lines in selling the exclusiveness of these developments. This was the stage when the great impetus to Negro migration occurred during World War I. Low-income colored Americans from the South poured into many Northern cities, replacing, as the new source of unskilled and semiskilled labor, the earlier European immigrants who were no longer available during and after the hostilities. Not only were the newcomers mostly poor and ill-prepared for urban life, but they were also dark skinned. As the readily-identified descendants of slaves, they had the least amount of social prestige of any ethnic group. Race and color joined class in rendering them forbidden neighbors.

Middle-class whites, led by the real estate fraternity, frequently resorted to racial housing covenants and zoning to contain non-whites in a restricted area. Low-income whites, only slightly less undesirable in the eyes of the middle-class, sometimes used intimidation, violence, and threats to assert their Americanism. On the part of the former, this was a manifestation of class as well as racial prejudice; on the part of the latter it was primarily racial. Yet lower-class whites and Negroes frequently shared the same residential areas and faced the same disabilities of poor neighborhoods. Class was often more important than color in neighborhoods which failed to offer prestige or adequate protection and public services to any residents, regardless of race. The early governmental policy of segregation in public housing subsequently served to accentuate color consciousness in low-cost housing at the same time that it reflected the strategic role of authority in establishing racial patterns.

World War II brought in a new stream of Negro, Mexican-American, and Puerto Rican migrants to the urban North and West. It also brought greater residential segregation. This too represented, first, resistance to the expansion of land space available to non-whites and, most recently, abandonment of segments of the central cities to them. Several factors played an important part in this. The federal government through the Federal Housing Administration had facilitated phenomenal expansion of suburban construction, and low down-payments and a longer period for mortgages had made a large part of this available to middle- and lower middle-income families. At the same time FHA accepted the concept of homogeneous neighborhoods and until 1947 the instrument of the racial restrictive housing covenants. Higher incomes during the war enabled a vast number of families to accumulate down payments and sustained prosperity facilitated their meeting monthly carrying charges. At the same time government housing policy made home ownership more attractive than rental and practically all new construction was in lily-white suburbs.

Not only was it possible for the upper-middle class to desert the central city but many of lesser means—if they were white—could follow suit. Even the low-income white family could hope for homogeneity—either in the suburbs with a little more money or perhaps in the grey areas of the core city if the expansion of non-whites was contained. Racially homogeneous neighborhoods had achieved a new prestige and this was increasingly apparent in slums and blighted areas where residents sought to emulate dominant racial attitudes.

Rapid movement of whites to the suburbs was but a part of the population trend. For example, over 7,000,000 persons entered the suburbs between 1940 and 1950. While a large volume of long-term residents left the cities, an even larger number of individuals moved from non-urban areas directly to the suburbs. Meanwhile a much smaller number of whites moved into than moved out of central cities while many non-whites entered the in-lying areas. "The process of losing one net migrant to the suburbs actually was the end result of a larger process whereby for each two non-white persons moving into the central city about three white persons moved out."

These movements have brought interesting changes in the housing market. Throughout the North and West, non-whites have acquired a much larger number of housing units and frequently a more diversified and a better quality of housing. In the process they have expanded into many areas which were formerly all white. The Chicago experience of 1940–50 suggests the human components of this development. Those who initiated the movement were long-term rather than newer residents, resulting in no significant changes in socio-economic characteristics; and the first arrivals had had to "pay a premium rental, which they are able to finance only by using residential space very intensively, e.g., by doubling up families in the household or by including relatives or lodgers in the household."

While it is true that only in a quite general sense has succession in Chicago followed a pattern of radial expansion of the Negro community outward from the center of the city, it is significant that:

. . . within both the Negro and the white community, high-status groups tend to share residential areas and to be residentially segregated from low-status groups. Apparently, the selective forces which produce differentiation of residential areas in the urban community operate in somewhat the same way upon the Negro and the white population. This is also in line with the finding that patterns of interarea differentiation with respect to physical characteristics of the area and social and economic characteristics of the residents tend to be maintained under the impact of succession from white to Negro occupancy.*

* Otis Duncan and Beverly Duncan, *The Negro Population of Chicago* (Chicago, Illinois: The University of Chicago Press, 1957), p. 298.

These developments in Chicago, which are fairly typical of larger northern industrial centers, reflect the interaction of many events. Such expansion of housing accommodations for Negroes as took place was facilitated largely by the decline in the white population. It reflected a growing demand for shelter on the part of an expanding non-white population in which a significant number were able to pay higher rents and prices for housing and it enabled some whites to sell profitably and buy new suburban houses. Even where sales were not profitable the availability of Negro purchasers and renters greatly accelerated the liquidation of property in the central city and the acquisition of new homes elsewhere on the part of previous residents in the core areas. To a degree, this greater effective demand for housing on the part of non-whites sustained property values in many parts of the central city and accelerated the purchase of new homes by whites who were replaced by non-whites, many of whom paid higher prices than could otherwise have been secured.

Had there been less racial segregation in the suburbs, a larger number of non-whites would have joined whites in moving from the central cities to the suburbs and going directly to them rather than to the central cities. Even in the face of a most effective color bar, about one-third of a million Negroes did join whites in the 1940–50 trek to the suburbs. Most of those involved were in the South but there was a pronounced desire of Northern middle-class Negroes to escape from central cities, and there are indications that some of the colored migrants to the North avoided the central city and moved directly to older Negro settlements elsewhere. This seems to have occurred in the industrial cities of New Jersey and the larger cities in New York's Westchester County.

One upshot of residential segregation has been to contain most Negro middle-class families in the core cities. Another, and much more serious consequence for the cities has been the concentration of demand for housing on the part of the growing middle-class Negroes on certain city areas. This too has often sustained property values but it has tended to accelerate the exodus of middle-class whites. Were middle-class Negroes able to compete freely in the total market, their volume in most neighborhoods would have been so slight as to have occasioned little concern. There would have been much less premium payment incident to initial non-white occupancy and white owners would have had less economic incentive to forsake attractive neighborhoods and homes. Even the real estate operators would have had slight impetus to engineer flight of middle-class whites since the principal source of effective demand—the middle-class Negro purchaser—would be more discriminating and less available for any one neighborhood.

For the process described above to have taken place, there would have had to have been a much larger volume of low-priced housing available to non-whites in metropolitan areas. Without such a supply the sheer pressure of numbers occasioned the growth of non-white areas of concentration. In some instances this involved expansion of one or several major Negro ghettos, engulfing surrounding housing regardless of its price or suitability. In other instances it involved the development of new pockets of non-white residential concentration. Invariably, it occasioned over-crowding, undesirably high densities, and blight.

However, in a situation where the supply of low-cost housing available to non-whites is limited, the entrance of middle-income, non-white families into a neighborhood and its subsequent desertion by whites has benefited the mass of colored home-seekers. For, had there been less turnover, there would have been less filtration. This, in turn, would have delayed the improvement in the quality of housing occupied by non-whites. In the present situation of enforced residential segregation in many segments of the housing market, rapid racial transition of desirable housing in parts of the central city has made a larger amount of physically good housing available to non-whites. It has also resulted in more intensive and often socially undesirable occupancy patterns in the areas recently accessible to non-whites and it has made it difficult to sustain the middle-class characteristics of the affected areas, even when higher-income non-whites have attempted to do so. Relatively high vacancy rates, as in Philadelphia and Cleveland, have accelerated racial transition in certain neighborhoods with the result of substantial upgrading in the quality of the occupied housing stock and instability in some middle-class housing areas.

Modern cities can absorb a large supply of low-income migrants without subjecting the newcomers to economic exploitation and greatly augmenting slums and blight only by building more low-rent housing on open sites, solving the problem of rehabilitation without excessive costs and providing a free housing market. The central city has a stake in open occupancy throughout the metropolitan area because it is necessary in order that the market may operate most efficiently. Under conditions of open occupancy a much smaller number of areas of middle-class housing need be threatened by inundation by non-whites and it is possible to make the most effective use of the existing supply of housing —particularly the low-rent sector.

Efforts to attract middle-class families to the central city

It is against this background that urban renewal programs' efforts to attract and maintain middle-class families in the central city must operate. Regardless of any social, political, or moral considerations, the economics of the situation require concern for retention of white middle-class families in central cities because their numbers far exceed those among non-whites. In any given locality the problem has three manifestations: creation of new areas in which middle-class families will establish stable communities, rehabilitation or partial renewal of areas which will attract and hold middle-class families, and the arresting or preventing the desertion of middle-class families from existing areas of residence.

In the larger cities of the South new, segregated middle-class Negro communities have been developed. This has been possible for several reasons. In some instances it results from annexation of new areas by the central city after informal agreements have been made concerning the color identification of land. Atlanta is a prime example, New Orleans has had somewhat similar experience. In cities like Charlotte, Greensboro, and Winston-Salem, North Carolina, and Austin, Texas, availability of vacant land contiguous to, or in the path of, existing centers of Negro concentration has afforded sites for new, segregated FHA-insured housing. In Houston, Texas, where availability of good housing has made the owning of attractive homes an important source of status among Negroes, there has been an appreciable amount of new construction and a significant source of excellent middle-class housing in a good neighborhood available to Negroes during the last decade.

Clearly, by creation of new segregated areas in most of these cities and restriction of Negro encroachments upon middle-class white neighborhoods to a few locations in others, the impact of the non-white market has had but limited effect upon the desertion of the central city by middle-class whites. In Houston, where there seems to have been a rather loose housing market, Negro expansion into one good neighborhood served to sustain values and thereby accelerated movement of the older residents to the suburbs. However, some of those who sold to Negroes may have replaced other central city whites moving to the suburbs and thereby supported property values elsewhere in the central city.

In Northern cities the establishment of all-Negro suburbs is usually impossible. This is due to the spatial distribution of non-whites and rejection of segregated patterns by non-whites in the North. The latter fact is, of course, supported by legislation: a score of northern states and cities have non-discrimination housing laws, and racial discrimination in urban renewal areas is banned in several states and many cities. In all of these and other cities, the capacity and willingness of Negroes to pay for better housing in middle-class neighborhoods has increased significantly during the last decade at the same time that the low-income non-white population has grown appreciably. Indeed, the growth of non-white urban populations has been much greater in border and northern cities than in their southern counterparts. Thus the pressure of Negroes for more housing has had greater impact in the North than in the South. Also it has had less outlet via expansion into new, vacant areas. The consequence is that Negroes have expanded to a much greater degree into areas formerly occupied by whites in northern than in southern cities.

Efforts to attract and retain middle-class families in the central urban centers of the North and border states must recognize the pressure for housing occasioned by a growing Negro population. Some of these cities also face the arrival of large numbers of Appalachian Mountain whites, Puerto Ricans, and Mexicans. Since the Negro presents problems of class as well as color, concentration upon his impact is fruitful. . . . Survival of healthy, central cities requires recognition and solution of this problem. First, there needs to be an acceleration of the size of the middle-class among non-whites. Second, this will be achieved in large measure in proportion to the degree that the middle-class Negro is accepted as his immigrant prototype was accepted. Third, unless the achievement of American norms of success on the part of Negroes is rewarded, as it has been among others who started at the bottom of the economic and social scale, there will be a loss of motivation (already apparent among Negroes) with consequences which are inimical to the economic, political, and cultural health of the central city. Fourth, such results would be tragic for the nation—and western democracy—in the world of the cold war and the emergence of Asian and African nationalism.

Northern cities, if they are to maintain a sound economic base, must strive to adjust to continuing in-migration of low-income Negroes, Puerto Ricans, Appalachian whites, and Mexicans. A first step in this direction is to understand the nature of cities and the historical precedents. A second step is to face up to the unique problems of the present migrant groups. These can be summarized in a single statement: All of certain ethnic groups, because of their physical identification, are assumed to be a threat to a middle-class neighborhood, regardless of the individual's or the family's income, education, or behavior. Centuries of slavery, generations of color discrimination, repeated instances of economic disadvantage via perpetuation of a color line, and a liberal amount of guilt have perpetuated color concepts. These are most apparent and effective in situations involving areas of living and schools.

Most liberals and many social scientists advocate heterogeneous neighborhoods. The majority of them would favor a community of homes in which low-, medium-, and upper-income groups lived; as a minimum, they would mix low- and medium-income people. Some have equally strong feelings about racial heterogeneity, affirming that in the modern world it behooves us in the United States to learn and demonstrate how a multi-racial society can live together under democracy. Recently an outstanding land economist has dissented, questioning the innate superiority of multi-income neighborhoods. In this paper no attempt will be made to pass moral, social, or political judgments on this issue;

rather, the problem will be treated from the point of view of the survival of central cities. Our orientation will be primarily economic, recognizing that enforced racial residential segregation is under attack and in the process of change in the nation.

From this point of view, it must be recognized that the middle class in America is keenly conscious of the threat of lower-class encroachments. As was pointed out above this has long been a national characteristic, perhaps an inevitable consequence of a socially mobile people who are status-conscious. During the last quarter of a century, it has become more acute. This leads to the conclusion that many middle-class families will not long voluntarily remain in an area which they believe threatened by lower-class engulfment; few will migrate to such areas. The second fact that has to be recognized is that the white middle class fears neighborhood deterioration on the entry of non-whites—an attitude that has partial roots in the history of decline in city services, lax enforcement of housing codes, and overcrowding in areas inhabited by non-whites. Actually, the degree of this fear is often a function of the speed and intensity of non-white penetration, although it is today an almost immediate reaction upon the first evidence of non-white entry. Most white middle-class families will not long remain in a neighborhood where they are a racial minority. Should they fear this eventuality, they usually act so as to assure its fruition. On the other hand, there are many evidences of whites' accepting a few Negro neighbors, particularly if they are of comparable economic and social status.

The impact of urban renewal

Urban renewal activity concerned with attracting and holding middle-class households in the central city must be geared to creating neighborhoods which offer good schools, a reasonable degree of cleanliness, protection from violence, and physical attractiveness. They need not be single-class neighborhoods, but there is a limit—a class tipping point—to which they can at the present be heterogeneous from a class point of view. Similarly, they can absorb some minority group families of middle-class attributes as well as some of lower-incomes. The class and racial mix will vary from new urban redevelopment sites, partial redevelopment and rehabilitation efforts, and conservation areas. The greatest flexibility is in the newly reconstructed redevelopment areas—if for no other reason because new areas and new houses have a snob appeal in themselves. . . .

With rare exceptions a small island of medium-cost redevelopment housing in a sea of non-white slums will not attract whites. This was the experience of the attractive—but not relatively competitively-priced—Longwood Redevelopment in Cleveland. An exception was the reasonably priced (single-family, sales house) and slow moving redevelopment project in Richmond, California. On the other hand, redevelopment in an area which is fairly large and marked for total treatment can attract middle-class whites when a minority of non-whites are housed in it. This has been demonstrated in architecturally attractive Capitol Park Apartments of the Southwest Redevelopment in Washington, D.C. and in the Gratiot Redevelopment in Detroit. Both of these are fairly high-rent and that fact alone has greatly limited non-white participation.

Partial redevelopment and rehabilitation present more difficult problems. In the first place, frequently the old neighborhood which is the symbol of the threat of lower-class and minority families is not destroyed. Even if a new type of area is planned the physical evidences of the old remain. Where, as in the area around the University of Chicago, there is a sizeable amount of good housing and an enduring institutional base, the possibilities of success are enhanced. The urban renewal plan for the West Side of New York, which also involved spot clearance and a great amount of rehabilitation, is also favorably located. On the north is a large middle-income redevelopment project partially occupied and nearing completion, on the east an attractive predominantly upper middle-class residential strip on Central Park West, on the south a middle-class strip on 86th Street, and on the west a traffic artery.

In the Chicago and New York projects there has been great controversy as to how much public housing will be provided. In both instances the amount has been limited so that low-income families will be a definite minority of those in the areas. New York's West Side will also have a sizeable amount of lower medium-rent facilities or reasonably priced cooperatives, but most of the shelter will be priced so as to attract middle-income households. There is no question that both the New York and the Chicago neighborhoods will be predominantly middle class. Both will have some non-white, low-income families and some non-white, middle-income households. But they will be predominantly middle- and upper-income white communities.

Since conservation areas are subjected to the least amount of physical change, they share characteristics with most of the standard areas of existing housing. While the structures in such areas of the old city may be imposing in size and appearance, frequently they are architecturally obsolete. This may occasion new property uses—rooming houses, conversions to apartments of varying degrees of adequacy, or other forms of multi-family occupancy. Seldom are they suited for small families and their utilization by low-income households usually involves undesirable economic and social consequences.

In some instances the location of conversion areas (in terms of proximity to present concentrations of non-white families) inspires acute fear of minority inundation on the part of present residents. Thus, the possibility of panic selling is real and immediate upon the entrance of non-whites. There is another complicating factor. Present residents of these areas have not elected to live with non-white neighbors. The latter have come in after the neighborhood has been established as a racially homogeneous one. Thus there may be a feeling on the part of old residents that they had lost the opportunity to exercise freedom of choice in selecting non-white neighbors. In this regard they differ from those who move into a new or existing bi-racial community. The physical attributes of conservation areas and the process of change involved in establishing racial mixture complicate the process in such neighborhoods.

Thus conservation areas present perplexing problems to those who would attract and hold middle-class whites in the central city. At the outset it must be recognized that many parts of the core city are destined to be occupied by non-whites. Under present conditions they will provide the almost sole supply of housing for Negroes and other non-whites who seek better shelter and are achieving or have achieved sufficiently high earnings to pay for it. In addition, if the past is any indication of the future, many areas of this type will, should they lie in the path of the geographic expansion of existing racial ghettos, be occupied by house-hungry lower-income non-whites.

The degree to which low-income minority families enter these areas depends upon several things. If there is an alternative supply of good housing which better fits the family needs and pocketbooks of non-whites, the process will be delayed. If housing and occupancy standards are enforced—a thing that is unlikely unless there is an alternative supply—this too will slow up racial displacement. And of course the extent to which the central city becomes more attractive to whites will lessen the availability of such housing to non-whites. At the same time, however, the volume of migration of non-whites to urban centers will be a major factor in determining the demand for housing on their part. Finally, in proportion as we continue to concentrate upon clearing slums inhabited by non-whites the process of racial displacement will take place elsewhere in the city.

In recent years there has been a series of attempts on the part of middle-class neighborhoods to stay the departure of whites with the arrival of colored residents. To date, most if not all of these have been delaying tactics at best. Perhaps if such efforts were a part of an over-all program involving new open-occupancy construction, action for spreading the non-white demand over a larger area of the central city, prevention of the engineering of panic selling by real estate operators, better enforcement of housing and occupancy codes and effective action to open the suburbs to non-whites, such programs might succeed in maintaining the bi-racial character of some well-located and attractive neighborhoods.

The role of good schools

Up to this point little has been said of family composition and its implications for middle-class residence in the central city. Most of the urban renewal projects mentioned are designed for small families and the most successful of them house few young people of school age. A recent analysis of the demand for renewal and redeveloped housing in downtown Philadelphia eliminates families with children as a source of occupants, suggesting that such families would gravitate to "the massive sections of slums and deterioration that lie beyond the central core." There they would look for single-family houses or garden-type apartments.

Obviously, the needs and requirements of upper- and middle-income families without children are quite different from those who have youngsters. For the latter, schools are important. Among those of large incomes (and to some degree among the less prosperous) the possibility of using private schools may cause little concern for public educational facilities. In many northern cities parochial schools serve a similar purpose.

Public schools are a symbol and an instrument of democracy. While their programs can and should be tailored to meet the needs of students, the whole trend in the nation, as dramatized by the Supreme Court decision of May 1954, is away from racial segregation. This of course is not to say that every child receives the same training but it does call for no arbitrary assignment to schools on basis of color or class. It is compatible with an open system which, within a given school, assigns pupils to educational programs which meet their needs, provided that the system is fluid and based upon some universally applied criteria for assignment. The latter must be a reflection of ability and not social status. The track system now in operation in Washington, D.C. is one which seems to meet these requirements.

But there is still another requirement. It is a system which avoids the implications or consequences of separate identification by tracks. This has been accomplished in one school on the West Coast where there are several curricula for students of differing aptitudes. However, all students of a given grade have a common homeroom or common homerooms, regardless of differences in educational programs. Such arrangement is not only productive of identification with a common institution for all but it is also compatible with the concept of a democratic public school.

Just as most middle-class families, if they have an alternative, will not long remain in a neighborhood where they are a minority so they will not long send their children to a school where they are a minority. Middle-class whites with children will remain in the central city in large numbers only if they have access to a middle-class oriented, educationally satisfactory public school or can afford private or parochial schools. The degree of possible class and racial mix in a neighborhood is lessened, therefore, when school-age children are involved. It can be conceived however that as the number of stable bi-racial neighborhoods increases, tolerance for this type of living will grow. In light of the importance of prestige considerations in the selection of housing, it may well be that this process will be accelerated through the creation of attractive, newly constructed, racially mixed neighborhoods in the central city. The efficacy of the latter will be minimized as long as the suburbs remain essentially racially homogeneous.

Public schools in the central city cannot compete with their suburban prototypes on terms of the latter. The city public schools can never match the snob appeal of many suburban ones. Seldom can they assure the same degree of class or racial homogeneity nor can they equal the spaciousness of the surrounding campus. But they can be good schools. Indeed if they are specialized high schools concentrating on specific fields, they can be better schools. This is demonstrated by certain technical schools, fashion schools, and performing arts high schools in New York City. Emphasis must be upon high scholastic standards, adequate discipline in the school, and exploitation of the opportunities for cultural enrichment which urban life offers. While these potentialities will not be given a chance to flower if middle-class white parents feel that low-income and minority group children are to be a large element in the student body, they are possible of achievement in a city school which is not homogeneous. Proof of this is the effort prestige private schools have made for years to attract and enroll children of poorer parents and from non-white households. The administrations and parents of many of these schools lament the fact that such enrollment is not larger.

At the same time the central city public school has a unique character to sell—a degree of class and racial heterogeneity which will teach young people to live with other children of varying backgrounds. Many middle-class families are acutely aware of the importance of this in a democracy; in the world today it has even more pressing international implications. Unfortunately, realization of its desirability is far from accepting situations in which there is heterogeneity. This is due largely to fear that some class and racial mixture will lead to an inevitable lowering of academic and discipline standards and an ultimate minority status for white children in the school. It is also manifestation of apprehension lest there may be loss of social status in living in a predominantly non-white neighborhood or having one's children in a school with large Negro enrollment. If, however, the public school is geared primarily to the educational goals of middle-class families, it can and will attract and hold many middle-class white children even though some lower-income and middle-class minority pupils are included.

Another attraction which the school in the central city can have is to afford a richer and more meaningful education. This suggests delineation and exploitation of the educational advantages of the central city. The many cultural institutions located in the central city—its theatres, museums, concerts, and the like—are great assets. The school program should utilize fully and dramatically these facilities of the central city.

With all of this, there will be fear and apprehension on the part of middle-class parents. Over the long run, this can be met only as the living standards, opportunities, and assimilation of those least advantaged in the city are increased. Here too the public schools have a basic but not an exclusive role. In those areas where the schools serve large numbers of migrant, low-income, and minority families, programs need to be developed to accelerate their adjustment to urban life. Included among these are activities for remedial work, the discovery and nurture of talent, curriculum enrichment, reaching parents and involving them in community problems related to schools, and the preparation of teachers who understand the cultural problems involved.

All of these programs and activities will hold only some of the middle-class families now in the central cities. They will be more effective in attracting back to the city others who are exhausted or disillusioned with suburban life. But unless we begin now to deal with them, the trend of certain groups away from the city will continue—and probably at an accelerated rate. Certainly, in assessing the potential demand for medium-priced housing in the central city, an important variable is the success we have in creating and maintaining public schools which have an appeal to the families involved.

The class and race mix of the city tomorrow

This analysis suggests that in northern and border cities there can be a degree of class and racial mixture compatible with attracting and holding middle-class whites. In the expensive and upper medium-rental apartments and sales houses this presents few problems of planning. The income structure assures only token participation by non-whites and of course eliminates the low-income group. If the desirable mix (from the point of view of maintaining large numbers of medium-income families) involves limited participation of low-income households, this too can be achieved by redeveloping or renewing areas large enough to establish their own identity and limiting the amount of low-cost housing. This however implies the responsibility for providing in attractive locations an adequate supply of low-cost units and cessation of such widespread dislocation of families as has typified urban renewal to date.

It is at the level of medium-cost housing that real problems arise. The non-white and particularly the Negro housing market includes a growing number of families ready, willing, and able to purchase or rent such shelter. If the market is open to them in only a few locations at any one time the "tipping point" may soon be reached in any one or two developments. As was indicated above, opening the suburbs to non-whites is one of the necessary prices for attracting and holding middle-income whites in the central city.

Cessation of widespread dislocation of low-income families was suggested in the earlier discussion of high and upper-medium-cost housing. It was proposed there from the point of view of political expediency and equity. It is pertinent to the discussion of medium-cost housing for another reason. As long as large numbers of low-income families are uprooted by slum clearance they are a potential source for the displacement of middle-income families elsewhere in the community. This is especially true when they are colored and limited to a racially restricted market.

A final approach, applicable chiefly to conservation areas, is to perfect techniques for stabilizing racially transitional neighborhoods. To be effective they must be an element in a comprehensive program for expanding the supply of housing available to non-whites at all price levels. Also, it must be realized that there are some neighborhoods which, because of location in relation to the growth of areas of non-white concentration, will not respond to this treatment. This only illustrates that cities are not static institutions. Their physical facilities change and their people move. The problems of class and color can never be solved in any one neighborhood. Today they cannot be solved in the central city. They are problems of metropolitan areas.

If this analysis is valid, it has significance for the kind of cities we may expect in the next generation. While the size and squalor of slums may be decreased we shall not clear all of them. Poverty, rejection, and a certain amount of individual choice will dictate their perpetuation. Through better schools—in terms of plant, quality of teaching and effective programs to reach low-income families—the economic and social status of many slum residents can be raised. If we perfect and apply techniques to give the newcomers a feeling of belonging and provide meaningful assistance to the normal as opposed to the problem family, there can be greater occupational, educational and residential mobility among this group. For these approaches to work, our urban populations will have to be less color-conscious; and anti-discrimination housing legislation affecting the suburbs as well as central cities will be required. We need also to develop more tolerance to variations from established middle-class values and behavior.

American urban centers will not soon, if ever, become a

total of class and racial heterogeneous neighborhoods. Realistic and courageous planning, constant progress toward open occupancy, continued economic advancement on the part of the disadvantaged, progress in dealing with transitional neighborhoods, an expanding supply of housing suited to the family needs and pocketbooks of low-income and lower medium-income households, good schools, and the development of techniques to upgrade at a reasonable cost much of the existing housing supply will enable our cities to develop and maintain neighborhoods with varying degrees of class and color heterogeneity. But most of these will be predominantly of one income level; some will be almost exclusively nonwhite; a few will have a small number of medium-income non-whites; and others will be integrated in varying degrees.

What of the central cities? They will survive. Indeed, their demise, largely on the same grounds cited as threatening them today, has been foretold many times in the past. Of course, they will be different. For years to come they will have trouble attracting and holding middle-income white families with children. As long as there are private and parochial schools, some such households will remain. To the degree that redevelopment, renewal, and conserved neighborhoods, as well as areas which are left alone, become or continue to be identified as middle class, there will be middle-income whites with children in the central cities. Good public schools and other satisfactory public facilities will augment the number. Almost equally important will be the success we have in utilizing housing codes and other tools to raise the general level of housing, in developing realistic school programs to raise motivation and achievement in all schools, and in applying effective techniques for accelerating the occupational, residential, and social mobility of the growing number of newcomers who are entering and will continue to enter our cities.

9

Social Disorganization in the City

There is some implicit theorizing contained in the title of this chapter, as the perceptive reader has doubtless noted. We have focused on social disorganization because we assume that some generally undesirable results will be produced by the play of social forces between the individual and the city. Without pushing this underlying assumption too far, we are entitled to raise such questions as: To what extent are overcrowding and crime related? To what extent does education enable an individual to escape from the slum? What is the role of the city in producing gangs, and what are the behavior patterns of these gangs? The fascinating interrelationship between geography and sociology is demonstrated by Marshall Clinard in the first selection, which plots deviant behavior in the city by place of residence. Clinard makes use of one of the older and less sophisticated theories of city growth in his analysis of delinquency and crime; but the approach is nonetheless provocative, and it lays the groundwork for the following two selections. In the first of these, Daniel Bell traces the connection between crime and the problems faced by three major immigrant groups in adjusting to their new environment. These newcomers—as foreigners—were immediately faced with problems of language and cultural differences. Moreover, large numbers of the immigrants were peasants, to whom the urban environment was unfamiliar. Bell describes one facet of this adjustment process by contrasting the rise to organized crime of three immigrant groups and the modern trend toward what he calls "the embourgeoisement of crime." By showing the path to the top of the crime heap that was followed in the past and by noting that urban crime is to a large extent being absorbed into the fabric of today's urban society, Bell raises a complex question: What will be the pattern of organized crime during the next decade?

Svend Riemer then examines the slum from the standpoint of the alcoholic, the immigrant, and the poverty-stricken. He reminds us that the slum is a two-way street; by harboring "both those on the way up and those on the way down," it has performed an important social function. There may be those who prefer to live under conditions that spell refuge from the urban pressures to conform. The sexual deviant and the chronic drunk may actually see the slum as the only environment that makes their lives possible—so that, repugnant as the suggestion may seem to the well-intentioned, it may be necessary and desirable to allow a bit of slum in any plans for the city's future. Indeed, many communities have been confronted by this problem in developing their own urban-renewal programs. Often one of the first areas to be cleared and redeveloped is the skid-road section of the city. But then the awkward question arises: Where are we going to put the displaced transient laborer, the drifter, the hard-core down-and-out? Failure to realize that in a certain sense slums play a positive role in the life of the metropolis may mean that slums are never eliminated, merely transplanted.

William F. Whyte offers an absorbing report on the functions and activities of the street-corner gang in the city. Once again, the positive role of the organism, rather than the usual stereotype of the destructive nature of gang life, is emphasized.

A less comfortable view of slum life, and of the relevance of that life for the future of the city, is offered by James B. Conant, who demonstrates the stultifying effect of the slum on white and Negro alike.

Deviant Behavior, Urban-Rural Contrasts*

Marshall B. Clinard

For centuries writers have been concerned about the de-
bauchery and moral conditions of the cities and have generally praised
rural life. Hesiod, for example, wrote about the corrupt justice of the
cities. The Greeks and Romans compared the city with agricultural areas,
noting the greater evils and sources of criminality in the cities. One of
the first systematic comparisons of rural and urban peoples was made by
Ibn Khaldun in the fourteenth century. This famed Arab historian compared life in the city with that among the nomadic tribes. He found that
the nomads had good behavior, whereas evil and corruption were abundant in the city; that honesty and courage were characteristic of the
nomads, whereas lying and cowardice were prevalent in the city; and
that the city caused decay, stultified initiative, and made men depraved
and wicked. In general, rural life has been, and still largely is, a world of
close personal relationships. . . .

Delinquency and crime

The types, incidence, and reactions to rural crime, as with
urban crime, are a function of the type of life and the various norms and
values of the communities. Delinquency and crime rates today are generally much lower in rural areas than in urban. In general, the differences
between rural and urban property crimes are greater than the differences
in crimes against the person.

Some delinquent and criminal acts committed in rural areas
are dealt with informally and not officially reported, and there are undoubtedly more opportunities to commit offenses in urban as compared
with rural areas. The differences between rural and urban rates, however,
are so great that differential reporting or opportunity could, at most, account for only a small part. Also, there is little evidence to support the
theory held by some that the city attracts deviants from rural areas.

As the table shows, burglary rates in the United States, as

---

* Marshall B. Clinard, *Sociology of Deviant Behavior*, rev. ed. (New York: Holt,
Rinehart and Winston, 1963), pp. 78–92. Copyright © 1963, Holt, Rinehart and
Winston, Inc. Reprinted by permission of the publishers.
Marshall B. Clinard is Professor of Sociology at the University of Wisconsin.

RATES PER 100,000 POPULATION FOR CRIMES KNOWN TO
THE POLICE IN RURAL AND URBAN AREAS,
UNITED STATES, 1960

	Rate	
Offense	Urban	Rural
Murder and nonnegligent manslaughter	4.9	6.4
Forcible rape	10.3	6.8
Robbery	70.7	11.9
Aggravated assault	88.7	42.2
Burglary—breaking or entering	568.9	210.9
Larceny—theft ($50 and over)	340.8	102.8
Automobile theft	243.7	42.1

SOURCE: Derived from Federal Bureau of Investigation, *Uniform Crime Reports* (Annual Bulletin, 1960; Washington, D.C.: Government Printing Office, 1960), p. 33. The population figures used were based on the 1960 census. Rates for the above are based on 1960 census data. "Urban areas" include Standard Metropolitan Statistical Areas.

a whole, are generally almost three times as great in urban areas as in rural, larceny is over three times as great, and robbery over six times. The rates for burglaries known to the police per 100,000 population in 1960 were, for example, 568.9 in urban areas and 210.9 in rural areas. Crimes such as murder, which are relatively infrequent as compared with property crimes, are about the same, with a somewhat higher rate in rural areas, where the rate is 6.4 as compared with 4.9 in urban. Rape rates are much higher in urban areas, 10.3 in urban as contrasted with 6.8 in rural.

Specific studies, rather than statistical comparisons, also seem to support the thesis that the urbanization of rural areas and an increase in crime go hand in hand. A study of the southern mountain villages showed that as the hill country was opened to outside contacts criminal activities increased. The most important factor associated with this increase was the growing lack of community identification on the part of individuals as the villages became more urbanized. A study of rural inmates in an Iowa reformatory revealed that characteristics associated with an urban way of life played a significant role in their criminal behavior.

Mental disorders

Most contemporary data on mental disorders, but not all, show that the rates are generally higher in urban than in rural areas. As with crime, many writers feel that the expansion of urbanism is significant in the production of mental illness in our society. One writer has stated that "the data also show that insanity is much more prevalent in urban than in rural areas, a fact of no little significance for the student of rural sociology. . . . there seems to be no doubt of the association between urbanity and insanity." After a study of the prevalence of mental disorder among the urban and rural populations of New York State, Malzberg concluded that the rural regions of the state had less mental disorder than the urban.

In another study, Texas rates for all persons who became psychotic for the first time were found to be two and a half times greater in urban areas than in rural, a difference which was statistically significant. The same differential held for the sexes with an average annual rate per 100,000 for males in urban areas of 76 in contrast with 44 in rural areas; for females an even greater difference—99 as compared with 36. Even the age-specific psychoses rates were consistently higher in urban areas than for the same rural age group. The disparity between rates for rural and urban areas increased with advancing age. Jaco has summarized the results of the Texas study as follows: "In examining the overall results concerning the incidence rates of mental disorders in the rural and urban areas, no significant evidence was found to support the notion that the large rate differentials between urban and rural areas were due to differences in accessibility to psychiatric treatment facilities or to the type of psychiatric facilities available in the two areas."

Not all the evidence supports the conclusion that the incidence of mental illness is much less in rural areas. The differences may actually be smaller than they now appear to be because of the likelihood that rural families may keep mentally disturbed members at home rather than hospitalize them. A study made in Tennessee concluded that mental health in rural areas is not necessarily as good as the smaller number of commitments to mental institutions might indicate, for almost half the psychotic individuals in rural areas were found to be cared for by their families. For this reason it is possible that mental deviants in urban society may be somewhat more socially visible, and that both unofficial and official tolerance of the deviation will be less.

Alcoholism

The chances that rural persons will become chronic alcoholics are less than half as great as those for urban dwellers, according to estimates made by Yale University's Section on Alcohol Studies. In 1940 the rate per 100,000 adult population in areas of less than 2500 population was 474 as compared with 972 in cities of 100,000 population or over. There were 821 male alcoholics for every 100,000 rural males, as compared with 1894 in large cities; the difference between rural and urban women, computed on a standardized population, is somewhat less. The rates of reported deaths from alcoholism per 100,000 adults in 1940 was nearly twice as great in cities of over 100,000 as in rural areas. Urban commitments for alcoholic psychoses are reported to be three and a half times the rate for rural areas.

The principal reasons for this lower rate of alcoholism in rural areas are the social norms and the amount of social control at the personal level over drinking or excessive drinking. Farm people in the United States are much less likely to drink alcoholic beverages than are city dwellers. One half of the rural people are abstainers, but this proportion decreases as the size of the city increases, until in cities with a population of over 500,000 only one fourth do not drink. Both farm rearing and farm residence are associated with lower proportions of heavy drinkers. A recent Iowa study showed that 58 percent of drinkers in the city were either moderate or heavy drinkers as compared with 43 percent of the farm drinkers. Moreover, the extent of drinking increased among the farm-reared who had migrated to the city but this increase was in moderate rather than heavy drinking.

Suicide

On the whole, persons living on farms and villages either in Europe or in America are much less likely to take their lives than persons living in cities. In London the standardized rate, expressed as a percentage of that for the whole of England and Wales, is 115, for the county boroughs 106, for other urban districts 97, and for rural districts 88. In Sweden, Denmark, and Finland wide differences exist between farm and city in the suicide rates, in Finland the urban rate being over twice as high. A detailed study of suicide in France showed that the chances that farm people and persons living in places of less than 2000 population would take their lives were considerably less than for city people. Only in the Irish Free State and the Netherlands have suicides been reported to be greater in rural than in urban areas. This has been partially explained as being due to the large number of old persons in rural areas who, feeling useless from an economic point of view, commit suicide.

The suicide rate in cities of the United States of a population of over 10,000 has generally been almost twice as great as that in smaller cities and rural areas. A student from a small western Kansas town has written of suicides in his community over the past twenty years.

I know of only four suicides in the last twenty years in the town and its agricultural hinterland. Two of these are dramatic memories of my childhood and occurred in 1932. Both suicides were men (one the president of the Citizens State Bank and the other the county treasurer) who had become involved in dishonest financial affairs. The other two suicides were individuals past middle age and without kinship or community ties. One, a man, whose wife had died several years previously and who was without children, had spent his savings in an attempted rejuvenation. The other suicide, a woman, was separated from her husband and son and was shunned by the women of the community because she talked incessantly. One of the local ministers created a sensation in connection with this woman's funeral sermon —he accused the women of the town of murdering the woman who had committed suicide by refusing to associate with her. To my knowledge, no farmers have committed suicide in this area in the last twenty years.*

The differential in rural and urban suicide rates appears to be declining because of the tendency for an urban way of life to characterize rural areas. An analysis of 3081 cases of suicide in Michigan between 1945 and 1949 revealed that rural males exhibited higher suicide rates than urban males. Although "farmers and farm managers" had a high suicide rate in Michigan, the majority of "rural" males who committed suicide were engaged in urban occupations and resided in urbanized fringe areas. It is possible that the high rural rate in this sample was due to two factors: as urban values become more widely disseminated in rural areas they create an intense personal conflict because of the disparity between urban and rural values as they affect behavioral alternatives; and the occupations of rural males who committed suicide are characteristic occupations of urban groups, thus suggesting exposure to conflicting values and norms. Although they lived in the country, these people were oriented to an urban way of life. . . .

According to the most generally accepted theory, the characteristic spatial pattern of cities is a series of concentric circles, with each circle having certain distinctive characteristics moving out from the central business district into increasingly better areas of housing. The ecological pattern of the city in terms of concentric zones leading out from the first circle are Zone I, the central business district; Zone II, an area known variously by a number of names such as the slums, zone in transition, or interstitial area; Zone III, an area of two- and three-family flats or dwellings; Zone IV, an area of single-family dwellings; and Zone V, the suburban or commutation area. These circles can be thought of as undergoing constant movement in the form of expansion outward, much like the movement taking place on the surface of water when a pebble is dropped into it. The central business district is constantly expanding into the slum much as many persons living in each successive zone may eventually move outward to another area.

Although this theory implies equal expansion in all directions, few cities ever completely approximate a series of concentric circles. Rivers, mountains—or a lake, as in the case of Chicago—interfere with this natural growth. Even so, there are some cities, such as Rochester, New York, which closely resemble this pattern. This abstraction of concentric circles is no different from the law of falling bodies wherein the principle of an equal rate of fall between an iron ball and a feather is valid only if both are in a vacuum.

* From an unpublished personal document.

The slum is an area of particular interest to sociologists. It is an area of high land values but cheap rents. This curious contradiction is the result of such land being held "in pawn," so to speak, on the assumption that the central business district will expand into the area and will bring its business firms, manufacturing establishments, and high-priced rental units such as hotels and apartment hotels. The landowners, who seldom live in the area, do not wish to improve slum housing since

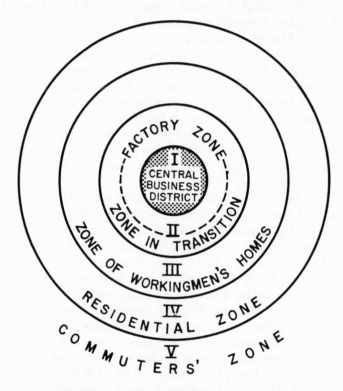

FIGURE 1. THE GROWTH OF A CITY

Source: Adapted from Burgess, "The Growth of a City," in Park and Burgess, *The City*.

it will eventually be torn down. This fact and the rather undesirable location make for cheap rentals. Yet the land remains so high-priced that when an occasional apartment hotel is erected in the area, as in the case of Chicago's Gold Coast, it must be of skyscraper proportions to be profitable. . . .

In each section of the city there are wide variations in age, sex, nationality and racial origins, occupation, social class, homeownership, condition of housing, literacy, and education. Differences in social class are one of the most important characteristics of various areas of a city. The shifting of persons under *ecological* pressures brings about an association of like with like and a tendency for population specialization in certain areas.

The central business district and the "zone in transition" have accentuated urban characteristics. The population of these areas is heterogeneous. The residents are chiefly unskilled workers and their families, and include migrants from rural and other areas, and various nationality and racial groups. People tend to move in and out of the areas with great frequency. For a long period of time prostitutes, vagrants, homeless men, delinquents, and criminals have often been concentrated in these areas. The norms and values of these areas, consequently, do not always agree with those of the more stable areas of the city. The residents of these areas are often more likely than those of other areas to regard delinquency and crime without as much disfavor as other areas of the city and to have different norms about sexual behavior, political honesty, or similar behavior. Considerable differences also exist in other social norms and values of various individuals and groups who live there. Patterns of parent-child relationships of persons residing there and in Zone III may be considerably different from those in the middle-class areas of Zones IV and V.

This does not mean that the slum is "disorganized," for about some norms and values there may be considerable agreement among all groups; moreover, each group may have a high degree of organization of its own. Whyte, in a study of an Italian slum of a large American city, found that both formal and informal groups among the Italians generally had a complex and well-established organization. Nationality and racial groups, however, tend to live in close association with one another even though there may be considerable social isolation from a different group living geographically close. This means in general that few close interpersonal relationships are developed among the diverse groups constituting the population of these areas.

Zone III has a more stable population, more skilled workers, and fewer foreign-born or racial groups. Second-generation immigrant groups moving out of the slum generally move here first. Zones IV and V largely consist of apartment houses, single-family dwellings, and commuters' houses, which means that they are chiefly upper-middle and upper class.

Over a century ago a few studies were made of the distribution of deviant behavior within a city, but most of this type of research began with the stimulation of sociological studies by Park, Burgess, and their students of the Chicago community in the 1920's. The spot-mapping of deviants by place of residence has revealed that, on the whole, certain types of social deviation tend to be concentrated in specific areas. For example, conventional crime, delinquency, mental illness in general and schizophrenia in particular, suicide, prostitution, vagrancy, dependency, illegitimacy, infant mortality, as well as associated problems such as high death and disease rates, have been found to vary with the areas of the city. The highest rates are in Zones I and II, and become successively lower out from this area. The evidence on alcoholism and the manic-depressive psychoses does not show quite this pronounced pattern for, although there are probably higher rates in Zones I and II, the differences are not as marked from one part of the city to another. White-collar crime, on the other hand, is greater in Zones IV and V of the city. Gambling and prostitution are prevalent not only in Zone II but sometimes beyond the suburban fringe of the city.

Delinquent gangs were found by Thrasher to be largely concentrated in the zone of transition. The spot-mapping of some 60,000 cases of delinquency, truancy, and crime by Shaw and McKay showed a close correlation among the rates of all three groups, with wide variation in their distribution among the local communities of the city. The slum area near the centers of commerce and industry had the highest rates, whereas those in outlying residential communities of higher economic status were uniformly low. In a later study of some 25,000 juvenile court delinquents, distributed over thirty-three years, Shaw and McKay reported additional evidence of the consistency of high rates of delinquency in Zone II.

Findings similar to those in Chicago have been reported for eight other large metropolitan cities and eleven other cities, all widely separated geographically, including Boston, Philadelphia, Cleveland, Richmond, Birmingham, Omaha, and Seattle. Higher rates of delinquency were found in the inner zones and lower rates in the outer zones, and in all nineteen cities, except for Boston, Birmingham, and Omaha, the rates also declined regularly from innermost to outermost zones. Even in these cities where rates in the outermost zones were somewhat higher than in the intermediate, as in Boston, the explanation may possibly be the fact that the industrial areas are near the periphery as well as the differences in the policies of the courts in the various areas. A study of Croydon, a large English city near London, revealed that the highest rates for delinquency were concentrated in areas of the city populated by unskilled and semi-skilled workers' families.

The correlation of delinquency rates with economic factors should not be interpreted as indicating any direct relation to poverty or bad housing, as Shaw and McKay have indicated. They point out that in rural areas there may be poverty but little delinquency. Poverty, moreover, does not produce a tradition of delinquency because of a lack of money in itself; rather, it may interfere with the realization of status or prestige. The explanation of delinquency, they believe, is to be found in the general social situations in delinquency areas.

The rate of arrests of adults per 10,000 population seventeen years of age and over was more than ten times as great in the central areas of Chicago as in the outlying areas of the city. The rates for nearly all 29 types of crimes known to the police in Seattle, and arrests for these crimes during the period 1949–1951 showed a decline as one moved out in six one-mile concentric zones from the highest land value in the central business district. There was a tendency for 23 out of the 29 types of crime known to the police to decrease more or less in direct proportion from the center of the city, in particular shoplifting, theft, arson, rape, sodomy, and burglary. Bicycle theft was the only crime known to the police which had a higher rate in Zone VI (149.5) than in Zone I (65.3). The differentials between inner and outer zones were relatively small for Peeping Toms, obscene telephone calls, indecent liberties, and carnal knowledge. Not a single category in the arrest series showed a higher rate in the peripheral zones. Arrest rates for fraud, rape, prostitution, lewdness, robbery, gambling, and common drunkenness showed the greatest difference, while auto theft and indecent exposure showed the least.

White-collar crime, as one might expect, follows a reverse pattern, with concentration in Zones IV and V of the city. In a study of wartime blackmarket offenders in the wholesale meat industry in Detroit, Hartung found that more than 80 percent of them lived in the most desirable areas of the city. . . . Of the ten who lived in the least desirable areas (4 and 5), three lived in good downtown hotels. . . .

The Embourgeoisement of Crime*

Daniel Bell

The Italian community has achieved wealth and political influence much later and in a harder way than previous immigrant groups.

---

* Daniel Bell, "Crime as an American Way of Life," *Antioch Review* 13, No. 2 (Summer 1953), as reprinted in Daniel Bell, *The End of Ideology* (New York: The Free Press, 1962), pp. 141–150. Reprinted by permission.
Daniel Bell is Professor of Sociology at Columbia University.

Early Jewish wealth, that of the German Jews of the late nineteenth century, was made largely in banking and merchandising. To that extent, the dominant group in the Jewish community was outside of, and independent of, the urban political machines. Later Jewish wealth, among the East European immigrants, was built in the garment trades, though with some involvement with the Jewish gangster, who was typically an industrial racketeer (Arnold Rothstein, Lepke and Gurrah, etc.). Among Jewish lawyers, a small minority, such as the "Tammany lawyer" (like the protagonist of Sam Ornitz's *Haunch, Paunch and Jowl*), rose through politics and occasionally touched the fringes of crime. Most of the Jewish lawyers, by and large the communal leaders, climbed rapidly, however, in the opportunities that established and legitimate Jewish wealth provided. Irish immigrant wealth in the northern urban centers, concentrated largely in construction, trucking, and the waterfront, has, to a substantial extent, been wealth accumulated in and through political alliance, e.g., favoritism in city contracts.

Control of the politics of the city thus has been crucial for the continuance of Irish political wealth. This alliance of Irish immigrant wealth and politics has been reciprocal; many noted Irish political figures lent their names as important window-dressing for business corporations (Al Smith, for example, who helped form the U.S. Trucking Corporation, whose executive head for many years was William J. McCormack, the alleged "Mr. Big" of the New York waterfront), while Irish businessmen have lent their wealth to further the careers of Irish politicians. Irish mobsters have rarely achieved status in the Irish community, but have served as integral arms of the politicians, as strong-arm men on election day.

The Italians found the more obvious big-city paths from rags to riches pre-empted. In part this was due to the character of the early Italian immigrant. Most of them were unskilled and from rural stock. Jacob Riis could remark in the nineties, "the Italian comes in at the bottom and stays there." These dispossessed agricultural laborers found jobs as ditch-diggers, on the railroads as section hands, along the docks, in the service occupations, as shoemakers, barbers, garment workers, and stayed there. Many were fleeced by the "padrone" system; a few achieved wealth from truck farming, wine growing, and marketing produce, but this "marginal wealth" was not the source of coherent and stable political power.

Significantly, although the number of Italians in the United States is about a third as high as the number of Irish, and of the thirty million Catholic communicants in the United States, about half are of Irish descent and a sixth of Italian, there is not one Italian bishop among the hundred Catholic bishops in this country or one Italian archbishop among the 21 archbishops. The Irish have a virtual monopoly. This is a factor related to the politics of the American church; but the condition also is possible because there is not significant or sufficient wealth among Italian Americans to force some parity.

The children of the immigrants, the second and third generation, became wise in the ways of the urban slums. Excluded from the political ladder—in the early thirties there were almost no Italians on the city payroll in top jobs, nor in books of the period can one find discussion of Italian political leaders—and finding few open routes to wealth, some turned to illicit ways. In the children's court statistics of the 1930's, the largest group of delinquents were the Italian; nor were there any Italian communal or social agencies to cope with these problems. Yet it was, oddly enough, the quondam racketeer, seeking to become respectable, who provided one of the major supports for the drive to win a political voice for Italians in the power structure of the urban political machines.

This rise of the Italian political bloc was connected, at least in the major northern urban centers, with another important development which tended to make the traditional relation between the politician and the protected or tolerated illicit operator more close than it had been in the past. This is the fact that the urban political machines had to evolve new forms of fund-raising, since the big business contributions, which once went heavily into municipal politics, now—with the shift in the locus of power—go largely into national affairs. (The ensuing corruption in national politics, as recent Congressional investigations show, is no petty matter; the scruples of businessmen do not seem much superior to those of the gamblers.) One way that urban political machines raised their money resembled that of the large corporations which are no longer dependent on Wall Street: by self-financing—that is, by "taxing" the large number of municipal employees who bargain collectively with City Hall for their wage increases. So the firemen's union contributed money to O'Dwyer's campaign.

A second method was taxing the gamblers. The classic example, as *Life* reported, was Jersey City, where a top lieutenant of the Hague machine spent his full time screening applicants for unofficial bookmaking licenses. If found acceptable, the applicant was given a "location," usually the house or store of a loyal precinct worker, who kicked into the machine treasury a high proportion of the large rent exacted. The one thousand bookies and their one thousand landlords in Jersey City formed the hard core of the political machine that sweated and bled to get out the votes for Hague. . . .

There is little question that men of Italian origin appeared in most of the leading roles in the high drama of gambling and mobs, just as twenty years ago the children of East European Jews were the most prominent figures in organized crime, and before that individuals of Irish descent were similarly prominent. To some extent statistical accident and the tendency of newspapers to emphasize the few sensational figures gives a greater illusion about the domination of illicit activities by a single ethnic group than all the facts warrant. In many cities, particularly in the South and on the West Coast, the mob and gambling fraternity consisted of many other groups, and often, predominantly, of native white Protestants. Yet it is clear that in the major northern urban centers there was a distinct ethnic sequence in the modes of obtaining illicit wealth and that, uniquely in the case of the recent Italian elements, the former bootleggers and gamblers provided considerable leverage for the growth of political influence as well. A substantial number of Italian judges sitting on the bench in New York today are indebted in one fashion or another to Costello; so too are many Italian district leaders—as well as some Jewish and Irish politicians. And the motive in establishing Italian political prestige in New York was generous rather than scheming for personal advantage. For Costello it was largely a case of ethnic pride. As in earlier American eras, organized illegality became a stepladder of social ascent.

To the world at large, the news and pictures of Frank Sinatra, for example, mingling with former Italian mobsters could come somewhat as a shock. Yet to Sinatra, and to many Italians, these were men who had grown up in their neighborhoods and who were, in some instances, by-words in the community for their helpfulness and their charities. The early Italian gangsters were hoodlums—rough, unlettered, and young (Al Capone was only twenty-nine at the height of his power). Those who survived learned to adapt. By now they are men of middle age or older. They learned to dress conservatively. Their homes are in respectable suburbs. They sent their children to good schools and sought to avoid publicity.* Costello even went to a psychiatrist in his efforts to overcome a painful feeling of inferiority in the world of manners.

As happens with all "new" money in American society, the rough and ready contractors, the construction people, trucking entrepreneurs, as well as racketeers, polished up their manners and sought recognition and respectability in their own ethnic as well as in the general community. The "shanty" Irish became the "lace curtain" Irish, and then moved out for wider recognition. Sometimes acceptance came first in established "American" society, and this was a certificate for later recognition by the ethnic community, a process well illustrated by the belated acceptance in established Negro society of such figures as Sugar Ray Robinson and Joe Louis, as well as leading popular entertainers.

Yet, after all, the foundation of many a distinguished older

---

* Except at times by being overly neighborly, like Tony Accardo, who, at Yuletide 1949, in his elegant River Forest home, decorated a 40-foot tree on his lawn and beneath it set a wooden Santa and reindeer, while around the yard, on tracks, electrically operated skating figures zipped merrily around while a loudspeaker poured out Christmas carols. The next Christmas, the Accardo lawn was darkened; Tony was on the lam from Kefauver.

American fortune was laid by sharp practices and morally reprehensible methods. The pioneers of American capitalism were not graduated from Harvard's School of Business Administration. The early settlers and founding fathers, as well as those who "won the West" and built up cattle, mining, and other fortunes, often did so by shady speculations and a not inconsiderable amount of violence. They ignored, circumvented, or stretched the law when it stood in the way of America's destiny and their own—or were themselves the law when it served their purposes. This has not prevented them and their descendants from feeling proper moral outrage when, under the changed circumstances of the crowded urban environments, latecomers pursued equally ruthless tactics.

Ironically, the social development which made possible the rise to political influence sounds, too, the knell of the rough Italian gangster. For it is the growing number of Italians with professional training and legitimate business success that both prompts and permits the Italian group to wield increasing political influence; and increasingly it is the professionals and businessmen who provide models for Italian youth today, models that hardly existed twenty years ago. Ironically, the headlines and exposés of "crime" of the Italian "gangsters" came years after the fact. Many of the top "crime" figures had long ago forsworn violence, and even their income, in large part, was derived from legitimate investments (real estate in the case of Costello, motor haulage and auto dealer franchises in the case of Adonis) or from such quasi-legitimate but socially respectable sources as gambling casinos. Hence society's "retribution" in the jail sentences for Costello and Adonis was little more than a trumped-up morality that disguised a social hypocrisy.

Apart from these considerations, what of the larger context of crime and the American way of life? The passing of the Fair Deal signalizes, oddly, the passing of an older pattern of illicit activities. The gambling fever of the past decade and a half was part of the flush and exuberance of rising incomes, and was characteristic largely of new upper-middle-class rich having a first fling at conspicuous consumption. These upper-middle-class rich, a significant new stratum in American life (not rich in the nineteenth-century sense of enormous wealth, but largely middle-sized businessmen and entrepreneurs of the service and luxury trades—the "tertiary economy" in Colin Clark's phrase—who by the tax laws have achieved sizable incomes often much higher than the managers of the super-giant corporations), were the chief patrons of the munificent gambling casinos. During the war decade when travel was difficult, gambling and the lush resorts provided important outlets for this social class. Now they are settling down, learning about Europe and culture. The petty gambling, the betting and bingo which relieve the tedium of small-town life, or the expectation among the urban slum dwellers of winning a sizable sum by a "lucky number" or a "lucky horse," goes on. To quote Bernard Baruch: "You can't stop people from gambling on horses. And why should you prohibit a man from backing his own judgment? It's another form of personal initiative." But the lush profits are passing from gambling as the costs of co-ordination rise. And in the future it is likely that gambling, like prostitution, winning tacit acceptance as a necessary fact, will continue on a decentralized, small entrepreneur basis.

But passing, too, is a political pattern, the system of political "bosses" which in its reciprocal relation provided "protection" for, and was fed revenue from, crime. The collapse of the "boss" system was a product of the Roosevelt era. Twenty years ago Jim Farley's task was simple; he had to work only on some key state bosses. Now there is no longer such an animal. New Jersey Democracy was once ruled by Frank Hague; now there are five or six men, each "top dog" for the moment, in his part of the state or faction of the party. Within the urban centers, the old Irish-dominated political machines in New York, Boston, Newark, and Chicago have fallen apart. The decentralization of the metropolitan centers, the growth of suburbs and satellite towns, the breakup of the old ecological patterns of slum and transient belts, the rise of functional groups, the increasing middle-class character of American life, all contribute to this decline.

With the rationalization and absorption of some illicit activities into the structure of the economy, the passing of an older generation that had established a hegemony over crime, the general rise of minority groups to social position, and the breakup of the urban boss system, the pattern of crime we have discussed is passing as well. Crime, of course, remains as long as passion and the desire for gain remain. But the kind of big, organized city crime, as we have known it for the past seventy-five years, was based on more than these universal motives. It was based on certain characteristics of the American economy, American ethnic groups, and American politics. The changes in all these areas mean that, in the form we have known it, it too will change.

The Slum and Its People*

Svend Riemer

The urban slum has always been a two-way station of social transition. It has harbored both those on the way up and those on the way down. The slum has furnished temporary shelter for new arrivals to the city. It also has received those members of the urban community who have lost their economic and social foothold in more elevated strata of urban society. The two-fold character of the slum's social function has not always been recognized.

In the early days of modern city growth, the slum environment was dominated by the task of providing a domicile for newcomers to the city. The slum provided cheap housing for single men and impecunious families. Such housing was often considered mere temporary shelter, to be abandoned for better quarters in the course of time and with the achievement of moderate financial success.

This function of the modern city slum was retained throughout the 19th century, through the recurrent arrival of immigrants in the urban settlements of this country. Temporarily, the slum became the seat of entire immigrant communities, as described by Upton Sinclair in "The Jungle," and analyzed by W. I. Thomas and Florian Znaniecki in their study of *The Polish Peasant in Europe and America.*

The slum quarters of these immigrants were intended for temporary occupancy only. Slum residence was a matter of emergency, not choice. During their first years in this country, many of the immigrants hoped to return to their place of origin after having accumulated some cash money. For many, these intentions were later changed, but even so, slum residence was never accepted as a permanent condition. If the immigrants changed their intention of returning home, they changed it toward advancement in the American way of life. They left the slum and settled elsewhere in the city.

If the immigrants left the slum before they were quite adjusted to the American way of life, they moved out in clusters, establishing elsewhere in the urban fabric secondary ethnic settlements on an economically and socially more advanced level. After complete assimilation, they lost themselves individually, spreading out over the entire city ac-

* Svend Riemer, *The Modern City* (Englewood Cliffs, N.J.: Prentice-Hall, Inc., 1952), pp. 139–150. Reprinted by permission.
Svend Riemer is Professor of Sociology at the University of California, Los Angeles.

cording to income, social and occupational affiliation, and individual preferences.

With the cessation of large scale immigration to this country in 1924, the second social function of the slum environment gained in relative importance. The German Club, the Polish Mission House, and the Swedish Station of the Salvation Army may still stand as reminders of a different past. Yet, with few exceptions such as those of the Puerto Rican immigration to New York City, the modern city slum has changed both face and function. It is not primarily a way station to success anymore. It has more and more become a receptacle for the driftwood of urban failure. . . .

The slum is an environment of contrast. It shelters populations in the process of either upward or downward mobility with regard to economic success and social advancement. The slum shelters the very cohesive ethnic group as well as highly individualized populations. Side by side, we encounter immigrants bound together by deep-seated loyalties, dedicated to the preservation of shared values and closely connected by friendship ties and mutual help, and also the human flotsam that wants to be left alone for various reasons.

In this urban slum, the deviants of our culture congregate. Deviant behavior is not necessarily inferior behavior. The anonymity of the slum environment is sought by the artist as well as the criminal, by the young writer as well as the sex pervert. In one respect, these different types of people find themselves in the same situation. They all try to escape from convention and from the control of environments where the individual is the concern of any neighbor who might want to pass judgment.

The refuge of urban anonymity in the slums is offered to all comers. They do come from the farm and the small town as well as from other parts of the metropolitan community. We stand without knowledge with regard to the background composition of these groups. There might be more young people from small towns in the artist colonies of our large cities than people with a metropolitan background. Many talented young people from the small towns are channelled through Greenwich Village in New York City before they are able to establish themselves professionally in the big city. Many of these artists and professionals remain in this location, once established. The "Village," partly because of its tourist appeal, has become the site of luxurious apartment buildings and expensive renovations, and deteriorated slum sections remain only at the edges. This bohemian part of the urban slum fills a nationwide function.

Anonymity is not always sought for constructive purposes. More conspicuous are the shady activities that cause one to seek cover in an environment where nobody cares what the next fellow does, where the entire neighborhood can be relied upon not to "squeal" to the police.

Apart from the so-called "bohemian" group, the criminal and the vice addicts are slum dwellers intent upon profiting from the shelter of anonymity.

The criminal may be either one who stayed in the slum, or one who found his way to the protective slum environment. There can be no doubt that the slum environment is crimogenic. On the other hand, it would be wrong to blame the slum alone for all the criminals who congregate within its confines.

Traditions of criminal behavior are certainly carried in the slum environment and handed down from generation to generation. The first American-born generation of immigrant stock is particularly tempted by the glamor and the rewards of crime. Their loyalties are divided and, obviously, confused. Temptation is bound to be challenging where prestige—otherwise missing—is easily gained within a value system that makes the most daring delinquent or criminal the idol of his associates. . . .

The clustering of deviant behavior is a truly metropolitan phenomenon. It is to some extent a question of numbers. There are enough deviants in the large city to make it possible for groups of them to congregate, to provide each other with sympathy in the isolation of illicit activities and to help each other and to instruct each other in the skillful pursuit of their vice.

The Street-Corner Gang*

William Foote Whyte

The corner-gang structure arises out of the habitual association of the members over a long period of time. The nuclei of most gangs can be traced back to early boyhood, when living close together provided the first opportunities for social contacts. School years modified the original pattern somewhat, but I know of no corner gangs which arose through classroom or school-playground association. The gangs

* Reprinted from *Street Corner Society* by William Foote Whyte (Chicago: The University of Chicago Press, 1943), pp. 255–263, by permission of The University of Chicago Press. Copyright 1943 by The University of Chicago.

William F. Whyte is Professor of Sociology at the New York State School for Industrial and Labor Relations, Cornell University.

grew up on the corner and remained there with remarkable persistence from early boyhood until the members reached their late twenties or early thirties. In the course of years some groups were broken up by the movement of families away from Cornerville, and the remaining members merged with gangs on near-by corners; but frequently movement out of the district does not take the corner boy away from his corner. On any evening on almost any corner one finds corner boys who have come in from other parts of the city or from suburbs to be with their old friends. The residence of the corner boy may also change within the district, but nearly always he retains his allegiance to his original corner.

Home plays a very small role in the group activities of the corner boy. Except when he eats, sleeps, or is sick, he is rarely at home, and his friends always go to his corner first when they want to find him. Even the corner boy's name indicates the dominant importance of the gang in his activities. It is possible to associate with a group of men for months and never discover the family names of more than a few of them. Most are known by nicknames attached to them by the group. Furthermore, it is easy to overlook the distinction between married and single men. The married man regularly sets aside one evening a week to take out his wife. There are other occasions when they go out together and entertain together, and some corner boys devote more attention to their wives than others, but, married or single, the corner boy can be found on his corner almost every night of the week.

His social activities away from the corner are organized with similar regularity. Many corner gangs set aside the same night each week for some special activity, such as bowling. With the Nortons this habit was so strong that it persisted for some of the members long after the original group had broken up.

Most groups have a regular evening meeting-place aside from the corner. Nearly every night at about the same time the gang gathers for "coffee-and" in its favorite cafeteria or for beer in the corner tavern. When some other activity occupies the evening, the boys meet at the cafeteria or tavern before returning to the corner or going home. Positions at the tables are fixed by custom. Night after night each group gathers around the same tables. The right to these positions is recognized by other Cornerville groups. When strangers are found at the accustomed places, the necessity of finding other chairs is a matter of some annoyance, especially if no near-by location is available. However, most groups gather after nine in the evening when few are present except the regular customers who are familiar with the established procedure.

The life of the corner boy proceeds along regular and narrowly circumscribed channels. As Doc said to me:

> Fellows around here don't know what to do except within a radius of about three hundred yards. That's the truth, Bill. They come home from

work, hang on the corner, go up to eat, back on the corner, up a show, and they come back to hang on the corner. If they're not on the corner, it's likely the boys there will know where you can find them. Most of them stick to one corner. It's only rarely that a fellow will change his corner.

The stable composition of the group and the lack of social assurance on the part of its members contribute toward producing a very high rate of social interaction within the group. The group structure is a product of these interactions.

Out of such interaction there arises a system of mutual obligations which is fundamental to group cohesion. If the men are to carry on their activities as a unit, there are many occasions when they must do favors for one another. The code of the corner boy requires him to help his friends when he can and to refrain from doing anything to harm them. When life in the group runs smoothly, the obligations binding members to one another are not explicitly recognized. Once Doc asked me to do something for him, and I said that he had done so much for me that I welcomed the chance to reciprocate. He objected: "I don't want it that way. I want you to do this for me because you're my friend. That's all."

It is only when the relationship breaks down that the underlying obligations are brought to light. While Alec and Frank were friends, I never heard either one of them discuss the services he was performing for the other, but when they had a falling-out over the group activities with the Aphrodite Club, each man complained to Doc that the other was not acting as he should in view of the services that had been done him. In other words, actions which were performed explicitly for the sake of friendship were revealed as being part of a system of mutual obligations.

Not all the corner boys live up to their obligations equally well, and this factor partly accounts for the differentiation in status among them. The man with a low status may violate his obligations without much change in his position. His fellows know that he has failed to discharge certain obligations in the past, and his position reflects his past performances. On the other hand, the leader is depended upon by all the members to meet his personal obligations. He cannot fail to do so without causing confusion and endangering his position.

The relationship of status to the system of mutual obligations is most clearly revealed when one observes the use of money. During the time that I knew a corner gang called the Millers, Sam Franco, the leader, was out of work except for an occasional odd job; yet, whenever he had a little money, he spent it on Joe and Chichi, his closest friends, who were next to him in the structure of the group. When Joe or Chichi had money, which was less frequent, they reciprocated. Sam frequently paid for two members who stood close to the bottom of his group and occasionally for others. The two men who held positions immediately below Joe and Chichi were considered very well off according to Cornerville standards. Sam said that he occasionally borrowed money from them, but never more than fifty cents at a time. Such loans he repaid at the earliest possible moment. There were four other members with lower positions in the group, who nearly always had more money than Sam. He did not recall ever having borrowed from them. He said that the only time he had obtained a substantial sum from anyone around his corner was when he borrowed eleven dollars from a friend who was the *leader* of another corner gang.

The situation was the same among the Nortons. Doc did not hesitate to accept money from Danny, but he avoided taking any from the followers.

The leader spends more money on his followers than they on him. The farther down in the structure one looks, the fewer are the financial relations which tend to obligate the leader to a follower. This does not mean that the leader has more money than others or even that he necessarily spends more—though he must always be a free spender. It means that the financial relations must be explained in social terms. Unconsciously, and in some cases consciously, the leader refrains from putting himself under obligations to those with low status in the group.

The leader is the focal point for the organization of his group. In his absence, the members of the gang are divided into a number of small groups. There is no common activity or general conversation. When the leader appears, the situation changes strikingly. The small units form into one large group. The conversation becomes general, and unified action frequently follows. The leader becomes the central point in the discussion. A follower starts to say something, pauses when he notices that the leader is not listening, and begins again when he has the leader's attention. When the leader leaves the group, unity gives way to the divisions that existed before his appearance.

The members do not feel that the gang is really gathered until the leader appears. They recognize an obligation to wait for him before beginning any group activity, and when he is present they expect him to make their decisions. One night when the Nortons had a bowling match, Long John had no money to put up as his side bet, and he agreed that Chick Morelli should bowl in his place. After the match Danny said to Doc, "You should never have put Chick in there."

Doc replied with some annoyance, "Listen, Danny, you yourself suggested that Chick should bowl instead of Long John."

Danny said, "I know, but you shouldn't have let it go."

The leader is the man who acts when the situation requires action. He is more resourceful than his followers. Past events have shown that his ideas were right. In this sense "right" simply means satisfactory to the members. He is the most independent in judgment. While his followers are undecided as to a course of action or upon the character of a newcomer, the leader makes up his mind.

When he gives his word to one of his boys, he keeps it. The followers look to him for advice and encouragement, and he receives more of their confidences than any other man. Consequently, he knows more about what is going on in the group than anyone else. Whenever there is a quarrel among the boys, he hears of it almost as soon as it happens. Each party to the quarrel may appeal to him to work out a solution; and, even when the men do not want to compose their differences, each one takes his side of the story to the leader at the first opportunity. A man's standing depends partly upon the leader's belief that he has been conducting himself properly.

The leader is respected for his fair-mindedness. Whereas there may be hard feelings among some of the followers, the leader cannot bear a grudge against any man in the group. He has close friends (men who stand next to him in position), and he is indifferent to some of the members; but, if he is to retain his reputation for impartiality, he cannot allow personal animus to override his judgment.

The leader need not be the best baseball player, bowler, or fighter, but he must have some skill in whatever pursuits are of particular interest to the group. It is natural for him to promote activities in which he excels and to discourage those in which he is not skillful; and, in so far as he is thus able to influence the group, his competent performance is a natural consequence of his position. At the same time his performance supports his position.

The leader is better known and more respected outside his group than are any of his followers. His capacity for social movement is greater. One of the most important functions he performs is that of relating his group to other groups in the district. Whether the relationship is one of conflict, competition, or cooperation, he is expected to represent the interests of his fellows. The politician and the racketeer must deal with the leader in order to win the support of his followers. The leader's reputation outside the group tends to support his standing within the group, and his position in the group supports his reputation among outsiders. . . .

The actions of the leader can be characterized in terms of the origination of action in pair and set events. A pair event is one which takes place between two people. A set event is one in which one man originates action for two or more others. The leader frequently originates action for the group without waiting for the suggestions of his followers. A follower may originate action for the leader in a pair event, but he does not originate action for the leader and other followers at the same time—that is, he does not originate action in a set event which includes the leader. Of course, when the leader is not present, parts of the group are mobilized when men lower in the structure originate action in set events. It is through observation of such set events when the top men are not present that it is possible to determine the relative positions of the men who are neither leaders nor lieutenants.

Each member of the corner gang has his own position in the gang structure. Although the positions may remain unchanged over long periods of time, they should not be conceived in static terms. To have a position means that the individual has a customary way of interacting with other members of the group. When the pattern of interactions changes, the positions change. The positions of the members are interdependent, and one position cannot change without causing some adjustments in the other positions. Since the group is organized around the men with the top positions, some of the men with low standing may change positions or drop out without upsetting the balance of the group. For example, when Lou Danaro and Fred Mackey stopped participating in the activities of the Nortons, those activities continued to be organized in much the same manner as before, but when Doc and Danny dropped out, the Nortons disintegrated, and the patterns of interaction had to be reorganized along different lines.

One may generalize upon these processes in terms of group equilibrium. The group may be said to be in equilibrium when the interactions of its members fall into the customary pattern through which group activities are and have been organized. The pattern of interactions may undergo certain modifications without upsetting the group equilibrium, but abrupt and drastic changes destroy the equilibrium. . . .

Slum Schools*

James B. Conant

In considering the relative abilities of whites and Negroes, let us examine the situation in an *all-white* slum in a city of considerable

* Reprinted with permission of McGraw-Hill Book Co., Inc., from *Slums and Suburbs* by James Bryant Conant (New York: McGraw-Hill Book Co., Inc., 1961), pp. 15–23. Copyright © 1961 by James Bryant Conant.
James B. Conant is a member of the Educational Policies Commission and a former president of Harvard University.

size. Perhaps the greatest handicap to good school work is the high mobility of the population in the neighborhood. It is not uncommon in such a school to have a turnover of the entire enrollment in one school year. A careful study of a group of children in grade 4 of one such school showed that their average achievement level was a full year below their grade placement—a typical situation in any slum area.

What the teachers in this school have to contend with is shown by a report from the principal, who writes:

"When a residential area composed of large, old homes formerly occupied by owners and single family groups changes economically and socially, conditions of general deterioration begin. Absentee owners rent the property by single rooms or small so-called apartments of two or three rooms to large families. . . . Such conditions attract transients (who either cannot or will not qualify for supervised low income housing), the unemployed, the unskilled and unschooled, and the distressed families whose breadwinners have either just been committed to prisons or mental institutions or who have but recently been released from such. The only possession most of these families have is children. . . . In such an environment all forms of evil flourish—the peddling of dope, drunkenness, disease, accidents, truancies, physical, mental and moral handicaps, sex perversions involving children. . . .

"The parents of at least one-third of the children are either in penal institutions, are on probation, or have prison records. At least 100 children are on probation to the Juvenile Court. There has not been a day since I've been at the school that there has not been one or more children in detention at the Juvenile Court. . . .

"Unless a school is able to educate its children so they may become competent and responsible citizens its work is a temporary stopgap that relieves immediate suffering only. Although the school is the only organization that has instruction as its primary responsibility, when a noble hearted teacher faces a barefoot, hungry, sick, distressed child, the result is an endless chain of efforts to relieve such a child.

"We realize that little or nothing can be done for or with the parents of the children who face such serious problems in their homes. These problems directly affect the child's health, attendance, emotional and personal adjustment, his learning and his progress (or lack of it) in every respect. In all probability at least one-half of our children will be school dropouts. In our opinion the children need, desperately, for desirable development, in addition to good schools—good homes, churches and communities."

I am quoting from an official report which, in acknowledging the generally low achievement of the white children in this school, makes the interesting statement that "There is no reason to believe that these students as a group are inherently or genetically less capable than average students, but apparently because of some types of experiences in their lives they have been unable to develop their intellectual skills." The belief expressed in the first part of this sentence can hardly be based on anything firmer than an assumption as to the genetic uniformity of white children whose ancestors have for several generations lived in the United States. Such an assumption, of course, leaves out of account the possibility of a selective process occurring over the generations as some tended to move to one type of occupation and settle in one type of community. However, since I see no way of investigating the role of selective migration, I would be inclined to let the assumption stand unchallenged. *Only I would argue strongly that to date we have no evidence to indicate that the assumption should not be broadened to include both white and Negro students.* For all the contrary evidence, namely the poor work in school and low scores on tests made by Negroes, is based to a large degree on the performance of children in what are essentially slum conditions.

In short, until we have a great deal more data about test scores and school records, especially with respect to large numbers of Negro children from stable high-income communities, I for one would reserve judgment as to the answer to the question whether there is a correlation between race and scholastic aptitude. And until the evidence is available, I suggest the only assumption to use as a working hypothesis is that there is *no* genetic or inherent difference as far as aptitude for schoolwork is concerned between large numbers of Negroes in the United States and large numbers of other children.

With this background sketched in, I can now take up the educational problems in the Negro slums of certain of our largest cities. I wish that I could do more than take them up. What I should like to do is to create in the reader's mind a feeling of anxiety and concern. For without being an alarmist, I must say that when one considers the total situation that has been developing in the Negro city slums since World War II, one has reason to worry about the future. The building up of a mass of unemployed and frustrated Negro youth in congested areas of a city is a social phenomenon that may be compared to the piling up of inflammable material in an empty building in a city block. Potentialities for trouble—indeed possibilities of disaster—are surely there.

Let me describe a slum that might be in any one of several of the large cities I have visited. The inhabitants are all Negroes and with few exceptions have entered the city from a state in the deep South anytime within the last month to the last three years. Often the composition of a school grade in such an area will alter so rapidly that a teacher will find at the end of a school year that she is teaching but few pupils who started with her in the fall. I recall the principal of one school stating that a teacher absent more than one week will have difficulty recognizing her class when she returns. This comes about because mothers move with their offspring from one rented room to another from month to month and in so doing often go from one elementary school district to another; I am told that resident tenements look more like transient hotels. I write "mothers" advisedly, since in one neighborhood, by no means the worst I have seen, a questionnaire sent out by the school authorities indicated that about a third of the pupils came from family units (one hesitates to use the word "home") which had no father, stepfather, or male guardian. This particular section was by no means homogeneous, of course. For while many moved about from room to room, a quarter of the parents reported that they owned their homes. Only 10 per cent of the parents had graduated from high school and only 33 per cent had completed the elementary school. Contrast the situation in which a third of the parents have completed elementary school with that in a high-income suburb where as many as 90 per cent of the parents have bachelor's degrees, if not graduate degrees from a university.

These Negro slums seem to vary considerably with respect to the social mores. In some there are very bad gangs with gang warfare among the boys. There are also vicious fights outside of school between Negro girls. The condition in one such neighborhood was summed up to one of my staff by a principal of a junior high school who said even he was shocked by the answers to a questionnaire to the girls which asked what was their biggest problem. The majority replied to the effect that their biggest problem was getting from the street into their apartment without being molested in the hallway of the tenement. He went on to say that the area had a set of social customs of its own. The women, on the whole, work and earn fairly good wages, but the male Negro often earns less than the woman and would rather not work at all than to be in this situation. As a consequence, the streets are full of unemployed men who hang around and prey on the girls. The women are the centers of the family and as a rule are extremely loyal to the children. The men, on the other hand, are floaters, and many children have no idea who their father is. Similar reports from principals and teachers can be heard by the attentive and sympathetic visitor to the Negro slums of any one of several cities. Racial discrimination on the part of employers and labor unions is certainly one factor which leads to the existence of so many male Negro floaters. What is terrifying is that the number of male *youth* in this category is increasing almost daily.

I have so far referred only to white and Negro slums. A few words are necessary to point out that in some cities, New York in particular, there are slum areas inhabited by recent arrivals from Puerto Rico. In these sections, the problems are similar to those I have been describing but complicated by the difference in language. Unlike the American Negro from the South, these recent arrivals bring with them a set of social mores closely associated with their own methods of communication. At the same time, they often, if not always, come with children whose schooling has been bad. Clearly the task of educating these Puerto Rican children involves both a reading and a foreign language problem. These problems are so special I shall not attempt to discuss them here. One hardly needs to point out that their existence adds one more complication to the tasks confronting the administrators and teachers in the New York City schools. Add to these problems the possibilities of interracial hostility and gang warfare between Negroes and Puerto Ricans and the resentment of both toward the whites, and one has a veritable witches' brew which comes to boil with unsavory violence in certain schools in certain areas—particularly in the junior high school years. The amazing feature of the whole situation is that pupils make any progress in schools in some areas of the city.

One needs only to visit such a school to be convinced that the nature of the community largely determines what goes on in the school. Therefore to attempt to divorce the school from the community is to engage in unrealistic thinking, which might lead to policies that could wreak havoc with the school and the lives of children. The community and the school are inseparable. For example, I have walked through school corridors in slum areas and, looking into classrooms, have seen children asleep with their heads on their hands. Is this situation the result of poor teachers without either disciplinary control or teaching ability? No, the children asleep at their desks have been up all night with no place to sleep or else have been subject to incredibly violent family fights and horrors through the night. Checking into one case, a principal told one of my staff that after climbing six flights of a tenement he found the boy's home—one filthy room with a bed, a light bulb, and a sink. In the room lived the boy's mother and her four children. I might add that it is not unusual for teachers in these schools to take home with them children with no place to go at night. The social attitudes found in this kind of slum neighborhood are bound to affect the atmosphere of the school. As one Negro teacher said to me, "We do quite well with these children in the lower grades. Each of us is, for the few hours of the school day, an acceptable substitute for the mother. But when they reach about 10, 11, or 12 years of age, we lose them. At that time the 'street' takes over. In terms of schoolwork, progress ceases; indeed many pupils begin to go backward in their studies!"

I ask the readers of this volume, many of whom live in wealthy suburbs, to ponder the contrast between the lives and the education of their children and the lives and education of the boys and girls in the neighborhoods I have been describing. It is after visits to schools like these that I grow impatient with both critics and defenders of public education who ignore the realities of school situations to engage in fruitless debate about educational philosophy, purposes, and the like. These situations call for action, not hair-splitting arguments.

Those who are deeply concerned with the education of the children in these slum areas are not waiting for others to change the social setting in which the schools operate. They are tackling the problem of getting the boys and girls from the poorest families to learn to read and write and do arithmetic. Foreign languages in grade 7 or algebra in grade 8 (recommendations in my junior high school report) have little place in a school in which half the pupils in that grade read at the fourth grade level or below. Homework has little relevance in a situation where home is a filthy, noisy tenement. Discipline, of course, is a problem. Many educators would doubtless be shocked by the practice of on-the-spot demotion of one full academic year, with no questions asked, for all participants in fights. In one junior high school I know of, a very able principal found so intolerable a situation that he established that very rule. As a consequence, there are fewer fights in his school among the boys, many of whom at one time or another have been in trouble with the police. In this school and in many others like it one finds the boys wearing ties and jackets to school, if not their one Sunday suit. When spoken to in the classroom, they rise to recite. Passing time between classes may be as short as one minute in order to preserve order in the halls. The school attempts to bring some kind of order to otherwise chaotic lives. And what is important, this formal atmosphere, at least in one school I know of, appears to work. School spirit has developed, and efforts are now being made to enlist the interest of the parents in the education of their children, who must stay in school till they are sixteen and whom the school will try to keep in school till graduation to prevent unemployed, out-of-school youth from roaming the streets.

In contrast to what one hears about "blackboard jungles," I think I am fairly safe in saying that the outward manifestations of discipline, order, and formal dress are found to a greater degree in the well-run slum schools of a city than they are in the wealthier sections of the same city. The contrast is especially noticeable between city slum schools and wealthy suburban schools, where informality in dress, deportment, and classroom procedure is the rule. I doubt that many suburban parents would stand for the regimentation and formal discipline meted out in many slum schools. It is not accidental that that part of the progressive movement in education which rebelled against formalism and authoritarianism found root in the suburban and private schools.

I should like to record at this point my impression of what my colleagues and I have seen in slum sections of big cities. Almost without exception we have seen white and Negro teachers and administrators struggling tenaciously and bravely against the adverse influences of the home and the street. As one of my associates who had spent the best years of his life as a principal of a suburban public high school put it, "I visited junior high schools in New York City in some of the worst areas. I expected to find blackboard jungles; instead I found schools with high morale, tight discipline, imaginative principals and teachers. My visits to New York City junior high schools," he went on to say, "have provided some of the most interesting and exciting experiences I have had. In bad neighborhoods with children from hopeless backgrounds these schools are really doing a magnificent job." My own visits were largely confined to similar schools in Chicago, Detroit, and St. Louis, and my admiration for what is being done in those cities is equal to that of my colleague for what he saw in New York City.

part four

Governing the Metropolis

The social changes and economic upheavals involved in the process of urbanization
ultimately find their expression in politics.
The methods by which people deal in an organized manner with the problems of urban
life result in a politics of urbanization, just as
the methods by which people select a chief
executive result in a politics of the presidency.
The politics of the presidency we have had
with us for a long time; the politics of urbanization are only now being hammered out.
The process is unlike anything seen before on
the American scene; for the scale of the en-
deavor is larger, and the pace of the shift to
urbanization gives the process an immediacy
sharper and more penetrating than earlier social changes. Nineteenth-century America had
the Civil War as its most piercing experience.
The urbanization of the United States, while
less bloody, is no less violent and far reaching
in its impact on people and institutions.

10

Government, Jurisdictions, and Finance

The shape of the new politics of urbanization will be determined by the interplay between the already existing political mechanisms and the kinds of problems to be solved. Where the traditional tools fail, new ones will have to be devised, even though they may conflict with other sectors of the already existing political establishment. Basically, the question seems to be: Will urbanization strengthen the power and responsibilities of the central government; will it produce a sort of regionalism of political power alignments, based on regional trade flows and other economic forces; or will it lead to revitalization of local government?

What are some practical methods that might be useful in dealing with the new metropolis? After setting the stage, Luther Gulick proposes four innovations in government. Essentially, Gulick's proposals represent a mid-point between the federal solution and the regional solution. He rejects the *ad hoc* device of turning to existing agencies; at the same time, he wants to preserve some flavor of localism in the new approach so as to assure preservation of the democratic processes. He is thus reluctant to abandon the state as the governmental unit with primary responsibility for handling urban problems. His four suggestions therefore, lean heavily on the state as the prime mover in metropolitan affairs. Does this

266

approach fit Jean Gottmann's theory that twentieth-century urbanization is a new problem requiring new approaches, or is it mere tinkering with the existing political mechanism?

If something like Gulick's metropolitan council were to be established, what kinds of problems would have to be faced? There has not been much direct experience with metropolitan government in America. Florida's experiment with this approach in Dade County has been beset with organizational problems, which have obscured some more fundamental issues. The situation is different in Canada, where metropolitan government has existed in Toronto since 1953. Webb Fiser describes this experience and, although he does not ignore the difficulties involved, concludes on a hopeful note: "For most of our smaller metropolitan areas the goal of county reorganization would seem to be an adequate solution and a natural development of our historic institutions and values."

Another approach to the task of devising methods for dealing with urban problems was given new life in 1962 by the President's proposal to establish a cabinet-level post for urban affairs. Actually, the idea of such a cabinet post was not new. In 1937, the National Resources Committee had urged such a step, after a long period of formal and informal support. But in 1962 the debate over the suggestion became sharper and more extended, primarily because for the first time the White House was strongly and publicly committed to the measure. The failure to set up the cabinet post in 1962 does not mean that the advocates of high-level authority for the purpose of centralizing planning and policy for urban problems will cease their lobbying. Pressure for some sort of organizational recognition of urban problems at the federal level will undoubtedly continue until such recognition is formally given. The arguments pro and con are typified by Senator Clark's statement in support of the bill to establish the cabinet post and by the response contained in the minority report of the Senate Committee on Government Operations.

Clark advocates the cabinet-level post on four grounds: It will provide proper status for consideration of urban affairs—status already granted to the farmers of America, who now constitute less than 25 per cent of the population of our Nation; it will increase the attention given to urban problems; it will provide coordination for action; and it will channel research. The minority report of the Senate Committee on Government Operations is in the standard tradition of resistance to expansion of the powers of the federal government and of reliance on action by local government.

The next two selections represent an attempt to peer into the future. Two widely differing views are presented here. Frank Zeidler advances the view that 1977 will see weaker state legislatures than exist today and that the pressures generated by the continued trend toward urban living will also produce or intensify certain group conflicts, such as that between labor and management, between the police and organized criminal elements, between minority groups and whites, and between gangs of youths led by demagogues and the more genteel members of the community. Countering Zeidler's gloomy view, Wallace Sayre describes some elements of strength in our traditional political mechanisms.

Those concerned with metropolitan financial problems often find themselves pulled in two directions at once. There is the citizen who wants better roads, more schools, increased police and fire protection, and generally high levels of municipal services. On the other hand, there is the taxpayer who objects to higher rates. Since the individual who wants more services is often the same person whose taxes provide the necessary funds, the pull of demand is the push toward higher taxes. And since the property tax, as of 1960, was the source of about 45 per cent of all state and local tax revenues in the United States, a major part of the discussion of metropolitan finance centers on the property tax as a revenue source and on the possibility of substituting other revenue-gathering devices for it. Another part of the discussion focuses on the spending side—i.e., on the extent to which expenditures for municipal services can be cut down, postponed, or eliminated.

But there are more complex issues to be faced. The revenue-gathering machinery of the local jurisdictions, which is relied upon in metropolitan finance, is a jungle inhabited by a complex variety of taxes and tax-collecting agencies. Lyle Fitch sketches the characteristics of the major taxes and draws an important distinction between taxes that are unrelated to the benefits resulting from their imposition and taxes that, like prices, do bear a direct relationship to the services provided. The property tax is merely one of a number of tools which can be used to generate revenues. The pertinent question for the harassed administrator and for the beleaguered citizen is: To what extent can changes in the tax structures provide relief for property owners and at the same time assure the provision of the services desired by the community? The answer, Fitch seems to indicate, lies not merely in juggling the makeup of the revenue sources but also in some fundamental governmental reorganization procedures, perhaps along the lines of those discussed by Gulick and Fiser.

It is fitting that the discussion of finance close with a description of the property tax as it is administered in California, which has been experiencing the growing pains of urbanization at a uniquely rapid rate since World War II. There are a number of views of the function of the property tax. Fundamentally, of course, it is regarded as a revenue-raising device. But some would wield the property tax as an instrument of social policy as well. Procter Thomson restricts himself to a penetrating examination of the administration and effectiveness of the property tax; he does not comment on the use of this fiscal device as a means of accomplishing desired social goals. Purely as a means of taxation, he finds the property tax inequitable, inefficient, and inflexible. This selection really functions as an irritant; for Thomson, in demolishing the property tax and in describing the overlapping governmental units, presents no solution, although his analysis clearly leads back to the reorganization proposals made in the earlier selections.

Innovative Techniques in Government*
Luther Gulick

A striking characteristic of the new metropolitan pattern of settlement in the United States is its amorphous structure, dynamism and unprecedented scale. The metropolitanized sections of the country now contain well over 60 per cent of the total population, while single "clusters" have three million, five million, or as many as 23 million human beings. In geographic extent the individual complexes run to as much as 18 thousand square miles.

The scale of what exists and is coming on top is so colossal that we are carried into a new dimension, a new world.

There are three aspects of scale and growth which must concern us as we think about the organization of government in the metropolitan regions. These are the management problems, the cost problems, and the problems of democracy. . . .

Every metropolitan area in the United States has many governments and much governmental activity. Many of the activities are federal, still more are state, and both operate through their several independent departments. In addition there are the activities of the cities, counties, "authorities," villages, towns, school, and other districts.

Even with all these governments severally at work, with the added influence of countless voluntary agencies, and with many intergovernmental arrangements and contracts, there are a number of clearly unmet requirements in most areas.

* Luther Gulick, "Metropolitan Organization," *The Annals of the American Academy of Political and Social Science*, 314 (November 1957), 57–65.
Luther Gulick is at the Institute of Public Administration, Columbia University.

The unmet needs give a clue to what is required. They differ from place to place. In some areas the work which falls between the many jurisdictions is water supply; in others it may be waste disposal, pollution control, education or housing, health, crime or flood and fire protection. Generally, there is an imbalance of local financial resources with resulting luxury for some and tax deficiencies for others. But everywhere there is chaos as to the major circulation system and pattern including highways, railroads, air facilities, mass transportation, and provision for traffic.

It is now evident that there are inherent reasons why such problems cannot be handled effectively by bits and pieces, each in the hands of independent jurisdictions.

And when it comes to zoning, land use regulation, and the system for circulation and traffic, the underlying problems become impossible of rational attack unless there is a single center for co-ordinated analysis, planning, and action. It is inherently impossible to "solve the traffic problem" within boundaries which are less than those of the normal area of circulation, that is, the entire metropolitan area; nor by separate and competing jurisdictions; nor by ignoring the fact that land uses and the transportation system and pattern are two sides of the same coin.

This statement does not prove that there must be "a single metropolitan government." It suggests, rather, that there must be several new area-wide governmental activities.

Some of these might be assigned to the federal government. The minimum civilized standards might be set and enforced by various federal and state departments. The states might be required to take over the broader metropolitan regional land use controls and to develop and enforce the general pattern of the highway system, controlling federal and state highway funds to this end. Tax difficulties and imbalances may be dealt with through state aid and various equalization formulas. And where some special service is required, like a single great sewage treatment plant or an interjurisdictional bridge or transit system, an "authority" may be set up with its own sources of support from charges or tolls.

Thus it may be possible to design governmental machinery to deal with each and every present need of the metropolitan regions without setting up any specific "metropolitan government." This *ad hoc* approach with a separate metropolitan agency of some sort for each metropolitan job is possible.

What does such an *ad hoc* approach lack? It lacks two very important elements:

First, the *ad hoc* approach lacks comprehensiveness. If we rely on existing state and federal departments each to take care of one or more of the area-wide needs of the metropolitan regions or set up special new agencies or authorities each to perform a specific service, it is evident that this arrangement cannot give a comprehensive or integrated treatment of the several metropolitan needs. Nor would fiscal resources be inter-related or pooled. There would be no possibility of over-all planning, integration, or mutual adjustment and compromise. Each activity would go it alone, and there would be nobody to hold things in balance or to tackle a new development not originally provided for.

Second, the *ad hoc* approach makes self-government by the people of the metropolitan area as concerns their own metropolitan prob-lems impossible as a practical matter. The state and federal agencies are democratically but distantly responsible to their larger electorates, not specifically to the metropolitan area. In fact, metropolitan areas are mark-edly underrepresented in most state legislatures and in the national politi-cal structure. The *ad hoc* agencies and authorities are legally parts of the state government, though in fact floating around in a sort of irresponsible political limbo. Even if such *ad hoc* agencies were made responsible en-tirely to local electorates, they would confront the electorates competi-tively with unresolved problems of balance and priorities in a form with which large-scale constituencies cannot deal directly.

These two inescapable deficiencies of the *ad hoc* approach, both of which are greatly accentuated by scale, lead one to explore the possibility of designing one or more governmental "models" planned to give the metropolitan area a government which is comprehensive as to area-wide matters and gives the region at the same time a large measure of local democratic self-government. . . .

Approaching our problem from this point, it will be found that there are situations, as noted above, in which we can turn to the federal government, to the states, to the counties, and to existing *ad hoc* agencies or to interjurisdictional contracts to handle the activities now called for.

Where none of these devices is available or adequate to meet the requirements we have laid down above, we shall need entirely new political invention.

With this in mind, four such "inventions" are here sketched, with no claim that they are original with the author. These are:

1. The creation of a state department of local affairs with an independent bureau or "desk" for each major metropolitan area within the state.

2. The reconstruction of the county so that the county may become the metropolitan government of its region.

3. The creation of a new limited purpose metropolitan service agency with a built-in power to expand as to functions, finance, and representation.

4. The creation of a new layer of local government above

the existing localities and below the state to be known as the metropolitan council of XYZ, having the authority and financial power to deal with broad but specified metropolitan activities. . . .

The proposed state department of local affairs would take over responsibility for handling all general relations of the state with county, city, village, town, and special district governments, and with their officials. The new department would collect local statistics, especially financial statistics, make administrative surveys and financial audits, offer "efficiency" advice and assistance, and would carry on extensive officer training and in-service-training programs for local elective and appointed personnel. The department would work directly with existing associations of local officials, participate in conferences, and defend the interests of the local governments as a group before the legislature and with all administrative departments.

Such a state department would not take the place of the state department of education in dealing with the local schools nor of the health department, the welfare department, the highway department, the state planning department, the tax department, or any other functional department in its specialized and professional functions. But the state department of local affairs would be concerned with the general impact of these specialized departments on local governments as such.

Under this concept, it would be desirable to set up in the proposed department a separate "desk" for each major metropolitan area of the state and to appoint to this desk a man of broad experience and competence. He would not only "clear" all state activities concerning their combined impact on "his metropolitan area" but would work directly with the local governments of his area. On occasions he would call their officials together for conference in order to develop the maximum co-operation and participation in the local solution of metropolitan problems and the fullest possible reflection of local needs and desires in all state decisions.

Co-operation in planning, the establishment of standards, and the development of services and compacts across state lines concerning metropolitan problems would be a responsibility of the "desk" and the department.

Under this plan, it would be most helpful if the local governments would set up voluntary regional councils like that developed in the New York tri-state region some years ago under the chairmanship of Mayor Robert F. Wagner.

The metropolitan county

A second possible approach is the complete reconstruction of the county government in densely populated regions so that it may add to its existing functions and become "the metropolitan government" of its area. Where the county already has an adequate geographical extent and a reasonable level of political responsibility and administrative competence, this might well meet the eight requirements stated above.

The major disadvantage of using the county as the foundation for metropolitan government is that the county is generally imbedded constitutionally in the state administrative, representational, and political structure. Its boundaries are most inflexible and its operation can be raised in managerial competence only with the greatest effort.

Wherever the county is used as the metropolitan government, issues of political representation arise as in the case of the new Dade County charter (Miami, Florida). Such a county falls into the same category as the great metropolitan city, or the city-county, in terms of political representation. The governing body must, preferably, be so designed as to represent the voters directly either by election at large, by districts, or by some combination of these methods. The size of the county council must be articulated to the form of county government. If a county manager is used, the council would be small and representative. If the county mayor is elected and assisted by an appointive chief administrative officer, then the council can be designed more freely in regard to size and methods of election. However structured in detail, the design of such a federated county council should be based on the representative system already tested in our great cities and city-counties and tailored to the political needs of the specific area.

The open-ended metropolitan commission

A third possible approach is the creation of a limited-purpose special "authority," service unit or commission designed to cover a large metropolitan area and to perform from the beginning some needed service, such as water supply or airport construction and operation, with the authority to add to its functions and powers by local action.

The recently enacted law in the State of Washington, the Metropolitan Council Act, is along this line although its possible added functions are rather narrowly limited. Presumably these could be extended by the state legislature in future years if occasion warrants.

Where this approach is adopted, it would seem important to establish something more than a small board of directors appointed by the governor, as is so often the case. If the board is to make extensive policy decisions as to planning, land use controls, and the general pattern of the transportation system, it is not likely that a small specifically chosen board can be effective.

A new metropolitan council

A fourth approach is the creation of an entirely new layer of local self-government, what we may call a metropolitan council.

This would be, first of all, a legislative body. It would be designed to bring together officially and regularly all of the major local governmental interests and problems of the metropolitan area so that the regional governmental shortfalls may be fully considered; remedial and developmental programs may be evolved with adequate planning; compromises arrived at, and decisions made and carried out.

These are primarily "policy" assignments; they are the stuff of politics.

We know from much experience that such functions cannot appropriately be left to experts or bureaucrats working alone. This kind of work calls for politically sensitive and responsible "representatives."

We know also that the real essence of the problem is the laying of the political foundation for the development of the metropolitan community as a political reality with rising political leadership, political education, and political following. This alone will make possible effective and balanced political action and community commitment for the metropolitan area as a whole.

Because of scale, we must have representative institutions, and for these to work we must have political leadership and political action. It is to this end that we need a political entity coextensive with the area and consequently a metropolitan political constituency.

Furthermore, we know that it is generally safer to build political institutions on what we already have, rather than to wipe the slate clean and start all over again.

From these considerations it follows that the membership of the metropolitan council should be made up initially from the chief elected officials of the local governments of the region which is being brought together. This would include, in most situations, the mayors of the larger cities and incorporated units and the chief elected official of each county comprised in the "metropolitan area." It might be desirable to add to this group a number of specifically elected representatives and a president of the metropolitan council to be elected at large, although these developments might well be postponed until the region is ripe for this type of leadership and direct representation.

The metropolitan council would establish a strong and well-staffed program development and planning unit, placing this directly under its chairman or president. The council would set up several special working committees for which the program and planning unit would furnish an appropriate staff.

The metropolitan council would do its administrative work, such as building a bridge or a water works or running a sewage treatment plant or a transit system, by using existing regional and local operating agencies as far as possible. Where no agency exists which can handle the operation, the council would by ordinance create such an administration. This could be done by setting up "an authority" or by creating an operating department under a manager to be appointed by the council president. Where one or more authorities or special district bodies exist already within the boundaries of the metropolitan council, these could be continued as they are, bringing certain of their powers under the supervision of the council.

Especially important is the definition of the responsibility of the metropolitan council. The effort would be made to assign to the council the over-all, inter-unit metropolitan matters and activities and to guarantee to the existing and underlying governmental units the responsibility to carry on their normal nonmetropolitan local activities. This can only be approached through trial and error: With a general statement of this principle, the listing of the arrangements with reference to a number of the more obvious services where the division of work is required, and by authorizing the localities which so desire to protect their unique advantages and to have local services of a higher standard than those of their neighbors.

While many of the metropolitan services and facilities developed by the metropolitan council will be "self-supporting" on the basis of prices and tolls collected, the council should not be required to rely solely on such receipts.

As to metropolitan areas which extend across state lines, as is already true of more than a score of such metropolises, the metropolitan council would be set up by joint action of the states involved, presumably utilizing the interstate compact procedure. In such cases the original compact should provide for territorial extension and for functional and fiscal modifications without requiring congressional reconsideration. As to modifications which do not change the arrangement fundamentally, it would be desirable for the contracting states to leave these to the area concerned, rather than to require the state legislatures to review the arrangement again.

Each such interstate metropolitan compact will have to be tailormade, primarily because of the required fiscal provisions. The present local government provisions, court decisions, and tax and debt systems are so diverse among neighboring states, that a great deal of constitutional ingenuity will be required to develop workable arrangements in all cases. It may even be necessary to consider the in-state members of an interstate metropolitan council as a separate "municipal corporation" with the right to act concerning matters within its state along lines agreed on jointly in the metropolitan council.

Character of the council

The metropolitan council as thus conceived is, first, an old-fashioned American "body of overseers" with authority limited to the over-all interests, concerns, and problems of the defined metropolitan region. It is democratically constituted from locally elected officials, with the eventual addition of directly elected members. As such it is also a federation of the existing local governments. The council is initially primarily a policy-developing and -adopting body; that is, a legislative agency. However, the council is given the authority, as are local legislatures generally, to develop such administrative units as may be required, using existing agencies as far as this is possible, or to create new units where necessary.

Under this proposal, the existing local governments—the cities, counties, towns, villages, and special districts—could be continued as they now are in relation to their local functions. Only the metropolitan aspects of functions would come under the oversight of the metropolitan council. At the same time, the existing local jurisdictions would be authorized to shift to the council by mutual consent any activities which they wish to handle in this way.

This proposal is not only elastic in its boundaries since it is not tied by definition to a specific set of existing city or county boundaries, but is extensible across state lines, following precedents already well established in many jurisdictions for more limited activities.

Under this proposal, finally, there is brought into legal and political existence what is now evolving naturally as a matter of social and economic life; namely, the metropolitan community. With a representative council, this emergent community is given political being. The metropolitan area becomes a single constituency for metropolitan representation, for metropolitan policy discussion, for metropolitan administration, and above all, for metropolitan political leadership and political action. While this in no way supersedes existing governmental organizations, it fills the vacuum and makes it possible for the rising metropolis to deal effectively and democratically with its now unmet metropolitan needs.

The Lesson of Toronto*

Webb S. Fiser

The act of the provincial legislature of Ontario in 1953 establishing the Municipality of Metropolitan Toronto raised hopes on the American side of the border that something might be done about reorganizing our own metropolitan areas. The critical role played by the province in achieving the federation suggests that we must be careful in drawing conclusions from this success. The principle of local home rule never developed in Canada to the same extent that it did in the United States. Consequently provincial intervention to reorganize Metropolitan Toronto did not offend Canadian sensibilities to the same extent that similar state intervention would in the United States.

Toronto had applied to the Ontario Municipal Board in 1950 for the progressive amalgamation of the thirteen municipalities in the area. The Town of Mimico had alternatively applied for the establishment of an inter-urban administrative area. In January, 1953 Lorne R. Cummings, Chairman of the Ontario Municipal Board, issued "The Cummings Report" dismissing both applications and recommending the establishment of a metropolitan municipal government. In the same year the provincial legislature passed "The Municipality of Metropolitan Toronto Act" creating a federal system of local government. The individual municipalities retain control over local matters and are directly represented in the Metropolitan Council which has authority over those matters deemed areawide in character.

The crucial element is the role of the province. The federation was created upon recommendation of the Ontario Municipal Board by the provincial legislature without requirement of local ratification. It is generally agreed that had a popular majority been required in each of the 13 municipalities the federation would not have been ratified. It is doubtful that a majority of the total area could have been mustered. It is also generally agreed that if the people of the metropolitan area were asked today whether they approved of the federation it would be overwhelmingly supported. This fact has led some people to suggest the desirability of placing greater responsibility in the state for reorganizing our metropolitan areas. Such a move has much to recommend it. In Vir-

---

* Webb S. Fiser, *Mastery of the Metropolis* (Englewood Cliffs, N.J.: Prentice-Hall, Inc., 1962), pp. 117–121. © 1962 by Prentice-Hall, Inc., Reprinted by permission. Webb S. Fiser is a member of the Maxwell Institute.

ginia there is a somewhat comparable procedure that is judicial rather than legislative.

We have a stronger tradition of home rule in the United States than does Canada. It is doubtful that many states could be brought to accept a system that did not provide for some form of local ratification. One can only hope that some state will find the courage at least to experiment with state adoption. A procedure somewhat more in keeping with our traditions would be the creation of a state agency with power to study and to recommend metropolitan reorganization in particular instances. This might be one of the duties of an Office of Local Affairs. Such a study could be initiated by application from a municipality or from the county. The objective of such a procedure would be to inject both expertness and impartiality into the recommended solution. The highest competence would be necessary to make such a process successful.

A means should be found of preventing small localized majorities from thwarting the general will of the metropolitan area. In some states traditions of home rule are so strong that the consent of each unit may still be required. The ultimate objective to be sought is a simple majority of the metropolitan area. A half-way solution would require concurrent majorities in the central city and in the area outside taken as a unit. In the end the health of a democratic society must rest upon the capacity of such majorities to recognize the distinction between what is truly local and what is an areawide concern. To continue to give a veto to a majority in a small jurisdiction means minority rule if the greater majority is prevented from taking action which they deem commensurate with the problem.

The recommended approach would require constitutional revision in most of our states. We certainly should not place all our hopes on such revision, since most state legislatures over-represent rural and small-town interests. Also, suburban communities often feel a strong attachment to home rule. Consequently, the path of constitutional reform will not be easy and other solutions must also be sought. In any case, constitutional revision will be the result of continuous public education over a long period of time. We cannot expect revision unless the need for it is generally recognized.

In many states constitutional revision could well take the tack of permitting the creation of urban counties. Such a provision does not exclude the procedure already suggested. The functions of counties have been expanding. They are becoming important administrative units for a wide variety of federal grant-in-aid programs. Constitutional revision permitting the adoption of home-rule urban county charters would be in line with existing developments. Such a procedure would permit transcending small local majorities. The best provision would be to require only a simple majority of the county taken as a whole to create such a charter. The requirement in New York, for example, that a county charter must have a majority in the central city and a majority in the rest of the county taken as a unit is an obstacle, but not a complete bar, to constructive action. New York law has the further disadvantage of requiring a majority in the villages of the county taken as a unit if any transfer of function is proposed.

In most of our urban counties a prior piece of business needs attention. Before we can seriously consider the urban county we need a modern and effective administration of that unit of government. It is still largely a collection of autonomous administrative units often with the political patronage system still in control, only loosely coordinated by the Board of Supervisors. Therefore, the creation of an effective county manager, county president or other elected executive, or county president-manager system is a prior condition to the transformation of an urban county into a general governmental unit. We need to raise the reputation and competence of county government before the people will feel secure in vesting it with broader powers. This requires both an over-all executive and possibly the election of at least some members of the legislative body from a large geographic area, possibly the county at large. We will probably not make maximum progress so long as county supervisors represent towns or townships. Political statesmanship will develop when the electoral base transcends the small vested interests.

Money is at the root of much of our difficulty. The competition between parts of the metropolitan area has resulted in tax inequalities. The value of property has become adjusted to the prevailing financial jumble. Consequently, it is impossible to revamp the financial base of support within the metropolitan area thoroughly without creating new injustices. To raise taxes substantially in a tax haven is to reduce the market value of the property and work injustice against recent purchasers who paid a price which capitalized the old inequity. A fair solution will probably require a gradual shifting of the tax burden from the property tax to sales or payroll taxes. The objective should be gradually to shift the financial support of governmental services to a metropolitan tax base in order to reduce over a period of time the relative importance of the existing inequalities. In this way we can gradually reduce the political importance of the present inequalities. To attack them directly is to invite failure.

For most of our smaller metropolitan areas the goal of county reorganization would seem to be an adequate solution and a natural development of our historic institutions and values. In all likelihood the transformation of the county will be a gradual process and take many forms. Therefore, we should not spend too much time trying to decide what the final outline will look like, but rather know in general where we are going and take one step at a time. First, improve the administrative machinery of the existing county; second, transfer welfare, or some other function, to the county; third, create a county planning body; fourth, transfer another function—public health, for example—to the county; and so on piece by piece. One must always remember that it is necessary for a consensus to be developed supporting a broader basis of operation. Often this agreement comes function by function. It is probably true that general schemes of reorganization will be both necessary and possible when a particular metropolitan area lets things get so bad that a general revolution becomes feasible. . . .

For a Department of
Urban Affairs*
Joseph Clark

. . . A Department of Urban Affairs and Housing would do four important things.

First, it would raise the status of a cluster of governmental programs which, taken together, have a tremendous impact on the development of communities of all sizes. As Mr. Norman Mason, the Housing and Home Finance Administrator in the Eisenhower administration, told the Housing Subcommittee of the Banking and Currency Committee of the Senate on May 9, 1960—

Functions of the Housing Agency now have a tremendous impact on the entire national economy. They closely affect the daily lives of many millions of our citizens: they play a vital part in the livability and the economic stability of towns, cities and metropolitan areas throughout the Nation; and they are closely related to the programs of many major departments of the Government. Finally, as your committee knows, our functions are necessarily very complex because they are addressed to so many difficult and closely interrelated problems affecting our urban communities.

Governor Rockefeller, in his 1957 memorandum, . . . pointed out that the HHFA then employed more than 10,000 persons, included 6 great bureaus, had obligational authority for that year of over

*From a speech on the floor of the Senate on February 7, 1962 in support of S. 1633, a bill to establish a U.S. Department of Urban Affairs and Housing. Joseph Clark is senior Senator from Pennsylvania.

$1 billion, was making commitments to insure mortgages and loans at a rate of $5 billion a year, and had insurance outstanding in excess of $24 billion. Citing its nonhousing functions, he said the HHFA was "already in important respects the Federal Urban Affairs Agency."

In Government, as elsewhere, status is important. The man charged with responsibilities of such magnitude deserves a rank equal to that of other officials with equal or lesser responsibility. The Federal Urban Affairs Agency deserves to be represented at the Cabinet table.

In short, we should not ask a major, or perhaps a colonel, to do a major general's job. But that is what we have been doing.

Second, the plan would bring greater attention to the problems of urban America.

In his message transmitting the plan, President Kennedy said:

Our cities and the people who live in and near them need and deserve an adequate voice in the highest councils of Government. The executive branch and the Congress need an adequate instrument to assist them in the formulation and execution of policy concerning urban affairs and housing. States and local governing bodies urgently need an agency at the departmental level to assist them in formulating and carrying out their local programs for dealing with these problems. All these needs can best be met through the establishment of the Department provided for in this reorganization plan.

It is true that the Housing and Home Finance Administrator now has a general concern for all of the problems arising from the explosive growth of urban and metropolitan areas, and he can propose legislative or executive action at any time. But a Secretary of Urban Affairs and Housing will be better able to make himself heard, partly because of his higher status, which I have already discussed, and partly because his new title will make clear to State and local officials, to the Members of the Congress, to the press and the public and all concerned that his interests are not limited to housing and home finance, but extend to urban affairs in general. Since, as Governor Rockefeller said in 1957, HHFA is already "the Federal urban affairs agency," this reorganization will fit the title to the fact.

Third, the reorganization would improve the coordination of Federal functions affecting communities. The Secretary would have no authority to direct the activities of other departments, but he would be responsible for initiating corrective action if, for example, highway programs conflict with urban renewal, or the Defense Department disrupts local planning. Governors, mayors, and county officials would have a central point of contact to straighten out conflicting or confused Federal policies.

The Housing and Home Finance Administrator, in his present subordinate status, is in no position to take the initiative for better coordination that is required. A Cabinet officer would have the rank and status that is necessary.

Fourth, the new Department would be in a better position to provide information and technical assistance to State and local governments on problems arising from urban growth. While any such activities would depend on congressional appropriations, the new Department, with its broader title, would presumably require more initiative than has HHFA in sponsoring research, and compiling and disseminating information on urban problems in general.

The Federal Government carries on extensive research on the causes and cures of potato blight, but not of urban blight. It knows much of farmland use, little of urban land use; much of the economics of transporting hogs, but little of the economics of mass commutation of people. The new Department would not conduct much research, but it would provide leadership, and a clearinghouse of information. . . .

Also consider that for 100 years the farmers of America, who now constitute less than 25 percent of the population of our Nation, have had a seat at the President's Cabinet table and a representative with Cabinet status, with all the influence that position implies.

Is it not right and just and fair that now, when 75 percent of the population are living in suburbs, metropolitan areas, small and large cities and towns, those three-quarters of our population should be given the same status, the same access, and the same right to be heard through a measure which authorizes no expenditure, creates no new functions, does not permit the Department to take any new steps or expand its activities without the consent of the Congress of the United States?

Against a Department of Urban Affairs*

Senate Committee on Government Operations

The introduction of legislation to create a Department of Urban Affairs and Housing carries this Nation toward the dangerous

---

* Senate Committee on Government Operations, Senate Report No. 879 (87th Cong., 1st Sess.). Minority Report, submitted September 6, 1961, to accompany S. 1633, a bill to establish a U.S. Department of Urban Affairs and Housing.

policies of political spending which hits hard at self-reliance. There has been a growing tendency to begin programs which aggressively make larger and larger segments of our population dependent on the Federal system, solely on the theory that local government cannot handle these special problems.

In the past 5 years, there have been a score of proposals put forward for new departments of Government.

Every pressure group in the Nation, looking for Federal funds, wants to have its representative crowding to the President's Cabinet table, not to advise and guide him on the problems of government, but to push for special favors for special interests.

The eventual demolition of power and authority of lesser levels of government such as city, county, or State, can be seen in the blueprints and the plans for a department of Government which will take over the handling of problems which are, in a large part, entirely local responsibilities. A line of communication will be set up directly from the city mayor's office to the center of the Federal Government. County commissioners, State legislatures, Governors will be ignored.

It should not be necessary to stress the value of keeping local controls over local problems, but, with the increased tendency to diminish the authority of Governors, State legislatures, and other levels of local government, such warnings must be sounded whenever possible.

Enactment of this legislation will not encourage the initiative of States or of cities, but will violate the principles of the Federal system, usurp authority vested in State governments, crumble the walls of self-determination, demolish local leadership, and build ever higher the stronghold of Central Government.

The people who live in the cities of this Nation, themselves, should be warned that the espousal of such a cause will eventually demean their own stature in a political sense. If Washington pays the bill, Washington will direct the action. It has been ever thus. We are, more and more, moving toward a directed economy in this country. The theory of those who support more Federal intervention is that Washington knows best, works best, pays best, and all lesser segments of government must change, they must reshape their concepts of self-determination, and accept the blueprint of the planners.

More than hopscotching over the State and county governments, this new Department can eventually nullify local city government.

A department of Government, which will carry out the functions envisioned by the supporters of the plan, will be the most powerful Cabinet post, and it will be the most expensive. There is a steady stream of pious protestations in Government that we need to cut down the deficit and the public debt, but we will, in one sweeping gesture, create a goliath which will drain our Treasury and which will keep a watchful, police eye on every urban community and its citizens, planning, spending, directing until citizens will not call city hall when streets need repair, or a water main needs replacing, but will notify their Congressman to contact the Cabinet member handling such problems, seeking repairs and services.

More than losing control over local city government, these citizens of urban areas may find corrupt administrations in certain city governments perpetuated. The attention of Congress should be called to the many scandals currently being aired, which involve the city governments of some of our largest cities, where, as one columnist expressed it, "there is a municipal system that is shoddy, incredibly inefficient, and complacently corrupt." Congress should consider carefully before making Federal funds available for the corrupt administrators to dispense for their own political gain. . . .

The assumption by proponents of this legislation is that the majority of our people, because they live in urban areas, have no Cabinet-level representation. The fact is that they are served in a variety of ways by every department of Government, including the Department of Agriculture.

The concept of a Department of Urban Affairs applies the principle of creating a Department to assist people because of their location and not because of functions which need to be performed in their behalf. In other words, this would be the only Department whose services would be denied some people merely on a geographic basis. It does not, as other departments do, have "something in it for everyone."

It should be pointed out that the sponsor of the bill, in his testimony in support of this argument, said that local governments could not finance the many planning and construction projects, thus revealing the aim behind the plan—to get more Federal aid for cities.

Statements before the committee suggested that cities had not yet utilized their own resources to solve their problems and it was pointed out that many cities had failed to continue to use existing programs when information was circulated that a Department of Urban Affairs was to be created.

If some of these populous, industrial, high-income areas do not now assume leadership in handling slum clearance and other metropolitan problems, the enactment of this legislation will discourage any such efforts at local control in the future.

The sponsor of the bill stated that lack of coordination of Federal programs creates difficulties in city planning. He cited, as an example, that a Federal highway program might disrupt a federally financed urban renewal program.

The Secretary of the Department of Urban Affairs would have no control over the activities of the Bureau of Public Roads, located in the Department of Commerce because this Bureau coordinates its work with State highway departments. How could such problems be resolved in any way that is superior to the present system? Would all such interdepartmental squabbles be referred to the President? Nearly every service which sponsors of this bill hope to have in the new Department is now provided in one of the existing agencies or departments of Government. . . .

Urbanism and Government, 1957-1977*

Frank P. Zeidler

I . . . look in this decade for increased state concern for some suburban areas in opposition to the central cities. This will occur largely because suburbanites will have considered their status and life improved to the point that they will leave the Democratic party and vote for the party of conservatism and the status quo, the Republican party. Legislation directed against the development and improvement of the urban centers will often be sponsored by wealthy suburbanites who make their living in the central area.

I also look for a continued migration of southern Negroes and southern white workers to northern cities. The core is the only part of these cities where they can go to live, and because of their numbers and poverty, this core will continue to deteriorate faster than local authorities, state governments, or the federal government can rebuild it. For political reasons, the state governments in this situation may try to lend their weight to increasing the density of population and making the minority problem in the central areas greater. They may do so because of their dislike of the central cities, their fear of the political philosophy held by people in them, and their desire to maintain the economic and class differences between the people of the suburban communities and the lower economic groups that migrate into the cities seeking work. . . .

* Frank P. Zeidler, "Urbanism and Government, 1957-1977," *The Annals of the American Academy of Political and Social Science*, 314 (November 1957), 77-81.
Frank P. Zeidler was Mayor of Milwaukee.

[Between 1957 and 1977], a great increase in population will occur in the urban centers of the United States; these centers will become much larger and more numerous. Many urban areas now separated by open country will become one continuous set of contiguous urban communities. The pressures of a large population and the need for critical services such as water and sewer in these areas will undoubtedly promote the creation of the metropolitan concept of government.

The unwillingness of state legislatures to face the growth of urban areas will impel certain urban groups to continue to seek grants in aid from the federal government. If the situation is bad enough, there may be attempts to have the major metropolitan areas made special wards of the federal government for certain purposes. As the metropolitan growth occurs, it is likely that hostility between the state governments and the central cities may grow. The political cleavage between the two, urban areas and state governments, will influence elections of the United States during the next two decades.

The need for furnishing special units of government to deal with regional sewer, water and traffic problems will introduce great complexities into the laws of state governments. Since state governments do not desire to see the growth of the political power of metropolitan areas, they will persist in seeking to fragment the metropolitan areas into urban and suburban conflicting groups as a means of dividing and ruling.

One can expect, also, that there will be a continued stratification of population in the urban areas with the wealthy and the people of white ancestry moving to the suburban areas where a kind of economic caste system will develop. People of colored ancestry may continue to move from the rural South into the core cities of metropolitan areas. This situation, in which the bloc of Negro voters in central cities grows greater, will further promote the desire of the controllers of state governments to isolate the central cities in metropolitan areas and to choke off their growing political strength.

The possibility in some areas of central governments being greatly influenced by Negro voting blocs would undoubtedly materialize in many cities in the next two decades. The development of the urban areas, therefore, in the northern part of the United States will be directly subjected to the policies of the southern states with regard to migrating Negro minorities. The presence of such blocs will bring demands for housing, fair-employment practices, civil rights, and welfare legislation. Other people, too, will continue to crowd into the cities to enjoy the convenience of living and the high wages that are to be found there.

The growth of urbanism will also tend to promote the conflict between public ownership and social welfare ideas and the concepts of private enterprise. Large numbers of people who are wage earners without any security other than their physical strength will tend to promote legislation which will guarantee their welfare and their security even in times of unemployment. This type of legislation, being considered hostile by the rural and suburban citizens, will result in struggles between the urban and the rural forces in the state legislatures and will spill over into the Congress. This same ideological conflict carried on in the field of housing will mean that the opponents of municipal housing will continue to be vigorous. As a result, there will be a constant shortage of adequate housing for urban residents of the United States since private enterprise will not be able to supply the urban population with adequate low-cost shelter because of fence-me-in economic laws.

The creation of express roads through the major cities will foster the spread of suburbanism. Within these cities there will be a development, though on a limited scale, of homogeneous, easily identifiable communities in the older areas. Some of these will be desirable; others will merely be unredeveloped slum areas bounded by trafficways which set them apart from surrounding communities. Out of each of these areas certain identifiable political yearnings will come. If urban redevelopment results in a mass dispossession of many small owners and the creation of a large tenantry, it is possible that federal and state laws will reflect the pressure of the tenants against the landlords.

The great growth of population without a proper expansion of resources to feed it and to provide it with fresh air and water may cause a significant deterioration in the standard of living for many people. A difficult problem will arise in the attempt to tax for educational purposes because of the larger number of children. It is possible that a resistance to property taxes for education will become so strong that the educational program of the nation will have to be seriously diminished.

The increased use of mechanical devices will also bring a rash of laws necessary to curtail their deleterious effects. Laws against improper uses of motor vehicles, against noise, dirt, and unsanitary conditions will undoubtedly result in the further concentration of population. Most of these laws will be developed in state legislatures but only after a resistance from the rural people who cannot conceive of the need for such laws.

Partly because the urban needs will be so great and the urban communities will put pressure on the federal government to solve these needs, state legislatures may make grudging concessions to the urban problems. However, it is not likely that state legislatures will bow in any direction toward legislation which might be described as socialistic if they can help it. In addition, there will be constant agitation in state legislatures to dismantle all of the operations of the federal government except those dealing with the development of military forces for an attack.

The increase in population in the urban centers may also

put a strain on the agriculture of the United States, and it is entirely possible that unless there is some better planning of agricultural development and water resources, the urban areas may suffer shortages of essential supplies some time within the next two decades. Even without the threat of atomic warfare, it is entirely possible that there may be recessions in business which will have their repercussions particularly on the urban communities and bring forth from them a demand for federal social legislation rather than state legislation to alleviate the conditions of unemployment.

The total results, therefore, of the pattern from 1957 to 1977, if the nation lives at uneasy peace with Russia, will be to diminish the strength of the state legislatures and to increase the strength of the federal government because of the pressures of urban living.

Over the next twenty years certain struggles between different groups in the great urban areas will also have their reflection on the federal system. The first of these is the struggle between two economic groups which are able to finance elections to gain a dominant hand in the voice of the communities. The one is a group represented by owners and management, most of whom are suburban dwellers, and the other is that reflected in organized labor.

There will be an attempt by both groups to attain ascendency in the government in metropolitan areas. Since most of the management people live in the suburbs, they will devote their attention particularly to changing state laws which will permit them to control the destinies of the central city by remote control or through special districts of government. In this action they will have the support of the rural legislators.

The labor movement will attempt to resist this move by maintaining control of the central cities independent of the legislatures. If the legislatures invade this control of the central cities too extensively, it is entirely possible that labor-elected city representatives will seek relief and protection from the federal government.

A second struggle will take place on the part of organized supporters of vice, gambling, and crime to gain control of the central areas. The central cities are oftentimes regarded as "play spots," and there is a tendency for local officials to wink at organized vice and crime in certain districts of their cities. This leads to the flourishing of gangs and organized hoodlums; and in most cities these organized hoodlums, working either through the management or labor groups, and sometimes working through both, have been enabled to control city government with the resulting deterioration of government and wholesale corruption.

This type of struggle will be intensified in the future because some people's appetite for vice and gambling will not be appreciably diminished. If the organized criminal elements gain control of the cities, they will use the same tactics and techniques to gain control of state governments. They are completely impartial as to their connections and are equally at home among management representatives as with labor representatives. They will "work" either group to gain control as conditions may require.

In many places, the organized criminal elements are working in close liaison with so-called leaders of respectable business. In other places, they have worked their way into influential positions in the central labor bodies. Federal legislation may be directed to overcome this problem because the state governments are often helpless, unable to act, or unaware of the problem.

The third major conflict which may find its reflection in the federal system is the conflict between migrating peoples, particularly between peoples of substantially diverse cultural background such as the southern Negro and the northern white of European extraction, or the Puerto Rican and the northern white. The great influx of Negroes into the northern areas, for the present, may increase the desire of the northern political leaders to call for increased activity in civil rights and fair employment practices. But it is possible that in the long run there may be a segregated caste system developed as the northern whites seek to withdraw from contact with the Negro community. This withdrawal will occur when the mental image that the northern white has of a Negro as a harassed and relatively helpless person is changed to an image of the Negro as a brutal attacker of women on the streets, one given to the use of narcotics, a brawler, and a slovenly person. Thus, by a relocation of the Negro population from the rural South to the northern cities there may be a greater tendency in the North to follow the pattern of the southern states, and this in turn would have its subtle reflections in the federal system.

Another problem which may have its bearing in the federal government is the growing number of young men who, kept apart from useful employment or from honest work necessary to support themselves, may readily lend themselves to gang formations. These formations can be shrewdly mobilized as a political force, even as youth movements in Germany were organized by political leaders. Any depression, in which the younger persons are deprived of money for automobiles and the pleasures which they are enjoying at the present time, might conceivably lead to a fascist development in the United States because many young people, unaware of the facts of economics, may follow a demagogue.

"Urbanism and Government, 1957-1977": A Rejoinder*

Wallace S. Sayre

[Mayor Zeidler] sees political and governmental wars, ethnic and racial turmoils, suburban snobbery in low alliance with rural lag, central city populations in poverty, hunger and thirst, the underworld seizing new opportunities, unemployed youth marching upon the city streets in cadence to demagogues; brooding over the whole unhappy scene is the unenlightened malice of the state governments. A few rays of hope are allowed to break fitfully through the ominous overcast: The federal government has a benevolent potential, and metropolitan area government may advance rapidly from infancy to maturity. But we are not to be encouraged into any easier breathing, Mayor Zeidler reminds us, for the odds remain stacked against all those who failed to keep the family farm.

These dismal forebodings arouse a political scientist to summon up all his optimistic resources. The Constitution, the federal union, the political parties, the urban and metropolitan community, the rationality of voters, the initiative of elected chief executives, the expertise of the bureaucracies, and even the vulnerability of state legislatures to urban ingenuity. The remainder of these comments will be devoted to a prayerful consideration of the possibilities that Mayor Zeidler's second-prophecy apparitions in our urban future may respond to this optimism.

Mayor Zeidler's first premise is his most hopeful one. If I may paraphrase it, this premise runs as follows: *The urban centers will form an alliance with the national government in a political contest against the state governments and suburbia.*

If this should come to fruition—and there are many signs to support Mayor Zeidler's prediction—then a political scientist would be disposed to anticipate victory for the cities. They have the votes to influence mightily the nominations for the presidency in both parties and to affect critically the presidential elections. This fact alone gives the cities a high status in the national party system, an asset which Mayor Zeidler seems to underestimate. Favored access to the presidency and to

* Wallace S. Sayre, " 'Urbanism and Government, 1957–1977': A Rejoinder," *The Annals of the American Academy of Political and Social Science*, 314 (November 1957), 82–85.
Wallace S. Sayre is Eaton Professor of Public Administration, Columbia University.

the national parties—especially in their presidential manifestations—is an asset of inestimable value. It should, if cultivated by urban initiative, lead —if not to a United States Department of Urbiculture—to a greater flow of aid from the national treasury to the urban centers; to closer ties between the executive branch of the national government and the cities; even perhaps to the national government's recognition of the metropolitan areas, less as "wards" perhaps than as favored protégés. We might actually envisage, if we were to indulge our optimism as boldly as Mayor Zeidler does his pessimism, the national government-metropolitan area alliance—especially if assisted by a similar alliance by the river-valley regions—as the solvent which would lead to an urban federal system substituted for our present rural one.

But Mayor Zeidler's second premise brings us back to the troubles closer home: He believes, if I may again paraphrase, that *the cities may be outflanked in the states by an aggressive determination on the part of the state legislatures and the suburban governments to "isolate" the central cities* by inhibiting the efforts toward metropolitan area integration, by increasing its fragmentation, and by resisting the cities' political strength in other ways.

These tendencies are visible, and Mayor Zeidler does not exaggerate their evident motivation. But perhaps he overlooks some urban resources and opportunities to protect the cities and perhaps even to envelop the opposition on its suburban flank. The first of these resources is the state governorship. The governor, like the president, is an asset of urban America. Urban influence is great in his nomination and election in every urban state; he cannot escape his urban commitments at home, and if he aspires to the presidency he cannot afford even the invisible wish to escape. The second resource lies in the fact that neither state party can afford to be caught in an overt alliance against the urban electorates; any such liaison would need to be a midnight affair. The staying power of such attachments is fragile in the daylight of political debate. Party leaders are among the most cautious and prudent of men when dealing with large electorates; they are not vindictive men; they are brokers. And for the third, the rural and suburban legislators typically work out their career aspirations within a political party whose leaders and "contributors" may live in the suburbs but mostly do their business in the cities where mayors and governors have the combined power to restrain, if not to humble, their exuberance. Further, the city government bureaucracies and the state government bureaucracies are usually in close alliance when "outsiders"—particularly rural and suburban "outsiders"—intervene; their influence will most likely be a moderating one, if not actively hostile to any effort to "isolate" the central cities. Finally, the urban-suburban hostility may have more surface than depth; as suburbia quickly becomes less than paradise, plagued by the same difficulties of urbanism as the central cities, its electorates may find more ties with the city electorates than with rural ones.

In short, the larger initiative in the states may belong to the cities. The suburban "third force" may come back home from its springtime escapade, anxious to be urban again even as junior partner in a metropolitan firm. In this event, the rural legislators rather than the central cities would be isolated.

Mayor Zeidler's third premise, if I may condense as well as paraphrase, is that *the central cities will be harassed by a rising tempo of ethnic and racial politics, by lower standards of living, by youthful unemployed, by an aggressive underworld*—with most of these related to a sharper conflict, on a broader stage, between the welfare state and the not-too-much-welfare state.

Again, I would read more favorable prospects into the future than does Mayor Zeidler. In the 1920's and 1930's, sociologists predicted the decay of the central cities, the flowering of suburbia—in the 1950's, thanks to the grace of federal urban redevelopment money and the urge of corporate America to work in air-conditioned glass-enclosed offices, the central cities are being reclaimed (for example, Clark's Philadelphia and Wagner's New York) faster than the slum dwellers can move to the suburbs. Ethnic and racial politics, juvenile delinquency, even gangsters are being distributed more evenly over the whole metropolitan landscape. To put the matter more soberly, ethnic and racial politics would seem to be moderating rather than intensifying (and they have always had their great solvent values as well as their irrationalities); the central cities are repudiating their premature obituaries; and the signs of a return to McKinley in our politics and public policies seem largely oratorical and semantic. The platforms of 1960, one may anticipate, will be a reaffirmation of the narrowly competitive goals of Stevenson and Eisenhower, not an endorsement of Byrd and Taft.

In summary, then— . . . I believe the cities are on the move, and that suburbia will, however reluctantly at first, follow in their wake —for the suburbs, too, belong to urban America and must soon see that nostalgia is less satisfying than common sense.

What do these more optimistic interpretations forecast in terms of the federal system? If I, too, may be bold, they suggest:

1. A gradual but steady political and governmental transformation within the urban states: The urban and suburban electorates —neither ever monolithic and to become rapidly less so—combining to make the state governments more urban in policies and arrangements; the rise of metropolitan area governments or treaties buttressing this trend as well as accelerating it; the leaders of the political parties—especially in

presidential, gubernatorial, United States senatorial, and "metropolitan" elections—responding to this urbanization of our politics.

2. An accompanying transformation of the relationships between these urbanized states and the national government: More direct dealings between the cities and the metropolitan areas, on the one hand, and the national government on the other—although the states may continue as the formal channel; the growth of national government bureaus with urban or metropolitan assignments; the greater interlocking of the multilevel bureaucracies, those increasingly potent participants in all our decision-making; the presidency becoming more and more the political magnet and the governmental instrument of urban-metropolitan America.

When and if these trends are fully under way, who will need to worry about—how long can anyone forestall—legislative reapportionment in the states? Who will say we cannot afford to indulge in the then largely symbolic debate about the virtues of suburbia versus the tensions of cities? Most of us would then even be willing to concede the values of preserving the traditional state boundaries as testimony of our rural past—including in our generosity toward institutions historic both "The Citadel" of the United States Senate, that most rural monument of our heritage, and the Office of Mayor in our central cities, overshadowed by the new Metrogovernors.

Metropolitan Financial Problems*

Lyle C. Fitch

. . . Metropolitan financial problems arise primarily from the lack of adequate machinery rather than from any lack of capacity. Presumptively, today's large urban communities, being typically the focal points of wealth and income, have the resources to meet their urban needs. The following deficiencies in the fiscal machinery charac-

* Lyle C. Fitch, "Metropolitan Financial Problems," *The Annals of the American Academy of Political and Social Science*, 314 (November 1957), 67–73.
Lyle C. Fitch is President of the Institute of Public Administration, Columbia University.

teristic of metropolitan areas seem to the writer to be the most important and the ones whose rectification will have greatest importance for the future.

1. Existing revenue-producing machinery is generally inadequate for the task of financing local government functions; this is true both of functions appropriate for the conventional (submetropolitan) local government and functions which can best be handled by metropolitan jurisdictions.

2. The extension of activities across jurisdictional boundary lines makes it more and more difficult to relate benefits and taxes at the local government level. In the modern metropolitan community, a family may reside in one jurisdiction, earn its living in one or more others, send the children to school in another, and shop and seek recreation in still others. But to a considerable extent, the American local financial system still reflects the presumption that these various activities are concentrated in one governmental jurisdiction.

3. In many areas there are great discrepancies in the capacities of local government jurisdictions to provide needed governmental services. At one extreme are the communities which have not sufficient taxable capacity for essential services. The most common case is the bedroom community of low- and middle-income workers which has little industry or commerce. At the other extreme are the wealthy tax colonies, zoned to keep out low-income residents.

Three main types of decisions must be made in setting up and financing functions on an area-wide scale. They concern:

The services and benefits which should be provided on an area-wide basis.

The question of whether services should be financed by taxes or charges.

The type and rate of tax or charge which should be imposed.

Some services and benefits, like health protection and air pollution control, can be provided efficiently only if they extend over a wide area and their administration is integrated; some, like hospitals and tax administration, are more economical if handled on a large scale; and some, like intrametropolitan transportation, can be controlled satisfactorily only by a central authority with powers to establish area-wide standards and policies and to resolve intra-area conflicts.

This discussion distinguishes mainly between general taxes bearing no direct relation to benefits of expenditures, like sales and income taxes, and charges, or public prices, which vary directly with the amount of the service provided, like bridge tolls, subway fares, and metered charges for water.

General taxes and public prices are at the opposite ends of the revenue spectrum. In between are benefit taxes, which are imposed on beneficiaries of a related service, with the proceeds being devoted largely or entirely to financing the service. Gasoline taxes used for financing highways are a familiar example; the real-estate tax is at least in part a benefit tax where it pays for services which benefit the taxed properties.

Local governments, within the generally narrow confines of state-imposed restrictions, have shown considerable ingenuity in tapping pools of potential revenue, however small; few things on land, sea, or in the air, from pleasures and palaces to loaves and fishes, escape taxation somewhere. However, most of the principal local taxes used today are loosely enforced or expensive to administer and dubious in their economic effect. Even the property tax is not exempt from this indictment, although its praises have long been sung and its vices excused on the ground that it is the only tax which can be administered successfully even by the smallest local government. The fact is that it has generally not been successfully administered at all, according to most criteria of equity and efficiency. It is capricious and inequitable even in what it purports to do best.

Part of the typical difficulties of local taxation arise from smallness, both in size of jurisdiction and scale of administrative organization. These, of course, may be obviated by metropolitan area-wide administration. Efficient collection of most types of revenues requires an organization large enough to afford trained personnel, costly equipment, and professional direction and research. Geographically, the taxing area must be large enough and isolated enough to discourage avoidance of taxes by persons who move their residences or business establishments over boundary lines or who go outside the jurisdiction to shop. When imposed by several neighboring local governments, many taxes involve issues of intergovernmental jurisdiction and allocation of tax bases.

Where taxes are imposed on an area-wide basis, one issue of metropolitan area finance—allocation of government service costs among communities—is resolved; allocation is a function of the type of tax imposed. Area-wide taxes also eliminate tax competition within the area; however this may not be an unmitigated blessing if competition by offering better services also is eliminated.

To date, the principal revenue sources of area-wide public agencies have been property taxes and user charges, although some metropolitan counties in New York and California, for instance, impose sales taxes and occasionally other nonproperty taxes. The problems of granting taxing powers to metropolitan jurisdictions which extend over several counties remain largely unexplored. A bill introduced in the 1957 session of the California legislature to establish a multicounty San Francisco Bay area rapid transit district went further in this direction than most legislative proposals by giving the proposed district power to impose both a property and a sales tax. The sales tax authority was eliminated in the version of the bill finally adopted.

The difficulties of working out harmonious tax arrangements between metropolitan jurisdictions and state and already-existing local governments have been great enough when only one state was involved to block all but the feeblest beginnings beyond the one-county level. They have thus far been considered insuperable where interstate arrangements are involved. For some time to come, interstate functions probably will be financed by user charges, supplemented where necessary by contributions from the state or local governments involved.

In the almost-perfect metropolitan area, we would expect to see metropolitan real-estate taxes assessed by an area-wide agency, with metropolitan levies for such metropolitan services as were deemed to be of particular benefit to property and additional local levies for local government activities. Only metropolitan jurisdictions would be authorized to impose nonproperty taxes. In general, the permissible nonproperty taxes would include general sales and amusements taxes and a levy on personal income. Business firms might be taxed, if at all, by some simple form of value-added tax.

The following are among the taxes not used at the local level in the almost-perfect metropolitan area: Gross-receipts taxes and taxes on utility services because of their excessively deleterious economic effect; and corporate income taxes and such selective excises as gasoline, alcoholic beverages, and tobacco taxes because they can be much better administered at the state level.

Along with several others, the revenue sources mentioned above are now being used by municipalities with two exceptions: The value-added tax and the general income tax. The so-called municipal income taxes now imposed in Pennsylvania, Ohio, and a few other states rest largely on wages and salaries. Considerations of equity manifestly require a broader tax base, and the need for administrative simplicity suggests a supplemental rate on an existing base where this is practicable.

The principal justification for the real-estate tax, aside from tradition, convenience, and expediency, is that by financing beneficial services, it benefits property. Another logical function, which it performs very inadequately, is to capture at least part of the unearned increments to land values accruing by reason of urban developments. Special assessments have been widely used to recoup at least part of land values accruing from public improvements, but no means has been devised, at least at the local level, of recapturing land values not attributable to specific public improvements.

The enormous increases of land values which typically occur as land is converted from rural to urban use and from less to more intensive urban use constitute a pool of resources which can be appropriately utilized to meet the social costs of urban development, if taxes can be devised to tap the pool. Such land value increases, however, seem characteristically to be concentrated in the expanding sections, mostly the suburbs. Available evidence suggests that land values in many core cities have lagged far behind general price levels and in some cities have not even regained levels reached in the 1920's. In such cases, urban redevelopment, unlike the initial urban development, cannot count on pools of expanding land values; on the contrary land costs often must be written down at government expense if redevelopment is to be economically feasible.

Clearly the real-estate tax must be adapted to the dynamic characteristics of the urban economy. The tax in its present form gives equal weight to the incremental values resulting from urban development, the values of land already developed, and the values of improvements. Several possible new features should be explored. Some of them are: A local capital gains tax on land value increments, special levies on property values accruing after the announcement of public improvements which benefit the whole community, and a differential tax on land values. Of these three possibilities, the last seems most promising, if only because the basic concept is familiar; it has been used in Australia, Canada, and elsewhere abroad, but by only a few cities in the United States.

There is a case for charging for a service instead of financing it by general taxation if the following conditions are met:

1. The charge must be administratively feasible. Among the other requirements, the service must be divisible into units whose use by the beneficiary can be measured, like kilowatts, gallons of water, trips across a bridge, or miles traveled on a turnpike.

2. The immediate benefits of the service should go mainly to the person paying for it. This condition, not always easy to apply, means that if a person refrains from using the service because of the charge, the rest of the community suffers relatively little loss. For example, the community is ordinarily not much damaged if a person uses less electricity or makes fewer long-distance telephone calls. In some cases, an additional use by a few individuals may greatly inconvenience many others; for example, a few additional vehicles on a roadway may produce traffic congestion.

3. The charge should encourage economical use of resources. Metered charges, for instance, encourage consumers to conserve water and electricity by turning off faucets and lights.

One of the most important functions of charges is to

balance demand and supply in cases where excess demand produces undesirable results. If the number of curb parking spaces is less than the number of would-be parkers, the space will be allocated on a first-come first-served basis, in the absence of any better device, and there is no way of assuring that space will go to those who need it most. In such cases, a charge may be the most efficient way of rationing space. This is frequently attempted by use of parking meters, although nearly always in a crude fashion. Meter systems could be much improved if the elementary principles of charges were better understood.

Conversely, a charge—or the increase of an already-existing charge—is not justified if it results in the underutilization or waste of resources. For example, as an immediate result of the increase of the New York subway fare from 10 to 15 cents in 1953, passenger traffic declined at least 120 million rides per year, the bulk of the drop being concentrated in nonrush hours and holidays when subways have excess capacity. Not only did the community lose 120 million rides per year, which could be provided at little additional cost, but traffic congestion increased because former subway riders switched to private passenger cars and taxis, and downtown shopping and amusement centers suffered to an undetermined extent.

The peripatetic propensities of metropolitan man and the fact that he may consume services in several jurisdictions while voting in only one have disjointed local government fiscal structures in several places. First, the separation of workshops and bedrooms may create disparities between taxable capacities and service needs. Second, the separation of political jurisdictions in which individuals are taxed and in which they require services handicaps the budget-making process; it makes more difficult a rational determination of how much of the community's product should take the form of government services. Third, the necessity of providing services to outsiders, particularly commuters, creates pressure for taxation without representation.

These considerations argue for a policy of structuring metropolitan governmental organizations in order to allow as much freedom as possible to the play of market forces in determining the kinds and quantities of government services to be supplied, subject to the general principles previously noted. . . .

The market system can operate at two levels: That of the individual or firm purchasing services or goods from a government enterprise and that of the group, for example, the smaller governmental jurisdiction, purchasing goods or services from a larger jurisdiction. The second level is exemplified by the city of Lakewood, California and several other cities which purchase their municipal services from Los Angeles County.

One of the principal decisions respecting any government service is the quantity to be furnished. The important distinction between ordinary government services and services provided under enterprise principles lies in the nature of the decision-making process. Budgetary decisions affecting regular government services are political decisions, reflecting judgments of legislatures regarding how much of the services are needed by the community and how much the taxpayers are willing to pay. Not infrequently, decisions are referred directly to voters. The amount of service to be provided under enterprise principles is dictated by consumers, by the usual market test of how much individuals or firms in the aggregate will buy at cost-of-production prices. In other words, the question of how much is decided by following the simple rule that where demand exceeds supply, the service should be expanded, and vice versa.

The price-market test of resource allocation greatly simplifies the problem of citizen participation in the governmental process. Where services and goods are bought by individuals, each consumer takes part in the decision-making process by determining how much of the service he will buy.

Where purchases are by groups, decisions as to how much to spend must be political ones; but the issue of citizen participation can be simplified in several ways as compared with the situation where budgetary decisions are made by large political units. If the purchasing group is more homogeneous than the whole community, any decision is more wholly satisfactory to a larger percentage of the members. Even if the small group is no more homogeneous than the large, individuals may participate more effectively in small-group decisions.

While user charges and the demand-supply rule can simplify the budgetary problem, they do not divorce public enterprise operations from the political process; political participation in many decisions is essential, including the crucial decisions respecting organizational form, investment policies, and integrating the particular function with other community services. For instance, the quantity of services to be supplied by a basically enterprise type of operation may be extended by public decision and public subsidy beyond the amounts which could be made available at cost-of-production prices. In some cases, public subsidies may be necessary to avoid waste of an already-existing resource. Public prices too often are fixed to achieve narrow objectives, such as meeting debt service on construction bonds, without regard for their over-all economic effect.

Some of the most urgent area-wide needs are appropriately financed partly or wholly by charges. They include the services which are frequently provided by private regulated utilities such as gas and electricity, water, and mass transportation and other transportation facilities, port development, waste disposal, many recreational services, and hospital services.

There have been few studies of the over-all relationship of costs and taxable capacity in metropolitan areas—although endless attention has been lavished on particular functions, notably education—and the subject still abounds with unsettled questions. Brazer's analyses indicate that the relative size of the suburban population is an important determinant of local government expenditures in large cities, a finding consistent with the hypothesis that cities assume considerable expense in providing services to suburban residents. Both Brazer's and Hirsch's studies indicate, moreover, that per capita expenditures on some functions—police, for instance—typically increase with population density; this may be due partly to the tendency of low-income groups to congregate in central cities. On the other hand, the worst cases of fiscal undernourishment appear to be in the suburbs.

This article has space only for several generalizations which may serve to indicate directions for further analysis:

1. Costs of essential services may be "equalized" over a metropolitan area, either by area-wide administration and financing, or by grants to local jurisdictions financed at least in part by area-wide taxes. Experience with state and federal subventions indicates that the subvention is a clumsy tool. On the other hand, putting services on an area-wide basis may deprive local communities of the privilege of determining the amount of resources to be allocated to specific services.

2. In many cases, the remedy for fiscal undernourishment may lie in area-wide planning and zoning; fiscal measures as such may strike only at symptoms rather than underlying difficulties.

3. Fiscal stress in the modern American community is often more psychological than economic. A common case is that of the former city apartment dweller who buys his own house in the suburbs and for the first time in his life is confronted with a property tax bill. It is not strange that he should resist taxes while demanding municipal services of a level to which he has been accustomed in the city, nor that he should seek outside assistance in meeting his unaccustomed burden.

4. The point has been made that intercommunity variations in the levels of services should allow metropolitan residents to satisfy their preferences as to levels of local government services and taxes and hence promote the general satisfactions of the entire community. While the argument may be valid within limits, the limits are narrow; they may extend, for instance, to the quality of refuse collection, but not air and water pollution control.

5. Services rendered to individuals in their capacity of workers, shoppers, and other economic functionaries may in some in-

stances be properly treated as a charge upon the business firm involved rather than upon the individual. Suburbanites, like other persons, create real property values wherever they work, shop, or play. This fact refutes the case for a general tax on commuters, although it does not damage the case for user charges where these would improve the allocation of resources. On the other hand, the maintenance of minimal service levels in poor communities and care for the economically stranded, wherever located, are the responsibility of the entire community.

Social Choice and Inconsistent Expectations —the Property Tax*

Procter Thomson

Follies and absurdities that would immediately be apparent in the management of an ordinary household are tolerated and even encouraged in the conduct of public affairs. The occasion for this churlish observation is the universal tendency of local communities to demand more services than they are willing and able to pay for. Within recent years in California, this particular variety of fiscal schizophrenia has become more virulent than usual since complaints about inadequate public services l..ve increased in equal measure.

To move to the same conclusion from another direction, complaints about the burdens of taxation can emanate from many sources. The four principal points of the compass are: (1) people whose preference for government services is lower than the community's in general, (2) people who disapprove of certain kinds of public expenditure, (3) people who believe that the tax system is unjust and that they bear too large a share of the burden, and (4) people who want government serv-

* Procter Thomson, "The Impending Crisis: Myth or Reality," reprinted from *California Local Finance*, by John A. Vieg and others, with permission of the publishers, Stanford University Press, the Haynes Foundation, and Claremont Social Research Center © 1960 by the Board of Trustees of the Leland Stanford Junior University.
Procter Thomson is John C. Lincoln, Professor of Economics and Administration at Claremont Men's College.

ices but object to paying taxes. The first three of these groups have logical and reasonable grounds for complaint; the fourth group suffers from an optical illusion, but this illusion is by no means uncommon. For obviously the link between costs and returns is far less direct for public goods, where individual taxes bear little relation to individual benefits, than it is for private goods where payment is proportional to benefits.

The members of a free society are, and must be, able to choose the government under which they live. As a result they may, and often do, prefer to live in a charming community that is too small to operate efficiently. They may be unwilling to consolidate their schools with someone else's schools in order to achieve a balanced and integrated program. They are reluctant to relinquish the autonomy of their local police force in order to achieve the economies of centralized record-keeping, fingerprinting, and reporting. They may prefer to deal with a host of elected officials, rather than with a small number of impersonal administrative agencies.

Students of local government can raise no legitimate objection to the consequences of these choices. They are entitled to enquire, however, whether all available alternatives were taken into account. Do people know the price they pay for the governments they have elected to establish? When a jealous regard for local autonomy animates some crossroads community to oppose school district reorganization, do parents know the fiscal and educational costs of operating these isolated districts? When some small municipality is hastily gerrymandered from a few scraps of unincorporated territory for a temporary advantage in lower taxes, do property owners realize how illusory these benefits will become with the passage of time? Or when the residents of some urban fringe area decide to form their own city in order to forestall annexation, do they realize how costly this privilege will become when they are forced to bear the expense of full-scale municipal operation?

The moral that lies behind these events is that in government as in other aspects of life one worthy objective frequently conflicts with another so that rational policy requires choices to be made between them. A citizen who prefers a small autonomous community, for example, must be willing to relinquish the prospect of securing governmental efficiency through large-scale municipal operation. And a harassed city dweller who moves to a no-down-payment suburban paradise, populated by small homes and large families, must be prepared to bear the burden of heavy school taxes with a certain degree of equanimity. To complain about the terms of these choices is only natural; but to fail to recognize the pattern of conflict among objectives, to expect the irreconcilable to be reconciled, and to refuse to accommodate to the necessity of making choices—these inconsistent and erroneous attitudes are a formidable barrier to wise policy in local government. . . .

The property tax, the main source of local revenue, illustrates the ancient maxim "uneasy lies the head that wears a crown." The property tax is both defective in principle and deficient in practice. "Its sole virtue," one writer states, "is its age." But according to some authorities, in addition to the virtue (if any) that age confers upon it, taxation of real property is the only source of revenue local units are competent to administer. If this contention is true, if other forms of taxation are too complex for cities and schools to handle or if the attempt to employ them would erode their economic base, then discussing the disabilities of property taxes is an invitation to despair. For nothing is either good or bad, to paraphrase the Bard slightly, save alternatives make it so. And if the property tax has no feasible alternatives—save loss of local initiative or wholesale reduction in local services—we must accept it as it is and pass on to more fruitful areas of inquiry.

But alternatives do exist. The principal sources of public revenue are wealth, income, and consumption. Of these three the taxation of wealth secures the minimum amount of revenue with the maximum amount of fiscal inequity, economic inefficiency, and administrative difficulty.

Fundamentally, the property tax is unjust because it fails to treat equals equally. Income from property is only a fraction of income in general, somewhere between ¼ and ⅓, in fact, for the U.S. economy as a whole, and different families have widely different ratios of wealth to income. To the extent, therefore, that taxes on property are ultimately borne by owners of property and to the extent that personal income represents the most equitable measure of that illusive magnitude, "ability to pay," the property tax violates one of the basic criteria of taxation in a democratic society.

The property tax distorts the pattern of investment between different communities. Communities with high tax rates have a lower volume of commercial and residential investment and those with low tax rates have a higher volume of investment. Differences in tax rates lead to improper allocation of resources.

Some of these effects, admittedly, take a very long time to work themselves out and all of them are mixed and interspersed with a number of other forces. A growing community with a high tax rate, for example, will not expand quite as rapidly as it otherwise would. But regardless of disturbing factors, the long-run return on capital in one area must be roughly equal to the return in any other area. As a result, buildings are relatively scarcer and their rents before taxes are relatively higher in high tax communities while the reverse is true in low tax communities so that net yields in both are approximately equal after taxes are paid.

How does this adjustment affect economic efficiency? It is bound to affect it adversely because the location of business, residential, and commercial activities no longer reflects the natural advantages of different communities. Differences in tax rates create artificial scarcity and artificial abundance. If X would have been a good place for a shopping center or an apartment house and Y a relatively poor site, the differences in taxes ought not to repeal the comparative advantage which nature establishes.

As most California communities have discovered, the property tax is inflexible. It is inflexible in principle because the market values of assets, which are the capitalized net worth of income streams running into the distant future, do not always keep pace with year-to-year changes in community income. It is inflexible in practice because assessed values tend to lag behind market values.

These twin disabilities create, in California as elsewhere, the sorry spectacle of wealthy communities and impoverished governments during periods of economic growth and cumulative inflation. And state legislatures have enthusiastically compounded the natural disabilities of the tax by imposing legal barriers on both the operating margin and the borrowing margin of cities, schools, and other local agencies. Altogether, no more perfect formula for fiscal mismanagement could be devised than to place the governments of expanding metropolitan areas upon a narrow fiscal base and then deny them the power to use that base when they need it. Legal limits on local tax rates are, in one sense, however, a kind of left-handed recognition of the inherent inequities and diseconomies of the property tax *per se*. The remedy, we trust, is sufficiently obvious that he who runs may read: Retire the property tax from active duty as rapidly as possible.

A favorite indoor sport of writers on public finance is to complain about the assessment practices and administrative standards of the local property tax. The bill of particulars varies little from one community to another. In the first place, property is never assessed at its full value; for California as a whole the assessed values are about a quarter of the market values and the ratio has been falling intermittently throughout most of the postwar period. Second, different tax areas have widely differing ratios of assessed to market value; as far as can be determined, California counties in 1957 varied from 20 to 27%, i.e., the highest level is 35% greater than the lowest. Third, different kinds of property within the same tax jurisdiction are assessed at different ratios of market value. Fourth, in all jurisdictions some property escapes assessment altogether; this is particularly true of the personal property tax, which falls mainly "upon those unfortunate individuals who are burdened either with a vigorous conscience or a groundless fear of legal consequences."

The causes of these variations are not hard to isolate. Apart from the inherent difficulties of identifying and measuring millions of parcels of residential property according to a fair and equitable formula, the virtual impossibility of conducting search and seizure operations to catch hundreds of millions of pieces of personal property, and the unbelievable complexity of the recording and reporting arrangements required by this bootless enterprise, there are six causes susceptible of remedy this side of Utopia:

1. The elected, often technically untrained, assessor who is subject to political pressure both to reduce individual assessments and to lower the general level of assessments in the area under his jurisdiction,

2. State aid programs which, however desirable on other grounds, provide an incentive for competitive underassessment because state money is paid to schools in inverse proportion to the amount of assessed value per child,

3. The ancient tradition of underassessment and differential assessment in local units which perpetuates itself by its own inertia,

4. The preoccupation of professional assessors with a metaphysical magnitude called "true value" which renders them incapable of recognizing the impact of inflation on asset prices,

5. The political climate which converts a technical issue, the value of property, into a power struggle between the taxpayer, or taxpayers as a group, and the assessor,

6. Failure to coordinate and centralize the assessment of property in the hands of a unified agency with effective power to achieve equalization between different tax jurisdictions.

The fascinating and interesting complexities of local organization in California defy analysis and frustrate generalization. The present (1958) structure, the joint product of historical development and ad hoc improvisation, consists of 351 cities, 57 counties, 1 city-county, 1,790 school districts,* and around 3,000 special districts. Except for the counties, whose boundaries have remained stable for nearly half a century, these numbers are constantly changing. New cities are incorporating; new special districts are spawning in the suburban hinterlands of metropolitan regions. But, as a welcome exception to this pattern of governmental fertility, the number of school districts has steadily decreased during the last few decades.

While the pattern of local government in California is a patchwork quilt of many hues and colors, its infinite variety bespeaks

* These numbered 1,818 on July 1, 1957.

both confusion and experimentation. In broadest outline the problem of "government"—the making of group decisions, the allocating of political power, expressing group loyalty—is inherently quite simple. But this problem admits of a multiplicity of solutions, solutions that must recognize the historical conditions of the locality, the geographical advantages and disadvantages of the region, the social composition of the area's population, the economic trends and prospects of the community, the personal ambitions of community leaders, the diverse expectations of interest groups, and so forth. Even in the absence of these sources of diversity, no one "correct" solution to the problem of government exists; there are many roads to the summit.

Consequently, the governments we observe in the municipalities and counties and districts of this state can be regarded as a series of viable experiments, a set of rough approximations to an ideal dimly visible beneath the mass of confusion and detail that confronts the observer on every hand. . . .

The infinite variety and vast complexity of public organization in a metropolitan community frustrate the efforts of the ordinary citizen to make rational decisions on public policy. Wholly apart from its other demerits, the multiplicity of governmental units taxes the voter's understanding of public issues, increases the number of agencies and authorities he must keep track of, diffuses his interest in any one public agency, multiplies the number of candidates he must examine and vote upon, and, finally, subverts the democratic process by encouraging neglect and disinterest. In addition, the uninstructed citizen who wishes to petition his government for some simple and ordinary service is shunted about the labyrinth like a character in a Kafka novel.

The ordinary citizen in California may deal with ten to a dozen different governments and encounter a roster of names at election time that would tax the memory of an insurance salesman. In addition to state and national governments, the list includes the city, the county, the school district, and half a dozen special districts. If he follows the prevailing California pattern, living in one locality and working in another, he will encounter another parcel of local agencies at his place of business. Inhabitants of unincorporated urban areas with their burgeoning quota of special districts have an even larger list to keep track of. To compound his difficulties the California custom of legislation by constitutional amendment—an inevitable outgrowth of an unrepresentative legislature— confronts him with an elongated ballot of state propositions.

Now *representative* democracy is itself a device for economizing on the labor of decision-making. The selection of representatives to decide complex issues of taxing, budgeting, administering, and staffing for local governments is designed to spare the ordinary citizen from the uncongenial and time-consuming task of examining those issues with the care their importance deserves. The citizen determines only the broadest and most general outlines of policy and trusts his elected representative to translate this policy into specific legislation. But the multitude of candidates and agencies and issues exceeds the citizen's span of attention and defeats one of the essential purposes of representative democracy.

The vast number of different governments erected on the same fiscal base and given autonomous power to draw up budgets and levy taxes means that no single agency reviews and compares the relative value of money spent for different purposes—no single agency, that is, except the voter himself in a very roundabout and indirect fashion. Each agency, of course, can reallocate funds between the various functions it controls but no agency can transfer money from the city to the school budget, or from the county to the independent district's budget to equalize returns at the margin between each field of use. This limitation is serious. It is as if one person in a household were empowered to decide how much should be spent for food, another to decide for clothing, another for recreation, etc., but no one could decide to transfer funds from clothes to food if the last dollar spent for the former brought less satisfaction than the last dollar spent for the latter.

Even in principle, with a unified decision on the allocation of resources between functions, maximum satisfaction from the expenditure of a given total is difficult to achieve and impossible to verify because the satisfactions accrue to different people. . . . Nevertheless, a kind of rough intuition about community values and relative satisfaction is available to guide this decision. But even this imperfect monitor cannot be mobilized when different bodies make independent decisions for different purposes.

Of equal if not of greater importance, the multiplicity of units means that no single agency decides whether the sum total of public money is either greater or smaller than the community desires. For the alternative to public expenditures is private consumption and investment (as any taxpayer well knows) and the ultimate cost of public goods is the clothing and cars and houses and books that do not get made and sold because resources are used for highways, clerks, prisons, teachers, and schools. The rationality of this decision also goes by default when a number of independent local bodies make autonomous expenditures and tax levies.

In practice, and as a result of precedent and experience, things are not quite so bad as we have indicated. Members of one taxing authority do communicate occasionally and informally with their opposite members in other governments; an underlying community consensus on both the pattern and the total emerges after much painful experience with unsatisfactory alternatives; and voters do pick and choose on the basis of their fiscal preferences among various functions. But adjustment is painful and prolonged and, moreover, in a new or rapidly growing community—as what town in metropolitan California isn't?—the consensus is difficult to sample at best and impossible to ascertain when decisions are diffused.

11
Politics and the Power Structure

There are essentially two views of the power structure in the city. C. Wright Mills, who has given us the term "the power elite," takes the position that this elite is the prime mover in the process of community decision-making. Furthermore, the power elite of each city, the metropolitan 400, is bound by ties of family and training to the power elites existing in all other metropolitan areas. "To the extent that the economy is national and big-city centered, and to the extent that the upper classes control its key places of big-city decision—the upper classes of each city are related to those of other cities." Mills places emphasis on the role of social status in lubricating the process. Speaking of the gentlemen's club, he says, "In it all the traits that make up the old upper classes seem to coincide: the old family, and the proper marriage and the correct residence and the right church and the right schools—and the power of the key decision."

Scott Greer provides the alternative view—that in a pluralistic society, such as exists in the metropolis, only the naïve can continue to believe in the type of power structure in which control is centered in the hands of the businessman. However, the confrontation between Mills and Greer is not a direct one. For Mills, the power elite consists of many elements other than the corporation owners and managers. But Greer's oblique reference to the power structure serves to reinforce his theme that the municipal polity,

309

democratic in nature, is a story of man functioning in a pluralistic social framework.

Both Mills and Greer speak in highly general and abstract terms. Edward Banfield, however, brings the argument down to earth with an examination of the gap between the idea of an elite and actual political events in Chicago. Banfield confines himself to the idea of a business elite and thus, like Greer, meets Mills's argument only obliquely. Although he virtually discards the notion that a business elite actually runs the city, Banfield does believe that this elite *could*, if it wished, "exercise a great, and probably a decisive, influence."

The final selection touches on another facet of the question of the power structure. Floyd Hunter makes use of an intensive case study of his mythical "Regional City" to supply some insights into the makeup of the power structure. At this point, the question may be raised: Does Hunter's description of the process of entré into the power structure shed any light on the nature of the power structure itself? If wealth and social prestige are not automatic guarantees of entrance into the elite group, does this mean there is no elite? Or must we return to Mills's position that the selection process is performed by a sort of interlocking directorate of prestigious clubmen?

Metropolitan 400 *

C. Wright Mills

In each of the chosen metropolitan areas of the nation, there is an upper social class whose members were born into families which have been registered since the *Social Register* began. This registered social class, as well as newly registered and unregistered classes in other big cities, is composed of groups of ancient families who for two or three or four generations have been prominent and wealthy. They are set apart from the rest of the community by their manner of origin, appearance, and conduct.

* C. Wright Mills, *The Power Elite* (New York: Oxford University Press, 1959), pp. 57–62. © 1956 by Oxford University Press, Inc. Reprinted by permission.
    C. Wright Mills was Professor of Sociology at Columbia University and author of a number of influential books—notably, *The Power Elite* and *White Collar*.

They live in one or more exclusive and expensive residential areas in fine old houses in which many of them were born, or in elaborately simple modern ones which they have constructed. In these houses, old or new, there are the correct furnishings and the cherished equipage. Their clothing, even when it is apparently casual and undoutedly old, is somehow different in cut and hang from the clothes of other men and women. The things they buy are quietly expensive and they use them in an inconspicuous way. They belong to clubs and organizations to which only others like themselves are admitted, and they take quite seriously their appearances in these associations.

They have relatives and friends in common, but more than that, they have in common experiences of a carefully selected and family-controlled sort. They have attended the same or similar private and exclusive schools, preferably one of the Episcopal boarding schools of New England. Their men have been to Harvard, Yale, Princeton, or if local pride could not be overcome, to a locally esteemed college to which their families have contributed. And now they frequent the clubs of these schools, as well as leading clubs in their own city, and as often as not, also a club or two in other metropolitan centers.

Their names are not in the chattering, gossiping columns or even the society columns of their local newspapers; many of them, proper Bostonians and proper San Franciscans that they are, would be genuinely embarrassed among their own kind were their names so taken in vain—cheap publicity and cafe-society scandal are for newer families of more strident and gaudy style, not for the old social classes. For those established at the top are "proud"; those not yet established are merely conceited. The proud really do not care what others below them think of them; the conceited depend on flattery and are easily cheated by it, for they are not aware of the dependence of their ideas of self upon others.

Within and between the various cliques which they form, members of these proud families form close friendships and strong loyalties. They are served at one another's dinners and attend one another's balls. They take the quietly elegant weddings, the somber funerals, the gay coming-out parties with seriousness and restraint. The social appearances they seem to like best are often informal, although among them codes of dress and manner, the sensibility of what is correct and what is not done, govern the informal and the natural as well as the formal.

Their sense of civic service does not seem to take direct political form, but causes them gladly to lead the charitable, educational, and cultural institutions of their city. Their wealth is such—probably several millions on the average—that they do not usually have to use the principal; if they do not wish to work, they probably do not have to. Yet their men—especially the more substantial older men—generally do work and sometimes quite diligently. They make up the business aristocracy of their city, especially the financial and legal aristocracy. The true gentleman—in the eastern cities, and increasingly across the nation— is usually a banker or a lawyer, which is convenient, for those who possess a fortune are in need of trusted, wise, and sober men to preserve its integrity. They are the directors and the presidents of the major banks, and they are the senior partners and investment counselors of the leading law firms of their cities.

Almost everywhere in America, the metropolitan upper classes have in common, more or less, race, religion, and nativity. Even if they are not of long family descent, they are uniformly of longer American origin than the underlying population. There are, of course, exceptions, some of them important exceptions. In various cities, Italian and Jewish and Irish Catholic families—having become wealthy and powerful —have risen high in status. But however important, these are still exceptions: the model of the upper *social* classes is still "pure" by race, by ethnic group, by national extraction. In each city, they tend to be Protestant; moreover Protestants of class-church denominations, Episcopalian mainly, or Unitarian, or Presbyterian.

In many cities—New York for example—there are several rather than one metropolitan 400. This fact, however, does not mean that the big-city upper classes do not exist, but rather that in such cities the status structure is more elaborate than in those with more unified societies. That there are social feuds between competing status centers does not destroy the status hierarchy.

The family of higher status may belong to an exclusive country club where sporting activities and social events occur, but this pattern is not of decisive importance to the upper levels, for "country clubs" have spread downward into the middle and even into the lower-middle classes. In smaller cities, membership in the best country club is often the significant organizational mark of the upper groups; but this is not so in the metropolitan status market. It is the gentleman's club, an exclusive male organization, that is socially most important.

Gentlemen belong to the metropolitan man's club, and the men of the upper-class stature usually belong to such clubs in more than one city; clubs for both sexes, such as country clubs, are usually local. Among the out-of-town clubs to which the old upper-class man belongs are those of Harvard and Princeton and Yale, but the world of the urban clubs extends well beyond those anchored in the better schools. It is not unusual for gentlemen to belong to three or four or even more. These clubs of the various cities are truly exclusive in the sense that they are not widely known to the middle and lower classes in general. They are above those better-known arenas where upper-class status is more widely recognized. They are of and by and for the upper circles, and no other.

But they are known and visited by the upper circles of more than one city.

To the outsider, the club to which the upper class man or woman belongs is a badge of certification of his status; to the insider, the club provides a more intimate or clan-like set of exclusive groupings which places and characterizes a man. Their core of membership is usually families which successfully claim status by descent. From intimate association with such men, newer members borrow status, and in turn, the accomplishments of the newer entrants help shore up the status of the club as a going concern.

Membership in the right clubs assumes great social importance when the merely rich push and shove at the boundaries of society, for then the line tends to become vague, and club membership clearly defines exclusiveness. And yet the metropolitan clubs are important rungs in the social ladder for would-be members of the top status levels: they are status elevators for the new into the old upper classes; for men, and their sons, can be gradually advanced from one club to the next, and so, if successful, into the inner citadel of the most exclusive. They are also important in the business life within and between the metropolitan circles: to many men of these circles, it seems convenient and somehow fitting to come to important decisions within the exclusive club. "The private club," one national magazine for executives recently put it, is becoming "the businessman's castle."

The metropolitan upper classes, as wealthy classes having control of each locality's key financial and legal institutions, thereby have business and legal relations with one another. For the economy of the city, especially of a metropolitan area, is not confined to the city. To the extent that the economy is national and big-city centered, and to the extent that the upper classes control its key places of big-city decision— the upper classes of each city are related to those of other cities. In the rich if gloomy quiet of a Boston club and also in the rich and brisk chrome of a Houston club—to belong is to be accepted. It is also to be in easy, informal touch with those who are socially acceptable, and so to be in a better position to make a deal over a luncheon table. The gentlemen's club is at once an important center of the financial and business network of decision and an essential center for certifying the socially fit. In it all the traits that make up the old upper classes seem to coincide: the old family and the proper marriage and the correct residence and the right church and the right schools—and the power of the key decision. The "leading men" in each city belong to such clubs, and when the leading men of other cities visit them, they are very likely to be seen at lunch in Boston's Somerset or Union, Philadelphia's Racquet or Philadelphia Club, San Francisco's Pacific Union, or New York's Knickerbocker, Links, Brook, or Racquet and Tennis.

The Urban Polity*

Scott Greer

There have always been many Americans who prefer to believe that power in the local community is tightly organized in the hands of a few persons who represent "the interests." Perhaps this is a rural survival, for in the small town there is some evidence of consistent domination by those who control land, credit, and wealth. Such an image can be easily transplanted to the city, where the mass media emphasize a few large-scale images connected with the polity, ignoring the supporting organizations and their dependence upon the citizens. The average urbanite, viewing these affairs from a great social distance, can easily believe that a small circle of the powerful exists and runs the city.

This image of the metropolitan area's power structure usually relies upon the assumption that local government is merely the executive committee of the bourgeoisie and the politicians hired hands of those who control the massive resources of the corporations. Floyd Hunter has documented such an image for Atlanta, Georgia, ending up with a list of a small number of people who are said to run things. Such studies are based upon "perceived influence" and they suffer from a curious solipsism. For, if the notion of monolithic power structure is diffused through the society, and if one approaches the study of power by asking people what they think occurs, he is very apt to document a myth—held sincerely and even fervently by his subjects, but quite likely to be as far from the truth as any other proposition about society upon which most people agree.

There is a touching naïveté in this faith, shared equally by left, right, and center. The ideologues of the left, confused and bemused by social transformations never posited in their theories, cling to the notion that *some* things do not change. The businessmen of main street have a vested interest in the image: it emphasizes their prestige and power and reinforces their own notions of who the first class citizens are, and what interests are legitimate. The vulgarized radicalism that has permeated American thinking leads diverse people to find reassurance in a conspiracy theory of local government.

* Reprinted with permission of the publisher from *The Emerging City: Myth and Reality*, by Scott Greer (New York: The Free Press, 1962), pp. 151–160, 163–167. Copyright 1962 by the Free Press of Glencoe, A Division of The Macmillan Company.

Scott Greer is Associate Professor of Social and Political Science at Northwestern University.

When, however, careful scholars investigate the way key *decisions* come about in the metropolis, they find neither the dominance of business interests nor the simple order assumed in the myth. Recent studies of New York, Philadelphia, Boston, St. Louis, Chicago, and Syracuse all present striking evidence that there is no simple structure, hierarchical and monolithic, deploying the power of the ruling classes and running the city (Kaufman and Sayre, Reichley, Baltzell, Norton Long, Long and Greer, Banfield, Banfield and Meyerson, Wilson, Freeman and associates). Instead, the businessmen are seen as limited in their influence, poorly organized and internally divided in their interests—frequently, in short, captives or pawns in a game where they do not hold the decisive advantage and frequently do not understand the play. Metropolitan politics, a continual interplay of other interests, has been given the felicitous name of "an ecology of games" by Norton Long. For the single pyramidal structure of control in the city, he substitutes a pluralistic political world where, like a continual game of musical chairs, the chief actors change positions as the issues revolve.

The myth of the economic ruling class makes two major assumptions about the metropolitan community in large-scale society. It assumes that there is a great commitment by businessmen to the fate of the local community, resting upon a great commitment of their corporate wealth and power. It also assumes that they have the instrumental ability to affect the local polity in the light of their corporate interests, to "call the shots" as the community agenda is formulated and acted upon.

Perhaps at one time, in the early decades of expanding scale, these assumptions held true. Perhaps, when the various large cities were all important headquarters of massive corporations, the latter were such citizens as elephants among chickens. Certainly today both assumptions can be questioned. Mills has pointed out the consequences of increasing scale for the corporation's commitment to the local area. Increasing scale means corporate merger, and the great and powerful corporate citizens in the community of yesterday are, today, branch plants of national organizations. The consequences, from the point of view of the career bureaucrats who now manage these plants, have been spelled out by Norton Long in detail; the effects of such changes upon the polity in a "satellite city" have been investigated by Schulze. Baltzell has demonstrated the diminishing concern of Philadelphia gentlemen for the local community, as their own interests focus more upon New York and Washington and they become part of a national upper class.

The manager of the branch plant is primarily a citizen in his national corporation, and his lodestar is company headquarters. To his own career, local affairs are relatively unimportant. His aim is to pursue the corporation's advantage (and thus his own) as quietly as possible, letting the sleeping community dogs lie. He makes a one-way gamble if he gets "involved" in local affairs—it can profit him little, and it can hurt him a great deal. His strategy is the limited one of protecting the company's public relations and trying to keep at least a consultative status and a veto on those issues that could cost the company dearly. And so his role is usually defined by headquarters. Proconsular in his position, each major commitment to the local community must be reviewed by his superior and every cent of his war chest accounted for. Powerful as he may be in the imaginations of local citizens, his power is usually the passive force of a bureaucratic instrument, part of a larger social machine.

In the corporation headquarters city matters may have another weight, for here the autonomy and the power coexist. But in the headquarters of a national or international organizational network, immediate local affairs usually appear trivial. In the light of the corporation's function, the chief advantage of *this* city, *this* community, may be no more than the residential preferences of the top staff and a relatively minute investment in a building or two. The geography of large-scale bureaucracy is quite different from that of the geography textbooks. Organizational space supersedes geographical space for most purposes.

So much for the real giants of American business and industry; they are, in large degree, neutral actors in the local community polity. However, there are other firms that are inevitably committed to a given city. The metropolitan newspapers are nontransferable assets, and their fate is linked to that of their city. So also are the local banks (particularly in states that forbid branch banking) and the closely related real-estate companies. Public utilities are earth-bound, their fortunes inextricably involved with those of the metropolitan community as a whole. Retail merchants also have, in plant and clientele, assets that have value in this city, but perhaps in no other. The civic leaders of Chicago or St. Louis, Boston, Los Angeles, or Cleveland, are drawn from the managerial and ownership ranks of these businesses (and such businesses are apt to be locally owned). They are committed: their liability is greater—they have nowhere else to go. They are, then, the chief corporate actors of business in the local community.

But there is a second assumption underpinning the classic myth of community control: the committed economic powers have the ability to call the tune for local government. Again, this may once have held, in smaller cities of a smaller-scale society. But in a society where the decisive actors of formal government are elected by the citizens, such political actors would have to share either a common normative system with voters and businessmen, or else have great freedom from the opinions of the voters and a great commitment to businessmen. The mechanisms assumed are usually (1) gross manipulation of votes and voters, insuring freedom from the electorate and its interests, and (2) the need for

money from businessmen, for elections, bribery, and the personal income
of politicians . . .

These conditions certainly do not obtain in the contemporary metropolitan area. Neither the amateur governments of the suburbs
nor the large-scale government of the central city can disregard the perceived interests of a majority with impunity. The increasing education,
income, and occupational level that have affected all of the diverse populations of the city have forced an increasing emphasis upon issues of the
community that are real to the residents. The absorption of the children of
immigrants into the middle ranks of the familistic neighborhoods has
weakened the power of the "ethnic name." Such devices as voting machines have made ballot-box stuffing increasingly dangerous. These
changes in the nature of elections and the electorate have shifted the
strategies of political victory from the simple disbursement of money to
manipulation of the local branch of the national political party—for it is
the party label that wins. As this occurs, the power of the businessman's
campaign donation has shrunken proportionately. While bribery is undoubtedly still effective in some cases, it should always be remembered
that the politician, like any organizational actor, usually will put the conditions for job security and progress in the job above everything else.
Bribery by business would be defined as "selling out" to the enemy. In
short, the businessman cannot often affect an official's political success one
way or the other.

The weakness of the businessman in politics is also partly
a result of the massive shift in residence within the governmentally bi-
furcated metropolis. The population that has moved outward has included the great majority of what was, once, the Republican basis of
strength in the central city. The familistic, nonethnic, higher-rank residents have moved to the suburbs, leaving a pathetic remnant of Republican
councilmen to represent the two-party system in most great American
cities.

Along with the Republican voters, the leaders of the business
community have gone to the suburbs. Equally important is the loss of the
middle-level cadres of the middle class—the aspiring junior executives
and young lawyers, the educated and politically inclined club women, the
small businessmen. These are the people who could constitute an effective
organizational middle class for the electoral contests of the city. Their
disappearance from the scene leaves those economic leaders who remain
in the city (in the town houses and private streets of yesterday) far up
in the organizational stratosphere, with no links to the mass of voters.
And the latter are, increasingly, union members, ethnics, and confirmed
Democrats. . . .

Thus, local government in the metropolitan area does not approach the image of the monolithic power structure at many points.

Instead of a pyramidal structure, controlled at the top by the representatives of economic interests, we find a pluralistic world of corporate citizens contending for power. The veto groups range from the corporation whose assets are captive to the polity of the central city, on one hand, to the Puerto Rican wards or the suburban municipalities on the other. This contention occurs within a framework dominated by the political organization—and in the central city, that organization is the local wing of the Democratic Party. But because of recent political transformations the governmental personnel are generally dominant. The team of the incumbents, especially the big city mayor, are the key actors. Among them, the heads of the giant bureaucracies loom large. They move consistently and continuously toward autonomy, security, and expansion. Fire, education, police, health, and other specialized agencies become organizational empires outlasting any given administration. Their professional commitments and relative freedom from party apparatus allow a genuine concern with universal norms. The mayor's autonomy allows him to concern himself also with the welfare of the city as a whole. The two kinds of actor, in combination, stand for political virtue and expertise. These attributes are frequently respected, in turn, by business representatives who see in a "clean" and professional mayor only another executive like themselves.

Big business has few "trading cards" for the game of big city politics. It can exercise real power only at the top, for it lacks the troops to contend in the electoral domain. Its chief political force derives from (1) bargaining rights due to party control elsewhere, in the State House or in Washington; and (2) the potency of the newspapers, which are usually Republican in their ideology and which are big business in their own right. As distinguished from "power," businessmen have influence insofar as their opinion, as experts and as folk heroes of American middle-class society, matters to the mayor and his team. Evidence indicates that, in certain respects, it matters a great deal. For the big city mayor, emancipated from his machine allies, behaves much like a respectable, suburban, middle-class citizen.

In the multitudinous municipalities of suburbia, a power structure does frequently exist. But it is a structure very democratic in its nature. The social homogeneity of the citizens, their equality in social honor and resources, their common image of the local community—all these result in a self-selected sample that holds the offices of government. This oligarchy overemphasizes the role of businessmen, for their prestige is transferable to the political realm in a community that accepts the ethos of Main Street as definitive. They often produce a "clean" government, run by a manager, supported by a good government caucus party whose ward-heelers are members of the League of Women Voters.

Within these frameworks of control, the everyday business

of governing a metropolis proceeds. In the central city the organizational subsegments of government are social machines organized as bureaucracies, governed by explicit norms and informed with professional codes. The public administrator and the jurisprudent, the specialist in police administration and the certified public accountant, are culture carriers who rationalize (and disenchant) the jungle of corruption and power that so fascinated Lord Bryce. For party conflict is substituted competition among the "different branches of the service," the lobbying of special interest groups and the struggle of party chieftains (who are usually elected officials) for the succession.

In the suburban municipalities the management-oriented administrator is also frequently dominant as is the city manager of a small city. He works patiently within the circle of his amateur politicians, trying to educate them to the necessities of operating a going concern (which the municipality is) within a context of public responsibility and visibility (which a business firm is not). In towns without professional managers, the reason for their absence is usually anemia of the fisc; though some corruption occurs in such places, it is much more likely to be the incompetence of the officials that strikes the observer.

The sum of these arguments then, is this. No polity can embrace the total metropolis: too many legally autonomous structures are in being and there is always the dichotomy between central city and suburbia. Nor is a powerful, consistent, and continuous program of change likely in a central city. The mayor has strength, but chiefly to arbitrate among competing bureaucracies, business interests, ethnic minorities, and party organizations. Banfield describes Chicago's major issues for a two-year period; the majority resulted in stalemate and were tabled. Sayre and Kaufman show the City of New York as a mandarin bureaucracy, dominated by an irresponsible and conservative Board of Estimate. In short, the only dynamic that is consistent through time is that resulting from the continuous efforts of the "nonpolitical" civic bureaucracies to expand. In the process, services are provided within the limits of precedent. A minimal order is maintained. The past is the basis for extrapolation into a future where its rules and rules of thumb may or may not work.

Janowitz has put it succinctly. "Let it be assumed that effective decision-making at the community level is the prerequisite for democratic procedures in the larger political system. Everywhere community leadership faces a common problem, . . . namely, the issue is not the manipulation of the citizenry by a small elite, but rather the inability of elites to create the conditions required for making decisions."

The Mythology of Influence*

Edward C. Banfield

Many Chicagoans, including some who are generally well informed about civic affairs, believe that a little group of private persons whose names are in some cases unknown to the general public have ample power to decide any public matter whatsoever. These alleged "top leaders" are the multi-millionaires who control the largest businesses, own the newspapers, and dominate the boards of directors of the civic associations, universities, hospitals, and other public service bodies. They are said to be at the top of a hierarchy of influence the lines of which are so well drawn as virtually to constitute a formal organization. When they give the word, lesser figures below them in the hierarchy—including other business leaders as well as politicians, university heads, clergymen, and so on—are supposed to hasten to do their bidding. According to one businessman who knows his way around Chicago (he owns a firm that grosses more than $100 million a year), the city is run by only four men: "Do you know who really runs Chicago? Who has the real money and power? Four young men: Brooks McCormick of International Harvester; Hagenah of Wrigley's; Calvin Fentress, son-in-law of General Wood, you know; and Marshall Field, Jr. These four young men control the wealth of Chicago. Not many people know that."

The head of a Negro civic association set the number of "top leaders" a little higher. According to him, "There are a dozen men in this town who could go into City Hall and order an end to racial violence just like you or I could go into a grocery store and order a loaf of bread. All they'd have to do is say what they wanted and they'd get it."

Sometimes the "top leaders" are regarded as a conspiracy of the rich to frustrate the workings of democracy. More often, it is assumed that they exercise their influence for the good of the community. The "top leader"—according to this view—is rich enough to put aside his private advantage in most matters (certainly in all small ones), and he is accustomed, by training and position, to take a statesmanlike view of public questions. He may be the representative of a family—the Fields, McCormicks, Ryersons, Swifts, or Armours, for example—that has devoted itself to public service for generations, or he may be the head of a large corporation—Inland Steel, Sears, Roebuck, Field's Department Store,

* Reprinted with permission of the publisher from *Political Influence* by Edward C. Banfield (New York: The Free Press, 1961), pp. 286–291. Copyright 1961 by The Free Press, a corporation.

Edward C. Banfield is Henry Lee Shattuck, Professor of Urban Government, Harvard University.

the Chicago Title and Trust Company, for example—that has a long-standing tradition of "civic responsibility." In any case, he is trusted to have good intentions. The Negro leader quoted above was confident that if the facts about racial violence were brought to the attention of the right men, they would give the necessary orders. It was reasonable for him to take their goodwill for granted: most of his organization's support came as gifts from corporations owned or controlled by them.

In Chicago, big businessmen are criticized less for interfering in public affairs than for "failing to assume their civic responsibilities." They themselves seem to agree with this view; those of them who do not exercise influence in civic affairs are apt to reproach themselves for failing in their duty. The general view seems to be that the "top leaders" ought to unite on some general plan for the development of the city and the metropolitan area.

Frequently, efforts are made in American cities to give official standing to the hierarchy of influence that is presumed to exist. The independent, unpaid planning commission, which is the organizational form into which the city-planning function has been cast in most cities, is, in intention (but not in practice), "top leadership" brought out from behind the scenes and made official. The assumption is that a plan can be carried into effect if—and only if—the principal private interests of the city agree upon it.

It may be, as Norton E. Long has conjectured, that "top leadership" is talked about because people feel the need of a government that has power to solve community problems, to deal with community crises, and to make and carry out comprehensive plans. Where the politicians who hold the offices do not regard themselves as governors of the municipal territory but largely as mediators or players in a particular "game" (the great game of politics), the public finds reassurance in the notion that there exists a "they" who are really running things from behind the scenes.

The notion that "top leaders" run the city is certainly not supported by the facts of the controversies described in this book. On the contrary, in these cases the richest men of Chicago are conspicuous by their absence. Lesser business figures appear, but they do not act concertedly: some of them are on every side of every issue. The most influential people are the managers of large organizations the maintenance of which is at stake, a few "civic leaders" whose judgment, negotiating skill, and disinterestedness are unusual and, above all, the chief elected officials. Businessmen exercise influence (to the extent that they exercise it at all) not so much because they are rich or in a position to make threats and promises as, in the words of one of them, "by main force of being right."

These findings do not, however, prove that there is no "they" behind the scenes. Possibly, they were not sufficiently interested in what was at stake in these cases to bestir themselves. Or, possibly they were well satisfied with what was done and saw no need to interfere. Or, again, they may, from considerations of policy, have restrained a desire to interfere (they may have thought interference "undemocratic" or "poor public relations"). Any of these theories, or all of them together, would explain the absence of "top leaders" from the scene and, incidentally, would leave open the possibility that in some future case—one in which their vital interests *are* at stake—they may issue the orders necessary to set in motion the lower echelons of the alleged influence hierarchy.

There is yet another possibility. It may be that the "top leaders" did not exercise their influence, or did not exercise it in earnest, for want of organization and that this want could easily have been supplied if they had cared to take the trouble. If, for example, the four young men who "have the real money and power" had got together for lunch one day and had talked things over, they might have set "policy" with regard to the Fort Dearborn Project, the Branch Hospital, the Exhibition Hall and, for good measure, racial violence. If they had done so, their decisions (according to the theory) would have been quickly communicated down the hierarchy of lesser business leaders, elected officials, managers, and civic association professionals. That they did not get together for lunch was—on this theory—only a matter of "accident" or "mere circumstance." (One of the young men may perhaps have been confined to his home with a painful case of gout, while another was busy skiing in Switzerland.) On this theory, there was nothing to prevent the "top leaders" from running things except the difficulties that normally stand in the way of concerting the activities of four busy people. Their failure to exercise influence, then, is to be explained as "mere want of organization." This theory leaves open the possibility that the four young men may some day meet for lunch. If they do, presumably they will then run the city. . . .

These theories are all plausible. It is unquestionably true that a very small number of men control the principal industries of the metropolitan area and, if they wish, can have a great deal to say about how civic associations and other private bodies are run. No doubt, any four of at least forty men could, if they acted together and if they exerted themselves fully, exercise a great, and probably a decisive, influence in such matters as have been described here. In the Branch Hospital dispute, for example, Maremont and others raised several thousand dollars to fight for a South Side site. They could have raised not thousands but hundreds of thousands or even millions if they had wished. (To have done so would have been out of proportion to any public or private benefit, of course, but it would have been possible all the same.) If they had gone to such lengths, the outcome of the controversy would probably have been different. It is not unlikely, for example, that if the Urban League had been given a very large contribution on condition that it support the South Side branch, its directors would have decided that strengthening the organization justified a sacrifice of ideological principles. Similarly, if Ryan had been told that a very large addition to his campaign fund was contingent upon his support of a South Side branch, he might have been more sympathetic to it. Evidence that the biggest businessmen of the metropolitan area were sufficiently aroused to make such an offer would no doubt of itself have put the matter in a different light in his eyes.

The political heads, even in the rather rare instances when they have decided policy preferences of their own, believe that they ought to be responsive to the wishes of the public and especially to the wishes of that part of the public which has the most at stake in the particular matter. As a rule, therefore, the "top leaders," if they were united and ready to back to the limit a project which was not obviously contrary to the interest of the community, would find the political heads ready to co-operate. And even if the political heads opposed, the "top leaders" might have their way, although perhaps not in the very short run. For if the twenty or thirty wealthiest men in Chicago acted as one and put all their wealth into the fight, they could easily destroy or capture the machine.

These remote and even fantastic possibilities are mentioned only to show that the notion of an elite having the ability to run the city (although not actually running it) is not inherently absurd. Indeed, if influence is defined as the *ability* to modify behavior in accordance with one's intention, there can be little doubt that there exist "top leaders" with aggregate influence sufficient to run the city.

Regional City's Power Structure*

Floyd Hunter

Society prestige and deference to wealth are not among the primary criteria for admission to the upper ranks of the decision-makers according to the study of Regional City. The persons who were included in the listing of forty top leaders purely on the basis of their wealth or society connections did not, with three or four exceptions, make the top listing of persons who might be called upon to "put across a community project." . . . a distinction is made between persons of wealth and social prestige who engage in work and those who do not. The persons of

* Floyd Hunter, *Community Power Structure* (Chapel Hill, North Carolina: The University of North Carolina Press, 1953), pp. 80–87. Reprinted by permission.
Floyd Hunter is director of the Floyd Hunter Company, a social science research and development firm for civic, governmental, and business organizations.

wealth are perhaps important in the social structure of the community as symbolic persons. They may be followed in matters of fashion and in their general manner of living. Their money may be important in financing a given project, but they are not of themselves doers. They may only be called decisive in the sense that they can withhold or give money through others to change the course of action of any given project. Gloria Stevens spends large sums of money on Regional City projects, but the expenditures are made through her lawyer, Ray Moster. She does not interact with any of the top leaders whom we interviewed, other than Moster, so far as could be ascertained. Hetty Fairly, another woman of wealth, spends her charitable monies through a foundation handled by a lawyer not on the list of leaders. The lawyers may be vigilant in serving the interests of their clients in both instances, and a part of the vigilance exercised is in keeping abreast of possible tax incursions on the "frozen wealth" of the foundations. In this there may be some connection with power, but it is rather obscure in terms of the definition of power as being the ability of persons to move goods and services toward defined goals. If there is power in the charitable foundation structures, it resides in the lawyers who operate them, rather than in the donors who are largely inactive in the affairs of the foundations.

Political eminence cannot be said to be a sole criterion for entry into the policy echelons of Regional City's life, generally speaking. The two exceptions to this statement are embodied in Mayor Barner and County Treasurer Truman Worth. Both Barner and Worth were successful businessmen before becoming involved in local politics to the point of seeking public office. Their interests may be said to be primarily business in the strict sense of the word. Both have a popular following that has kept them in office, but their close associates are businessmen. Mayor Barner had only one picture in his office—that of Charles Homer, the biggest businessman in the community. Both Barner and Worth look to businessmen constantly for advice before they make a move on any project concerning the whole community. Furthermore, they do not ordinarily "move out front" on any project themselves, but rather follow the lead of men like Delbert, Graves, or any one of the other leaders of particular crowds.

The point made at this turn of the discussion is not a new one. Businessmen are the community leaders in Regional City as they are in other cities. Wealth, social prestige, and political machinery are functional to the wielding of power by the business leaders in the community. William E. Henry puts the matter this way:

The business executive is the central figure in the economic and social life of the United States. His direction of business enterprise and his participation in informal social groupings give him a significant place in community life. In both its economic and its social aspects the role of the business executive is sociologically a highly visible one.

The "visibility" suggested by Henry is a highly applicable concept in connection with an analysis of Regional City leadership. One need not labor the point. This study has already shown that business leaders take a prominent position in Regional City civic affairs.

In the general social structure of community life social scientists are prone to look upon the institutions and formal associations as powerful forces, and it is easy to be in basic agreement with this view. Most institutions and associations are subordinate, however, to the interests of the policy-makers who operate in the economic sphere of community life in Regional City. The institutions of the family, church, state, education, and the like draw sustenance from economic institutional sources and are thereby subordinate to this particular institution more than any other. The associations stand in the same relationship to the economic interests as do the institutions. We see both the institutions and the formal associations playing a vital role in the execution of determined policy, but the formulation of policy often takes place outside these formalized groupings. Within the policy-forming groups the economic interests are dominant.

The economic institution in Regional City, in drawing around itself many of the other institutions in the community, provides from within itself much of the personnel which may be considered of primary influence in power relationships. A lengthy discussion on institutions per se is not proposed. Their existence as channels through which policy may be funneled up and down to broader groups of people than those represented by the top men of power is easily recognized. Some of the institutions would represent imperfect channels for power transmission, however. For example, the family as an institution is not a channel of itself for bringing about general community agreement on such a matter as the desirability of building a new bridge across Regional River. On the other hand, the church might represent a more potent force on this question. The preacher could preach a sermon on the matter in any given church, and the members could sign petitions, attend meetings at the behest of the church bureaucracy, and go through a whole series of activities motivated by the institution in question.

It may be noted here that none of the ministers of churches in Regional City were chosen as top leaders by the persons interviewed in the study. The idea was expressed several times by interviewees that some minister *ought* to be on the listing, but under the terms of power definitions used in the study they did not make "top billing." It is understood, however, that in order to get a project well under way it would be important to bring the churches in, but they are not, as institutions, considered crucial in the decision-making process. Their influence is crucial in restating settled policies from time to time and in interpreting new policies which have been formed or are in the process of formulation. Church leaders, however, whether they be prominent laymen or professional ministers, have relatively little influence with the larger economic interests.

One cannot, in Regional City at least, look to the organized institutions as policy-determining groupings, nor can one look to the formal associations which are part of these institutions. But let us briefly be specific concerning the role of organizations. There is a multiplicity of organized groups in Regional City. The Chamber of Commerce lists more than 800 organizations from bee-keeping societies to federated industrial groups. The membership lists of some of these organizations often run into the hundreds. In this study organizations were considered as being influential in civic affairs and some ranking of the most important was deemed necessary. Consequently, all persons interviewed were asked to give their opinion on a selected list of supposedly top-ranking organizations in the community. An initial selection of thirty organizations was made by a panel of judges from lists supplied by the Chamber of Commerce and the local Community Council. The persons interviewed in the list of forty leaders narrowed their selections of organizations to seven—organizations to which the majority of these top leaders belonged. They were (in rank order of importance) the Chamber of Commerce, Community Chest, Rotary Club, Y.M.C.A., Community Council, Grand Jurors' Association, and Bar Association. There was a scattering of votes for the Christian Council and for one of the larger labor organizations. The Retail Merchants Association was added to our list by two merchants. The under-structure professional personnel in civic and social work who were interviewed indicated that they recognized the influence of the same organizations chosen by the top leaders. It may be noted that they generally belonged to only the Community Chest and the Community Council in conjunction with the top leaders. . . .

None of the men interviewed considered any of the associational groupings crucial in policy determination. Their role, like that of the organized institutional groupings, is one of following rather than leading. They may provide a forum for discussing and studying community issues, needs, and policies; but, when decision is called for, another structure must come into play before action becomes the order of the day. The organizations may serve as training grounds for many of the men who later become power leaders. Most of the leaders had "graduated" from a stint in the upper positions of the more important organizations. Most associational presidents, however, remain in the under-structure of the power hierarchy. The organizations are not a sure route to sustained community prominence. Membership in the top brackets of one of the stable economic bureaucracies is the surest road to power, and this road is entered by only a few. Organizational leaders are prone to get the publicity; the upper echelon economic leaders, the power.